Hospitality
Marketing
Management

Hospitality
Marketing
Management

Fifth Edition

Robert D. Reid
James Madison University

David C. Bojanic
University of Texas at San Antonio

WILEY
John Wiley & Sons, Inc.

Library of Congress Cataloging-in-Publication Data

Reid, Robert D.
    Hospitality marketing management/Robert D. Reid, David C. Bojanic.—5th ed.
        p. cm.
    Includes bibliographical references.
    ISBN 978-0-470-08858-6 (cloth)
    1. Hospitality industry—Marketing. 2. Food service—Marketing. 3. Restaurants—Marketing.
I. Bojanic, David C. II. Title.
    TX911.3.M3R443 2008
    647.94068′8—dc22   2008021436

Printed in the United States of America
10 9 8 7 6 5 4 3 2 1

Contents

Preface

As the hospitality and tourism industry matures and changes, marketing for the industry matures and changes, as well. Today's hospitality marketing student needs to be as concerned with service as with marketing plans or Internet optimization. The *Fifth Edition* of *Hospitality Marketing Management* presents many new ideas along with established marketing principles, exploring not only the foundations of marketing in the hospitality world but also new trends in the industry.

Hospitality Marketing Management explores marketing and themes unique to hospitality and tourism. **Part 1** provides an introduction to marketing and the roles of service and customer satisfaction in hospitality marketing. **Part 2** focuses more specifically on how to better identify target markets by utilizing the principles of consumer behavior and market segmentation and positioning. This section of the book explores influences on decision making and buyer behavior, the strategies of segmentation, and the product-service mix. **Part 3** weaves application with theory in the discussion of the marketing plan and needed information for marketing decisions or market research. **Part 4** looks at the product-service mix in more detail, including strategies for marketing through channels, and takes a close look at the rapidly evolving world of e-commerce, which offers many marketing opportunities. **Part 5** explores strategies for promotion, including advertising in different forms of media, sales, merchandising, and public relations. **Part 6** presents pricing strategy, which includes techniques and procedures as well as revenue management, and includes a **new chapter** on destination marketing.

New to the Fifth Edition

The changes to this *Fifth Edition* were made with the goal of improving the text and keeping it up to date. They include:

- **New chapter on destination marketing.** In keeping with current industry trends, a new chapter has been written on destination marketing. Chapter 16 focuses on the specific branding and marketing challenges faced by tourism destinations.

- **More coverage of the Internet and technology.** Greater emphasis was placed on the use of the Internet and technology in hospitality and tourism, especially in the chapters on advertising (Chapters 11 and 12) and e-commerce (Chapter 10). Also, Internet exercises have been added to some chapters to help students see the usefulness of the Internet for gathering relevant information.

- **Key Terms and Glossary.** The book now includes a comprehensive glossary of key terms and concepts. In addition, definitions appear in the margins where the terms and concepts are introduced.

The most important concepts from the menu design as a marketing tool chapter are now incorporated into other parts of the book. For example, the concept of menu engineering is now included in Chapter 8, as an application of resource allocation models.

- **More coverage of international marketing throughout.** The importance of a global economy directly affects the hospitality and tourism industry. As in past editions, an effort was made to provide more international examples and references throughout the book to illustrate this trend.

- **More coverage of the tourism industry.** In addition to the new chapter on destination marketing, an effort was made to include more tourism marketing examples, visual aids, and industry profiles. The book is now more comprehensive in its coverage of the hospitality and tourism industry.

- **Expanded coverage of important topics.** Certain areas of the text were expanded based on comments by instructors and reviewers. For example, the discussion of reference groups in Chapter 3, "Understanding the Behavior of Hospitality Consumers," includes more information on opinion leaders, such as travel writers and food critics. In addition, the discussion of marketing planning in Chapter 5 was expanded to include more material on the practical application of marketing planning.

PEDAGOGICAL FEATURES

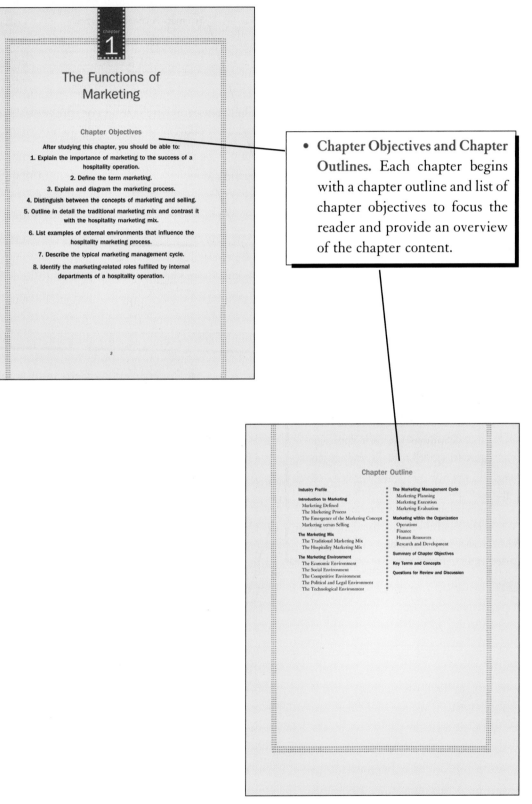

- **Chapter Objectives and Chapter Outlines.** Each chapter begins with a chapter outline and list of chapter objectives to focus the reader and provide an overview of the chapter content.

- Correspondingly, each chapter culminates with a more detailed **summary of chapter objectives** to bring the discussion full circle and reiterate key points.

- **Key Terms and Concepts.** Each chapter contains a list of key terms and concepts at the end. The terms and concepts appear in **bold** throughout the chapter, and definitions for each appear in a glossary as well as in the text margins at the point they are introduced. The goal is to provide students with a thorough understanding of the terms and concepts, and the ability to apply them in real-world situations.

Summary of Chapter Objectives

This chapter discussed the role of marketing channels in planning the marketing strategy for hospitality and tourism services. Decisions must be made regarding channel width (how many outlets) and channel length (number and type of intermediaries). If the decision is made to use an indirect channel (at least one intermediary), then the firm must examine channel management issues such as channel leadership and channel power. Finally, the extent of the relationships with other channel members will need to be considered.

Some type of vertical marketing system can be used to provide more certainty in the relationships. Franchising is probably the most common form of vertical marketing system.

Intermediaries exist in channels because they perform certain channel functions more effectively than the other channel members. One advantage of using intermediaries is the fact that they often have access to markets that are desired by a manufacturer or producer. Travel agents and tour operators specialize in packaging trips and selling them to groups and individuals for pleasure travel, and meeting planners and travel bureaus work more with business groups for conferences and conventions.

Key Terms and Concepts

Administered vertical marketing system
Central reservation systems (CRS)
Channel length
Channel power
Channel width
Coercive power
Contractual vertical marketing system
Convention and visitors bureau (CVB)
Corporate vertical marketing system
Destination management company (DMC)
Destination marketing organization (DMO)
Direct channel
Electronic commerce
Exclusive distribution
Expert power

---

in the early 1990s, occupancy and profitability reached all-time highs for many lodging companies. In the early 2000s, and especially after the events of September 11, 2001, and the recession of the early 2000s, hotel occupancies fell and many properties suffered operating losses. Since 2005, occupancy percentages have improved and in many cases, profitability has been excellent.

- Variations in consumer purchasing power have led the hospitality and travel industry to offer products and services at different price levels. For example, most of the major lodging chains now have established multiple brands, ranging from economy to luxury, based on prices and amenities. Each brand targets a specific market segment.

Some of the issues in the economic environment are closely related to the trends in the social environment that will be discussed next.

The Social Environment

There are constant changes in the social environment as consumers evolve. The social environment is affected by all of the other environments. Changes in the economy, advances in technology, competitive actions, and government regulations all shape the way consumers view the world. These changes may be sudden, or they may take place over a number of years or even decades. First, there have been changes in **demographics**, or characteristics that describe the population, such as age, income, education, occupation, family size, marital status, and gender. Second, there have been changes in consumers' attitudes, interests, and opinions that determine their lifestyles.

Some issues related to the social environment affect the hospitality and travel industry:

- The proportion of two-income families and the impact that the increased discretionary income and time pressures have on their lodging, dining, and travel behaviors. These families take more but shorter vacations to fit their busy lifestyles. Also, they are quality-conscious and focus on brand names.

- The proportion of older Americans and their purchasing power are continually increasing. Senior citizens are becoming a very important market segment because people are living longer. Further, there is an improved quality of life among seniors, and their disposable income continues to

Demographics
Characteristics that describe the population such as age, income, education, occupation, family size, marital status, and gender.

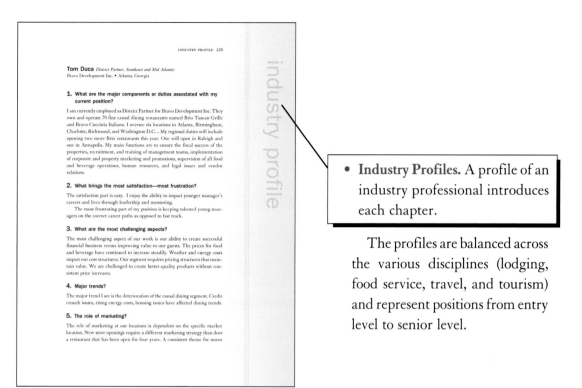

- **Industry Profiles.** A profile of an industry professional introduces each chapter.

The profiles are balanced across the various disciplines (lodging, food service, travel, and tourism) and represent positions from entry level to senior level.

- **Case Studies.** Several new case studies have been added to this edition and the case studies that have been replaced are archived and available to instructors on the book's Web site: **www.wiley.com/college/reid**. The case studies contain enough information to be used as group projects but also are concise enough for individual class assignments and discussions. The cases are based on real-world situations, whether they reference an actual company or disguise the name for proprietary reasons.

- **Questions for Review and Discussion.**
There are questions provided at the
end of each chapter to give students a
chance to test their knowledge of the
material. Instructors can use the questions to initiate class discussions, or to
review for exams. The Instructor's
Manual contains the answers for the
questions for easy reference.

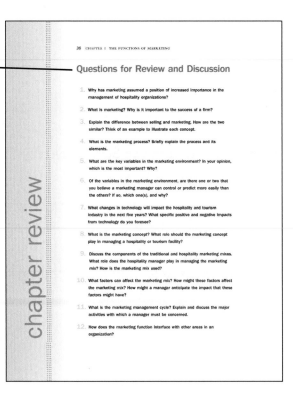

Supplementary Materials

The *Instructor's Manual* (978-0-470-25404-2) with test questions has been
updated. An electronic version of the *Instructor's Manual* is available to qualified instructors on the companion Web site at **www.wiley.com/college/reid**.
In addition, **PowerPoint slides** can be downloaded from the same Web site.

Information about **WebCT** and **BlackBoard** resources available with this
book are also available on the companion Web site: **www.wiley.com/college/reid**.
Links to WebCT and Blackboard are provided within the Title Information
categories listed on the home page. For more information on the valuable
resources included, click on the link for WebCT or Blackboard, or contact your
Wiley representative.

We hope you find these improvements and changes to the *Fifth Edition*
of *Hospitality Marketing Management* useful in your quest to learn about the
exciting world of marketing in the hospitality and tourism industry.

Acknowledgments

We are grateful for the assistance of talented educators who have contributed to this edition through their constructive criticism. They include:

Jeffrey A. Beck, Michigan State University
Kimberly A. Boyle, University of Alabama
Steve Fixman, J. Sargeant Reynolds Community College
Valerian A. Ginter, Fiorello H. LaGuardia Community College of the City University of New York
Amy Hart, Columbus State Community College
Kyungmi Kim, Southern Illinois University
Stuart Levy, Florida International University
Lauren Maguire, Bunker Hill Community College
Ian McVitty, Algonquin College
Juline Mills, Purdue University
Shaun M. Murie, Florida Gulf Coast University
Emily Grace Newkirk, Sandhills Community College
Susan Stafford, State University of New York

Robert D. Reid
Dean and Professor
James Madison University, Harrisonburg, Virginia

David C. Bojanic
Anheuser-Busch Foundation Professor of Tourism
University of Texas at San Antonio, Texas

part 1

*Courtesy of The Breakers, Palm Beach,
Florida.*

Courtesy of Wyndham Worldwide.

The Functions of Marketing

Chapter Objectives

After studying this chapter, you should be able to:

1. Explain the importance of marketing to the success of a hospitality operation.

2. Define the term *marketing*.

3. Explain and diagram the marketing process.

4. Distinguish between the concepts of marketing and selling.

5. Outline in detail the traditional marketing mix and contrast it with the hospitality marketing mix.

6. List examples of external environments that influence the hospitality marketing process.

7. Describe the typical marketing management cycle.

8. Identify the marketing-related roles fulfilled by internal departments of a hospitality operation.

Chapter Outline

Industry Profile

Introduction to Marketing
Marketing Defined
The Marketing Process
The Emergence of the Marketing Concept
Marketing versus Selling

The Marketing Mix
The Traditional Marketing Mix
The Hospitality Marketing Mix

The Marketing Environment
The Economic Environment
The Social Environment
The Competitive Environment
The Political and Legal Environment
The Technological Environment

The Marketing Management Cycle
Marketing Planning
Marketing Execution
Marketing Evaluation

Marketing within the Organization
Operations
Finance
Human Resources
Research and Development

Summary of Chapter Objectives

Key Terms and Concepts

Questions for Review and Discussion

Jenny Lucas *Director of Education and Career Development*
Loews Hotels • New York, New York

1. What are the major components or duties associated with your current position?

Ultimately, my role is to ensure that we are able to deliver four diamond *and more* service through training our team members and developing programs that allow them to grow their careers. The education piece includes the facilitation of manager workshops throughout the company. We facilitate several FranklinCovey workshops, including Stephen R. Covey's *The 7 Habits of Highly Effective People* and *The 4 Disciplines of Execution*, which our executive committees and managers across the company attend. In addition, we develop and facilitate our own management and hourly workshops, designed to reinforce our company culture, share basic skills, and ensure that our team members are able to deliver our brand promise. Maintaining, measuring, and monitoring adherence to our standards is also a big component of the role— every position and every task each position performs has service standards associated with it.

For management development we meet individually with managers at all properties who are interested in growing with Loews and relocating from one hotel to another. Participants work with their managers to develop a personal career development action plan. With the information discussed during our session, we look to match each manager with open positions throughout the company. Over the past two years, with the implementation of our career development program, we have seen internal management promotions increase from 32.9 percent to 52.5 percent. We also oversee the program for our high-potential managers. This program allows them to work on additional projects through the year, preparing them for their next role. One on one time is spent with each of them to create a plan, touch base throughout the year, and evaluate the final portfolio each creates to document the managers' projects for the year.

2. What are the components of your position that bring you the most satisfaction? What about your position causes you frustration?

I guess it's pretty much a cliché to say people—but in this field it's all about seeing someone reach their goal and hearing how excited or proud they are of their accomplishment. I enjoy taking my ten-plus years of hotel operations experience and using it to help managers throughout the company. Whether I am sharing Covey principles or company culture, having real-life hotel experiences that I can share to help others better understand or get excited about a concept is very rewarding. Great satisfaction comes from seeing people make the connection—the light goes on, that "Aha, now I get it!" Follow-up e-mails and phone calls from the people out at the properties after a workshop or seeing a familiar face in a new position and hotel makes all the traveling worthwhile!

The greatest frustration for me is that there is simply never a good time to train—it's either too busy or too slow. Unfortunately, training is oftentimes seen as an unnecessary cost—a luxury, especially if the economy takes a turn down. Usually, the red line goes through training dollars as soon as times get tough. A couple of months down the line, when managers are wondering why the guest satisfaction scores are lower, you just have to bite your tongue and ask what you can do to help. Failing to make that investment can lead to an apathetic staff providing average service at best. It is easy to forget that training, even in small doses every day, helps energize the team—when employees see the investment being made in them, they put in extra effort to deliver the standards and exceed our guest expectations.

3. What are the most challenging aspects you're facing?

Fewer and fewer managers are willing to relocate to another city, which makes it difficult as we look to grow the brand. The best way to ensure the company culture comes to life at a new hotel is by having Loews managers in key positions. Once upon a time, to grow with a company you had to be willing to go anywhere the company asked you to, but times have changed, and people are looking more and more to stay close to home. It can be difficult to keep a high-potential manager who isn't interested in relocating challenged in his or her current position until an opportunity comes available. As an organization, we need to find ways to encourage people to relocate and make it easier and more attractive to do so.

4. What major trends do you see for your segment of the hospitality and tourism industry?

In training we are seeing more and more blended learning adding Web-based and virtual training to the traditional classroom training. The hospitality industry isn't always on the cutting edge of technology so, while other industries set trends, we tend to follow a few years behind. The nature of our industry is one where many team members attending workshop do not have access to computers, so we'll always have a need for traditional classroom instruction. That being said, with different generations in the workplace today, we need to constantly evaluate what available tools and technology we could better use to engage the younger generations.

5. What role does marketing play within your company?

In the training world we work to market our programs to our internal guests—our managers and team members. Developing our team members is part of our brand promise, so our department is charged with making that a reality. Our new-hire orientation program ensures that all new team members are given the proper tools to succeed. We show them from day one that we are committed to their success. Each of our programs is marketed on the property to encourage attendance and reinforce the importance of continuing education throughout one's career.

Training and education does play an outside marketing role as well. We are recognized on *Training* Magazine's Top 125 Training Companies. When preparing a presentation to potential investment partners or hotel owners, our vice president of development includes this honor and an overview of our different education and development programs, as well as the measurement tools we have in place to ensure that our standards are being upheld throughout the company. While financial results certainly play a major role in an owner's decision, many companies may offer a similar return—our investment in our team members can be what makes us unique.

6. If you could offer one piece of advice to an individual preparing for a career in the hospitality and tourism industry, what would you suggest?

Be proactive and take responsibility for your career—now. There's no substitute in this business for hands-on experience—think of it as the hospitality school of life. That experience can be what separates you from your peers. Worse yet, don't wait until a required internship to find that this industry isn't for you. You've got to have a passion for what you do—to love the service business and taking care of people. Be willing to put in the energy and effort right from the beginning so that you can stand out from the rest of the graduates just starting out on their careers.

INTRODUCTION TO MARKETING

In recent years, most of the growth in the hospitality industry has occurred in chain operations or in the industry's corporate segment. The hospitality industry leaders, such as Marriott International, Hyatt, Hilton, McDonald's, Subway, Choice International, and Starwood Lodging, continue to increase their share of the market at the expense of smaller chains and independent operators. While independent operators have continued to prosper, especially in the food service sector, the marketplace is much more competitive. An increased level of competition has meant greater emphasis on marketing. No longer is it possible for an individual to open and operate a food service facility successfully on good food alone. To ensure a steady flow of customers, a hospitality manager must possess a thorough understanding of marketing. Without the marketing management skills the hospitality industry demands, a hospitality manager is less likely to achieve success today. With this continual change and increased competition, what are the marketing functions that a successful hospitality manager must fulfill? This chapter introduces basic marketing definitions and concepts, including the marketing mix, the marketing environment, the marketing management cycle, and the role of marketing within the operation of a hospitality and tourism organization.

Marketing Defined

The term **marketing** encompasses many different activities, and it is necessary to discuss some of the terms used in the definition of marketing, and throughout the text. First, the term **product** refers to all of the goods and services that are bundled together and offered to consumers. For example, computers and automobiles are sold as tangible goods, but they include warranties and service contracts as part of the overall product. Therefore, the term **product** refers to both goods and services, but it is often thought of as a good or commodity. Nearly every product sold includes both tangible and intangible elements. Another term that is used to refer to the product as a bundle of goods and services, and eliminate the confusion, is the **product–service mix**.

A **service** is defined as an intangible product that is sold or purchased in the marketplace. A meal purchased at a fast-food restaurant or an occupied room in a hotel is considered a part of the service segment. Why? Simply stated, after the meal is consumed and paid for or after the individual checks

Marketing

Marketing encompasses merging, integrating, and controlling supervision of all company's or organization's efforts that have a bearing on sales.

Product

The goods and services that are bundled together and offered to consumers.

Product–service mix

A bundle of goods and services offered by an organization.

Service

An intangible product that is sold or purchased in the marketplace.

out of the hotel, the individual leaves the facility and does not have a tangible product in exchange for the money spent. This individual has consumed a service that is a part of the hospitality and travel industry, one of the largest service industries.

Each year, millions of individuals spend billions of dollars vacationing and traveling for business and pleasure; when the trip is over, nothing tangible remains. To more clearly reflect the role of service industries, such as the hospitality and tourism industry, the definition of marketing can be expanded to include references to services. This will eliminate the confusion caused by the semantic differences between products, goods, and services, discussed earlier. According to the American Marketing Association, "Marketing is an organizational function and a set of processes for creating, communicating, and delivering value to customers and for managing customer relationships in ways that benefit the organization and its stakeholders.[1]

The vast majority of hospitality establishments, however, are operated to generate a satisfactory return on investment in the form of profits or excess revenue. These profits are used to pay dividends to stockholders and are reinvested by the organization to promote expansion and further development. Even nonprofit hospitality operations, such as selected hospitals, nursing homes, college or university hospitality operations, and government-run hospitality operations must be concerned with marketing. Managers of nonprofit operations must still understand the wants and needs of their consumers and provide goods and services at a satisfactory level to as many individuals as possible. A universal concern of all hospitality managers is the financial condition of the organization. Whether a manager is trying to achieve a 20 percent annual return on investment (ROI) or is instead aiming to break even on a very limited budget, the overriding concern is still financial.

Another factor that any definition of marketing must include is a focus on the exchange that takes place between a producer and a consumer. In order for an exchange to take place, both parties must receive something they are satisfied with. In most cases, consumers give producers money in exchange for products and services that meet the consumers' wants and needs. However, the exchange can include anything of value to the parties. Before there was a monetary system, people would **barter**, or exchange goods and services rather than money. There are still companies that engage in bartering today. For example, PepsiCo chose to exchange its soft drink product with a company in Mexico for wine and other products to avoid incurring the foreign exchange risk associated with the peso, which was devalued at the time.

Barter
A process of exchanging goods and services rather than money.

The Marketing Process

Marketing concept

The marketing concept is based on the premise that firms determine customer wants and needs, and then design products and services that meet those wants and needs, while also meeting the goals of the firm.

Marketing mix

The first layer around the target market, or consumers, is referred to as the marketing mix. The marketing mix has four components: price, product, place, and promotion, which are often called the four P's of marketing. Managers can control those variables.

The process of marketing can be best understood by examining the diagram presented in Figure 1.1. As you can see, the target market, or those groups of consumers that the firm chooses to target with its marketing efforts, is at the center of the process. The **marketing concept** is based on the premise that firms determine customer wants and needs and then design products and services that meet those wants and needs while at the same time meeting the goals of the firm. This concept is an extension of earlier concepts that focused on the production process as a means to design products and services, or the selling of already produced products and services. Today, most firms realize the value of customer input in the new product design process. Chapter 2 looks at the issues unique to marketing services, Chapter 3 focuses on the behavior of hospitality consumers, and Chapter 4 discusses the process of choosing target markets and positioning products in the market.

In Figure 1.1 the first layer around the target market, or consumers, is referred to as the **marketing mix**. The marketing mix has four components: price, product, place, and promotion. These are often referred to as the four P's of marketing, and they are the variables that managers can control. Firms will manipulate the marketing mix variables to formulate strategies that are

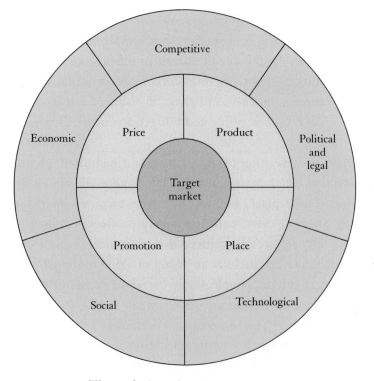

FIGURE I.I • *The marketing mix.*

combined in a **marketing program** for a product or service. This program is the basis on which the firm's products and services compete with the offerings of other firms in the competitive environment. The marketing mix will be discussed in more detail later in this chapter. The product component is covered in Chapters 7 and 8, the place (distribution) component is covered in Chapters 9 and 10, the promotion component is covered in Chapters 11 through 15, and the price component is covered in Chapter 15.

The outside layer of the diagram represents the **external environments** that influence the marketing process. The state of the economy, trends in society, competitive pressures, political and legal developments, and advances in technology all affect the performance of a product or service. Firms cannot control these environments, but they must monitor the changes and trends in the respective environments and look for opportunities and threats. Later in this chapter, the different environments and some of the current trends that affect hospitality and travel firms will be examined in more detail.

Firms must continually monitor environments and make changes in their marketing programs. The **marketing management cycle** involves marketing planning, marketing execution, and marketing evaluation. This cycle is discussed briefly in this chapter, and Chapter 5 covers the marketing planning process in depth. To be successful in marketing planning, firms need to conduct research and collect information that can be used to evaluate their programs. Chapter 6 discusses the **marketing research process** used to gather information to be stored in **marketing information systems** and used to make marketing decisions.

The Emergence of the Marketing Concept

If a hospitality organization is to market its product–service mix successfully, it is essential that the marketing concept be thoroughly understood and fully implemented. Understanding the marketing concept is not difficult, but implementing it may prove to be very challenging for management. Simply stated, the marketing concept is a consumer-oriented philosophy that focuses all available resources on satisfying the needs and wants of the consumer, thereby resulting in profits. As an old rhyme states, "To sell Jane Smith what Jane Smith buys, you've got to see things through Jane Smith's eyes."

Clearly, it is difficult to sell something to someone who has no need for it. If the firm adopts a consumer-oriented marketing philosophy, however, the product–service mix will be designed in direct response to unsatisfied consumer needs. As a result, very limited actual selling will be necessary. In such

Marketing program
Firms will manipulate the marketing mix variables (e.g., price, product, place, and promotion) to formulate strategies for a product or service that are used to form a marketing program.

External environments
The environments that influence the marketing process. The state of the economy, trends in society, competitive pressures, political and legal developments, and advances in technology reflect external environments and affect the performance of a product or service.

Marketing management cycle
The marketing management cycle involves marketing planning, marketing execution, and marketing evaluation.

Marketing research process
A process used to collect information about consumers and markets.

Marketing information systems (MIS)
The structure of people, equipment, and procedures used to gather, analyze, and distribute information used by an organization to make a decision.

instances, supply and demand are in balance, and both the consumer and the hospitality providers are satisfied.

Table 1.1 illustrates the two different philosophies of the marketing concept that are often practiced in the hospitality and tourism industry. One demonstrates the actions of a manager who applies the marketing concept; the other demonstrates actions that are not consistent with the marketing concept. The key question to ask when trying to distinguish between the two approaches is whether consumers are given priority, or whether the operation is run to suit the needs of the employees, management, or owners.

A manager of a hospitality operation has a difficult series of daily challenges. First, a manager is expected to successfully satisfy the needs of the hospitality consumers. Second, the owners expect a manager to maintain the level of expenses within certain predetermined limits that are usually defined in actual dollars or as a percentage of sales. Third, a manager is expected to generate a satisfactory return on investment (ROI) for the owners.

This return might be the break-even point in a nonprofit operation or a 10, 15, or 20 percent rate of return in a commercial operation. Whatever the expected return, a manager is faced with a series of difficult objectives to achieve, and these objectives often conflict with one another. Even in the most successful companies, there are limited resources that must be used to accomplish seemingly unlimited goals and objectives. Regardless of how well the company has performed in the past, owners and senior management will always expect a little more in the future. Guests develop ever-increasing expectations for all aspects of the product–service mix. Owners want increased profits, and the employees want a little more each year. The manager's task is to balance the three objectives mentioned in the preceding paragraph. Managers often view profitability as the single most important objective of the firm. Yet for the long-term financial well-being of the firm, profits may not be the most important objective. It is quite possible, as many shortsighted owners and managers have demonstrated, to achieve high levels of short-term profitability at the expense of long-term consumer satisfaction and long-term profits. After a period of time, however, consumers will perceive that they are not receiving a high level of value for their money, and the operation will develop a reputation for being overpriced and/or offering poor service. As a result, the number of patrons is likely to decline, and so will profitability.

By contrast, if management establishes a consumer orientation and places customer satisfaction as the number one priority, the firm's products and services are more likely to meet customers' expectations. As a result, they will return more frequently to the hospitality operation, and this will have a positive influence on long-term sales and profits. In addition, by telling their friends and

DECISIONS	WHEN THE MARKETING CONCEPT IS APPLIED	WHEN THE MARKETING CONCEPT IS NOT APPLIED
Menu design	"Let's conduct focus group interviews using our current and target market customers to determine which potential new menu items we should add to our menu."	"Let's add two steaks to the menu; that's what I like to eat."
Pricing	"How do you think our guests will perceive the price value of our new weekend package if we increase the price by 5 percent?"	"Let's increase the price by 5 percent; that's what we did last year."
Guest service	"I'm very sorry that you had to wait 20 minutes for your breakfast this morning. May I offer you a complimentary breakfast today, or would you like the credit applied toward your breakfast tomorrow?"	"I'm sorry you had to wait, but we were short-handed today. One of the servers called in sick."
Guest requests	"We don't have any rooms with a king bed available at this time, but I can have one ready for you in 30 minutes. Can I have the bell staff check your bags until then?"	"We don't have any rooms with a king bed left. You'll have to take a room with two double beds."
Reactions to negative guest comments	"That is a very good idea. I'll talk about it at our staff meeting tomorrow and see if we can use your suggestion to improve service. Thanks for suggesting that."	"Your idea isn't feasible, and besides, it's against our policy."

TABLE I.I • *Marketing Concept Philosophies*

Word of mouth

A spoken communication that portrays either positive or negative data.

acquaintances about their positive experiences, satisfied consumers are likely to influence others to patronize the establishment. This **word of mouth** passed on by satisfied customers can become a very important part of a firm's promotional efforts. It doesn't cost anything, yet it can be a very powerful influence on sales, and as sales increase, so does profitability. Experience shows that when the marketing concept is understood and applied by all of a firm's employees, substantial changes have often been made in the establishment's manner of operation, and the financial results have often been improved significantly.

Marketing versus Selling

Many hospitality managers engage in activities that they incorrectly refer to as marketing. Many people confuse advertising or personal selling with marketing. Although such activities are without question a part of the marketing function, alone and unsupported they cannot be referred to as marketing. Marketing refers to the entire process that is illustrated in Figure 1.1. Advertising and personal selling are merely forms of promotion, and promotion is just one component of the marketing mix. Managers engaging in activities of this type are merely attempting to sell their products and services.

The product–service mix is composed of all the tangible and intangible products and services that make up a hospitality operation. The product–service mix includes the food, beverages, guest rooms, meeting facilities, tabletop appointments, and personal attention by service personnel, as well as a host of other tangibles and intangibles. Advertising or personal selling performed alone focuses only on the hospitality operation's product–service mix, and the goal is to convince the consuming public to purchase and consume a portion of the product–service mix. Little consideration is given to the needs and wants of the consuming public; instead, the hospitality manager is hoping that a sufficient number of consumers will patronize the operation to allow the operation to achieve its financial objectives.

The hospitality and tourism industry, especially the foodservice segment, is filled with examples of operations that have failed because the owners created operations they liked or "always wanted to operate," yet the owners and managers failed to consider fully the needs and wants of potential consumers. The results are predictable: low volume, poor sales revenue, and frequent bankruptcy. Because this mistake is so prevalent in the foodservice segment, restaurants have one of the highest failure rates of any type of business in the United States. In some instances, the failure rate of new independently owned restaurants may reach 90 percent in the first 12 months of operation.[2]

The difference between selling and marketing is very simple. **Selling** focuses mainly on the firm's desire to sell products for revenue. Salespeople and other forms of promotion are used to create demand for a firm's current product(s). Clearly, the needs of the seller are very strong. Marketing, however, focuses on the needs of the consumer, ultimately benefiting the seller as well. When a product or service is truly marketed, the needs of the consumer are considered from the very beginning of the new product development process, and the product–service mix is designed to meet the unsatisfied needs of the consuming public. When a product or service is marketed in the proper manner, very little selling is necessary because the consumer need already exists and the product or service is merely being produced to satisfy the need.

A brief example will illustrate the critical difference between selling and marketing. If you had asked many successful hospitality owners in the middle 1980s if they thought that an operation specializing in coffee and tea beverages, as well as baked pastries, sandwiches, salads, musical CDs, and a retail coffee selection, made available in a casual atmosphere in which customers could relax and enjoy conversation, could be successful, many would not have been positive. They might have provided many reasons that the concept could not work, or could not be scaled to multiple units. How wrong they might have been. What began as a single Starbucks™ in 1971 located in Seattle has grown significantly. Today, Starbucks™ has 6,566 company-owned stores and 3,729 licensed stores that operate in more than 40 countries.

Table 1.2 illustrates the growth that Starbucks™ has enjoyed.

YEAR	NUMBER OF STORES
1990	84
1995	677
2000	3,501
2005	10,241
2006	12,440
	Source: http://www.starbucks.com/aboutus/Company_Timeline.pdf

TABLE 1.2 • *Starbucks Growth*

Selling

In contrast to marketing, selling focuses mainly on the firm's desire to sell products, and to a lesser extent on the needs of the potential buyer.

To achieve success in marketing a hospitality operation, a manager must closely examine and understand all of the components of the marketing mix. To be successful, these components must be combined into well-conceived marketing programs and managed properly. There is no magical formula that will guarantee success. If there were, no hospitality operation would ever fail or go out of business. Yet each year, many hospitality operations fail because they are not able to combine the elements of the marketing mix into effective marketing programs, or they fail to implement them properly.

The Hospitality Marketing Mix

Hospitality marketing mix

Hospitality marketing mix consists of five components: product–service mix, presentation mix, communication mix, pricing mix, and distribution mix.

Just as researchers have demonstrated distinct differences between goods and services, some researchers believe that the traditional four P's approach to the marketing mix does not apply to the hospitality industry. Rather, a modified marketing mix is more appropriate. This **hospitality marketing mix** consists of five components:[3]

1. Product–service mix

2. Presentation mix

3. Communication mix

4. Pricing mix

5. Distribution mix

PRODUCT–SERVICE MIX. This is a combination of all the products and services offered by the hospitality operation, including both tangible and intangible elements. For example, it includes such things as the type of guest room, the amenities offered, and the broad array of elements offered to the consumer. Chapter 2 addresses further the unique nature of services. Keep in mind that once a hospitality consumer leaves the hotel or restaurant, there is nothing tangible to show. Because the consumer has purchased and consumed the service, the largest part of the hospitality industry product–service mix is indeed the intangible elements of service.

PRESENTATION MIX. This includes those elements that the marketing manager uses to increase the tangibility of the product–service mix as perceived by the consumer. This mix includes physical location, atmosphere (lighting, sound, and color), and personnel.

COMMUNICATION MIX. This involves all communication that takes place between the hospitality operation and the consumer. It includes advertising, marketing research, and feedback about consumer perceptions. The communication mix should be viewed as a two-way communication link, rather than as a simple one-way link with the hospitality operation communicating to the consumer. This two-way link allows for the traditional advertising and promotion that flow from the seller to the buyer, but it also allows for marketing research and other data collection vehicles. In these cases, the seller is seeking information and data from the consumer, thereby establishing open communication with the various market segments.

There are some similarities and differences between the traditional marketing mix and the hospitality marketing mix. In the hospitality version, the product component is expanded to include some aspects of distribution. People are part of the production process in services, and distribution occurs in the presence of the consumer. The communication mix is almost identical with the promotion component in the traditional marketing mix, although it does include some additional communications such as marketing research. Finally, the presentation mix represents the largest departure from the traditional marketing mix. It includes price and some of the aspects of the place component such as location, and it adds elements such as atmosphere and the personal contact between customers and employees.

PRICING MIX. In addition to the actual price a firm charges, the pricing mix encompasses the consumer's perception of value. The pricing mix includes such variables as volume discounts and bundling multiple products together for an overall discounted price. This bundling approach is used extensively by fast-food chains as a method to increase spending per customer.

DISTRIBUTION MIX. This includes all distribution channels available between the firm and the target market. Historically, distribution occurred at the point of production, such as the restaurant where the food was produced. This has changed since newer distribution channels, such as the Internet and e-Commerce have developed; the importance of the distribution mix has increased.

The marketing mix, whether designed in the traditional or modified hospitality services format, is an important concept for managers of marketing functions. Initially, the marketing mix is used to formulate a marketing strategy and plan (see Chapter 5), but it pervades all aspects of marketing management. Several external factors can reduce the effectiveness of the manager's efforts to successfully implement all the components of the hospitality marketing mix. These factors, which may have either direct or indirect influence, are consumer perceptions, attitudes, and behavior; industry practices and trends; local competition; broad national and international trends; and government policy and legislation.

THE MARKETING ENVIRONMENT

During the past decade, many changes have had an impact on the hospitality industry in the United States. The industry has confronted and adapted to such diverse situations as economic recession, overbuilding, increased competition, increased emphasis on technology, increased emphasis on the environment, newer forms of distribution and sales using technology, increased foreign ownership of previously American brands, changes in dining habits, changes in food consumption patterns, the ever-increasing globalization of the hospitality and tourism industry, and the impact of international terrorism. Each of these external forces has brought with it changes that hospitality firms have had to make to remain competitive in a global marketplace.

When marketing managers consider changes in marketing strategy or tactics, they often examine the changes in five major marketing environments: competitive, economic, political and legal, social, and technological. Firms cannot directly influence their external environments, but they can monitor changes and be somewhat proactive. It is critical for firms to engage in some level of **environmental scanning**, so they can take advantage of marketing

Environmental scanning
Environmental scanning can be a formal mechanism within a firm, or merely the result of salespeople and managers consciously monitoring changes in the environment.

Hotels such as the Wingate Tulfarris Hotel and Golf Resort in County Wicklow, Ireland, offer a range of room rates and amenities for guests with differing levels of purchase power. Courtesy of Wyndham Worldwide.

opportunities while at the same time anticipating any threats to their business. Environmental scanning can be a formal mechanism within a firm, or merely the result of salespeople and managers consciously monitoring changes in the environment. The larger the firm, the more likely it will have a structured approach to scanning the environment and documenting trends. The following section contains brief descriptions of each of the external environments.

The Economic Environment

The goal of all marketing activity is to create and satisfy customers. Consumers' **purchasing power**, or ability to purchase products and services, is directly related to the economic health of the city, state, and country. As marketers study the economic environment, they are concerned about such things as inflation, recession, unemployment, resource availability, interest rate trends, personal income growth, business growth and performance, and consumers' confidence in the economy. There are other key economic terms that relate to marketing and will be used throughout the text. The **consumer price index (CPI)** is a measure of the relative level of prices for consumer goods in the economy. As this measure rises, there are more concerns about inflation and a poor economy. The term **disposable income** refers to the portion of an individual's income that is left for spending after required deductions such as taxes. **Discretionary income** is probably a more important measure for most marketers because it refers to the income that is available for spending after deducting taxes and necessary expenditures on housing, food, and basic clothing.

Some examples of issues and trends related to the economic environment that affect the hospitality and travel industry:

- The percentage of independently owned hospitality operations has declined, resulting in a concentration of power among large hospitality chains. In turn, these chains have become large, multinational firms based in the United States or abroad.

- An increase in the amount of discretionary income has resulted in an increase in the percentage of the household food budget spent outside the home. The hospitality industry today receives in excess of 50 percent of all consumer expenditures for food.[4]

- After a period of excess supply due to overbuilding in the 1980s, hotel occupancy percentages fell to the low 60s. This trend later reversed itself because of the strong economy and business growth. Following a recession

Purchasing power
Consumers have the ability to purchase products and services.

Consumer price index (CPI)
A measure of the relative level of prices for consumer goods in the economy.

Disposable income
An individual's income that remains for spending after required deductions such as taxes.

Discretionary income
An individual's income that is available for spending after deducting taxes and necessary expenditures on housing, food, and basic clothing.

in the early 1990s, occupancy and profitability reached all-time highs for many lodging companies. In the early 2000s, and especially after the events of September 11, 2001, and the recession of the early 2000s, hotel occupancies fell and many properties suffered operating losses. Since 2005, occupancy percentages have improved and in many cases, profitability has been excellent.

- Variations in consumer purchasing power have led the hospitality and travel industry to offer products and services at different price levels. For example, most of the major lodging chains now have established multiple brands, ranging from economy to luxury, based on prices and amenities. Each brand targets a specific market segment.

Some of the issues in the economic environment are closely related to the trends in the social environment that will be discussed next.

The Social Environment

There are constant changes in the social environment as consumers evolve. The social environment is affected by all of the other environments. Changes in the economy, advances in technology, competitive actions, and government regulations all shape the way consumers view the world. These changes may be sudden, or they may take place over a number of years or even decades. First, there have been changes in **demographics**, or characteristics that describe the population, such as age, income, education, occupation, family size, marital status, and gender. Second, there have been changes in consumers' attitudes, interests, and opinions that determine their lifestyles.

Some issues related to the social environment affect the hospitality and travel industry:

- The proportion of two-income families and the impact that the increased discretionary income and time pressures have on their lodging, dining, and travel behaviors. These families take more but shorter vacations to fit their busy lifestyles. Also, they are quality-conscious and focus on brand names.

- The proportion of older Americans and their purchasing power are continually increasing. Senior citizens are becoming a very important market segment because people are living longer. Further, there is an improved quality of life among seniors, and their disposable income continues to

Demographics
Characteristics that describe the population such as age, income, education, occupation, family size, marital status, and gender.

increase. This segment has specific needs, and the American Association of Retired Persons (AARP) is one of the strongest political lobbying organizations in the nation.

- The dietary habits of the American people have also changed, and in some ways are bipolar: the percentage of individuals characterized as overweight or obese is at an all-time high, yet many individuals are showing an increased concern for their health. The trend has been toward healthier, more natural foods. In support of this, the United States Department of Agriculture publishes *Dietary Guidelines for Americans*, which outlines the dietary goals for the nation. The American Heart Association provides menu review and recipes that meet their dietary guidelines for good health. Many foodservice operations now feature menu items that have been approved by this organization. The National Restaurant Association has also been active in this area, especially in educating its members.

Fast-food restaurants, extended-stay hotels, and the growth in the cruise industry are all the result of changes in the social environment. These changes can offer opportunities for new products and services, while posing a threat to existing companies. For example, the increasing emphasis on brand names has resulted in tremendous growth in restaurant chains such as Outback Steakhouse, Starbucks, Panera Bread, Subway, Chili's, and Applebee's. This growth of regional and national brands has come at the expense of many independent restaurants.

The Competitive Environment

Within all markets, a variety of competitors seek to win the favor of the consumer. Each offers what it believes will be the best combination of products and services designed to result in maximum consumer satisfaction. The **competitive structure** in an industry can range from a **monopoly**, with one seller and many buyers, to **perfect competition**, with many buyers and sellers of homogeneous products that are almost exactly the same. In between, there is the **oligopoly**, with a few sellers and many buyers, and the most common form of competitive structure, **monopolistic competition**, where there are many buyers and sellers with differentiated products. The **price elasticity of demand** is a measure of the percentage change in demand for a product resulting from a percentage change in price. The price elasticity of demand normally increases as the competitive structure changes from monopoly to oligopoly to monopolistic competition and ends with perfect

Competitive structure
A combination of buyers and sellers in a market.

Monopoly
A competitive structure in an industry with one seller and many buyers.

Perfect competition
The competitive structure in an industry with many buyers and sellers of homogeneous products that are almost exactly the same.

Oligopoly
A competitive structure in an industry with a few sellers and many buyers.

Monopolistic competition
A common, competitive structure where there are many buyers and sellers with differentiated products.

Price elasticity of demand
A measure of the percentage change in demand for a product resulting from a percentage change in price.

competition. The hospitality and tourism industry is highly competitive, with new companies entering the industry every day. In the business world, four levels of competition must be considered in order for firms to be able to protect their positions in the market:[5]

- **Product form competition exists among companies that provide similar products and services to the same customers at a similar price level.** For example, McDonald's competes with Burger King and Wendy's; Delta Airlines competes with United Airlines and US Airways; Hertz competes with Avis and National; and Four Seasons Hotels competes with Ritz-Carlton and other luxury hotels.

- **Product category competition exists among companies that make the same class of products.** In this case, McDonald's competes with other fast-food restaurants such as Pizza Hut, Taco Bell, and KFC; Delta Airlines competes with charter airlines and commuter airlines; Hertz competes with all the local rental car companies; and Four Seasons Hotels competes with nonluxury hotel chains such as Marriott and Sheraton.

- **General competition exists among companies that offer the same basic service that fulfills the same basic consumer needs.** For example, McDonald's competes with all restaurants as well as with convenience stores and supermarkets; Delta Airlines and Hertz compete with all forms of transportation, such as bus and rail; and Four Seasons Hotels competes with all forms of lodging, such as bed-and-breakfasts and boutique hotels.

- **Budget competition exists among all companies that compete for consumers' disposable incomes.** Most consumers have limited budgets that can be used for purchasing products and services, and all companies compete for these consumer dollars, especially discretionary income. The hospitality and travel firms discussed earlier would compete with department stores, movie theaters, health clubs, and financial institutions for consumers' limited resources.

As companies examine the competitive environment, three important questions need to be addressed. The questions may seem straightforward, but the answers are often difficult to determine, and many firms do not make the correct decision:

1. Should we compete?

2. If we compete, in what markets should we compete?

3. What should our competitive strategy be?

The response to the first question should be based on such things as the firm's resources and objectives. The company must examine the level of potential sales, potential profitability, and the overall feasibility of competing. A firm may decide that it should not compete if the risks outweigh the potential returns or if the projected returns are not as high as it would like to see.

The second question relates to the markets in which a firm wishes to compete. Most firms elect not to compete in all potential markets. For example, although many firms, such as Marriott International, have developed brands that compete in all price segments of the lodging industry (economy through luxury), others, such as Hyatt Hotels and Resorts, initially did not chose not to compete in all price segments. They believed that the single brand strategy would serve its best long-term interests. More recently, Hyatt has adopted the multibrand strategy. The following information was posted at www.hyatt.com. This area is covered in more detail in Chapter 5.

Hyatt brands and affiliates in addition to Hyatt Hotels:

Andaz—Simple luxuries. Unexpected details.

Hyatt Place—A new kind of Hyatt for today's relaxed lifestyle.

Hyatt Summerfield Suites—Upscale all-suite hotels with full kitchens.

Hyatt Vacation Club—Own a vacation for a lifetime.

AmeriSuites—Great rates, spacious hotel rooms.

Hawthorn Suites—For business travel or for pleasure.

The third question relates to marketing strategy. How should the firm attempt to gain a competitive advantage? These decisions, which will be explored in much greater depth throughout the text, are related to issues such as products and services, pricing, distribution, and promotion.

The Political and Legal Environment

Understanding the political and legal environment means understanding the rules and regulations by which the competitive game is played. At all levels of government—local, state, national, and international—there are laws and regulations that businesses must follow. To compete successfully, a firm must understand not only the current laws and regulations but also any new ones that might come into play in the future. Most professional hospitality and tourism managers belong to one or more professional associations. One of the goals of these associations is to help members not only understand developing laws and regulations, but have influence in how they are written through lobbying efforts with politicians and government officials. Two examples of hospitality industry associations are the National Restaurant Association (NRA) and the American Hotel & Lodging Association (AH&LA). Here are some examples of issues related to the political and legal environment that affect the hospitality and tourism industry:

- **Changes in the federal tax codes have made hotel development less desirable than under previous tax codes.** So-called passive investments, in which the investor is not an active participant in the daily management of the facility, are not treated as favorably under the new federal tax codes as they were in the past. As a result, future hotel development decisions are based more on operational feasibility and less on the real estate investment aspects of the project.

- **As a means to reduce the federal budget deficit, costs are being shifted to state and local governments.** To raise tax revenues at the local level without incurring the disapproval of local voters, many localities have implemented or increased taxes on lodging and restaurant meals. These user taxes serve to increase consumer perceptions of the prices for hospitality and travel products and can have a major negative impact on operations.

- **Another related tax issue that affects the hospitality industry is the reduction in the tax credit for business meals and expenses.** The lobbyists for the NRA argued that this tax change would have a major negative impact on restaurant sales.

- **National, state, and local governments also pass laws that can affect firms' operations without using taxes.** For example, while the national government has chosen to stay on the sidelines, local and state governments are taking on the issue of smoking in public places such as restaurants and arenas. This directly affects the competitive structure of the industry when regulations do not affect all firms equally. For instance, in some areas with smoking bans, consumers can go to restaurants in nearby towns and smoke.

The idea of a level playing field is critical when governments evaluate new taxes and regulations. It is often difficult for firms to address social issues as a priority over profits, especially small firms with very limited resources. However, governments can make sure that their laws and regulations do not distort the balance of competition.

5 The Technological Environment

We live in an increasingly technological and interconnected society. With the evolution of the personal computer from an expensive desktop machine to either a notebook computer, a smartphone, or a personal digital assistant (PDA) and the pervasive access to the Internet via both wired and wireless connections, our lives have changed in ways we perhaps could not have even dreamed about before. The power of computers doubles roughly every 18 to 24 months, with prices constantly dropping. Computers are being used for more and more applications every day. Although the hospitality and tourism industry remains a highly labor-intensive and personal-contact-oriented industry, computers and technology have had and will continue to have an impact. The area in which technology will have the greatest impact in the next ten years is in direct marketing and mass customization, where a product–service provider can customize the experience for each individual customer. Through the use of database software technology, marketers have improved their ability to target their customers, track their behavior and preference, and then provide exactly what the customers desire when they want it. Through the careful use of technology, marketers can monitor guests' purchasing behavior and then tailor service offerings to meet their needs.

Direct marketing
The firm contacts consumers at home or work with promotions.

Mass customization
When a firm customizes the experience for each individual consumer.

Hotels now provide Internet stations to their customers. Courtesy of Wyndham Worldwide.

Some examples of issues related to the technological environment that affect the hospitality and travel industry:

- New technologies have helped to combat labor shortages and the high cost of labor by enabling hospitality and travel firms to shift some of these duties to consumers through self-service operations. Examples include automated check-in and checkout. This is occurring within all segments of the industry, from fast-food restaurants to luxury hotels and resorts. The very competitive environment in which commercial airlines operate has made them leaders in cost-saving applications of technology.

- The increasing sophistication and decrease in price of computer technology have had a significant impact. Most of the larger firms maintain relational databases and use resource management systems that can provide managers with the potential to better serve customers. This technology is becoming more accessible to smaller firms through service contractors and consultants.

- The development and growth of the Internet has changed the competitive structure in the hospitality and travel industry. Even small firms can now market on a national or international basis. Selling on the Internet also reduces the costs associated with service delivery, thereby increasing the profit potential for service firms. The trend toward consumers' evaluating service alternatives and making online purchases has been significant.

Along with these changes, the hospitality industry has experienced growth. Most of the leading hospitality experts are projecting continued industry growth, albeit somewhat slower rate. Certainly, a few large obstacles loom on the horizon. Existing economic cycles will cause some upward and downward shifts in the hospitality industry, and further changes in the tax codes may have some negative impact on business travel and entertaining.

THE MARKETING MANAGEMENT CYCLE

Marketing is an ongoing process. It needs constant attention to be successful. Management must regularly obtain feedback and use it to revise strategic plans. Management's role in the marketing effort is critical, for without diligent effort, the results will be less than satisfactory.

Large hospitality and tourism organizations normally have a director of marketing who is responsible for the management of all marketing activities. However, in most hospitality and tourism units, and especially in independent firms, the marketing function is the responsibility of an operations manager who must be concerned with other functions as well. This, together with the lack of a sizable budget, results in a low priority for marketing in these situations. For the larger organizations, the units are all treated the same, which could lead to some missed opportunities and competitive disadvantages. For smaller organizations, it is difficult to compete with larger chains that benefit from national and regional marketing campaigns.

The successful marketing of a hospitality operation is not something that can be accomplished overnight or with only a few hours of attention each week. Establishing and maintaining a successful marketing program requires significant management time and effort. The management activities in marketing a hospitality operation can be divided into three major areas that form a marketing management cycle: marketing planning, marketing execution, and marketing evaluation. Each of these areas will be discussed in more depth in later chapters; however, a brief overview of the major functions of each element of the marketing management cycle is presented in Figure 1.2.

Marketing Planning

The **marketing planning** process is discussed in detail in Chapter 5. There are three basic questions that should be addressed during this process. The first question is "Where are we now?" A situation analysis should be performed to determine the company's strengths and weaknesses. This information is based on past trends and historical performance, and it should include an analysis of the market and the competition. In addition, it is necessary to scan the environment for opportunities and threats. Once the company has a good grasp of the situation, it is time to move on to the next question.

Marketing planning

Managers focus on three basic questions that should be addressed during this process: Where are we now? Where do we want to go? How are we going to get there?

FIGURE 1.2 • *The marketing management cycle.*

The second question is, "Where do we want to go?" It is at this point that a company must set its goals and objectives for operating in the future. These goals and objectives should be clear, concise, and measurable over a specific time frame. All employees and stakeholders should be made aware of the strategic direction of the firm. Also, these goals and objectives become targets for evaluating the performance of the company's employees. Finally, these goals and objectives should be consistent with the company's mission statement.

The third question is, "How are we going to get there?" Once the company determines its direction for the future, it is necessary to devise strategies and action plans that can serve as a road map. Basically, marketing managers develop marketing programs that are consistent with the goals of the firm. The components of the marketing mix are under the direct control of managers, and they can be used to form strategies that will help the company to reach its goals. The actions taken with price, the product–service mix, promotion, and distribution should be integrated and lead to a common end.

Marketing Execution

Once the objectives and strategies are determined, the next step is to implement the action plans developed during the planning process, using the specific timetable that was part of the marketing plan. This is accomplished using the promotional, advertising, personal selling, and direct marketing materials and methods that were devised in the planning stage. Employees should be informed about the company's plans for its service offerings and receive additional training if necessary. Unit managers and franchisees should be made aware of the changes in the marketing plan so that they can implement them in their respective units.

Marketing Evaluation

The final step in the marketing management cycle is to monitor and control the elements of the marketing plan. Data are collected and evaluated using a variety of marketing research methods and stored in forms that allow for easy retrieval. Organizational performance needs to be analyzed in comparison with goals and objectives, looking for the underlying reasons for the difference between stated performance goals and actual performance.

Specifically, the company should analyze the effectiveness of its marketing programs, including its strategies for pricing, promoting, and distributing its products and services. The firm's performance can be evaluated relative to its competitors, using measures such as sales, market share, and customer satisfaction. Finally, at this point, firms can return to the planning stage of the marketing management cycle and make any desired changes in their objectives or their strategies.

MARKETING WITHIN THE ORGANIZATION

Marketing management, as practiced today, differs tremendously from the techniques used earlier. Marketing within the hospitality and travel industry is in a constant state of flux, as corporations plan, implement, and evaluate new marketing strategies and tactics. Marketing management practices and techniques should be analyzed and used as guidelines, but it is necessary for each hospitality organization to adjust and modify these general guidelines and techniques as dictated by the competitive environment. The competitive environment is ever changing, and this serves to attract management personnel who want to be continuously stimulated and who don't want to work in a repetitive environment.

It is also important to remember that marketing is but one of the key result areas with which management must be concerned. Within large hospitality organizations, specialists are hired to staff positions within each of the functional areas. In small organizations, however, managers must wear many hats and successfully perform all or some of these managerial functions. The following discussion places marketing in its proper place as a major part of the successful management of any hospitality organization. To fulfill an organization's potential, management must integrate its various key result areas and manage them successfully. The key result areas are interdependent and must support each other, thereby increasing the overall strength of the organization. The primary focus of all marketing efforts is to create and sustain customers. In order to do this successfully, marketers must understand and work with other managers who have responsibilities in the other key result areas discussed in this section.

Operations

Management is responsible for the day-to-day operation of the hospitality facility. This includes diverse activities such as purchasing, receiving, inventory control, production, service of guest rooms, and all of the other activities that take place each day within a successful hospitality or tourism operation. Without a strong focus on operations, the quality of the product–service mix is likely to be poor or inconsistent. Problems in the operations area of a firm can lead to declining customer counts and possible business failure. People in operations are mainly concerned with efficiency and cost containment, which are best achieved by limiting product flexibility and standardizing production and delivery. Conversely, marketing personnel are concerned with pleasing customers by providing them with the types of products and services they prefer. This requires a good deal of variety and individual customization that conflicts with the goals of production personnel. Management must balance the goals of the two areas with the goals of the firm in order to be successful.

Finance

A central and overriding goal of all businesses, including hospitality and tourism organizations, is to increase the wealth of the owners or stockholders. In periods of economic uncertainty, such as during high rates of inflation, high interest rates, or periods of recession, skilled management of the financial function becomes even more critical to the success of the hospitality organization. All hospitality organizations need to focus considerable attention on this function to manage the organization's assets and financial affairs successfully. Most areas within a firm have bottom-line financial responsibility, and managers need to understand the fundamentals of finance and accounting. All firms have limited resources, regardless of size, and it is important to invest in areas that demonstrate a high potential for meeting the targeted return. For example, financial considerations must be applied when developing new products and services, creating advertising campaigns, and setting pricing policies.

Human Resources

As a service industry, the hospitality and tourism industry places a heavy emphasis on customer service. The success of a hospitality venture depends greatly on the ability of its employees to provide a consistently high level of customer service. Management is responsible for establishing the overall direction, but it is left to each employee to implement management's strategies and action plans. The major activities of human resources include recruitment, selection, orientation, training, professional development, benefits management, compliance with laws and regulations, and other aspects of personnel relations. Historically, the turnover rate in the hospitality industry has been much higher than in other industries. Wages tend to be low in relation to responsibility, and in some cases, there is a lack of upward mobility unless the employee is willing to relocate. High rates of turnover for all positions adversely affect the entire organization. It is the responsibility of the human resources department to select employees who fit the profile of a dedicated service employee and then train them and provide support throughout their careers. In essence, the human resources department must market the firm to employees, who will then be motivated to market the firm and its products to customers.

Research and Development

To compete successfully in the years ahead, hospitality firms must invest time and money in the key result area of research and development. These efforts typically focus on developing new market segments and new elements of the product–service mix. The growth of new concepts and new types of product–service mixes is an example of the outgrowth of research and development efforts. Lodging organizations such as Choice Hotels International, Marriott International, Starwood Hotels and Resorts, Promus Hotel Corporation, and others developed all-suite hotel brands and other segmented brands in response to research and development efforts that identified a substantial consumer market for a specific set of product–service mix attributes at varying price points. Each year, they further refine their products and services offered to the traveling public with the goal of meeting and exceeding customer expectations. Because it is unlikely that a single hospitality concept will be successful indefinitely, management must be future-oriented and must anticipate necessary changes. Research and development efforts must be attuned to what consumers will want in the future. Being ready and able to change to meet future consumer needs is the real challenge of research and development. Examples of recent product–service mix enhancement within the lodging industry include such improvements as better-quality bedding and pillows, more functional desks and workspaces for business travelers, installation of larger flat-screen televisions, and wireless networks throughout the hotel. Although none of these changes are revolutionary, all address specific guest needs and enhance the guests' experience. The goal of each is to improve the guest experience and build loyalty.

Summary of Chapter Objectives

This chapter serves a vital function in introducing many concepts that will be used throughout the book. First, it provides an introduction to marketing, including the definition of marketing, the marketing process, and the difference between marketing and selling. For the purposes of this book, marketing is defined as the process of determining consumer needs, creating a product–service mix that satisfies these needs, and promoting the product–service mix in order to attain the goals and objectives of the firm.

The marketing process starts with research to determine the wants and needs of consumers so that products and services can be developed to fulfill those needs. Then, once the product–service mix is determined, the firm develops a marketing program using the other three elements of the marketing mix: price, place, and promotion. The strategies for each of the four P's are combined into a marketing program that is used to position the firm's products and services in the marketplace. The marketing management cycle consists of marketing planning, execution, and evaluation. Finally, the firm scans the environment throughout the marketing management cycle to identify any potential opportunities or threats that should be addressed. The external environment can be divided into five subenvironments: economic, social, competitive, political and legal, and technological.

Marketing is different from selling because marketing focuses on the needs of consumers, whereas selling focuses on the needs of the seller. In addition, the marketing concept advances the philosophy that the needs of the consumer should be given priority over any financial goals that the firm may have. The concept holds that if the consumer's needs and wants are totally satisfied, then financial success will follow.

Finally, it is management's responsibility to understand the role of marketing within the organization. It is important to understand how marketing interfaces with the other key result areas in the firm: operations, finance, human resources, and research and development. These key areas are normally well defined within large organizations. However, it may be difficult to separate these functions in smaller firms because the same employees are often responsible for more than one key area. One of the most critical issues is to balance the often-conflicting goals of the operations area and the marketing area with the overall goals of the firm.

chapter review

Key Terms and Concepts

Barter

Competitive structure

Consumer price index (CPI)

Demographics

Direct marketing

Discretionary income

Disposable income

Distribution

Environmental scanning

External environments

Hospitality marketing mix

Marketing

Marketing concept

Marketing information systems (MIS)

Marketing management cycle

Marketing mix

Marketing planning

Marketing program

Marketing research process

Mass customization

Monopolistic competition

Monopoly

Oligopoly

Perfect competition

Place

Price

Price elasticity of demand

Product

Product–service mix

Promotion mix

Purchasing power

Selling

Service

Word of mouth

chapter review

Questions for Review and Discussion

1. Why has marketing assumed a position of increased importance in the management of hospitality organizations?

2. What is marketing? Why is it important to the success of a firm?

3. Explain the difference between selling and marketing. How are the two similar? Think of an example to illustrate each concept.

4. What is the marketing process? Briefly explain the process and its elements.

5. What are the key variables in the marketing environment? In your opinion, which is the most important? Why?

6. Of the variables in the marketing environment, are there one or two that you believe a marketing manager can control or predict more easily than the others? If so, which one(s), and why?

7. What changes in technology will impact the hospitality and tourism industry in the next five years? What specific positive and negative impacts from technology do you foresee?

8. What is the marketing concept? What role should the marketing concept play in managing a hospitality or tourism facility?

9. Discuss the components of the traditional and hospitality marketing mixes. What role does the hospitality manager play in managing the marketing mix? How is the marketing mix used?

10. What factors can affect the marketing mix? How might these factors affect the marketing mix? How might a manager anticipate the impact that these factors might have?

11. What is the marketing management cycle? Explain and discuss the major activities with which a manager must be concerned.

12. How does the marketing function interface with other areas in an organization?

Notes

[1] American Marketing Association Dictionary website,
http://www.marketingpower.com/_layouts/Dictionary.aspx?dLetter=M, 2008.

[2] American Express Open Services, television commercial, 2003.

[3] Leo Renaghan, "A New Marketing Mix for the Hospitality Industry," *The Cornell Hotel and Restaurant Administration Quarterly* (April 1981), pp. 31, 35; Robert C. Lewis, Richard E. Chambers, and Harsha E. Chacko, *Marketing Leadership in Hospitality: Foundations and Practices*, 2nd ed. (New York: John Wiley and Sons, Inc., 1994), pp. 394–395.

[4] William Fisher, president of the National Restaurant Association, presentation at the annual conference of the Council on Hotel, Restaurant and Institutional Education, July 1994.

[5] Donald R. Lehman and Russell S. Winer, *Analysis for Marketing Planning*, 2nd ed. (Homewood, IL: Richard D. Irwin, Inc., 1991).

Case Study

Location, Location, Location?

Bruce Adams stood in the parking lot facing an empty restaurant building. The restaurant had closed 60 days earlier, after being in business for about eight months. As he visually surveyed the area he noticed several things of interest. The building itself was fairly new, having been built ten years ago by a franchisee of a national budget steakhouse chain. In the current configuration, the building had three separate dining areas, with seating for 40, 50, and 30 in the respective areas. In addition, there was a lounge that had 12 seats at the bar and space for an additional 16 seats. The quality of the building was very good, and the equipment, while not new, was certainly better than what he'd seen in other locations.

Bruce, who owned three other restaurants in another city within the state, believed that the local area offered potential. A successful 130-room, four-story Days Inn was located next to the restaurant, and it was positioned at an interchange of an interstate highway. There was a small residential community north of the restaurant that consisted of approximately 100 single-family homes priced slightly above the average for the city. To the east and south of the restaurant were over 1,500 apartments, occupied predominantly by students attending a local university. The city in which the building was located had a rapidly growing population of 50,000, and the effective trading area population for businesses in the city was over 200,000. Several universities and a community college were within a ten-mile radius of the restaurant. The local industrial base consisted of a number of small manufacturing operations. The largest employers manufactured parts for the automotive industry, published books for national and international distribution, manufactured equipment for the agricultural industry, produced beer for one of the nation's largest brewers, and provided trucking and transportation services. In addition, there was a growing service economy, and the city was home to a regional medical center and a strong professional community. At the present time, overall economic conditions in the area were good. Unemployment was very low, less than 2 percent, well below both the state and national levels.

As he stood in the parking lot, Bruce discussed the restaurant site with a business associate and a commercial real estate agent. He asked what he felt was an obvious question: "With what appear to be so many positive attributes for this location, why hasn't anyone been successful here?" In the ten years since the building was constructed, there had been five different restaurant concepts, none of them successful. The failed concepts included a budget steakhouse, a southern barbecue restaurant, two different midpriced casual dining concepts, and most recently a somewhat upscale fine-dining concept. All had proven to be unsuccessful. Most closed their doors within 9 to 12 months. The longest-running restaurant remained open for 22 months. The only individuals making any money from this location were the commercial real estate agents. As the discussion continued, Bruce wondered aloud, "What type of product–service mix might be successful here? What type of concept might attract and retain customers? How might we approach the development of a successful restaurant?"

Case Study Questions and Issues

1. How can the marketing concept be applied to this situation?

2. Should Bruce be considering the potential product–service mix for a restaurant at this location at this time? Or should he be focused on other issues? If so, what might they be?

3. What information does Bruce need in order to make a decision about the possible purchase or lease of this site?

4. How should he go about gathering this information? What should his action steps be?

5. Based on what Bruce has said, do you perceive him to be a marketer or a seller? Why?

6. Based on the information you have, assess the marketing environment.

Several reasons underlie the remarkable growth in services. Two leading services marketing experts, Christopher Lovelock and Lauren Wright, cite numerous reasons for this growth:[2]

- **Changing patterns of government regulation.** The reduction in government regulation has spurred the growth of services. In recent years, there has been a very noticeable shift toward the government taking a much less active role in the regulation of business activities. The most noteworthy of these shifts have been in the airline, trucking, telecommunication, and electrical generation and distribution industries. All of these industries have seen significant changes, as the barriers to entry have been removed and regulations governing such marketing elements as price have also been relaxed or entirely removed.

- **Relaxation of professional association restrictions on marketing.** A new element of competition has been introduced into professions such as law and medicine as more of the practitioners in these areas advertise their services. Bans or restrictions on promotion have been largely removed. Within the hospitality and tourism industry, standards have also changed. We have seen an increase in advertising focusing on direct comparisons, or attacks, on competitors' products and services. This type of advertising

The front desk agent often sets the tone for guest service. Courtesy of Hilton Hospitality, Inc.

strategy creates, or sustains, the perception of superiority in the mind of the consumer in favor of the brand being advertised.

- **Privatization of some public and nonprofit services.** The term **privatization** was first used in Great Britain when the government adopted the policy of returning national industries from government to private ownership. This transformation has resulted in a greater emphasis on cost containment and a clearer focus on customers' needs. Later, in Central and Eastern Europe, following the fall of communism, we witnessed a continuing transformation from planned or central government-run economies to market-driven economies fueled by private companies. Many of these countries' governments have released the control of airlines and other travel related agencies to private firms.

- **Technological innovation.** Technology continues to alter the way firms do business and interact with consumers. In all types of businesses, consumers take a more active role in the service delivery process. For example, airlines, in an effort to reduce labor costs and increase speed of service to customers, have aggressively promoted self-check-in, both at the ticket counter and through their Web sites prior to arrival at the airport. Customers print boarding passes, receipts, and other documents without intervention by an airline employee. Express checkout for hotel guests has been in place for many years, but hotel chains continue to experiment with ways to enhance the service, thereby reducing labor costs and/or increasing the customers' **perceived value.** In other settings, touch-screen computers collect feedback from guests, in much the same manner that comment cards have been used previously. The ease with which a company can maintain and access a database has permitted the development of sophisticated reservation systems and has led to more sophisticated frequent traveler programs. The use of more sophisticated reservations and property management systems has allowed hospitality and tourism firms to improve the level of service provided to guests. Guest history data serve as another example of how a hospitality organization can use technology to gain a competitive advantage. If a hotel guest requests a specific type of pillow, staff can record this preference within the individual's guest history file. When this guest checks into another hotel operated by the chain, the items that were previously requested can be waiting, without the guest even having to request them.

- **Growth in service chains and franchise networks.** Much of the growth in service firms, including the hospitality industry, has been the direct result of franchising efforts by some of the major companies. **Franchising** represents a contractual arrangement whereby one firm (the franchisor) licenses a

Privatization

A process whereby the government allows an industry or business to change from governmental or public ownership or control to a private enterprise.

Perceived value

This represents the perceptions that a consumer has about a product.

Franchising

A contractual arrangement whereby one firm licenses a number of other firms to use the franchisor's name and business practices.

The Nature of Services: Differences between Goods and Services

Along with the growth in services, an appreciation for the ways in which services are different from products has developed. The traditional ways of marketing tangible products are not equally effective in services marketing. In many industries, marketing involves tangible manufactured products, such as automobiles, washing machines, and clothing, whereas service industries focus on intangible products such as travel and foodservice. However, before we can explore how services get successfully marketed, we need to examine the ways services differ from products. Lovelock and Wright have identified nine key differences:[3]

1. **No ownership by customers.** A customer does not take ownership when purchasing a service. There is no transfer of assets.

2. **Service products as intangible performers.** The value of owning a high-performance car or the latest computer lies in the physical characteristics of the product and, to some extent, the brand image it conveys. The value of purchasing services lies in the nature of the performance. For example, if you decide to celebrate a birthday or anniversary by dining at an expensive restaurant, the value lies in the way in which the service actors perform. When servers come to the table and present all the entrees simultaneously, the choreographed presentation appears in the same manner as a choreographed play or performance.

3. **Greater involvement of customers in the production process.** Because consumers tend to be present when receiving service within a hospitality operation, they remain involved in the service production. In many instances, they are directly involved through the element of self-service. Examples of this can be seen in fast-food restaurants as well as in hotels that provide automated check-in and checkout by means of either a machine or a video connection through the television. Airlines have greatly expanded self-service within their operations as a means of reducing labor costs. In any case, the customer's level of satisfaction depends on the nature of the interaction with the service provider, the nature of the physical facilities in which the service gets provided, and the nature of the interaction with other guests present in the facility at the time the service is provided.

4. **People as part of the product.** People or firms that purchase services come in contact with other consumers as well as the service employees. For example, a hotel guest waits in line at the front desk or the concierge desk with other guests. In addition, the guests share facilities such as the pool,

the restaurant, and the fitness center. Therefore, service firms must also manage consumer interactions to the best of their abilities to ensure customer satisfaction. For example, a hotel's sales office would not want to book group business with a nondrinking religious group at the same time as a reunion of military veterans. The two groups are significantly different in behavior, and the expectation is that they would not mix well within the facilities at the same time. Similarly, restaurants separate smokers and nonsmokers, and they should try to separate other patrons that show some potential for conflict.

5. **Greater variability in operational inputs and outputs.** In a manufacturing setting, the operational production can be controlled very carefully. For example, staff carefully manage inventory and precisely calculate production times. Services, however, are delivered in real time, with many variables not being fully under the control of managers. For example, if a guest has been promised an early check-in but all of the guests from the preceding night are late in checking out, it becomes more difficult for the hotel to honor the arriving guest's request. A service setting remains a more difficult site in which to control quality and offer a consistent service experience. Service firms try to minimize the amount of variability between service encounters, but much of the final product stays situational. There are many uncontrollable aspects of the delivery process, such as weather, the number of consumers present, the attitudes of the consumers, and the attitudes of the employees. Therefore, it becomes impossible to consistently control the quality for services in the same manner as the quality of manufactured products.

6. **Harder for consumers to evaluate.** Consumers can receive considerable information regarding the purchase of products; however, they often do not obtain it for services. Prior to buying a product, a consumer can research the product attributes and performance and use this information when making a purchase decision, especially an important one.

7. **No inventories for services.** Due to the intangible nature of services, they cannot be inventoried for future use. Therefore, a lost sale can never be recaptured. When a seat remains empty on a flight, a hotel room stays vacant, or a table stays unoccupied in a restaurant, the potential revenue for these services at that point in time becomes lost forever. In other words, services are perishable, much like produce in a supermarket or items in a bakery. It remains critical for hospitality and tourism firms to manage supply and demand in an attempt to minimize unused capacity. For example, restaurants offer early-bird specials and airlines offer deeply discounted fares in an attempt to shift demand from peak periods to non-peak periods, thereby increasing revenue and profits.

8. **Importance of time.** Hospitality services are generally produced and consumed simultaneously, unlike tangible products, which are manufactured, inventoried, and then sold at a later date. Customers must be present to receive the service. There are real limits to the amount of time that customers are willing to wait to receive service. Service firms study the phenomenon of service queues, or the maximum amount of time a customer will wait for a service before it has a significant (negative) impact on his or her perception of service quality. Airline companies offer curbside check-in for the most time-conscious passengers, and restaurants have devised practices such as providing guests with pagers and expanding the bar area in order to reduce the negative effect that results from waiting for service.

9. **Different distribution channels.** The distribution channel for services is usually more direct than the traditional channel (i.e., manufacturer-wholesaler-retailer-consumer) used by many product firms. The simultaneous production and consumption normally associated with service delivery limits the use of intermediaries. The service firm usually comprises both the manufacturer and the retailer, with no need for a wholesaler to inventory its products. Consumers are present to consume the meals prepared in a restaurant, to take advantage of the amenities in a hotel, and to travel between cities by plane.

Intangible products, such as a cruise, are the basis of services marketing.
Courtesy of Carnival Cruise Lines.

Search, Experience, and Credence Qualities

Consumer behavior is covered in greater depth in Chapter 3, but a brief introduction to the subject as it relates to services becomes useful at this point. When consumers make purchase decisions, they move through a series of steps that explain the thought process leading up to and following the purchase of a product or service. Prior to making a purchase decision, consumers look for information about the product or service. **Search qualities** are attributes that the consumer can investigate prior to making a purchase. When purchasing hospitality and tourism services, consumers rely heavily on word of mouth and on promotional elements such as advertising and publicity. Since services are intangible, search qualities can be difficult to evaluate. However, advances in technology and the increase in consumer advocacy groups have resulted in more information being available to consumers prior to purchase.

Search qualities
Attributes that the consumer can investigate prior to making a purchase.

The second set of qualities consumers use to evaluate services are **experience qualities**. These refer to the attributes that can be evaluated only after the purchase and consumption of a service. The intangible nature of services forces consumers to rely heavily on experience qualities in the final evaluation of services. Therefore, a high risk remains associated with the purchase of services. For example, consumers who want to purchase an automobile will test-drive the car and review and consult the consumer performance data that are available on that model. Conversely, consumers who rent cars cannot evaluate their purchases until after they have committed their payment. Few consumers will take the time or make the effort to test-drive potential rental cars prior to making a decision at the time of rental. Similarly, consumers are taking a risk when they choose a restaurant because they cannot sample meals before they are purchased.

Experience qualities
Attributes that can be evaluated only after the purchase and consumption of a service.

Finally, **credence qualities** are those attributes that are difficult to evaluate even after the service is consumed. Even though you arrive safely at your destination after a flight, you cannot evaluate the pilot's work in any real depth. In many cases, you know a service was not performed correctly only when an obvious mistake exists. For example, bacteria often appear on food served in restaurants, but the public becomes aware of it only when major ramifications such as food poisoning or deaths get publicized.

Credence qualities
Attributes that are difficult to evaluate even after the service is consumed.

Purchase decisions related to services are more difficult to make because of the lack of search qualities and the difficulty in evaluating credence qualities. Consumers tend to rely on their own past experiences and those of others when making purchase decisions. Therefore, service firms must obtain as much feedback from consumers as possible. If consumers do not return, the firm may not know why, and the consumers will probably tell others about their experience. Service firms should know if consumers are not satisfied so that appropriate actions can be taken to improve the quality of service and increase repeat business.

SERVICE QUALITY

Firms use two basic strategies to compete: Become a low-cost provider of a particular service and focus on price competition, or focus on quality and try to differentiate your service from those offered by your competitors. Firms that can project high-quality images can charge higher prices. Pricing strategies are discussed in detail in Chapter 15, but the concept of quality will be introduced in this chapter.

Service quality is a perception resulting from attitudes formed by customers' long-term, overall evaluations of performance.[4] Maintaining high-quality service in the hospitality and tourism industry remains difficult because of the variability in service delivery mentioned earlier in this chapter. Service quality is affected by all of the individuals who have contact with customers. If one employee provides below-standard service or fails to satisfy the customer, a negative experience could result. Therefore, it is important to understand the entire process of service delivery that leads to consumer perceptions of quality.

Service quality

A perception resulting from attitudes formed by customers' long-term overall evaluations of performance.

Satisfied customers are repeat customers, one of the goals of managing service quality.
Courtesy of Gaylord Opryland Resort & Convention Center, Nashville, TN

The Service Quality Process

The service quality process is the product of the expectations and perceptions of a firm's management, its employees, and the customers it serves (see Figure 2.1).[5] Whenever there are differences in expectations or perceptions between the people involved in the delivery and the consumption of services, a potential for a gap in service quality exists. Firms should diagnose any service quality gaps because there is a direct relationship between service quality and customer satisfaction. Simply stated, when customers are satisfied, they are much more likely to purchase from the service provider again. Over time, if they remain satisfied, they become loyal customers. The **service gap** is the final gap that exists when there is a difference between customers' expectations of a service and their perceptions of the actual service once it is consumed. When this difference occurs, it is the result of one or more gaps that occur earlier in the service quality process.

Service gap

The final gap that exists when there is a difference between customers' expectations of a service and their perceptions of the actual service once it is consumed.

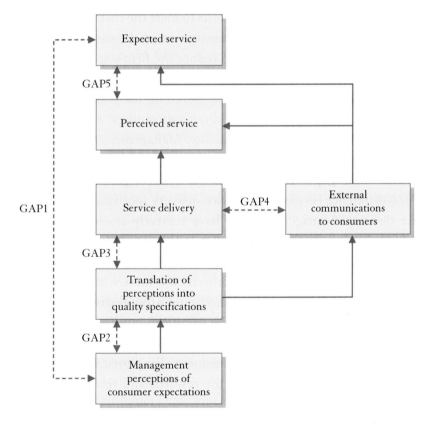

FIGURE 2.1 • *Service quality process.* Reprinted with permission of the *Journal of Marketing,* published by the American Marketing Association.

customers know that the airline provided high-quality service, and (2) it gave employees an idea of the firm's service expectations.

Finally, firms need to provide employees with rewards and recognition when they perform at a high level of discretionary effort. This motivates service providers to continue performing at high levels and to remain loyal to the firm. Retaining good employees is important in providing high-quality service, and it reduces the costs associated with turnover. It takes a great deal of time and effort to hire and train good employees. Firms can use extrinsic rewards such as salary increases and bonuses or intrinsic rewards such as recognition and job satisfaction to motivate employees. Many firms recognize "employees of the month" by honoring them with plaques displayed where customers can see them or allowing them to use special parking spaces close to the building.

CUSTOMER SATISFACTION

Benchmarking

A process whereby a firm establishes a level of performance by comparing current performance against past performance, or by comparing current performance against the performance of other companies or an entire industry.

Most firms understand the importance of customer satisfaction and will provide basic training to their employees. The more sophisticated firms actually have instruments that they use to measure customer satisfaction and establish benchmarks for future comparisons. **Benchmarking** is a process whereby a firm establishes a level of performance by comparing current performance against past performance, or by comparing current performance against the performance of other companies or an entire industry. Data are used to create benchmarks, which then become the standard against which current and future performance is evaluated. Unfortunately, many firms still only pay lip service to customer satisfaction and the complaints received from customers. The following information was collected through the efforts of the Technical Assistance Research Program several years ago, but it remains accurate today:[8]

- The average business does not hear from 96 percent of its unhappy customers.

- For every complaint received, 26 other customers have the same problem.

- The average person with a problem tells 9 or 10 people, and 13 percent will tell more than 20.

- Customers who have their complaints resolved to their satisfaction tell an average of 5 people about the experience.

- Complainers are more likely to do business with you again than non-complainers who have a problem: 54 to 70 percent if resolved, and 95 percent if resolved quickly.

These statistics support the contention that a dissatisfied customer tells people about a bad experience more often than a satisfied customer tells people about a good experience. However, firms should take note that it is beneficial to have customers voice their complaints so that they can be resolved and increase the likelihood that the customers will return.

Improving Customer Service and Customer Satisfaction

Improving customer service should be a top priority of all managers working in the hospitality and tourism industry. Superior **customer satisfaction** occurs when a firm's service, as perceived by customers, meets or exceeds expectations. Firms that can consistently meet or exceed customer expectations will develop good reputations and often good-quality images. When we travel, we encounter service providers in hotels and restaurants who provide exceptional service. This type and consistency of service does not happen by accident; it begins with a commitment by management to make it that way. Conversely, when the opposite occurs, the finger should be pointed at management as well.

Quality Service: The Restaurant Manager's Bible by William Martin remains an excellent source for methods to improve service.[9] Martin recommends the five-step process for improving customer service that is shown in Figure 2.3.

1. **Define your standards of quality service with measurable indicators.** Before you can evaluate the level of service provided by employees within your organization, you must establish the standards by which they will be judged. These standards, or benchmarks, should be observable and measurable. For example, it might be reasonable to expect front desk agents to answer the telephone within four rings or room service to deliver meals within 30 minutes of when the order was received. Once these standards are developed, they must be communicated to all personnel. It remains crucial that standards be clearly defined before any plans are developed to improve the level of service.

Martin suggests two major dimensions to define quality service: the **procedural dimension** and the **convivial dimension.** The procedural dimension includes incremental flow of service, timeliness, accommodating consumer needs, anticipating consumer needs before they occur or are

Customer satisfaction
This occurs when a firm's service, as perceived by customers, meets or exceeds their expectations.

Procedural dimension
This refers to the procedures used in the service delivery process.

Convivial dimension
This refers to the human element (e.g., body language, saying the guest's name) in the service delivery.

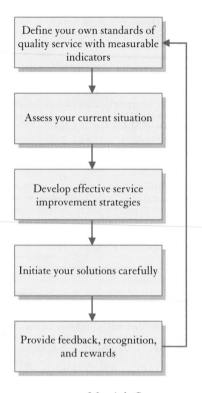

FIGURE 2.3 • *Martin's five-step process for improving customer service.*

requested by the consumer, communicating in a clear and concise manner, obtaining consumer feedback, and coordinating through proper supervision. The convivial dimension includes displaying a positive attitude and body language, using the guest's name as a means of delivering personal attention, attending to the guest on a personal basis, providing guidance to guests who are indecisive, and solving problems that arise.

2. Assess your current situation. As in any continuous improvement program, before you move forward, you must determine your current position. This can be done by objectively assessing the level of service currently provided within the organization; this involves conducting an audit of the services provided by service personnel within the organization. As a result of the audit, the strengths and weaknesses of the firm can be determined. This will provide a means of building on the aspects of service that are positive and improving the areas that are deficient. Audits can be conducted using mystery shoppers, or corporations may use staff members to audit the performance of units within the company.

3. Develop effective service improvement strategies. This must be accomplished through well-planned and thorough training of service providers. Attention must be paid to identifying objectives for the training and providing specific instructions and clear descriptions of the expected outcome(s) of the training.

4. **Initiate your solutions carefully.** As with any plan, implementation is the most critical stage. You should proceed with caution, taking steps incrementally rather than all at once. You should build on small successes, rather than trying to accomplish too much too soon.

5. **Provide feedback, recognition, and rewards.** Positive feedback must be provided if the change in behavior continues. A reward structure must be provided that will maintain the level of interest and enthusiasm among the service providers throughout their careers. This represents a major challenge for management, but one that is well worth the effort.

Finally, management must continually evaluate the performance of its employees and make the appropriate changes. Over time, customers' expectations of service firms change, and competitive firms may increase the level of service that is considered the standard in an industry. Therefore, firms must constantly reassess their strategies and redefine their service standards. Service performance and customer satisfaction should be measured and evaluated using benchmarks established during previous periods. Also, direct comparisons with the performance of firms considered industry leaders are an excellent way to establish goals for future improvement.

Service Failures, Customer Complaints, and Recovery Strategies

Service failures occur at **critical incidents**, or "moments of truth," in the service encounter, when customers interact with a firm's employees. It is important to provide service personnel with the authority and the recovery tools necessary to correct service failures as they occur. This section will discuss the types of service failures, common consumer complaints, and **recovery strategies** that can be used to repair the service failures.

SERVICE FAILURES. The timeliness and form of response by service providers to service failures will have a direct impact on customer satisfaction and quality perceptions. Service failures are assigned to one of three major categories: (1) responses to service delivery system failures, (2) responses to customer needs and requests, and (3) unprompted and unsolicited employee actions.

The first category, **system failures**, refers to failures in the core service offering of the firm. These failures are the result of normally available

Service failures

Service failures are assigned to one of three major categories: (1) responses to service delivery system failures, (2) responses to customer needs and requests, and (3) unprompted and unsolicited employee actions.

Critical incidents

"Moments of truth" when customers interact with a firm's employees and have a positive or negative experience.

Recovery strategies

Strategies used to recover from service failures. Common service recovery strategies include conduct cost/benefit analysis, encourage and respond to complaints, anticipate the need for recovery, train employees, and empower the front line of employees.

System failures

When a failure or service breakdown occurs in a core service provided by the firm.

services being unavailable, unreasonably slow service, or some other core service failure that will differ by industry. For example, a hotel's pool may have a leak and be closed, a customer may have to wait a long time for the shuttle to an airport car rental agency, or an airline might mishandle a passenger's luggage.

Customer needs failures

These are based on employee responses to customer needs or special requests.

The second category, **customer needs failures**, are based on employee responses to customer needs or special requests. These failures come in the form of special needs, customer preferences, customer errors, and disruptive others (i.e., disputes between customers). For example, a hotel guest may want to have a pet in the room, a customer may want to be switched to an aisle seat on an airplane, a customer at an event may lose his ticket, or a customer in a restaurant may be smoking in a nonsmoking section.

Unsolicited employee actions

Actions, both good and bad, of employees that are not expected by customers.

The third category, **unsolicited employee actions**, refers to the actions, both good and bad, of employees that are not expected by customers. These actions can be related to the level of attention an employee gives to customers, to unusual actions that can be performed by employees, to an action's reinforcement of a customer's cultural norms, or to an employee's actions under adverse conditions. For example, a hostess in a restaurant could anticipate the needs of a family with a small child, a hotel front desk clerk could give a free upgrade to a guest who waited in line too long, a flight attendant could ignore passengers with children, or a cruise ship employee could help to evacuate passengers during a crisis.

CUSTOMER COMPLAINT BEHAVIOR. As mentioned earlier in this chapter, certain undesired outcomes are associated with dissatisfied customers. Two of the most common are to engage in negative word of mouth and to change service providers. A third, less common reaction is to engage in some form of retaliation. This retaliation can range from a negative word-of-mouth campaign to causing physical damage or launching a major protest. The way a firm approaches and handles complaints will determine its long-term performance. Some firms show a dislike for customers who complain, while other firms create an atmosphere that encourages customers to voice their concerns. For example, Bertucci's Brick Oven Pizzerias, headquartered in Massachusetts, offers customers a toll-free number that they can call to register a complaint. One of the primary reasons for doing this is to provide dissatisfied customers with an outlet to have their concerns heard and to take immediate steps to resolve the complaint. By doing so, the firm hopes to reduce negative word of mouth and to retain customers.

Most customers complain in an attempt to reverse an undesirable state. Other more complicated reasons for complaining are to release pressure, to regain some form of control over a situation, or to get the sympathy of others. Whatever the reason, the outcome is that customers are not completely satisfied, and it is in the firm's best interest to know when this occurs. There are many other dissatisfied customers who do not complain because they don't know what to do or they don't think it will do any good.

RECOVERY STRATEGIES. When customers complain, firms are presented with the opportunity to recover from service failures. **Recovery strategies** and actions occur when a firm's reaction to a service failure results in customer satisfaction and goodwill. In fact, customers who are involved in successful service recoveries often demonstrate higher levels of satisfaction than customers who do not report service failures or complain. The following list describes popular service recovery strategies:

- **Cost/benefit analysis.** Service firms should conduct a **cost/benefit analysis** to compare the costs of losing customers and obtaining new customers with the benefits of keeping existing customers. Most firms place a high value on retaining customers. However, some guests take advantage of satisfaction guarantees and complain on every occasion. Many hotel chains, such as Doubletree, maintain a database on complaints and will flag chronic complainers.

- **Actively encourage complaints.** It is better to know when customers are not satisfied so that action can be taken to rectify the situation. It is important to note that while unhappy customers may not complain to service firms, they will often complain to their family and friends. Hospitality and tourism firms use comment cards and toll-free numbers to encourage customers to provide feedback. Also, service personnel are trained to ask customers whether everything was satisfactory.

- **Anticipate the need for recovery.** Service firms should "blueprint" the service delivery process and determine the moments of truth, or critical incidents, where customers interact with employees. The process can be designed to avoid failures, but recovery plans should be established for use in the event that a failure occurs.

- **Respond quickly.** The timelier the response in the event of a service failure, the more likely that recovery efforts will be successful. Once a customer leaves a service establishment, the likelihood of a successful recovery falls dramatically. Based on this principle, firms such as Marriott International provide service hotlines at each hotel to help resolve problems quickly. Managers and associates know that the speed with which they respond is often as critical as what the final resolution becomes.

Recovery strategies
Strategies used to recover from service failures. Common service recovery strategies include conduct cost/benefit analysis, encourage and respond to complaints, anticipate the need for recovery, train employees, and empower the front line of employees.

- **Train employees.** Employees should be informed of the critical incidents and provided with potential strategies for recovery. For example, some hotel training programs use videotaped scenarios of service failures to show employees potential problems and the appropriate solutions.

- **Empower the front line.** In many cases, a successful recovery will hinge on a frontline employee's ability to take timely action and make a decision. Firms should empower employees to handle service failures at the time they occur, within certain limits. For example, Ritz-Carlton allows its employees to spend up to $1,000 to take care of dissatisfied customers.

One of the classic examples of a service failure involved Northwest Airlines during a major winter storm at the Detroit airport. Unfortunately, due to the heavy snow, many outbound flights were canceled, and no gates were available for unloading passengers from the inbound flights. This traffic jam left many passengers stranded as the airplanes sat on the tarmacs and taxiways for several hours. Northwest's inability to provide the passengers with information or a solution resulted in hundreds of unhappy passengers and a class-action lawsuit. Having delayed flights and a shortage of gates is not a new phenomenon at airports in climates such as Detroit's, and Northwest Airlines should have had a viable service recovery program in place that could have lessened the severity of the problem.

Techniques to Assess Customer Satisfaction

One of the critical components of a firm's commitment to customer satisfaction is feedback that provides an assessment of the firm's performance. Then benchmarks can be established and future progress can be evaluated. Also, these measures can be used to reward service personnel in a way that stays consistent with a firm's customer satisfaction goals. The following section describes the most common techniques used by firms to assess customer satisfaction.

SPOKEN COMMENTS AND COMPLAINTS. Listening to consumer comments and complaints remains the most straightforward way to evaluate customer satisfaction. Service firms should set up formal systems that encourage customer and employee feedback regarding service experiences. Management should not overlook the value of the information obtained by boundary-spanning personnel through their normal contact with customers. One of the most recent approaches is providing toll-free numbers so that customers can call to voice complaints.

SURVEYS AND COMMENT CARDS. Many hospitality and tourism firms leave comment cards in guest rooms, on tables in restaurants, and at other points of contact so that they can obtain feedback. One of the problems associated with this method is the lack of representation. The response rate is small, and it tends to be biased toward those who are most upset and chronic complainers. Larger operations will conduct surveys through the corporate offices by either telephone or mail. Surveys will normally be more representative than comment cards and provide more detailed information. These types of surveys also provide for a more representative sample of customers.

NUMBER OF REPEAT CUSTOMERS. Service firms can gauge customer satisfaction by keeping track of repeat business. Higher levels of satisfaction would be associated with higher percentages of repeat customers. This models an unobtrusive method of assessing customer satisfaction, but it does not provide much detail.

TRENDS IN SALES AND MARKET SHARE. Another way to evaluate customer satisfaction without direct contact with customers is to examine the firm's internal sales records. Comparisons can be made on a month-to-month basis and with the same period of the previous year. Higher levels of satisfaction would be associated with increases in sales. However, firms should be careful with this method because there are many possible explanations for increases in sales. For example, the firm may have launched a new advertising campaign, a competitor may be renovating or going out of business, or the firm may have decreased its prices. In addition to examining sales records, firms should also look at market share. This measure considers sales in relation to the competition, which is a more accurate assessment of improved market performance. However, there could also be other explanations for changes in market share besides customer satisfaction.

SHOPPING REPORTS. Another approach used by hospitality and tourism firms involves having someone consume a service just like any other customer. The "secret shopper" can be an employee of the firm, an outside person chosen by the firm, or an employee of an outside firm that specializes in this service assessment activity. These shoppers are normally equipped with detailed evaluation forms based on company guidelines that can be used to record the desired information. It is often recommended that someone outside the firm be used in an attempt to maintain some level of objectivity. It is important to have a particular operation evaluated by more than one shopper on several occasions throughout the desired period. Doing so will result in a more representative sample of service experiences.

SERVICE TRENDS AFFECTING THE HOSPITALITY AND TOURISM INDUSTRY

Identifying trends within any business is one of the keys to success. Being in a position to identify what is occurring and what is likely to occur in the future remains very important. As discussed in Chapter 1, when studying trends in a broad sense, one should examine five major areas: the competitive environment, the economic environment, the political and legal environment, the social environment, and the technological environment.

Several issues and trends are critical to understanding hospitality and tourism marketing. They help put into proper perspective what occurs within the competitive marketplace. Three trends that are having an impact on the hospitality industry and will continue to do so are shrinking customer loyalty, increasing customer sophistication, and increasing emphasis on the needs of individual customers.

Shrinking Customer Loyalty

Advertising and promotion for the hospitality and tourism industry's product–service mix have traditionally focused on the product, the services provided, and the physical plant or atmosphere in which the customer enjoys the product–service mix. Today, many hospitality and tourism firms focus their promotions on price; that is, heavy price competition exists along with a good deal of discounting. Unfortunately, price discounting exists as a short-term strategy that seldom builds brand loyalty. Consumers often shop around for the best deal and are loyal only to organizations that give them a consistently superior one. Recognizing this, companies have sought ways to increase brand loyalty, especially among heavy users of the product–service mix. The best examples of this approach are the frequent flyer programs promoted by the airlines and the frequent traveler programs promoted by the lodging companies. These loyalty programs are commonplace in the lodging industry; all of the major chains use loyalty programs to encourage and reward frequent guests. The strategy behind loyalty programs is to hook the customer with points that can be redeemed for products or services. The more frequently the customer stays at a hotel operated by the company, the more points are earned. The basic concepts common to all of these programs are as follows:

- Identify individuals who frequently purchase your product–service mix.

- Recognize the contribution those individuals make to the success of your company.

- Reward those individuals with awards and incentives that will increase their loyalty to your company and its brands.

Tie-ins with other companies providing travel-related services are also frequently used. For example, airlines, hotels, and car rental companies frequently offer bonus points within their programs if the traveler uses the services offered by one of the companies participating in the tie-in. Both the airlines and the hotel companies are constantly making minor alterations to their programs.

Increasing Consumer Sophistication

The budget segment of the lodging industry has undergone significant growth in the last several years. This growth has been fueled by the consumer demand for affordable accommodations that provide good value. In fact, consumers focus more on value and less on quality or price alone. Consumers have become more sophisticated and understand the concept of value at any price level. Companies have responded with brands that offer good quality at an affordable price (e.g., Hampton Inn, Comfort Inn, Holiday Inn Express, and Fairfield Inn). Each of these brands features nicely appointed guest rooms, limited or no public meeting space, limited or no foodservice provided on the hotel site, and a complimentary continental breakfast for guests. These limited-service brands incur lower development and operating expenses and thereby can provide guests with a lower price and good value, something that all consumers are seeking.

Hotels in the upscale segment are also trying to increase the consumer's perception of value. They continually provide a broad assortment of amenities, such as health clubs on the property, business centers, rooms that provide more work space for business travelers, and personalized concierge service. These properties are striving to become "one-stop" destinations, providing a complete product–service mix that includes many food and beverage outlets, in-house office services, a wide variety of meeting room configurations, and other services, such as recreation, that will appeal to potential guests. Within

Affordable price and familiar brands are important in a global market. Visitors to The Forbidden City in Beijing, China, can stay at this Days Inn. Courtesy of Wyndham Worldwide.

Hotels provide amenities, such as health clubs, to increase the consumer's perception of value. Courtesy of Gaylord Opryland Resort & Convention Center, Nashville, TN.

the fast-food service segment, companies often "bundle" their products in an attempt to increase sales and provide a better value for their customers. For example, they combine a sandwich, a large order of french fries, and a large soft drink at a price lower than what the items would cost if purchased separately. Similarly, tour operators and travel agents attempt to provide customers with more value by "bundling" the various components of travel (e.g., airline ticket, hotel room, car rental, and tickets for tourist at-service attractions) at a price lower than the sum of the individual components. This approach is known as **product bundling**.

Product bundling

An approach in which menu items are bundled with other items, often at a price that is less than if the individual items were separately ordered.

Increased Emphasis on the Needs of Individual Customers

The markets within both hospitality and tourism segments have been segmented for a long time. In the past 20 years, this trend has become even more pronounced. Mass marketing has become a thing of the past as more firms extend their product lines to meet the specific needs of smaller segments of travelers and diners. This phenomenon has become most apparent in the lodging industry. During the last decade, most of the major lodging chains

20 or 30 minutes for our turn. We were assigned to a room, but at this point we had a few bags and my son was fast asleep and had to be carried. When I asked for assistance with our luggage, I was told that no one was available at that time of night. The hotel was large, having over 1,000 rooms, and the rooms were spread out among several adjacent buildings. Our room was two buildings away from the lobby area. My wife and I struggled to carry the luggage and our son to the room. We arrived there about 11:30 and attempted to enter the room. The key unlocked the door, but the door would not open. After a couple of attempts, we heard a woman's voice in the room. Obviously, the room had been double-booked and the woman woken from her sleep. I used the house phone to call the front desk and explain the predicament. The front desk manager offered a quick apology and said that she would send someone with a key to a nearby room. About ten minutes later, a housekeeper happened to be going through the hallway, and she let my family into the room that I had been given over the phone. However, the housekeeper had no idea what was going on and took my word. After we had been in the room for ten minutes, the phone rang and I spoke with the front desk manager. She acted as though she had sent the housekeeper to open the room, but she still needed to send someone with the room keys. She apologized one last time and told me to call the front desk if I had any other problems."

Case Study Questions and Issues

1. What steps should Kristen recommend to the general manager?

2. What action steps and timetable should she recommend? How should decisions be made about which steps should be done initially?

3. Develop a service blueprint of the check-in process. How might this be used to improve the situation?

4. Discuss the gaps in the service quality process that Bill Foster experienced.

5. What kind of service failures occurred and what recovery strategies were employed?

6. How did the Excelsior Hotel fail to meet Mr. Foster's expectations?

7. What other actions could have been taken?

Case Study

Service Quality at Express Airlines

Ben Kidd was a relatively new associate with Express Airlines, a national carrier with extensive routes in the eastern half of the country. On one particular night, Ben was working the gate in Chicago, getting ready to load a flight to Washington, D.C. The flight was scheduled to be about 90 percent full, so he wanted to begin boarding passengers as quickly as possible after the plane landed, the passengers deplaned, and the cleaning crew got the plane ready for the next flight. When the plane landed 20 minutes later than scheduled, the pilot reported a small mechanical problem that would have to checked by the airline mechanics prior to when the outbound passengers boarded the aircraft and departed for Washington, D.C.

There was a crew change for the flight as well. The crew—pilot, first officer, and flight attendants—boarded the plane as soon as the inbound passengers deplaned. The outbound pilot spoke with the inbound pilot and the mechanics concerning the mechanical problem. There was some uncertainty, but the mechanics felt that the problem was minor and could be repaired within the next 30 minutes. The pilot reported this to Ben, who then provided an update to the outbound passengers about the 30-minute departure delay. A few passengers approached the desk in the gate area to speak with Ben about travel options, while other passengers immediately pulled their mobile phones out of their pockets, placing calls to the airline and other travel agencies to explore options. Ben felt he had done an excellent job in informing the passengers about the delay caused by the mechanical problem and couldn't quite understand why passengers were so "edgy" about the delay and were pressing him for more information and assurances that the flight would depart after the 30-minute delay while the mechanics made the necessary repairs.

After about 15 minutes, Ben checked with the outgoing pilot, the mechanics working on the repair and his supervisor. It was determined that the repairs were progressing on schedule and that the passengers should be loaded in anticipation of a 30-minute delayed departure. Ben immediately began to load the plane, beginning with the premier-level passengers. That entire process took about 20 minutes, during which time the mechanics continued to work on the repair. As the last passenger took her seat, the mechanics informed the pilot and Ben that the repairs could not be completed and that the plane would need to be returned to the hanger to complete the repair. The plane would not be available for service until sometime the next day, as an additional part needed to be installed and would not be available until the next day. As Ben hung up the phone after talking with the pilot, the pilot announced to the seated passengers that the repair could not be made and that all passengers would have to leave the aircraft. He apologized for the delay and indicated that airline personnel would be available to assist passengers with modifying their plans.

Case Study Questions and Issues

1. Assess the actions that Ben undertook. What were the positive actions? What might he have done differently?

2. Develop a service blueprint of the preboarding and boarding of the flight to Washington, D.C. How might this be used to improve the situation?

3. What specific action steps and timetable would you recommend to Ben at this point?

4. Are there other individual airline personnel that might become involved? What role(s) might they play?

5. Discuss the gaps in the service quality process that passengers experienced.

6. What other actions could have been taken by Express Airlines personnel?

case study

part 2

UNDERSTANDING AND TARGETING
HOSPITALITY CONSUMERS

Courtesy of Mobile Bay CVB.

SELF-ACTUALIZATION NEEDS. The highest-level needs within Maslow's hierarchy focus on an individual's need to reach his or her full potential. For the most part, these needs are often beyond the scope of what hospitality and tourism marketers can expect to fulfill. However, there are examples from within the hospitality and tourism industry regarding the consumer's attempt to satisfy self-actualization needs. For example, when guests are attracted to sports programs at five-star resorts focusing on how to play the best golf or tennis possible, they are seeking to reach a state of self-actualization with regard to the sport.

An alternative approach combines the work of Maslow with the work on personality development by Erik Erikson.[3] In this model, adults pass through three life stages, and each stage will help to determine the kinds of experiences that they will seek as consumers (see Figure 3.3). Consumers purchase products either because they need them, because they desire them, or both. Purchases based on need are considered nondiscretionary, while purchases based on desire are considered discretionary. Consumer satisfaction is achieved mainly through discretionary purchases.

In the first stage, young adults (age 40 or younger) are seeking satisfaction through purchasing *possession experiences* in their early career-development and family-building years. Examples of products purchased during this stage are cars and houses. Then, as they grow older (age 40 to 60), consumers focus more on purchasing *catered experiences* such as travel, restaurants, education, and sports. Finally, the third stage (age over 60) finds consumers shifting their focus toward *being experiences* associated with interpersonal relationships and simple pleasures. In this context, hospitality services would be purchased more in the second stage, although they would be purchased merely for survival throughout a consumer's life span. Some resorts, spas, and travel destinations target the third stage as well. For example, some destinations market themselves to older travelers who are seeking a more spiritual experience.

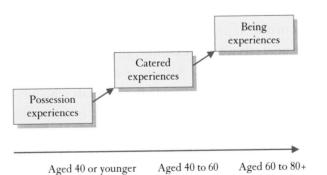

FIGURE 3.3 • *Consumer discretionary purchasing over a life span.*

Psychologist David McClelland identified three social motives: achievement, affiliation, and power.[4] Achievement causes an individual to work harder to reach a goal. Affiliation causes individuals to belong to groups or to seek the approval of others. Each person has the need to belong and to be accepted. Finally, McClelland identified individuals' need for power. Individuals want to feel that they have some control over their immediate environment.

EXPERIENCE. Experience is also a major internal influence on consumer behavior. As individuals encounter new situations, such as dining in a particular restaurant for the first time, they integrate their perceptions into an experience framework that influences future decisions. The old adage, "First impressions are important," applies directly to the hospitality and tourism industry. If consumers are turned off the first time that they walk up to the front desk in a hotel or are greeted by a host in a restaurant, they are unlikely to return. One of the factors that have led to the success of Walt Disney World is that the staff, called "cast members," focus on the guests' needs from the moment they arrive on site until they depart. In the morning when carloads of excited families arrive, they are greeted by smiling parking-lot cast members who help to get everyone's day at Disney off to a memorable start. These initial impressions are the start of a great day for the guests.

Hospitality managers must remember that people (consumers) are products of their environments. Each new experience is integrated into a frame of reference against which new situations are evaluated. This frame of reference includes each individual's beliefs, values, norms, and assumptions. Consider the following example. A guest who travels more than 100 days each year checks into a hotel at which she has not previously stayed. As the guest checks in, she is evaluating the quality of the service received against prior check-in experiences. Based on her prior experience, she may believe that the check-in process should not take more than 60 seconds to complete. Any time in excess of 60 seconds will likely result in dissatisfaction with the hotel. In this example, the guest has a belief that check-in should be accomplished quickly and easily. This is the norm against which the guest will judge all check-ins.

PERSONALITY AND SELF-IMAGE. Each individual consumer develops a unique **personality** and self-image over a period of time. For marketing purposes, individual personality types can be grouped into various classifications such as swingers, conservatives, leaders, and followers. The important thing for hospitality managers to remember is that no hospitality operation can be all things to all people. Firms must select one or more target markets that are subsets or segments of the total market and then appeal directly to these consumers. Many hospitality organizations experience difficulty when attempting to appeal to too wide a segment of the total market. The result is

Personality
An individual's distinctive psychological characteristics that lead to relatively consistent responses to his or her environment.

quite predictable: failure to satisfy any of the target markets, which leads to poor financial performance and often failure.

One example of this type of thinking involved a restaurant that featured a beef and seafood menu, with moderate to high prices and a semiformal atmosphere. This restaurant had been successful, but the owners and managers felt that more profits could and should be generated. In an attempt to broaden the target market, the atmosphere was made more informal, and the menu was changed to include hamburgers, snacks, sandwiches, and pizza, as well as steaks and seafood. Thirty days after the change was made, sales volume had increased by 15 percent. Within three months, however, volume had fallen by 38 percent, and what had once been a profitable operation was now running a deficit. Following careful examination of the performance of several hospitality organizations, one finds that it is normally those with well-defined target markets that are the most successful. Those attempting to be all things to all people often fail.

PERCEPTION AND ATTITUDE. Each day, consumers are exposed to thousands of stimuli. Some of these stimuli are consciously received, resulting in a thought process, while others are simply ignored. **Perception** is the process by which stimuli are recognized, received, and interpreted. Each individual consumer perceives the world differently. Perceptions are manifested in attitudes. As stated earlier in the chapter, attitudes are learned predispositions to act in a consistently favorable or unfavorable manner. For example, some individuals' attitudes are that fast-food meals are very good because they are of high quality and low cost and come with fast and courteous service. Other individuals' attitudes are that fast-food meals are of low nutritional value and poor culinary quality and that they are not visually attractive. Both types of individuals hold attitudes based on their perceptions. Their perceptions may or may not be valid, but it is important for the marketing manager to remember that perceptions are the way an individual sees the world. In the mind of the individual consumer, the perceptions and resulting attitudes are correct and valid. It is very difficult to change the perceptions and resulting attitudes that individuals have developed over time.

Perception

The process by which stimuli are recognized, received, and interpreted. Each individual consumer perceives the world differently.

Consumer Adoption Process

Hospitality consumers today are demanding more sophisticated dining and lodging experiences. Consumers are better educated, earn more money, and are more confident when they travel and dine outside the home. Today's hospitality consumers are seeking products and services tailored to meet their specific needs. They are more concerned about nutrition and safety, and they know more about value. Some of the following trends in individual behavior are affecting consumerism:

- Receiving instant gratification rather than the concept of self-denial

- Feeling terrific rather than feeling responsible

- Improvising rather than planning

- Choosing simplicity over complexity

- Showing concern for status rather than egalitarianism

These trends shape the way firms develop and market their products and services. There are consumer models that aid marketers in understanding consumers and determining strategies.

Individuals have been classified according to willingness to change. Some are not upset by change, while others resist change in any form. Figure 3.4 illustrates the diffusion of consumers over a typical product life cycle. Consumers will adopt new products at different rates depending on their level of aversion to risk and change. When a new hospitality operation opens, it is very important that individuals representing the innovators and early adopters are reached by marketing efforts. These individuals offer excellent potential as early customers, for if they are satisfied, they will tell friends and associates, and these people, in turn, may become customers. People falling into the early and late majority categories will not usually try a new hospitality operation until they have heard positive comments from others.

This process of influencing the innovators and early adopters is called *diffusion and adoption*. The key is to get the consumers who are most likely to

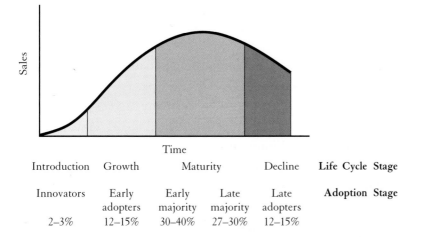

FIGURE 3.4 • *Diffusion and adoption across the product life cycle.*

try new products and services to make a trial purchase—that is, to dine at the restaurant, stay in the hotel, rent a car, or purchase a flight. If they are satisfied with the products and services received, they will then help to spread the positive word to others, and the number of customers will increase over time. How quickly consumers adopt a new product depends on the actual need for the product and the risk associated with the product's purchase.

First, products that are necessary will be adopted more readily than products that are not essential. For example, a fine-dining restaurant may take longer to build a clientele than a fast-food restaurant in a growing suburb. Second, the more risk involved with a product's purchase, the slower the adoption process. Several types of risk are associated with the purchase of a product or service:

- **Financial risk.** The monetary loss that would result from a wrong decision.

- **Performance risk.** The chance that the product or service will not meet a consumer's expectations.

- **Physical risk.** Any mental or physical harm that could occur.

- **Social risk.** The possibility that the product will not meet the approval of one's peers.

For example, a cruise can be expensive, it carries a certain prestige, and consumers have high expectations. Also, there have been instances in which passengers have been harmed or even killed, as the result of fires, taking on water, and terrorists.

CONSUMER DECISION-MAKING MODEL

When consumers make decisions concerning the purchase of goods and services, a very complex decision-making process takes place. Numerous variables influence this decision-making process, as the many models of consumer behavior demonstrate. Figure 3.5 draws together several theories into a model that shows both the external and internal influences we have just discussed, as well as the process by which consumers make purchase decisions.

This model illustrates the major steps in the decision-making process, as well as the role external and internal influences play as the individual makes purchase decisions. Because both external and internal variables influence consumers' decision-making processes, hospitality managers need to develop

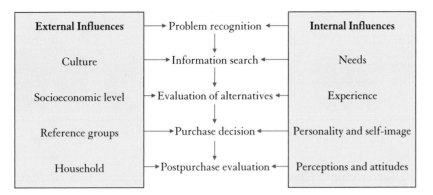

FIGURE 3.5 • *A consumer decision-making model.*

awareness of the specific influences that are most important to their particular target market segments. Figure 3.5 shows five key elements in the decision-making model: problem recognition, information search, evaluation of alternatives, purchase decision, and post-purchase evaluation. Each element is affected by external and internal influences.

Problem Recognition

The decision-making process begins with problem recognition, which occurs when a consumer realizes a difference between her actual state and her desired state. Thousands of different stimuli can trigger the awareness of a need or a problem. For example, if one feels hungry when driving down an interstate highway, this may trigger a need to search for a restaurant to satisfy the hunger need. In another situation, the need to feel important and be treated with the utmost respect may lead a potential guest to search for an upscale hotel with a concierge floor when making a reservation. The need may not begin within a single individual. For example, if a couple comes home after both have worked all day, and one says to the other, "Let's go out tonight; I'm too tired to cook," this manifests a joint need that only one of the individuals may have felt. Hospitality marketing managers should recognize the wide variety of needs that consumers are attempting to satisfy when they dine out.

Information Search

Once the need is raised to a conscious level, the model holds that consumers seek to retrieve information. This search can involve a variety of information

INFORMATION SOURCE	EFFORT REQUIRED	CREDIBILITY
Internal (past experience)	Low	High
External		
Personal (friends and family)	Low	High
Marketing (advertising, promotions, salespeople)	High	Low
Public (consumer information, Internet)	High	High

TABLE 3.1 • *Comparison of information sources.*

sources, including reference groups and members of the immediate household, as well as the mass media in the form of advertising. Table 3.1 provides a comparison of information sources based on the effort required and the credibility of the source.

If the felt need is as basic as the need to eat because of hunger, the information retrieval process is likely to be brief. That is, the restaurant facility selected in this case is likely to be chosen primarily because of convenience, and the number of sources of information consulted is likely to be quite small. In other situations, the number of sources consulted could be much larger. Consider the meeting planner who is coordinating the annual meeting for a professional association. This individual is likely to consult several sources of information before selecting an appropriate hotel for this important event. The important thing for the hospitality marketing manager to remember is that consumers rely to a certain extent on the mass media for information.

The amount of information to research and the length of the consumer decision-making process will increase with the consumer's level of involvement. Consumers tend to be more involved when there is a greater perceived risk of making a wrong choice, which is normally associated with products or services with higher prices, more visibility, or greater complexity. Consumers tend to compare the benefits of search (e.g., value, enjoyment, self-confidence) with the costs (e.g., money, time, convenience) to determine the perceived risk. There are also many other situational factors that will affect the amount of information search, such as product knowledge, demographics (e.g., income and education), and the market environment.

Evaluation of Alternatives

Once the consumer has gathered a sufficient amount of information, the third element in the decision-making process is to evaluate alternatives. Consumers who ask, "At which one of several possible restaurants should I dine tonight?" go through a cognitive process in answering this question, whereby they weigh the positive and negative aspects of each alternative. They also examine the attributes of the product–service mix of each restaurant. Consumers consider the relative importance of each attribute of the product–service mix by making trade-offs between the various attributes and their levels. The final result is an **evoked set**, or group of brands that will be considered in the final purchase decision.

Marketing managers in other industries have long recognized this cognitive process and have used it to their advantage in advertising and promoting their products and services. Rather than simply discussing their products or services as if they existed in a vacuum, firms make direct comparisons with the competition. This assists the consumer's cognitive process of evaluating alternatives. Of course, every advertiser makes certain that its product or service compares favorably with those of the competition based on the criteria selected.

The following example illustrates how a hospitality firm can gain a better understanding of the consumer decision-making process. Assume the information in Table 3.2 represents one consumer's evaluation of the importance of hotel attributes and the ratings of three competing hotels on those attributes. (This is the kind of data that could be collected using a comment card or some other type of survey.) The first column under each hotel represents the actual rating and the second column represents the weighted rating based on the importance assigned to the attribute by the consumer. The consumer was instructed to divide 100 points between the three attributes based on their relative importance. The figures were converted to decimals and the weighted

Evoked set

A set of brands that will be considered in the final purchase decision.

ATTRIBUTE	IMPORTANCE	HOLIDAY INN		MARRIOTT		FOUR SEASONS	
		Actual	*Weighted*	*Actual*	*Weighted*	*Actual*	*Weighted*
Price	.50	4	2	3	1.5	2	1
Location	.30	3	.9	3	.9	4	1.2
Service Quality	.20	2	.4	3	.6	4	.8
Average		3.00	3.30	3.00	3.00	3.33	3.00

TABLE 3.2 • *Evaluation of Alternative Hotels*

rating was computed by multiplying the importance rating by the actual rating. The final average for the weighted rating is simply the sum of the scores for each attribute. The ratings were based on a four-point scale: 1 = poor, 2 = fair, 3 = good, 4 = excellent.

The hospitality manager can see from the information in Table 3.2 that this consumer feels that price is the most important factor in choosing a hotel, followed by location, and then service quality. The manager can also tell how each hotel is perceived on the same list of attributes. In this example, the consumer prefers the Holiday Inn based on her perceptions of the hotel and her relative importance rating for each of the attributes. The Holiday Inn received the highest weighted average total across the three attributes (price, location, and service quality). This same process can be used for a market segment by combining the scores of a sample of consumers and using the aggregate figures. However, the section on consumer problem-solving strategies explains how consumers employ different heuristics for making purchase decisions.

Purchase Decision

The fourth stage in the consumer decision-making model is the purchase decision. It is at this point that the individual actually makes the decision. All external and internal variables come together to produce a decision. This decision is made based on the perceived risk associated with each alternative and the willingness of the individual to take risks. This risk factor offers a tremendous competitive advantage for hospitality chains. When consumers step through the front door of a McDonald's, Burger King, Red Lobster, or any other nationally recognized chain, they are taking a much smaller risk than if they entered an independent restaurant about which they knew very little. There is less risk with the chain operation because the product–service mix is well known to customers. Independent hospitality operations must work very hard to establish themselves and thereby reduce some of the risk consumers associate with patronizing a restaurant where the product–service mix is not well known.

There are other factors, in addition to perceived risk and risk aversion, that affect the consumer's purchase decision. The actual purchase is based on the consumer problem-solving strategy used by each individual. Some consumers base the decision on their evaluation of all the product or service attributes simultaneously, while others evaluate the attributes one at a time. Also, it depends on the consumer's involvement with the product or service category and the resultant problem-solving technique. Both of these topics are discussed in the next section, following the discussion of the final stage in the consumer decision-making process—postpurchase evaluation.

Postpurchase Evaluation

Following the product–service mix consumption, the final stage is postpurchase evaluation. How did the actual experience compare with the expectations prior to purchase? Was the product–service mix better than or not quite up to the standards anticipated? Postconsumption feelings are based on two factors: the consumer's expectations and the actual performance by the hospitality operation. For this reason, it is very important for any hospitality operation to deliver the product–service mix promised in advertising promotion or personal selling. Failure to perform at or above the level anticipated by the consumer is likely to lead to negative postconsumption feelings. These negative feelings produce dissatisfaction and reduce the level of repeat patronage. From a management perspective, it is important to promise less and deliver more—underpromise and overdeliver. This is a key concept in producing satisfied customers.[5] Finally, there is a period of time between the purchase of hospitality or tourism services and when they are consumed. During this period, consumers may have second thoughts or negative feelings about the purchase that are referred to as **cognitive dissonance**. That is why it is important for hospitality firms to run advertisements that depict satisfied customers.

Cognitive dissonance
Consumers may have second thoughts or negative feelings after they have purchased a product or service.

Consumer decision making is extremely complex. Marketing managers constantly strive to learn more about the way consumers reach decisions. As with other forms of human behavior, consumer behavior may never be totally understood.

CONSUMER PROBLEM-SOLVING PROCESSES

Consumers, either consciously or subconsciously, employ certain processes to integrate the information that they have obtained over time to evaluate and choose among the various alternatives. These formal integration strategies can be termed compensatory, noncompensatory, or a combination of the two.

Compensatory strategies
Consumers use a product's strength(s) in one or more areas to compensate for deficiencies in other areas. This strategy allows products' strengths to compensate for their weaknesses.

Compensatory Strategies

When consumers use **compensatory strategies**, they use a product's strengths in one or more areas to compensate for deficiencies in other areas. In other words, consumers view products and services as bundles of attributes. The set

ATTRIBUTE	IMPORTANCE	HOLIDAY INN		MARRIOTT		FOUR SEASONS	
		Actual	*Weighted*	*Actual*	*Weighted*	*Actual*	*Weighted*
Price	.50	4	2	3	1.5	2	1
Location	.30	2	.6	3	.9	4	1.2
Service Quality	.20	2	.4	3	.6	4	.8
Average		2.66	3.00	3.00	3.00	3.33	3.00

Compensatory Strategy: highest average score
Conjunctive Strategy: all scores above minimum threshold of 3.0 for all attributes
Disjunctive Strategy: highest score on most important attribute (price)
Lexicographic Strategy: highest score starting with most important attribute (price)

TABLE 3.2(A) • *Evaluation of Alternative Hotels*

of alternatives that a consumer is considering for purchase will contain products or services that have various combinations of these attributes and their levels. This multiattribute approach assumes that consumers are capable of evaluating each of a product's attributes and then arriving at an overall assessment, or score, for the product that can be compared to alternative products. It is believed that consumers make these complicated comparisons and trade-offs and then choose the product that achieves the highest rating.

For example, the consumer information in Table 3.2(a) can be used to illustrate the differences between the various consumer problem-solving processes. According to the information in the table, if all of the attributes were equally weighted, the consumer would choose the Four Seasons because it received the highest average score (3.33) based on the actual ratings. Even though the hotel received a lower rating for price, its higher ratings on location and service quality compensated for the deficiency. However, if the weighted averages are used, the Holiday Inn received the highest average score because this consumer (or market segment) is relatively price sensitive and Holiday Inn's higher rating on price offset the lower ratings on location and service quality.

Noncompensatory Strategies

Noncompensatory strategies

Consumers place more emphasis on individual attributes and, in some cases, develop minimum thresholds to use in evaluating products and services. There are three main noncompensatory strategies that are used by consumers: conjunctive, disjunctive, and lexicographic.

When using **noncompensatory strategies**, consumers do not allow product strengths in one area to compensate for deficiencies or weaknesses in another area. Instead, consumers place more emphasis on individual attributes and in some cases develop minimum thresholds to use in evaluating products and services. There are three main noncompensatory strategies that are used by consumers: conjunctive, disjunctive, and lexicographic.

CONJUNCTIVE. A conjunctive approach involves setting minimum thresholds for each attribute and eliminating brands that do not surpass this threshold on any one salient attribute. The consumer determines which attributes will be important in choosing between brands. For example, a certain individual might consider location, food quality, food variety, and price to be the salient attributes in choosing a restaurant while on vacation. Upon examining the menus that are posted in the windows of restaurants in a busy tourist area, the individual can quickly eliminate restaurants that are deficient on menu variety or have prices that are too high. In addition, restaurants with good reputations for food quality and menu variety that are within the acceptable price range will be eliminated if they are not within walking distance.

Referring to the example in Table 3.2(a), assume that the consumer has a minimum threshold of 3.0 (good) for all of the attributes. Even though the Four Seasons received the highest scores for location and service quality, it did not meet the threshold for price. Therefore, the consumer would choose the Marriott if he was using a conjunctive strategy. It is the only hotel that received a minimum of three on all of the attributes.

DISJUNCTIVE. Some consumers do not get as involved in the purchase process and may prefer to take a less complicated approach to making purchase decisions. With the disjunctive approach, consumers still establish minimum thresholds for their salient attributes. However, a brand will be acceptable if it exceeds the minimum standard on at least one attribute. Consumers applying this approach tend to have only one or two salient attributes, the products or services tend to be very similar, and they are not as highly involved in the decision-making process. For example, a truck driver might consider price, location, and basic quality in choosing a hotel or motel to stop for the night. However, it is not unusual for truck drivers to choose the closest hotel or motel when they are starting to get tired. Similarly, an international tourist might choose the first hotel that looks clean or fits his price range.

Once again, the information in Table 3.2(a) can be used to illustrate the thought process behind a disjunctive strategy. Assume that the consumer was concerned about only one attribute. In this case, it would probably be price, since it received the highest importance rating. The consumer would choose the hotel that received the highest rating for price, which would be the Holiday Inn. This strategy would assume that location and service quality weren't as important, given that the Holiday Inn received the lowest ratings on both.

LEXICOGRAPHIC. The lexicographic approach falls somewhere between conjunctive and disjunctive choice processes in terms of complexity. Just as in the other two approaches, the consumer determines a set of salient attributes, or choice criteria. Next, the consumer places these choice criteria in rank order from most important to least important. Then the consumer evaluates the alternative brands, starting with the most important attribute. The brand that rates the highest on the most important attribute will be selected. If two or more brands tie or are closely rated, then those brands are evaluated using the second most important attribute. This continues until one brand remains or the list of attributes is exhausted—forcing a choice between the remaining brands. It is important to note that all brands are not evaluated on all criteria. For example, a business traveler might rank the most important attributes in airline travel to be convenience, comfort, food quality, and price, in that order. Depending on the airport where the flight is going to originate, the traveler might be able to narrow the choices down to two airlines that offer direct flights at the preferred time. The final choice might then be made based on the fact that one of the airlines is perceived by the traveler to provide better service or comfort.

Finally, the information in Table 3.2(a) can be used to demonstrate this last noncompensatory strategy. This strategy would make use of the actual ratings based on the importance, or priority assigned to each of the attributes. The consumer put the attributes in order of price, location, and service quality based on importance (highest to lowest). Therefore, the first step is for the consumer to evaluate all three hotels on price. Since the Holiday Inn received the highest rating for price, the consumer would choose that hotel. However, if one of the other hotels also received a 4.0 rating for price, the consumer would have eliminated the one that didn't and move to the next attribute. This process would be repeated until there was one alternative left.

Combination Strategies

One of the main questions regarding problem-solving strategies is the ability of consumers to obtain, integrate, and evaluate the information available on the myriad brands in most product categories. The compensatory approach is particularly cumbersome in this respect, as can be noncompensatory approaches such as conjunctive or lexicographic strategies. And in many cases, the disjunctive approach would seem overly simplistic. Therefore, it could be argued that consumers actually use a combination of approaches in an attempt to adapt to the purchase situation and simplify the decision process. For example, using a conjunctive strategy, a family might eliminate all restaurants that don't have children's menus. Then the remaining restaurants could be evaluated using a more complicated compensatory strategy or a more simple disjunctive strategy.

CONSUMER PROBLEM-SOLVING TECHNIQUES

The consumer decision-making process differs in the length of time and effort expended on each stage based on the consumer's level of involvement and experience with a product category. Also, the level of involvement may change depending on the purchase situation. For instance, a young man's choice process for a restaurant could differ greatly when it is for a date versus a dinner with his buddies. Table 3.3 provides a comparison of the three levels of problem solving: routine response behavior, limited problem solving, and extended problem solving.

CHARACTERISTICS	ROUTINE RESPONSE BEHAVIOR	LIMITED PROBLEM SOLVING	EXTENDED PROBLEM SOLVING
Amount of search	Minimal	Moderate	Substantial
Number of brands considered	One	Few	Many
Number of attributes evaluated	One or two	Few	Many
Cognitive processing	Minimal	Moderate	Substantial
Number of external information sources used	None	Few	Many
Level of involvement	Low	Medium	High
Total amount of effort	Low	Medium	High

TABLE 3.3 • *Problem-solving techniques.*

Chapter Outline *(continued)*

Tom Duca *District Partner, Southeast and Mid Atlantic*
Bravo Development Inc. • Atlanta, Georgia

1. What are the major components or duties associated with my current position?

I am currently employed as District Partner for Bravo Development Inc. They own and operate 70 fine casual dining restaurants named Brio Tuscan Grille and Bravo Cuccinia Italiana. I oversee six locations in Atlanta, Birmingham, Charlotte, Richmond, and Washington D.C... My regional duties will include opening two more Brio restaurants this year. One will open in Raleigh and one in Annapolis. My main functions are to ensure the fiscal success of the properties, recruitment, and training of management teams, implementation of corporate and property marketing and promotions, supervision of all food and beverage operations, human resources, and legal issues and vendor relations.

2. What brings the most satisfaction—most frustration?

The satisfaction part is easy. I enjoy the ability to impact younger manager's careers and lives through leadership and mentoring.

The most frustrating part of my position is keeping talented young managers on the correct career paths as opposed to fast track.

3. What are the most challenging aspects?

The most challenging aspect of our work is our ability to create successful financial business versus improving value to our guests. The prices for food and beverage have continued to increase steadily. Weather and energy costs impact our cost structures. Our segment requires pricing structures that maintain value. We are challenged to create better-quality products without consistent price increases.

4. Major trends?

The major trend I see is the deterioration of the casual dining segment. Credit crunch issues, rising energy costs, housing issues have affected dining trends.

5. The role of marketing?

The role of marketing at our locations is dependent on the specific market location. New store openings require a different marketing strategy than does a restaurant that has been open for four years. A consistent theme for stores with ages of 18 months and more is to be very active in the community. Our same-store sales are typically driven by well-operated properties that have created a core group of repeat guests. Local charities, the fire and police, libraries, are community partners who we focus on creating great relationships with by supporting them and their causes.

6. Advice?

My piece of advice would contain several elements:

- **Use your academic advantage.** I have managed over 400 food and beverage managers in my career. Eighty percent of these managers ended up in this industry by being promoted through line level positions. Your education is a huge advantage if used correctly.

- **Choose your first company wisely.** Stability is a very attractive quality when recruiting. It shows commitment and loyalty. Do not take a position to "get your foot in." You will probably not last there.

- **Decide what you want most out of your work.** Is it financial reward? Is it quality of life? Different jobs will have pros and cons (this is obvious); however, there are no dream jobs. Typically, the jobs that pay more result in less quality of life. You need to decide ahead of time what is important to you.

- **Invest into your career.** Everybody works hard. Most upper-level managers recognize those who work harder than their peers. These leaders will also reward people who go above and beyond. I admire younger managers who come to work early, stay late, and come in on their scheduled days off to complete their work ahead of time. These are the personality types who get promoted quicker.

industry profile

Case Study

Segmenting and Positioning in the Cruise Industry

The cruise industry has increased in popularity over the past two decades. This has led to higher volume, including more market segments than just affluent travelers. However, the cruise lines have to be careful that they don't try to mix too many different groups of customers on the same ship. In response, the cruise lines have added more ships and designed them to appeal to the varied customer segments. Also, there are many outlets for purchasing cruise travel, including traditional travel agents, online travel agents, airline agents and Web sites, and the cruise line agents and Web sites.

The purpose of this exercise is to research the various distribution outlets and determine the make-up of the cruise line industry. That is, identify the popular cruise lines in the United States, how they are positioned, and what market segments they serve. The following is a description of how you can find this information through two of the more popular online travel agents, but you can use other sources as well. You should limit your search to Bahamas cruises of 3–6 nights/days. It doesn't matter what month you use as long as it is a popular cruising month for the Florida ports (i.e., Fort Lauderdale, Miami, and Tampa).

First, you can go to www.expedia.com and click on "Cruises." Put in the criteria listed above (i.e., Bahamas, 3–5 nights, all lines) and choose a month. Next, click on "Choose and Continue" for the various selections and scroll down to "About the Ship."

Next, you can go to www.travelocity.com and click on "Cruises." Put in the same criteria (except it is 3–6 nights) and choose the same month. Then, click on "More Info" for each of the selections, followed by "Reviews."

Case Study Questions and Issues

1. What cruise lines are available, and how are they positioned in the market? Explain your answer based on actual evidence and construct a simple perceptual map based on price and quality.

2. What are the primary market segments for cruise lines based on your review of the Web sites? What ships are available within the Carnival Cruise Line, and how are they targeted to each of these segments?

3. What other websites are available for obtaining useful information for how the cruise lines, and their ships, are segmented?

case study

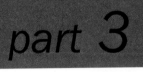

part 3

MARKETING PLANNING AND INFORMATION

Courtesy of Corbis Digital Stock.

Courtesy of PhotoDisc/Getty Images.

Developing A Marketing Plan

Chapter Objectives

After studying this chapter, you should be able to:

1. Compare and contrast two types of marketing plans—strategic and tactical.

2. Outline the advantages and disadvantages of planning.

3. Define the terms *mission, goals and objectives, organizational resources, market risks and opportunities, evaluation plans, marketing strategies,* and *action plans.*

4. Describe in detail the four steps of the marketing planning process.

5. Develop a preliminary marketing plan.

6. Explain qualitative and quantitative techniques for developing sales forecasts.

7. Evaluate criteria to select appropriate sales forecasting techniques.

Chapter Outline

Chris Gabaldon *Vice President, Sales Strategy and Operations*
The Ritz-Carlton Hotel Company • Washington, D.C.

1. What are the major components or duties associated with your current position?

I develop and manage sales strategy for the Ritz-Carlton Hotel Company worldwide. That includes sales deployment, business development, market research and analysis, customer research and analysis, and sales measurement and evaluation. I also manage sales operations, including sales systems, operating procedures, capital budgeting for sales initiatives, budget management, sales programs and initiatives, and general operational needs. Furthermore, I manage and develop sales-related relationships with the parent company, Marriott International.

2. What are the components of your position that bring you the most satisfaction? What about your position causes you frustration?

Enhancing and building a world-class sales organization for the most recognizable luxury hotel brand in the world (according to Future Brands survey, 2002). Also, providing leadership and stimulating change that continually grows revenue and brand equity.

Change is difficult and takes longer than anyone ever would like. Also, the hotel industry is continually behind the technology curve. We are making great strides, but there is still a lot of opportunity in inventory management and guest recognition.

3. What are the most challenging aspects you're facing?

Balancing growth while maintaining and enhancing the power of the Ritz-Carlton brand. Also, managing cost while investing in new markets and new strategies in the volatile post-9/11 environment.

4. What major trends do you see for your segment of the hospitality and tourism industry?

Customer recognition is more and more important. The Internet threatens to push lodging toward being a commodity, similar to what happened in the airline industry. Brands must continue to look for ways to differentiate their products and provide unique experiences.

5. What role does marketing play within your company?

Marketing funds are limited, so the majority of the effort is focused on brand image campaigns. Secondarily, marketing is used to build awareness in new markets and for new products such as spas or enhanced group capabilities. At the property level, most marketing is very tactical and call-to-action-oriented.

6. If you could offer one piece of advice to an individual preparing for a career in the hospitality and tourism industry, what would you suggest?

Gain practical experience. When it comes down to it, this is still and always will be a people-to-people business. Understand what really makes the difference between guests who leave satisfied and beyond, who will likely return, and the ones who will never come back.

industry profile

INTRODUCTION

Planning focuses on the future. It involves assessing current environmental trends and determining what is most likely to occur in the future. People who are responsible for developing marketing plans chart a course of action that they believe will allow the firm to achieve its stated objectives. Planners can never be 100 percent certain that they will achieve their stated objectives, but well-developed plans have a much higher probability of accomplishing the desired results.

In general, a marketing plan can be defined as a written document containing the guidelines for the business's center's marketing programs and allocations over the planning period."[1] Several key parts of this definition must be discussed. First, marketing plans are written documents, requiring managers to analyze the company, its products and services, and the environment so that they can prepare well-organized documents to guide their companies. Second, marketing plans are written for the appropriate business center as defined by the organization. Such a business center is referred to as a **strategic business unit (SBU)** because it consists of products that share common characteristics and have the same competitors. For example, within a large multibrand lodging company such as Marriott International, an SBU might be classified as one of the brands, such as Fairfield Inns or Courtyard. Finally, marketing plans are developed for a specific time period that varies from product to product or unit-to-unit based on the scope or breadth of the planning activity. For example, strategic plans are broad, have far-reaching implications, and often extend three or more years into the future. Conversely, tactical plans are more short-term in focus, with an emphasis on implementation.

Strategic marketing plans result from a careful examination of a firm's core business strategy and primary marketing objectives. When involved in this type of planning, firms should focus on key areas, starting with the type of business the firm is in or wishes to be in. Next, the firm should ask where it is now and whether it is where it would like to be. If not, what should the firm do to get there? Questions such as these are not easy to answer, but they are the foundation on which strategic plans are developed. Strategic planning is the process of determining the firm's primary goals and objectives and initiating actions that will allow it to achieve those goals and objectives. All types of hospitality and tourism firms conduct strategic marketing planning, but it is an absolute necessity for multiunit firms or chains.

Tactical marketing plans focus on implementing the broad strategies established in the strategic plan. For example, if a hotel's strategy is to increase occupancy by 2 percent by focusing on a specific target market, how will this market segment be approached? What specific steps need to be taken to

Strategic business unit (SBU)
Strategic business units represent business centers consisting of products that share common characteristics and have the same competitors.

Strategic marketing plan
These plans result from a careful examination of a firm's core business strategy and primary marketing objectives.

Tactical marketing plan
These plans focus on implementing the broad strategies that are established in the strategic plan.

achieve the stated goal? The actual methods used are part of the tactical plan. Tactical plans typically cover a period of one year and primarily focus on specific activities that must be implemented if the firm is to achieve the goals and objectives stated in the longer-range strategic plan. One of the focal points for tactical plans is the allocation of resources to achieve the stated objectives. Tactical plans may get modified, based on the actions of the primary competitors and the availability of resources, but strategic plans are normally not modified without considerable reflection.

Within small chains and independent operations, the unit management is often granted great autonomy. Within larger chain organizations, most aspects of the marketing function are tightly controlled, and the manager of an individual unit is more involved in implementing rather than planning. Planning is conducted at a higher level within the organization to ensure coordination of marketing efforts and consistency throughout the chain. Corporate-level marketing managers normally work with managers of the individual units to help them formulate and implement tactical plans that allow the unit to remain successful, while at the same time supporting the overall corporate marketing strategic plan.

Tactical plans prepared for a one-year time horizon are based on the answers to questions similar to those listed here:

- What is our market share? Is it increasing or decreasing?

- How have the strengths and weaknesses of our firm changed in the last year?

- How has our mix of guests changed in the last year?

- What advertising and promotions were the most and least successful during the last year?

- What types of promotions and sales efforts should we use to build business during our slow periods?

- What specific promotion and advertising schedules will lead to success?

- What in-house promotions should we schedule?

Advantages and Disadvantages of Planning

Formulating an organized and well-conceived marketing plan can have a tremendously positive impact on a hospitality firm. There are five main advantages of marketing planning:

1. **It helps the firm cope with change more effectively.** If the competitive environment changes rapidly, a firm that has developed strategic plans with several contingency options is in a better position to effectively deal with the change.

2. **Developing marketing plans ensure that the firm's objectives are achieved.** The plans serve as guides to help the firm achieve the objectives. If, in some unforeseen circumstances, the objectives are not attainable, objectives and plans can be modified. This is done after a very careful analysis of the situation, investigating why the original objectives could not be achieved.

3. **Establishing a marketing plan aids management in decision making.** The established plans can easily serve as a point of reference for management to consult when confronted with a difficult decision. Given the alternatives, managers can decide which ones will contribute the most to the achievement of their objectives.

4. **Planning forces managers to examine the firm's operations.** Marketing plans make it necessary for managers to relate employee tasks and resource allocation to the firm's objectives. There must be a clear delineation of how the use of resources and employee time will help the firm achieve its objectives.

5. **Developing both strategic and tactical marketing plans helps management when evaluating the marketing efforts.** Results of marketing efforts are compared with projected results, giving management a control process for the marketing function.

Although establishing a marketing plan has many advantages, there are also some disadvantages associated with marketing planning. Five main disadvantages of marketing planning follow:

1. **Establishing objectives and formulating a marketing plan are very time consuming.** The time that management invests in planning can be expensive, and the results of planning must be cost-effective. The overall benefits of these efforts, however, normally far exceed the cost to the firm.

2. **If planning is to be successful and have the desired impact on an organization, it must have the support and commitment of the top management.** If those involved in the planning process perceive that they are merely going through the motions and that their activities will not have any impact, they will have a negative opinion about planning. Under these circumstances, managers perceive the planning process as an extra duty. Therefore, they give it a low priority, resulting in an inferior plan.

Inherent in this analysis is the need for managers to examine what the business does well and what could be improved. At the same time, a critical assessment of the market is needed to determine, as specifically as possible, the threats and potential opportunities that exist outside the firm. Management must ask, "What do we have or offer that is different, unique, or superior to what the competition offers consumers?" Management must also examine the organization's shortcomings by asking, "What do we provide that is below average?"

The process of identifying internal strengths and weaknesses or external threats and opportunities is similar to examining a balance sheet with assets and liabilities. The strengths and opportunities are used to promote the business and to make decisions about new directions that should be taken. Conversely, managers must make every effort to correct or neutralize the weaknesses and threats. Many managers find it difficult to identify an organization's weaknesses or threats clearly, tending to overlook or downplay negative factors. Successful managers can usually predict the future and adapt to meet the changes that are occurring in the marketplace. Although this may not be entirely true, those who are successful seem to know what will occur in the marketplace before it actually happens. Is it luck or successful planning? One definition of luck is "preparation meeting opportunity." Successful managers are students of trends. They carefully watch the broad marketing environment discussed in Chapter 1, looking for subtle changes in the economic, political and legal, social, and technological environments that may potentially influence their businesses. They carefully study the moves made by their competitors and do everything they can to stay close to their customers. In doing so, they attempt to match their product–service mix to the ever-changing needs and wants of their customers and potential customers.

Goals

Goals are broad statements of what the firm seeks to accomplish.

Objectives

Objectives are more detailed statements of what the firm intends to achieve. Well written objectives should state (1) what will be accomplished in measurable terms, (2) within what specific time frame it will be accomplished, (3) which individual or group will be responsible for achieving the objective, and (4) how the results will be evaluated.

Defining the Firm's Goals and Objectives

A firm's goals and objectives should evolve from the mission statement. **Goals** are broad statements of what the firm seeks to accomplish. For example, a firm may develop a goal that states, "We are seeking to achieve the number one market share in the mid-Atlantic region." The goal does not tell how the results are to be achieved; rather, it states, in broad terms, the desired result. **Objectives** are more detailed statements, or refinements, of what the firm intends to accomplish. A good objective includes (1) what will be accomplished in measurable terms, (2) within what specific time frame it will be accomplished, (3) which individual or group will be responsible for achieving the objective, and (4) how the results will be evaluated.

PURPOSE OF OBJECTIVES. The objectives serve several functions. For one thing, they enable management to arrive at a consensus concerning the primary activities of the organization. In addition, responsibility for specific objectives gets assigned to specific managers, thereby establishing accountability. If a well-defined objective is assigned to a specific manager, that individual assumes responsibility for following through and seeing that the objective is completed. Therefore, the results are likely to be more positive than if no one individual is assigned responsibility.

For objectives to achieve their greatest purpose, they must be established with the input of many individual managers. The process of defining objectives can serve as a brainstorming and motivational tool. When individuals have input into formulating the organizational marketing objectives, they develop a sense of ownership and allegiance toward the objectives. As a result, employees are likely to work more diligently to achieve stated objectives. Formulating well-written and measurable objectives takes time, and care should be taken to ensure that the objectives remain feasible. Several characteristics of good objectives follow:

- **Objectives should be specific and easy to understand.** They should not be too broad and difficult to define. Everyone involved in formulating the objectives should clearly understand the precise objectives toward which the organization seeks to move.

- **Objectives should identify expected results.** They should be quantitative so that no gray area will exist for purposes of evaluation. When managers state an objective in quantitative terms, the expected results are more readily understood.

- **Objectives must be within the power of the organization to achieve.** When establishing objectives, management must keep in mind the relative abilities of the organization.

- **Objectives must be acceptable to the individuals within the organization.** Management must come to a consensus concerning the objectives. It is extremely difficult for a firm to achieve the stated objectives if the managers, who have input into the formation of the objectives, do not agree.

Table 5.1 provides examples of both objectives that are well stated and some that are poorly stated. It is easy to see how the two types differ in their abilities to steer firms and allow for the measurement of performance. The well-stated objectives are clear and concise. They provide a specific time frame for completion, and they contain quantified targets. In addition to stating objectives, it is necessary for firms to explain how the results will be evaluated

WELL-STATED OBJECTIVES	POORLY STATED OBJECTIVES
Our objective is to increase occupancy rate from 70% to 75% within one year by decreasing group rates by 5%.	Our objective is to increase occupancy rate.
Our objective is to increase our awareness rating from 60% to 70% within one year by allocating $200,000 to advertising for an awareness campaign.	Our objective is to increase awareness over the next year.
Our objective is to increase the average check by 10% within six months by providing waiters with a 2-hour suggestive selling training program.	Our objective is to increase the average check by training waiters.

TABLE 5.1 • *Examples of Objectives*

and who has the actual responsibility for attaining the objective. Finally, adequate resources must be committed to achieving each objective, including personnel, facilities, and financial resources.

TYPES OF OBJECTIVES. Objectives are grouped into four main categories: financial, sales, competitive, and customer. Table 5.2 contains a list of specific objectives that can be used under each of the four categories. *Financial objectives* focus on the firm's ability to generate enough money to pay its bills, offer investors an adequate return, and retain some of the earnings for investing in the firm. *Sales objectives* focus on the level of sales in units or dollars, and the firm's sales relative to its competitors (i.e., market share). *Competitive objectives* focus on the firm's ability to compete in the marketplace. The firm positions itself against the competition, determines the best strategies for survival, or tries to keep pace with the competition in terms of sales growth, market share, and/or marketing expenditures. Finally, *customer objectives* focus on the firm's ability to make consumers aware of its products, provide them with a product–service mix that meets their expectations, and create a level of goodwill among customers and other stakeholders.

Firms can use a combination of objectives, such as a desire to maximize profit and increase customer satisfaction. In most situations, objectives do not conflict, so the firm can work at attaining both. However, it is necessary to prioritize multiple objectives and allocate resources appropriately. One potential

MAIN CATEGORY	SPECIFIC OBJECTIVES
Financial	Maximize profit Target rate of return Increase cash flow
Sales	Increase or maximize sales revenues Increase volume (number of units sold) Increase or maximize market share
Competitive	Position against competitors Long-term survival Maintain competitive parity (market share or marketing expenditures)
Customer	Increase market awareness Increase customer satisfaction Improve or change perceived image Create goodwill

TABLE 5.2 • *Types of Objectives*

problem with multiple objectives is that there could be a conflict between them. For example, consider the case of a firm that wants to increase market share and maximize profit. In the short run, increases in market share are accomplished by lowering price and/or increasing marketing expenditures on changes in the product–service mix and promotion. Either decreasing price or increasing marketing expenditures will result in a decrease in short-term profits. The firm must rethink its objectives or make a distinction between short-term and long-term profits.

Formulating Marketing Strategies and Action Plans

A strategy is the manner by which an organization attempts to link with, respond to, integrate with, and exploit its environment. In other words, a firm's strategies integrate its mission, goals, objectives, and action plans. When well formulated, strategies help firms maximize the use of their resources. This, in turn, puts them in a viable position within the competitive environment. Timing is everything. Managers must always look for a

It is crucial that firms examine the income statement to determine why net profit is negative or does not meet the target set in the marketing plan. Often, firms approach profitability from a cost perspective without having a good understanding of pricing strategy. Chapter 15 covers pricing in detail, but it is important to know how consumers' price sensitivity impacts the firm's products and services. There is no simple solution for obtaining desired profit levels. It is not easy to maximize sales revenue and minimize costs simultaneously. Decreases in costs can lead to lower quality and decreased sales and profits. In some cases, sales revenue can increase when the firm incurs additional costs to improve the product–service mix and raises prices. A classic example of this situation involved Smirnoff vodka competing with Wolfschmidt vodka. With the goal of increasing market share, the brand managers for Wolfschmidt decided to reduce the price of the product. The brand managers for Smirnoff noted this change and considered alternatives. A normal reaction might have been to reduce the price to the level set by the competition, with the goal of retaining market share. Smirnoff decided to take a different course. It increased the price of the product and allocated additional resources for advertising and promotion. The results are classic: Smirnoff increased both gross sales and market share and for a time became the market leader. The income statement is a very useful tool for marketers. It should be studied carefully to determine the level of profitability, and if the desired results are not being achieved, the source of the problem can be determined by tracing it back through the sections of the income statement to determine the cause or causes. Once the cause is identified, a plan for corrective action can be developed.

Consumer feedback is the final area of performance evaluation, and it is a key element in understanding the results of the financial analyses. Consumer feedback provides firms with information regarding awareness, knowledge, attitudes, purchasing behavior, and customer satisfaction.

Chapter 3 discussed consumer behavior, and Chapter 6 discusses the research methods used to obtain this information. In many cases, the financial data are merely a symptom of problems within the firm. It is often necessary to obtain consumer feedback to gain a true understanding of the problem.

It can be detrimental if managers focus too much on numbers and not enough on consumer needs. For example, a hotel in Boston was experiencing a decrease in occupancy rate in relation to other hotels in the area. Management tried to approach the issue by discounting prices, but it had very little effect. After speaking with customers, the hotel realized that business travelers found the rooms too small. Business travelers are not as price-sensitive as other travelers, but they are quality-conscious, which explained the ineffectiveness of the

Consumer feedback
This is the final area of performance evaluation and is a key element in understanding the results of financial results, based on how well the firm has met consumer needs.

price discounting strategy. As a result, the hotel decided to focus on the government market because of the hotel's location.

The government market is price-sensitive (there is an allowable per diem) and not as quality-conscious, and the hotel could selectively discount to this large-volume market. Once again, it is important to point out that marketing planning is a continuous process. Marketing managers must evaluate the situation and adapt to changes that occur. Evaluating the success of the marketing plan is the moment of truth. Managers develop a plan to increase the probability of success, and once the plan is implemented, it is important for management to monitor the results. Any variance from the predicted results should be identified, evaluated, and corrected.

As the environment changes or the results vary, management may need to return to the appropriate step to reformulate marketing strategy or the action plans. The marketing planning process continues as a dynamic procedure, with sufficient flexibility allowing for changes in strategies, action plans, or implementation schedules.

SALES FORECASTING

One of the most critical components of a marketing plan is the forecast for sales. **Sales forecasting** is the process for determining current sales and estimating future sales for a product or service. The success of the firm often results from the accuracy of forecasts. The decisions about the elements of the marketing mix—product–service mix, price, promotion, and distribution—that are made during the situation analysis are based on sales forecasts.

Sales forecasting
The process for determining current sales and estimating future sales for a product or service.

Sales Forecasting Techniques

Sales forecasting techniques are separated into two broad categories: quantitative techniques and qualitative techniques. Quantitative techniques use past data values and employ a set of rules to obtain estimates of future sales. Qualitative techniques rely on judgment or intuition and tend to be used when data are not readily available. Quantitative methods can be further classified as either causal or time series. Both types of quantitative methods use trends in historical data to predict future sales; however, **causal analysis** techniques establish a cause and effect relationship between variables and the results. Using historical data to establish the relationship between sales and other factors that are believed to influence sales. These techniques model the relationships between sales and other variables that can help predict changes in sales. Time series techniques extrapolate future sales estimates based on the trend in historical sales. In other words, past sales are used to predict future sales, assuming all other factors that affect sales will continue to have a similar effect in the future. The forecasting techniques described in this chapter are presented in a conceptual framework. Use of these techniques requires a sound statistical background. The techniques are presented so that marketing managers will have a better understanding of the range of techniques that are available.

QUALITATIVE FORECASTING TECHNIQUES. The goal of qualitative forecasting techniques is to forecast changes in the basic sales pattern as well as the pattern itself. Qualitative techniques are often difficult to apply, and they tend to be very time-consuming and costly. Therefore, these techniques are used mainly for long-term forecasts and in situations that are of major importance to the firm. It is important for firms to predict changes in sales patterns so they can take advantage of opportunities and minimize the impact of threats. To predict these changes, firms enlist the aid of experts, or individuals with an intimate knowledge of the product and its markets. The following basic approaches are classified as qualitative forecasting techniques:

- **Expert opinion.** Marketers look to a panel of experts with knowledge of the industry and the marketplace to provide a forecast. A variety of sources are consulted, and the results are combined to form a consensus forecast based on **expert opinion**. These experts can be from within the firm or from outside the firm. Often, secondary sources, such as forecasts published in major trade journals or business journals, are used. The resulting forecast can be obtained by simply averaging the individual forecasts, or a more complicated weighting system can be used based on the experience and knowledge of the panel members.

- **Delphi technique.** The **Delphi technique** involves several rounds of forecasting and review by a panel of experts. It can be very time-consuming, but it is often quite accurate. This technique involves collecting forecasts, developing composites, and sending the data to those participating several times until a consensus results. The Delphi technique is normally used when the decision is an important one and there are no time constraints. Panel members are able to adjust their forecasts after seeing the forecasts of others on the panel.

- **Sales force forecast.** The **sales force forecast** technique aggregates the sales forecast of each salesperson or unit, depending on the level of the forecast. For example, a hotel may have each of its salespeople provide a

Expert opinion

Marketers look to a panel of experts with knowledge of the industry and the marketplace to provide a forecast.

Delphi technique

The Delphi technique involves collecting forecasts, developing composites, and sending the data to those participating several times until a consensus results.

Sales force forecast

This technique aggregates the sales forecast of each salesperson or unit, depending on the level of the forecast (e.g., a hotel may have each of its salespeople provide a forecast for his or her territory and then combine the forecasts to obtain an overall estimate).

forecast for his or her territory and then combine the forecasts to obtain an overall estimate. Alternatively, a hotel or restaurant chain may have each unit provide a forecast and then combine the forecasts to obtain an overall estimate for the chain. The rationale for using this technique is that it may be more accurate to forecast the sales for each territory or unit rather than to obtain a higher-level forecast and break it down for operational purposes. Each salesperson, or unit manager, is in touch with the customers and changes in the environment.

- **Survey of buying intentions.** Firms can use marketing research to ask potential customers about their future purchase intentions and then estimate future sales. This type of forecast, or **survey of buying intentions,** is very subjective because there is no clear relationship between purchase intentions and actual purchase behavior. However, this kind of information is readily available from published sources such as *Sales & Marketing Management.*

> **Survey of buying intentions**
> Firms use marketing research to ask potential customers about their future purchase intentions and then estimate future sales.

The experts employed in these methods may base their judgment on prior experience, or they may use sophisticated quantitative techniques to model the effects of other factors that influence the level of sales. However, the ultimate outcome is to predict changes in sales patterns.

QUANTITATIVE FORECASTING TECHNIQUES. The common element in quantitative forecasting techniques is that they are based almost exclusively on historical data. These forecasting techniques tend to be quicker and less costly because the data are readily available through existing sources. Quantitative forecasting techniques are also gaining in popularity due to their level of proven accuracy and improvements in computer technology. Many spreadsheet software packages, such as Microsoft Excel, have statistical applications that can be used for quantitative forecasting, and other statistical programs and forecasting packages are available at a reasonable price. In addition, these programs are easy to use, and many are compatible with software for preparing reports and charts. The two basic quantitative forecasting techniques are time series analysis and causal methods.

TIME SERIES ANALYSIS. The **time series analysis** method uses statistical techniques to fit a trend line to the pattern of historical sales. The trend line is expressed in terms of a mathematical equation that can be used to project the trend forward into future periods and predict sales. The trend line can be linear (a straight line) or nonlinear (a curved line) depending upon the pattern of the historical data. Four major components of a time series should be considered in choosing a technique: (1) trend, or the long-term pattern;

> **Time series analysis**
> This method uses statistical techniques to fit a trend line to the pattern of historical sales. The trend line is expressed in terms of a mathematical equation that can be used to project the trend forward into future periods and predict sales.

(2) cycle, or medium-term changes due to business and economic changes; (3) seasonal, short-term movements based on buying patterns; and (4) residual, unpredictable influences or disturbances. Here are the most common methods of time series analysis:

Trend extrapolation

The simplest method for forecasting sales is the linear projection of past sales.

- **Trend extrapolation.** The simplest method for forecasting sales is the linear projection of past sales, or **trend extrapolation**. It assumes that the factors that influenced sales in the past will have the same effect on future sales, and all data points are weighted equally. This is somewhat naive, but firms' basic marketing programs and competitive situations normally do not change drastically from year to year. This method is very simple, the data requirements are minimal, and it can be very accurate for products in industries with low growth rates.

Moving average

This technique uses short-term forecasts (e.g., monthly) and takes the average of the most recent periods to predict future sales.

- **Moving average.** The **moving average** technique uses short-term forecasts (e.g., monthly) and takes the average of the most recent periods to predict future sales. For example, next month's sales are forecast using the average of the monthly sales for the last three or four months. This method is simple and can be used when sales are fairly stable throughout the year, with only small fluctuations.

Exponential smoothing

This technique uses the trend line to predict future sales; however, it places more weight on the most recent periods.

- **Exponential smoothing.** The technique of **exponential smoothing** uses the trend line to predict future sales; however, it places more weight on the most recent periods. This method is better at picking up trends than the previous time series methods, and there are more complex formulas that allow for cycles and seasonal effects.

There are more sophisticated time series techniques, but they are beyond the scope of this text. For example, there is a group of methods referred to as autoregressive moving averages (ARMA), which express forecasts as a linear combination of past actual values and/or past errors. These methods are becoming more widespread, but they require more than a rudimentary knowledge of forecasting.

CAUSAL METHODS. These are often referred to as explanatory methods because they use historical data to establish the relationship between sales and other factors that are believed to influence sales. The other factors, or causal factors, can differ based on the level of the forecast. The higher the level or the more macro-oriented the forecast, the more likely the variables are to be economic, such as disposable income, unemployment, and consumer prices. As the forecast becomes more specific, or micro-oriented, the causal factors become more specific, such as price, advertising expenditures, and competitors' prices and advertising.

However, to forecast sales based on these causal factors, one must forecast the causal variables as well. In addition, the data requirements for causal methods are more extensive than for qualitative or time-series forecasting techniques. The two most common causal methods are as follows:

1. **Regression analysis.** A **regression analysis** identifies the causal factors, or independent variables, that can be used to predict the level of sales, or the dependent variable. Single regression analysis uses one independent variable, and multiple regression analysis uses more than one independent variable. Trend extrapolation is actually a simplified form of regression analysis that uses time as the independent variable and sales as the dependent variable. For example, a manager might want to study the impact that the growth rate of the economy or intensity of competition has on annual sales.

> **Regression analysis**
> This technique identifies the causal factors, or independent variables, that can be used to predict the level of sales, or the dependent variable.

2. **Econometric models.** In **econometric models**, statistical techniques are used to solve a simultaneous set of multiple regression equations. In this case, a causal factor may be predicted as a dependent variable from several other causal factors and then used as an independent variable in an equation to predict sales. This method is more complicated and requires some expertise in statistical modeling. In addition, this technique requires the largest amount of data because of the number of variables being used in the various equations. Econometric models are best used within a corporate or multiunit competitive situation and are not readily adaptable for use at the single-unit level.

> **Econometric models**
> This model uses statistical techniques to solve a simultaneous set of multiple regression equations.

Selecting a Forecasting Technique

All of the sales forecasting techniques discussed earlier have advantages and disadvantages based on the situation. Therefore, it is important to apply a set of selection criteria in choosing the appropriate technique. The following criteria can be used in forecasting to evaluate the situation and choose the technique that is best suited to the firm's needs:

- **The time horizon.** The period of time over which a decision will have an impact will clearly affect the selection of the most appropriate technique. Time series methods perform best for short-term (one to three months) and medium-term (three months to two years) forecasts, whereas qualitative techniques are best for long-term (more than two years) new product forecasts. Causal methods perform best in the short term, but they can also be used quite effectively for medium-term forecasts.

- **The availability of data.** The type and amount of data available can have a major effect on the choice of technique. If only historical sales data are available, then time series methods would be most appropriate. However, if very little data are available (e.g., for new products), then the qualitative techniques would be most appropriate. If data are available for a large range of variables, then causal methods can be employed, providing a good deal of information regarding relationships between variables.

- **The pattern of the data.** The majority of quantitative forecasting techniques assume a particular pattern in the data to be forecast. Time series methods work best when there are defined patterns (trends), including cycles and seasonal changes. However, causal methods and qualitative methods work best in high-growth markets and when there may be turning points in the pattern.

- **The desired level of accuracy.** The desired level of accuracy will vary based on the use of the forecast. Forecasts for control purposes tend to be short-term and need to be more precise, whereas forecasts for planning tend to be longer-term and can be less precise. Causal methods will normally be the most accurate in the short term under various conditions. However, time series methods can be very accurate when there is a strong trend in the data. Qualitative methods will tend to be most accurate for long-term forecasts because they use the combined forecasts of experts.

- **Cost.** It is necessary to trade off the benefits of the various methods based on the other criteria with the cost involved in using the technique. Cost will be a function of data collection, storage, and analysis. The time-series methods require the least amount of data and expertise, resulting in the lowest cost. Causal methods can be costly because they require the most data and expertise, while qualitative methods incur a large expense for data collection.

- **Ease of application.** The ease with which the various forecasting techniques can be employed depends on factors such as the firm's computer capabilities, the expertise of its employees, and the availability of data. Time-series methods are the easiest to employ, while causal methods and qualitative methods are somewhat more complicated.

When making decisions, managers must use all of these criteria in selecting the appropriate forecasting technique. Certain interrelationships among the criteria may help simplify the selection task. For example, when good historical data are available, time series methods provide accuracy for short-term forecasts. Choosing the best forecasting technique is important because many of the elements of the marketing plan are based on the sales forecasts.

Summary of Chapter Objectives

This chapter has discussed the essential process for formulating marketing plans. Strategic marketing planning (i.e., building on the firm's mission) focuses on goals and objectives to develop long-term plans. Conversely, tactical planning is more short-term and implementation-oriented. Effective marketing planning includes both strategic and tactical components. Although there are numerous advantages and disadvantages to planning, several research studies have clearly demonstrated that firms that engage in marketing planning hold a decisive advantage over the competition and exhibit improved financial performance.

The marketing planning process includes four important stages: (1) conducting a situation analysis, (2) defining the firm's goals and objectives, (3) formulating marketing strategies and action plans, and (4) implementing action plans and evaluating performance. The situation analysis includes a historical appraisal and a SWOT analysis to determine where the firm is in terms of internal strengths and weaknesses, and external opportunities and threats. SWOTs are the basis on which strategic marketing plans are developed.

Strengths and opportunities are leverage items on which firms develop competitive advantages. Conversely, weaknesses and threats are problem areas that must be minimized if the firm is to achieve maximum success. Goals are broad statements of what the firm seeks to accomplish. Objectives are more detailed statements of what the firm wants to achieve. Well-written objectives should state (1) what will be accomplished in measurable terms, (2) within what specific time frame it will be accomplished, (3) which individual or group will be responsible for achieving the objective, and (4) how the results will be evaluated. The firm's marketing strategies will guide the firm to achieve its objectives, and the entire process should be monitored and the performance evaluated so that necessary changes can be made.

The last section of the chapter reviewed sales forecasting, including both qualitative and quantitative techniques. Sales forecasts are crucial in establishing objectives and strategies and are used to set budgets for marketing planning. Firms must understand the advantages and disadvantages of the various forecasting techniques so they can select the appropriate technique for a given situation. The selection of a forecasting technique is based on the time horizon, availability of data, pattern of data, desired level of accuracy, cost, and ease of application.

chapter review

Key Terms and Concepts

Causal analysis

Consumer feedback

Cost control data

Delphi technique

Diversification strategy

Econometric models

Expert opinion

Exponential smoothing

Goals

Historical appraisal

Market development strategy

Market penetration strategy

Mission statement

Moving average

Objectives

Position statement

Product development strategy

Profit control data

Regression analysis

Sales control data

Sales force forecast

Sales forecasting

Strategic business unit (SBU)

Strategic marketing plan

Strategic window

Survey of buying intentions

SWOT analysis

Tactical marketing plan

Time series analysis

Trend extrapolation

chapter review

Questions for Review and Discussion

1. What is the difference between strategic and tactical marketing plans?

2. Provide examples of the types of questions tactical marketing plans seek to answer.

3. What are the advantages and disadvantages associated with planning?

4. Why do marketing plans fail? What steps might a marketing manager take to increase the probability of success?

5. Illustrate and discuss the steps in the marketing planning process.

6. What is a SWOT analysis? How can SWOTs be leverage or problem items?

7. Conduct a SWOT analysis for a restaurant located in your area. How might this restaurant leverage elements of its SWOTs?

8. What are the criteria for well-written objectives?

9. What are the four product development strategy options? Provide examples and justification of hospitality and tourism firms that you believe use each of the four options.

10. What are the types of control data that are used to evaluate performance?

11. What is sales forecasting? Why is it important?

12. Explain the difference between qualitative and quantitative forecasting techniques.

Notes

[1] Donald R. Lehmann and Russell S. Winer, *Analysis for Marketing Planning*, 2nd ed. (Homewood, IL: Richard D. Irwin, Inc., 1991), p. 1.

[2] http://www.tia.org/pressmedia/pressrec.asp?Item=706, 2006.

[3] Arthur A. Thompson Jr. and A. J. Strickland, *Strategy Formulation and Implementation* (Homewood, IL: BPI/Richard D. Irwin, 1989), p. 214.

[4] Robert E. Stevens, David L. Loudon, and William E. Warren, *Marketing Planning Guide* (New York: Haworth Press, 1981), pp. 244–251.

chapter review

Case Study

Planning at the Westwind Resort

When Wendell Adams became the general manager at the Westwind Resort, he knew that it would be a challenge. His predecessor, Manfred Gunlock, was highly regarded and had been in the position for over 20 years. During that time, the resort enjoyed success by building a new lodge, adding more than 1,000 time-share units, and adding more snow-making equipment that extended the ski season. During Mr. Gunlock's tenure, Westwind Resort became a four-season resort. The golf course was very good, with golfers playing more than 25,000 rounds annually. These rounds were divided evenly between resort guests and year-round permanent residents.

The resort catered to families, as it featured a modest pricing structure and a focus on providing maximum value for them. About 60 percent of the resort business came from families. Many of them had children between the ages of 5 and 17.

Wendell also knew that the resort faced challenges. Westwind Resort had begun to slip. Sales were down 4 percent, and the quality of the product–service mix was perceived to have declined slightly as well. While still profitable, the resort was not producing the level of cash flow that it had in previous years. When Wendell accepted the job, he worried that maybe Manfred Gunlock had retired because he saw trouble ahead for Westwind Resort. Wendell had taken some very positive first steps. He assembled the management team for a half-day off-site planning session. Westwind had been run in a very entrepreneurial fashion, with Mr. Gunlock making all the important decisions without much input from other managers or even the board of directors. Although this approach had been successful in the past, Wendell believed it was time to implement a more systematic approach. He wanted to develop a mission statement and a complete marketing plan for the resort.

"Without a road map, how will we know where we are going?" he told his staff during the planning meeting. Wendell had hoped to develop a mission statement during the planning meeting, but the members of his management team felt it would be better to complete an assessment of the resort's current position prior to developing a mission statement. They also felt that the mission statement should come from the board of directors, not from the managers. In the end, Wendell agreed with them, and they developed a SWOT analysis. The results of their work are shown here.

SUMMARY OF THE STRENGTHS, WEAKNESSES, OPPORTUNITIES, AND THREATS (SWOTS) FOR WESTWIND RESORT

STRENGTHS

- More than 1,500 year-round residents reside in private homes at the resort.
- The resort has a good reputation for food and beverage service.
- Westwind offers four-season sports, including skiing and golf.
- The airport on the property is suitable for up to six-passenger turboprop aircraft.
- There is low turnover among staff.
- Westwind Resort is located approximately 90 minutes from a major metropolitan area.
- The resort carries only a small amount of long-term debt. The mortgage on the lodge (built 15 years ago) is paid off.

WEAKNESSES

- Lodge occupancy has declined slightly, to 65 percent year round. Peak weekends during the ski season are overbooked.
- The average daily room rate for lodge guests has not kept pace with inflation for the past three years.
- There has been some management turnover since the retirement of Manfred Gunlock.
- Due to the location of the resort in the mid-Atlantic region, the ski season is limited to approximately 60 to 75 days.
- The lodge, while only 15 years old, lacks a freshness in the décor. It appears to be older than 15 years.
- Cash flow, while positive, is lower than in past years, due to a decline in profits.

OPPORTUNITIES

- Westwind has established a reputation as being a family-oriented resort.
- No competing resort has an airport.
- The four-season recreational offerings can be expanded.

THREATS

- Two other four-season resorts are located within a 90-minute drive of Westwind. Both are newer and offer more amenities.
- Sales of time-share units have slowed in recent years, as buyers have sought time-share units offered by major chains rather than independent resorts.
- Of the three competing resorts within a three-hour driving radius, two are owned by major corporations with significant resources and borrowing capacity.

case study

Having completed the SWOT analysis, the managers were feeling very good. This was the first time that many of them had ever been involved in such an activity. They enjoyed having the opportunity to talk about the future of the resort and how their individual contributions could positively impact the future.

Case Study Questions and Issues

1. What should the mission statement for Westwind Resort be?

2. How should the mission statement be developed? Who should review it and have input?

3. How could Wendell use the SWOTs that the management team had developed to form the basis for a marketing plan?

4. How should he lead the team in the development of a marketing plan? What should be the next steps?

5. What additional components of the marketing plan need to be developed? What additional data and input would be necessary to complete the plan?

Courtesy of Hilton Hospitality, Inc.

Information Systems for Marketing Decisions

Chapter Objectives

After studying this chapter, you should be able to:

1. Define the term *marketing information system*.

2. Outline key components and requirements of an effective marketing information system.

3. Identify primary and secondary data sources for marketing information.

4. Describe in detail the marketing research process.

5. Identify ethical issues surrounding marketing research and information systems.

Chapter Outline

(continues)

Chapter Outline *(continued)*

Sean O'Neill *Chairman and CEO*

Newmarket International • Portsmouth, New Hampshire

1. What are the major components or duties associated with your current position?

As chairman and CEO of Newmarket International, my primary duties revolve around maintaining the continued growth of the company in our current target markets while positioning Newmarket International to expand its market base through the development of new solutions and services in non-traditional verticals and business lines. There are several key factors critical to the success of meeting these objectives:

- World-class support and services to deliver the highest levels of customer satisfaction

- Continual investment in R&D to bring new products and services to market with improved quality and at a reduced cost

- Recruitment and retention of high-performance employees—"The Best Team"

- Refinement and use of business metrics to guide our decisions

- Achievement of steady earnings growth year over year

2. What are the components of your position that bring you the most satisfaction? What about your position causes you frustration?

The areas of my job that bring me the most satisfaction vary. They include:

- Meeting and exceeding our customers' expectations

- Creating a measured environment where we can successfully meet or exceed the expectations of each of our constituents: customers, associates, investors, and partners

- Continuous improvement in every area of our business through objective measurement

- Development of leading technology solutions as measured by our customers' adoption and subsequent business result

industry profile

- Striving to establish and motivate the strongest team in our industry

- Being guided by integrity when faced with the many difficult decisions this role brings with it

- The fact that I'm still learning something new every day

- Successfully bringing new products to market

- Achieving large-scale global expansion of our business

- Achieving growth for our business through the addition of new industry segments

Many executives likely share the areas that bring the greatest frustration. They include:

- Time—never enough hours in the day

- Missed opportunities

- Our desire to bring high-quality products and solutions to market faster

3. What are the most challenging aspects you're facing?

There are several challenging aspects:

- Maintaining growth in a complex global economy where our solutions need to change at a rate equal to or greater than the marketplace

- Keeping ahead of the pace in an ever-changing market, and implementing processes and business practices throughout the company that recognize and adapt to new ways of conducting business

- Attracting and developing the strongest team in our industry

4. What major trends do you see for your segment of the hospitality and tourism industry?

I see the following trends:

- A more global customer base with a growing set of complex needs

- Continued demand throughout the industry for integration among disparate system applications for "best of breed" product selection

- An increase in demand for low-cost, simple automation applications for midscale properties—hosted solutions—"Software as a Service"

- Continued adoption of B2B business models among the various business lines within the hospitality marketplace

5. What role does marketing play within your company?

Marketing plays a critical role in the company on a number of levels. Marketing serves:

- As the "voice" of the company through press releases, Web site design and content, and outbound communications to customers and prospects

- As brand agent for the company bringing the look, feel, and high-level messages and themes to market

- As the platform vehicle to bring new products to market through participation in key industry events, analyst meetings, Web seminars, ad and direct marketing campaigns, and more

- As a source to promote and accelerate the sales cycle through prospect acquisition and qualification

6. If you could offer one piece of advice to an individual preparing for a career in the hospitality and tourism industry, what would you suggest?

Information is an enormous asset. If you're better informed and educated, you make better decisions. For people interested in pursuing a career in the hospitality and tourism industry, the one thing I would recommend is that they get an education in the industry by attending one of the many universities that have a curriculum focused on this industry.

INTRODUCTION

Since the advent of personal computers, the world has experienced an information explosion, and all industries have made substantial advances in information collection, analysis, storage, and retrieval. The hospitality industry was very much a part of this trend. As the external environment becomes more intricate and more competitive, informational needs become more complex. Organizations that employ a systematic approach to collecting, analyzing, storing, retrieving, and using information effectively and efficiently are likely to be the most successful in the future. Without the proper types of information available on a timely basis, management is more likely to make decisions that will adversely affect the performance of the organization.

A simple example will illustrate this point. Suppose that the management of a small restaurant chain must make a decision concerning the allocation of the advertising budget among the available media for the upcoming quarter. The advertising objectives of this restaurant are to increase the rate of repeat patronage by 10 percent by reinforcing the chain's high level of perceived value among current customers, and to increase the number of customers who are patronizing one of the chain's restaurants for the first time by 10 percent. To make an effective decision about media allocation, the management of this chain has specific informational needs. Management needs access to the following types of information:

- The characteristics of the current clientele

- The characteristics of the target market segments most likely to patronize the chain's restaurants for the first time

- The media habits of both of these groups

- The profile of the consumers of all available media (e.g., television, radio, print) and the individual media vehicles (e.g., individual radio stations)

Without all of this information, the management of this restaurant chain will increase the uncertainty surrounding the decision. The results of a less-informed decision could adversely affect the advertising effectiveness of the organization and directly affect its financial performance.

All too often, management is forced to make critical decisions without the necessary marketing information. On many occasions, managers must work with information that is not complete, or information that is not in the desired form. The new versions of hotel reservation systems and restaurant point-of-sale systems are capable of obtaining more forms of data that can be used in making managerial decisions. Revenue-management and yield-management software are available to help organize data for pricing decisions, and statistical programs are available for analyzing data and making forecasts.

Definition of a Marketing Information System

A **marketing information system (MIS)** is the structure of people, equipment, and procedures used to gather, analyze, and distribute information needed by an organization. These are the data to be used as a basis for marketing decisions. *Marketing information system* is a broader and more encompassing term than *market research* and a variation of the term *management information system*. Market research indicates that information is collected for a specific reason or project; the major objective is a one-time use. For example, a potential restaurant owner may undertake a feasibility study and use market research to determine whether to build a new restaurant. Such an information-gathering study is designed to answer a very specific question: "Should we open this type of a restaurant in this area?"

A marketing information system, by contrast, is part of an ongoing data-gathering process involving initial data collection as well as routine and systematic data collection procedures. For example, a hotel manager may choose to collect data by means of a zip code analysis of guest registration information to determine the geographic profile of the guests of a hotel. This systematic and routine information gathering is not intended to address one specific question but is instead part of an overall system designed to monitor the degree of marketing success that the operation is able to achieve.

A well-designed marketing information system satisfies four basic criteria:

- It must include a structured organization or established system of people and information-gathering procedures.

- The system should be designed to generate a continuous flow of information to provide accurate and current marketing information for management.

- Information should be gathered from inside and outside the organization. External information-gathering methods include consumer surveys, while internal information-gathering methods involve employee meetings, guest comment cards, analyzing point-of-sale data, all guest registration information, and in-house guest surveys.

- Information should be compiled so that management can use it as a basis for marketing decisions.

Marketing information systems (MIS)

The structure of people, equipment, and procedures used to gather, analyze, and distribute information used by an organization to make a decision.

It would be extremely difficult and quite hazardous for the management of a hospitality organization to make decisions without accurate and up-to-date marketing information. Professional management demands that decisions be based on sound information. Managers can reduce the uncertainty surrounding marketing decisions when valuable information is available.

McDonald's Corporation serves as a good example. For many years, this corporation has relied on a widely based decision-making process to determine its locations and menus. The resulting decisions have consistently been very good and have allowed McDonald's to establish and maintain a leadership position in the quick-service restaurant segment of the hospitality industry. For instance, McDonald's is normally the first fast-food restaurant to locate in a rural area, or relatively new suburban development. The company is known in the retail industry for having one of the best location-analysis programs. In fact, instructors often joke with their students and ask how Burger King or Wendy's makes location decisions. The answer: They wait for a McDonald's to open and then they put a restaurant next to it. This is not to say that a very good marketing information system alone will allow an organization to achieve financial success, but it will be of tremendous benefit to management.

Components of a Marketing Information System

A key component of an effective marketing information system is having accurate information about the environment. The foundation for this data collection is environmental scanning, which refers to a process whereby external factors that could affect an organization are continually evaluated. Based on an initial evaluation, those factors with the greatest potential impact, either positive or negative, are examined in greater detail. From a theoretical standpoint, if management is to make rational decisions, all information that could affect the hospitality organization should be examined and evaluated. Realistically, however, this is not possible because of the finite limits on the valuable resources of time, money, and personnel. Instead, only those environmental variables that appear to be the most important or most critical are examined in greater detail.

In short, a marketing information system that uses environmental scanning provides an overview of the entire environment as well as further detail concerning those variables within the environment that are most critical to the successful operation of the hospitality organization. The firm's overall environment can be divided into three subenvironments: the macroenvironment, the competitive environment, and the organizational environment.

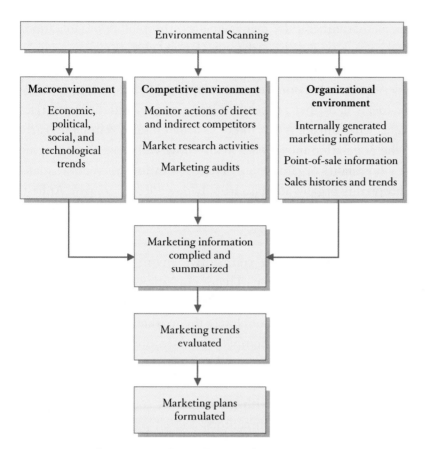

FIGURE 6.1 • *Components of a marketing information system.*

A conceptual model of the components of a marketing information system is shown in Figure 6.1. Data are generated for each of the three subenvironments through an environmental scanning process. The data are then compiled, summarized, and stored until needed by management. At the appropriate time, management can readily retrieve data summaries, evaluate marketing trends, and formulate marketing plans and strategies. There are three overriding objectives of a marketing information system:

1. To collect relevant data concerning each of these subenvironments

2. To compile, summarize, and store the data

3. To have data readily available for management on a timely basis

MACROENVIRONMENT. The macroenvironment concerns the broadest possible effects. Macroenvironmental effects are those that the individual hospitality organization is almost powerless to control and include economic, social, political, and technological aspects of the environment. As conditions change within the macroenvironment, the management of hospitality organizations should collect data concerning these changes. Knowledge of existing conditions will provide a basis for calculating the impact that these variables will have on the operation of the firm. For example, if the federal tax deductibility of business meals is further reduced or if the annual inflation rate rises by 3 to 4 percent, what impact is this likely to have on sales volume? Nearly 20 percent of the population moves each year—how will these demographic changes affect a hospitality organization? These are influences that the management of a hospitality organization is virtually powerless to control. At best, management can monitor the variables of the macroenvironment and gauge the effects they might have on business.

COMPETITIVE ENVIRONMENT. The competitive environment immediately surrounds the hospitality organization. The organization exerts some degree of control over this environment but can never control it totally. The major concern for management is to monitor closely the marketing and operational actions taken by direct and indirect competitors. Attention should be focused initially on changes made in the marketing mix, guest profile, room and menu prices, and sales volume as measured in both dollars and in guest counts. Management should also be concerned with the degree of concentration of competition, entries and exits among competitors, and changes in market share among competitors. Exact figures are not likely to be available, but all competitors should be monitored closely so that management can be prepared for changes before or when they occur, rather than weeks or months later. By monitoring competition in this way, management can prepare an appropriate competitive response, thereby gaining a differential competitive advantage.

The two other aspects of the competitive environment for a marketing information system are market research activities and marketing audits. Market research encompasses a wide range of activities undertaken to generate information about a firm's products, customers, and external environment. Marketing audits are evaluations of the effectiveness of current marketing practices. In particular, marketing audits are used to monitor marketing plans on an annual basis.

ORGANIZATIONAL ENVIRONMENT. The third subenvironment that is a part of a marketing information system is the organizational environment. Data collection in this subenvironment involves examining all relevant information sources within the hospitality organization. The basis for data collection in this subenvironment is guest histories, although information can be generated from other sources as well. Guest histories are records that a hotel maintains for all types of guests, both individual and groups. In addition, histories should be maintained within all retail outlets, especially food and beverage.

Within the food and beverage area, all sales should be recorded and broken down by menu group and menu item. Only when managers have access to records of previous sales are they able to make informed decisions concerning the product–service mix for the organization.

Requirements for a Successful Marketing Information System

The basic task of gathering data is important to an organization, but an effective marketing information system is one that is able to organize this task and supply the firm with useful information. To generate data that are useful for managers and decision makers, a marketing information system should fulfill three requirements:

1. **It should be objective.** Management should be able to quantify and analyze the information gathered. Management needs as much purely objective data as possible to make sound decisions. For example, which of these two statements seems to provide better information for decision-making purposes?

   Statement A: "As the owner of this restaurant, I think we should modify our menu so that we can appeal to more family business."

   Statement B: "A recent study has indicated a 10 percent increase in the number of families with children under the age of ten in our area."

   Statement B would appear to be more objective and to offer quantitative data on which to base a decision. On the other hand, Statement A is merely an opinion and is not supported by any quantitative data. Too many hospitality managers rely heavily on subjective opinions for decision-making purposes, and their decisions are often incorrect. Decisions based on purely personal opinion are often less than successful when implemented. Decisions based on a combination of data and managerial insight and experience generally yield higher-quality decisions.

2. **It should be systematic.** The marketing information system is not an on-off process; it is a system that should be designed to provide a continuing continuous stream of information source for management. When information is collected in a systematic and continuous manner, the quality and quantity of data improve. For example, many conference hotels only receive feedback from meeting planners on an ad hoc basis, rather than develop a system requiring feedback from each meeting.

3. **It should be useful.** Many studies produce information that is of little value. This is obviously not the purpose of a marketing information system. One

rule of thumb to follow is this: collect, compile, and store information only if it is used actively; do not collect information and then file it away without using it. This is a needless and expensive waste of time and effort, yet many hospitality operators, in an attempt to gather any quantitative information, maintain data that are never used and are truly useless. For example, many hotels still collect comment cards without inputting the results in the computer. Managers simply read over the comments and ratings and then manually file the cards. The advent of low-cost and increased-capacity hard disk storage within personal computers has made it easy to compile data to be examined using some type of analytical software (e.g., MS Excel, SPSS, etc.).

SOURCES OF MARKETING INFORMATION

Secondary data

Data that have already been collected by another source and made available to interested parties either for free or at a reasonable cost.

Primary data

Data that are collected for a current study or project and tailored to meet the specific information needs for that study or project.

A variety of sources can be used to obtain the information necessary to fuel a marketing information system. These information sources can be grouped into two main categories: secondary data and primary data. **Secondary data** were previously collected for another purpose. **Primary data** are generated for a specific purpose when the information is not available elsewhere. It is normally advisable to search for secondary data before engaging in a primary data collection process. The secondary data may provide the information necessary to make a decision, and even if they don't, they may be useful in developing the collection process for primary data. Figure 6.2 illustrates the possible sources of information for marketing decisions.

Secondary Data

As mentioned before, this type of data is already available from other sources and summarizes information about operations, marketing, human resource management, financial performance, and other topics of interest to management. A shrewd manager will make a thorough check of all available secondary data sources before undertaking primary data collection. Secondary data can save many personnel hours and a great deal of money. Here are the major advantages of using secondary data:

- **Cost.** It is much less expensive to obtain information from existing sources than to develop entirely new data. These existing sources may require a

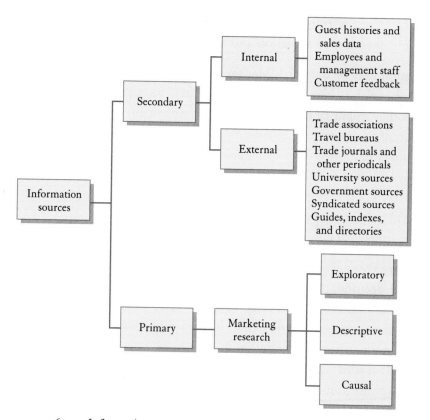

FIGURE 6.2 • *Information sources.*

nominal charge for the information, but it will be much less than the cost of undertaking primary data collection.

- **Timeliness.** Secondary data are available almost instantaneously. A manager can have access to data very quickly and therefore does not have to wait weeks or perhaps months for primary data to be collected, analyzed, and summarized. By using secondary data whenever possible, a manager avoids the frustration of developing the research methodology design, designing the data collection instrument, pretesting the instrument, devising a sampling plan, gathering the data, checking all data for accuracy and omissions, analyzing the data, and summarizing and reporting the results. Instead, a manager can merely locate the appropriate source and access the information desired. This process can be completed in a few hours or days, whereas primary data collection can take weeks or months to complete. However, secondary data collection does have the following disadvantages.

- **Limited applicability.** A manager has no assurance that information gathered by others will be applicable to a particular hospitality operation. For example, information obtained in New York about the popularity of a specific menu item is not necessarily useful to a manager operating in another part of the country. Information that pertains to one operation may apply only to that operation and be of limited value to anyone else.

- **Information may be outdated.** Managers need current and accurate information on which to base decisions. All too often, secondary data are not as useful as they might be merely because they are not current. For example, the results of a consumer attitude survey conducted by a restaurant four years ago would be of limited value to a manager making plans today. During the four years, a number of changes in consumer attitudes are likely to have taken place. These changes in attitudes will make the original data outdated and useful only in a historical sense. If a hospitality manager makes use of less-than-timely data, the results are likely to be less than satisfactory.

- **Reliability.** Whenever a hospitality operator uses secondary data as the basis for a decision, the manager runs the risk that the information may not be reliable and accurate. A manager would do well to determine who collected the data and what method of data collection was used. Information is only as good as the individuals who collect it and the methods they use. If a study is administered in a haphazard manner, the results and conclusions should be viewed with caution.

Pertinent guest information should be obtained by hotels for the purpose of analyzing sales data. Courtesy of Wyndham Worldwide.

There are two main types of secondary data that can be used by managers within a firm (see Figure 6.2). *Internal data* exist within the firm and can be obtained with minimal time and effort. Advances in computer technology have made it easier to obtain this information and provide it to managers in a form that is useful. *External data* are not readily available within the firm. Managers must obtain this data by spending more time and/or money contacting outside sources. The Internet has made this a much easier task, but there is still a fair amount of effort involved. The various sources of internal and external data are discussed next.

INTERNAL DATA. The component of a marketing information system that is the simplest to design and implement is an internal system, or the component designed to collect data from within the organizational environment. When considering the organizational environment, management needs to be concerned only with information available from within the physical confines of the organization's units, whether they are hotels or restaurants. This component of a marketing information system requires less time and money than does the competitive environment or externally generated marketing information.

The internal component of a marketing information system is very valuable to management because it provides a wealth of information. Management has three main sources of internal marketing information: guest histories and sales data, employees and management staff, and customer feedback:

- **Guest histories and sales data.** No rules can tell a manager exactly what records should or should not be maintained. The management of every hospitality organization must make this decision based on individual needs. Within a hotel operation, the minimum records that should be maintained are both individual and group guest histories. These will permit management to have knowledge and monitor changes in zip code origin of guests, length of stay, guest expenditure per day, and other pertinent data concerning guests. Within a restaurant operation, the records maintained should include customer counts for each meal period and sales for each menu item over a specified period of time. Many larger organizations have a sophisticated management information system in place. However, for the smaller organization, the design of a management information system is much easier than it has been in the past. Many point-of-sale terminals interface with personal computers, making the transfer of data to off-the-shelf database management and accounting software relatively easy. By using a personal computer, a manager is better able to manage the data. The quality and ease of use of off-the-shelf business software such as Microsoft Office make it far easier for a manager to capture and analyze large databases. It is more common for managers to conduct more sophisticated statistical analysis of the database of customers and to mine the database for keys to increasing the volume of business from current customers. It is obvious that, with accurate information readily available, a manager is more likely to consult such marketing information prior to making a marketing decision.

- **Employees and management staff.** All too often, hospitality management ignores the wealth of information that is informally gathered by hourly employees such as front desk personnel, telephone operators, restaurant service people, and hosts and hostesses. These individuals are in constant contact with guests, yet they are rarely asked to relay customer comments and reactions to operational changes, such as new menu items or guest room décor changes. These employees represent an excellent source of information, although the information they provide may not be totally objective. It is a good idea for management to meet with employees on a regular basis to discuss problems and opportunities. Employees crave recognition from their supervisors; this recognition increases the employee's satisfaction and commitment to the organization. All employees need to be exposed to some motivational techniques, although managers often ignore the simple and basic needs of employees as individuals.

- **Customer feedback.** The focus of the marketing concept is the hospitality operation's clientele. All aspects of the entire operation should be aimed at satisfying these individuals. The purpose of using an internal marketing information system is to solicit opinions and comments from the current clientele. This can be done in a number of ways, such as having the manager talk with a few of the customers or having service personnel check with the customers. One method used frequently is the comment card. These cards are placed in guest rooms or are provided to the guest upon checkout or when they have finished a meal in a restaurant. The purpose is to solicit their opinions and comments concerning the operation's quality.

All three internal sources of marketing information are very valuable. Together, they can provide a great deal of useful information with which to make decisions. Historically, hospitality managers have failed to use these sources to maximal advantage, but the current competitive situation in the hospitality industry dictates that all sources of information be used to gain a competitive advantage and to earn maximal financial rewards.

EXTERNAL DATA. Although externally generated marketing information is extremely valuable, it is normally not collected on a daily basis, as is the case with internally generated marketing information. This is due to a much larger investment of time, money, and other scarce resources required for externally generated information. Management should consider using a wide variety of sources of external marketing information. Literally thousands of sources are available, and these sources are limited only by management's own efforts to locate them. A few typical sources of external marketing information are:

- **Trade associations.** Many industries form trade groups that provide data for their members. These trade associations collect information from their members and then provide industry averages that can be used to measure a firm's relative performance. Some of the popular trade associations for the hospitality industry are the National Restaurant Association, the American Hotel & Lodging Association, and the Hospitality Sales and Marketing Association International. Two of the more popular tourism associations are the World Tourism Organization (WTO) and the Travel and Tourism Research Association (TTRA). However, most of the data for the tourism industry are collected by government travel bureaus.

- **Travel bureaus.** Cities, states, and countries usually form organizations that are responsible for promoting travel to the area. Most cities have a chamber of commerce that is responsible for promoting business in the city and, in some cases, tourism as well. Larger cities and regions form convention and visitors bureaus for the sole purpose of promoting business and leisure travel to the region. A chamber of commerce has member firms from all types of industries, whereas convention and visitors bureaus tend to have member firms from travel-related industries such as lodging, restaurants, and tourist attractions. Finally, most states and countries have government travel and tourism bureaus that are responsible for promoting travel to that state or country. It should also be noted that many of the tourism and destination Web sites provide access to arrival data and surveys regarding visitor profiles and travel motivations.

- **Trade journals and periodicals.** Many industry, or trade, journals are available to firms. Trade associations often publish their own journals, but many other organizations publish periodicals covering certain industries. Some of the more popular hospitality publications are *Restaurants & Institutions, Restaurant Hospitality, Nation's Restaurant News, Restaurant Business, Lodging Hospitality, Lodging Magazine,* and *Hotel & Motel Management*. The articles in these publications provide information on new products and advertising campaigns, as well as current trends in the industry. These articles also provide a valuable resource for case studies involving successes and failures of industry firms.

- **Other periodicals.** In addition to trade journals that specialize in a certain industry, other publications cover business in a variety of industries. Some of the more popular business publications that cover the hospitality and tourism industries are *BusinessWeek, Wall Street Journal, Fortune, Barron's,* and *Forbes.*

- **Internet.** The growth in both the quantity and quality of information available on the Internet is well documented. Using one or more of the available Internet search engines will uncover information, some of which will be highly valuable for managers. A key consideration for managers is being able to determine the accuracy and usefulness of information gathered from the Internet.

- **University sources.** Universities and colleges have well-stocked libraries that can be a valuable resource for firms in the area. These institutions often have access to many of the other sources of external data. In addition, universities and colleges form centers to research specific areas such as hospitality. This information is often free to the public or available for a reasonable fee.

- **Government sources.** Local, state, and federal governments maintain detailed data on all aspects of the economy; the data are free or available for a nominal fee. The U.S. Census gathers detailed information about the population and retail business, and the *Statistical Abstract of the United States* contains similar information in abbreviated form. Census and statistical documents are now available in electronic form, enabling quicker searches and data retrieval. The federal government also collects information about foreign countries and provides specialists to answer specific questions and address inquiries.

- **Syndicated services.** Firms such as Harris and Gallup polls, Target Group Index, Nielsen, and W. R. Simmons specialize in collecting and distributing marketing information for a fee. These syndicated services provide information about consumer profiles and shopping behaviors, consumer responses to sales promotions and advertising, and consumer attitudes and preferences. This information is useful in focusing on market segments using aggregate data. These services often advertise in trade publications and marketing periodicals.

- **Guides, indexes, and directories.** Other valuable sources of external information include guides, indexes, and directories that are available at most university libraries and larger public libraries. Guides such as the *Business Periodicals Index* provide references by subject matter for articles in major

Rick Casey *President*

Capitol Representation, Inc. • Basye, Virginia

1. What are the major components or duties associated with your current position?

As a company that handles all the meeting and hotel needs of a number of major organizations, I am responsible for the total operation of the company. My daily routine includes developing highly specific RFPs of guest room and functions, security initiation if the events are attended by heads of state of other dignitaries, contract review, assigning the on site planners with all appropriate information, promoting strong relationships with our clients and hospitality professionals and handling all daily aspects of running a small business.

2. What are the components of your position that bring you the most satisfaction? What about your position causes you frustration?

The strong relationships I have with both our client base and other hospitality professionals make the task of bringing a win-win situation about for everyone a pleasure. Going to work each day is like spending time with people I truly enjoy.

The ever-changing cycles of the market economy applies pressures on those I deal with. As there are many nonhospitality professionals in the ultimate decision making positions, occasionally, the "hospitality business" becomes the "hostility business." My goal is to conduct business in the same manner, regardless of the market economy.

3. What are the most challenging aspects you're facing?

Working with younger people who have not had the benefit of seeing markets shift from buyers to sellers and back. Even more difficult is dealing with experienced professionals who have not retained the knowledge they should have while experiencing such market shifts.

4. What major trends do you see for your segment of the hospitality and tourism industry?

There will be more third-party components becoming involved in all aspects of the industry...and I am not convinced that is a positive thing. I have seen many people with a nonhospitality mentality performing services in areas they are not well versed in, albeit, they proclaim to be "experts."

industry profile

Identifying and training a work force to balance the high demand of new properties under development will continue to be a challenge. Domestically, in particular, work force issues will prove to be a major issue in the coming years.

5. What role does marketing play within your company?

Marketing for our company has always taken the "rifle-shot" approach instead of a "shotgun" one. Intense research is done before devising any strategy to attract new clientele. We are strong proponents of "relationship marketing" where others are very instrumental in assisting our action plan.

6. If you could offer one piece of advice to an individual preparing for a career in the hospitality and tourism industry, what would you suggest?

Work anywhere, anytime you can to gain practical experience in all aspects of business, particularly the hospitality industry. Also, spend as much time as you can with industry professionals you respect, as they will offer great knowledge to help understand the complexities that cannot be learned in education and training.

industry profile

INTRODUCTION

No matter how successful a hospitality or tourism concept is, if the company associated with the concept does not evolve and change, then it will be left behind. If we were to consider the top 100 companies in the lodging and food service segments, we would find that each year, some companies drop off the list and get replaced by new ones. Corporations such as Marriott International, Carnival Cruise Lines, Hilton, Starbucks, and Disney continue to lead the industry because they have been very successful in developing products and services that enhance their market position. However, it has become increasingly difficult for hospitality firms to expand sales and market share simply by adding new units.

Today, growth must be accomplished within existing units by developing and implementing a superior product–service mix or by opening new units in untapped markets that may require a good deal of research and effort. For example, many firms have expanded their product–service mix offerings into international markets.

To further illustrate this point, consider the following examples. Since the number of great potential locations for restaurants has been reduced through market saturation, the leading companies have taken innovative steps to increase sales and grow their respective companies. First, they have sought new locations and venues to sell their product–service mix. For example, Pizza Hut, through an agreement with Marriott International, began selling a scaled-down version of its product–service mix in selected Marriott hotels. This scaled-down version, or kiosk style of operation, offers a limited menu with no seating within the immediate kiosk facility. In addition, Pizza Hut participates in some of the noncommercial foodservice accounts operated by contract foodservice companies such as ARAMARK. This allowed Pizza Hut to reach new markets, ones that they had not previously reached. The result has been increased sales and increased consumer satisfaction. This is a **win-win relationship** for both Pizza Hut and its partners. Win-win relationships are defined as situations in which both parties benefit, without one being a winner and the other a loser. When companies attempt to negotiate win-win agreements, they seek long-term relationships that over time benefit both organizations.

Win-win relationship
A situation that results when both parties are satisfied at the end of negotiations.

A second example of using product–service mix development to increase sales would be fast-food restaurants that introduce new products on a regular basis. Each of these companies routinely introduces new products or a bundle of products that will be available for a limited time. The goal is to increase patronage and market share by taking customers away from the competition.

A second goal is to increase brand loyalty, or the repeated purchasing of a firm's brand over time. These limited-time offerings are often a bundling of several products with a reduced price and/or increased portion size to convey a high level of perceived value to the consumer. Companies often call such bundling "value meals," "meal deals," or a similar term to convey better value.

The third example is best illustrated by the manner in which theme parks extend the life of their product–service mix life cycle by engaging in product–service mix development. Each year, thrill seekers want to try the newest and greatest rides at the many theme parks around the country. Among the leaders in this market are Disney, Six Flags, and Paramount. Each of these companies develops new rides each year in an effort to attract consumers to their respective parks. Having the latest, largest, or greatest of these thrill-type rides can have a very positive impact on theme park attendance, sales, and profitability.

Finally, product–service mix development includes additions to and enhancements of the service elements. For example, several restaurant chains, such as Outback™ and Chili's™, have increased sales by encouraging customers to purchase meals via a drive-up or take-away service. This added service allows them to increase unit sales without adding seats in their restaurants. Slight additions to staffing levels allow them to provide this service profitably.

Product development takes two forms: **innovation** and **follow the leader**. Innovators are the risk takers, always seeking to be the first in the market with a new product or service. The leader, or innovator, will benefit from being the first to market with a new product or concept. Customers may associate the innovation with the leader or become loyal to that brand. For example, it is not unusual to hear customers at Burger King order a "happy meal" (a McDonald's product).[1] However, given the ease with which hospitality products and services can be duplicated, those who subscribe to the follow-the-leader approach can introduce their competing products and services soon after the market leader introduces its own products and services.

The Importance of Product Lines

For the continued success of a hospitality or tourism firm, it is important to have a **product line**, or portfolio of products and services. Few firms can survive and sustain long-term growth with only one or two products or services, because of the high risk associated with the lack of diversification. In addition to diversifying a firm's operating risk, there are several other reasons for developing new product lines, discussed in the following sections.

Innovation

An approach that seeks to be first to market with a new product or concept.

Follow the leader

An approach that introduces competing products and services soon after the market leader introduces its products and services.

Product line

Firms develop and maintain a portfolio of products and services.

The sunburst brand is recognizable whether it is for Days Hotel, Days Inn, or Days Inn Suites. Courtesy of Wyndham Worldwide

GROWTH OPPORTUNITIES FOR THE BUSINESS. When a company limits itself to one product or a limited number of products, it limits the firm's growth potential. Consider a firm such as Baskin-Robbins. It was quite successful selling ice cream, but when consumer tastes shifted toward lower-fat and healthier items, the firm developed and offered new products such as frozen yogurt that met this demand.[2] This allowed Baskin-Robbins to appeal to more consumers and increase sales. McDonald's is another good example of a firm that has expanded its product line to attract additional business. In addition to the hamburgers, french fries, and children's fare, it added salads and other menu items that are targeted toward adults. In recent years, McDonald's has enhanced its coffee products, in an attempt to compete successfully against Starbucks and Caribou Coffee.

EFFICIENT AND EFFECTIVE USE OF COMPANY RESOURCES. As more products are developed or as a firm develops additional brands, it can make better use of corporate resources. For example, Choice Hotels International operates and franchises several brands of lodging products, including such brands as Clarion Hotels and Suites, Clarion, Quality Inns and Suites, Comfort Inns and Suites, Cambria, MainStay Suites, and Sleep Inns. Marriott International uses a similar strategy, offering traditional Marriott Hotels and Resorts, as well as J.W. Marriott Hotels and Resorts, Courtyard, Residence Inns, Fairfield Inns, Renaissance Hotels and Resorts, TownPlace Suites, SpringHill Suites, and Marriott Vacation Club. Operating multiple brands allows Choice Hotels International and Marriott International to make better use of corporate resources by segmenting the market and tailoring their offerings to the various segments using separate marketing programs.

Increasing Company Market Share and Importance of the Company within the Overall Market. When multiple products or brands are made available to the public, sales will increase and overall market share will also increase. This affords the firm a stronger position in the market and increases the importance of the firm.

Diversifying a Firm's Business Risk. Without a steady flow of new products and services, a hospitality or tourism firm could have serious problems if the sales of existing product–service mix start to decline. However, increased sales from new products and services can counteract poor sales from the current ones. The larger the portfolio of products and product lines, the smaller the firm's business risk.

PLANNING FOR NEW PRODUCTS

It is critical for firms to take a systematic approach to developing and marketing new products and services. The potential rewards are high for successful new products or services, but the potential risks of failure are equally high. A firm must do a thorough analysis of a new product idea to determine if it is compatible with the firm's goals, if the firm has the necessary resources, and if the environment is favorable. Marketing plans should contain information regarding new product development, as well as the goals and strategies for existing products. As with strategies for existing products, strategies for new products can be either **reactive strategies** or **proactive strategies**.[3] Reactive strategies are developed as a response to a competitor's action, while a proactive strategy is one that is initiated as a preemptive effort to gain a competitive advantage.

> **Reactive strategies**
> Strategies that respond to changes in the marketplace.

> **Proactive strategies**
> These strategies anticipate changes in the marketplace.

Reactive Strategies for New Product Development

> **Defensive strategy**
> A defensive strategy is used to counter the effects on an existing product from a competitor's new product.

A **defensive strategy** is used to counter the effects on an existing product from a competitor's new product. Initially, this strategy involves minor changes in a firm's marketing mix such as advertising, packaging, and/or pricing. This will negate some of the impact from the competitive product until more information can be obtained and substantive changes made, if necessary. These changes could involve the development of a new product or service, or some major modifications to the current product–service mix. Normally, when new restaurants open, the other local restaurants counter with increased

Hotels such as the Wingate Inn are targeted at specific markets, such as business groups. Courtesy of Wyndham Worldwide.

promotions and/or discounts. Similarly, when small airlines have tried to start a new service in niche markets, the larger airlines serving those same markets have retaliated with price cuts and promotions for their routes in those markets. The goal of the larger airlines is to prevent the smaller airline from gaining market share and profitability.

An **imitative strategy** involves copying a new product or service before it can have a large impact in the market. This strategy is particularly appealing when the product or service is not unique or when it can be easily duplicated.

Imitative strategy

An imitative strategy involves copying a new product or service before it can have a large impact in the market. This strategy is particularly appealing when the product or service is not unique or when it can be easily duplicated.

This strategy is heavily relied on in the fast-food industry. Every time McDonald's launches a successful new product, Burger King and some of the other competitors are quick to respond with similar offerings and prices.

Second but better strategy

An adapted version of the imitative strategy where firms are responding to competitors' new products; however, the firm's primary goal is to improve on the initial product.

An adapted version of the imitative strategy is the **second but better strategy**. Once again, firms are responding to competitors' new products; however, the firm's primary goal in this case is to improve on the initial product. Marriott International's introduction of its Courtyard division and extended-stay properties was eventually followed by competitors with similar products. For example, both Wyndham Hotels and Hilton introduced a line of garden hotels that are targeted at business travelers with modest budgets and a dislike for large hotels. These new product lines or brands will compete directly with Marriott International's Courtyard brand, but their ultimate goal is to be better. This strategy is more common for products or services that require a large investment and a longer period of time to develop.

Responsive strategy

A strategy where firms are responsive in that they react to the demands of customers.

The final reactive strategy is referred to as a **responsive strategy**. Firms are responsive in that they react to the demands of customers. These new products are truly market-driven. Hotels often modify their offerings and design new properties based on the observed behavior of their guests. The way guests tend to rearrange a room, common complaints, and frequency of use of amenities and services are all factors that affect the design of hotel products. A recent response to guests' changing demands has been the addition of spa services at many hotels. Previously, spa services were normally offered only at resorts.

Proactive Strategies for New Product Development

Research and development strategy

A popular, proactive strategy where firms conduct research to design and develop new products or services.

Another approach to developing new products is to be proactive and initiate change, rather than react to it. A popular proactive strategy used by manufacturing firms is a **research and development strategy**. Service firms also do research in an attempt to design and develop new service concepts. Hospitality and tourism firms are continually searching for new ways to improve facility designs and computer systems for reservations and resource management. Marriott International developed proprietary computer systems for conducting business, whereas many other firms choose to use systems developed by outside vendors.

Marketing

Marketing encompasses merging, integrating, and controlling supervision of all company's or organization's efforts that have a bearing on sales.

Another proactive strategy used by service firms is **marketing**. This strategy embraces the marketing concept and the notion that it is important to determine customer wants and needs and then design products and services to meet those needs. Most hotels and restaurants use marketing research, comment cards, and other methods to gather information from consumers. Firms such as Ritz-Carlton Hotels take a comprehensive approach to gather information on service quality and satisfaction. Ritz-Carlton was selected to receive the Malcolm Baldrige National Quality Award as a result of its efforts to meet customer needs. The hotel firm obtained feedback from customers, employees, and suppliers in an attempt to completely understand the process of delivering high-quality service to its customers.

Firms that are innovative and tend to be leaders in their respective industries try to create an **entrepreneurial strategy** for their employees. These firms are looking for new ideas that are generated internally through means other than research and development. Employees are a great source for ideas on improving existing products and services and developing new ones. After all, what employee does not have an opinion about how to improve his or her firm's products or services? Rather than have this be a negative influence on the organization, some firms choose to encourage employees to share their ideas and opinions. As a result, some of the new service concepts become separate operating divisions or separate components of current operations.

Another way to add products or services to a firm's portfolio is through mergers or **acquisitions.** A firm can acquire the rights to new products or services by entering into a legal arrangement with another firm, thereby combining the two firms' products and services. Acquisitions are plentiful in the hospitality and tourism industry. At one time, PepsiCo developed a major presence in the hospitality industry through its acquisitions of brands such as Pizza Hut, Taco Bell, and KFC. The advantage is that the individual firms do not have to diversify their offerings because the diversification has occurred at the corporate level. Later PepsiCo reassessed this strategy and divested itself of these brands, which were acquired by Yum! Brands.

Finally, some firms choose to form **alliances** for a specific goal or purpose instead of combining ownership. Alliances are designed to take advantage of synergies that exist between companies by pooling resources such as marketing, research, and distribution. Many airlines, hotels, and car rental agencies have formed strategic alliances to help promote and sell their products and services. The firms benefit from cooperative advertising and shared databases, among many other areas. For example, United Airlines Mileage Plus members earn free miles which can be redeemed with lodging companies Marriott, Carlson Hotels Worldwide, Starwood, Hilton, Omni, Wyndham or Choice Hotels, as well as rental car partners Hertz, Alamo, Budget, Avis, Dollar and National. Alliances have been used most effectively by airlines. The most well known of these alliances is the Star Alliance, which brings together 15 airlines to provide a more seamless travel experience. Aimed primarily at business travelers, the Star Alliance allows airlines to

Entrepreneurial strategy
Firms looking for new ideas that are generated internally through means other than research and development. Employees are a great source for ideas on improving existing products and services, and developing new products and services.

Acquisitions
A firm can acquire the rights to new products or services by entering into a legal arrangement with another firm, thereby combining the two firms' products and services.

Alliances
Firms pool resources for a specific goal or purpose instead of combining ownership.

share information about travelers, as well as allowing travelers to have better access to route information and reservations among the airlines that are members of the alliance. Product development is a highly complex issue. It requires critical thinking and careful planning. The next section addresses issues related to how companies organize for product development and how it is conducted.

ORGANIZING FOR NEW PRODUCT PLANNING

Firms use a variety of organizational structures to develop new products and services. No one way is best, and each has inherent advantages and disadvantages. The primary organizational structures are new product committees, new product departments, product managers, and venture teams. Each of these structures is explained in the following paragraphs.

New Product Committees

New product committee

New product committees consist of individuals representing cross-functional areas of the firm. Usually, representatives provide input from operations, marketing, finance, and accounting.

A **new product committee** consists of individuals representing cross-functional areas of the firm. Usually, representatives provide input from operations, marketing, finance, and accounting. Committee members are charged with the responsibility of reviewing new product ideas and with determining the impact that new products will have on each of their respective areas. The process of using new product committees is often slow, and members normally have their own day-to-day responsibilities within their respective functional areas of the firm. Although these committees typically make decisions about which new products or services to offer, they do not develop the actual products or services.

New Product Departments

New product department

Some firms establish full-time new products departments. It is still important for members of this department to solicit input from all cross-functional areas of the firm.

Some firms establish a full-time **new product department**. This addresses the problem of product development being a part-time responsibility of members of the product development department. It is still very important for members of the product development department to solicit input from all cross-functional areas of the firm.

Product Managers

Some firms appoint **product managers** or brand managers to assume complete responsibility for determining marketing objectives and marketing strategies for a specific brand. Included in these responsibilities is product development as it relates to that brand. For example, suppose that someone was responsible for the brand Holiday Inn Express. In the role of a marketing manager, the individual would be responsible for all elements of the marketing mix: the product–service mix, the presentation mix, the communications mix, and the distribution mix. The marketing manager would also have the responsibility of establishing and implementing marketing strategies for the brand. Among the additional responsibilities of this role is being involved in product development.

Product managers

Manager who assume complete responsibility for determining marketing objectives and marketing strategies for a specific brand.

Venture Teams

Venture teams are similar to new product committees, but they are formed to complete a specific product assignment. Venture teams bring together expertise from operations, marketing, accounting and finance, and, if necessary, architecture and construction. The venture team is charged with new product planning, development, and implementation. Unlike new product committees, which normally only review and make decisions about whether new products should be developed further, the venture team is expected to stay on the project through the entire new product development process.

Venture teams

These teams are similar to new product committees but are formed to complete a specific product assignment. Venture teams bring together expertise from operations, marketing, accounting and finance, and, if necessary, architecture and construction.

NEW PRODUCT DEVELOPMENT PROCESS

Developing new products and services is time-consuming and risky, but it is essential to the continued long-term success of a firm. Many methodologies can be used to develop products and services. In this section, we will explore the steps in **new product development** within the hospitality and tourism industry (see Figure 7.1). Many firms, especially foodservice firms, use this process when developing new products and services. The examples used in this section relate to how new menu items are developed by foodservice firms. Comparable product development processes are used in the development of lodging products

New product development

Developing new products and services is time consuming and risky, but it is essential to the continued long-term success of a firm.

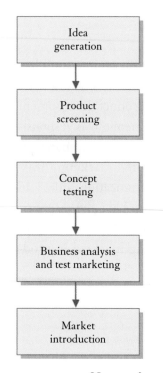

FIGURE 7.1 • *New product development process.*

and other types of products and services within the hospitality and tourism industry. Similar techniques are used to develop new services and elements of the total customer experience. The stages of the product development process are (1) idea generation, (2) product screening, (3) concept testing, (4) business analysis and test marketing, and (5) market introduction.

Idea Generation

New product ideas should take advantage of opportunities and trends in the dynamic marketplace, while matching the firm's strengths and overall mission. Ideas for new products can be generated internally as an assigned function for research and development groups or result from brainstorming by the structures covered in the previous section—a process called **idea generation**.

Other internal sources for ideas include salespeople and other employees. Many of the employees in a service firm are in customer contact positions. This enables them to get direct feedback concerning problems and to detect problem areas as they perform their normal job functions. This type of information is invaluable in improving customer satisfaction with service enhancements and new services.

Idea generation

Ideas for new products can be generated internally as an assigned function for research and development groups, or result from brainstorming.

Some of the external sources for new product ideas are competitors, suppliers, trade shows, and trade magazines. A firm can produce new product ideas from following the actions of competitors and reading about new developments in trade magazines. These new developments are also the focus of companies attending trade shows, whether they are direct competitors or simply similar firms in other markets. Finally, suppliers can sometimes have a keen insight into a firm's operations. They deal with many different firms and often generate ideas for improvement based on their own developments.

Firms should seek ideas from all potential sources. For example, menu items should be sought that expand, extend, or enhance the current menu. Currently, new menu item development appears to be most active in breakfast foods, light and healthy menu items, new tastes in foods such as regional cuisine, foods that cannot be easily prepared at home, foods that lend themselves to take-out, and food that is delivered.

Product Screening

Once ideas have been generated, the focus should turn toward **product screening**—evaluating the list of potential products to select the ones with the greatest potential for success. Managers should perform both qualitative and quantitative analyses to evaluate new product ideas. The qualitative standards involve answering the following questions:

Product screening
After product ideas have been generated, the focus turns toward screening the list of potential products to select the ones with the greatest potential for success.

- To what extent will the product increase sales and profits?

- Will the product attract new customers, and to what extent will it cannibalize from the sales of current products?

- What price would consumers pay for the product?

- Do we have the expertise and capacity to produce this product within our units?

- Does the competition offer a similar product? If so, how can we differentiate our product?

The quantitative analysis involves developing a weighted scoring for each new product idea to determine those with the greatest potential for success. The scoring is normally based on the following criteria:

- How the potential product or service contributes in a positive way to the image of the product and the company

- How the potential product contributes to achieving the overall company goals

- The strengths, weaknesses, opportunities, and threats (SWOT) that the firm faces

- Impact on current and potential customers

- Voids in the current product–service mix

- Equipment necessary to produce the new item

- Potential sources of supply for the new product or the necessary ingredients

Once the two types of analysis are completed, new product ideas with the most potential are selected for further development.

Concept Testing

Concept testing

A written or oral description and/or a visual representation is shown to consumers in the target market.

After new product ideas are screened, the ones that show signs of promise are subjected to **concept testing**. At this stage, a written or oral description and/or a visual representation is shown to consumers in the target market. This can be done through focus groups or using a more extensive marketing research data collection method. The consumers are asked a series of questions regarding the concept and its value in relation to competitors' products. The results of this analysis are used to refine the new product's design and assess its market potential. At this point, only products with a high probability of success are moved forward because the resources necessary to proceed begin to escalate.

At this stage in the menu design process, the products are typically tested further in corporate test kitchens. The emphasis at this stage is on recipe development to refine the product so that it can be consistently produced. Standards are established for portions, preparation, holding times, and presentation. If the development plan proceeds according to schedule, the product is tested in a few units. At this stage of development, focus groups representing individuals from the target markets evaluate the product. The focus groups, led by a skilled facilitator, assess the product's potential impact by conducting taste tests and soliciting consumer feedback about the product, price, appearance, and other attributes. If this process continues to be successful, the product is then ready to undergo limited test marketing in more units.

Business Analysis and Test Marketing

The information obtained from potential consumers, representing the target market, in the concept testing stage is used in a **business analysis** to evaluate the business potential of the new product. Consumer responses are used to estimate potential sales and market share so that costs can be allocated and potential profitability assessed. It is important to run more than one scenario (e.g., best case, worst case, and most likely case) for different market conditions. If the figures are promising, then the new product is prepared for test marketing.

Test marketing is the limited introduction of a new product in selected locations. It is necessary to extend the testing period long enough to view consumers' true purchase patterns, including repurchase (approximately 3 to 12 months). During the test market period, the product is evaluated based on (1) consumer feedback concerning quality, price, and various forms of sales promotion and advertising, (2) sales figures during various days of the week and times of day, and (3) the financial contribution that the new item has made.

Locations chosen for test markets should possess some common characteristics. First, the city or location should be similar to the planned market for the final product. It should have the same forms of media, the same demographic and psychographic backgrounds for potential customers, and the same or similar competitors. Second, the city or location should be somewhat isolated and of manageable size. There should not be any influence by competitors or media from neighboring locations. The most important point to remember when conducting test marketing is to make sure the test market locations are representative of the planned market to ensure the reliability and validity of the results.

Business analysis

Business analysis represents the qualitative and quantitative assessment of a firm's potential or a firm's strategies.

Market Introduction

The final stage in the new product development process is **market introduction**—introducing the new product to the entire market, or rolling it out market by market. New products that demonstrate favorable business projections and test-market results are given the green light by management. It is very costly to launch a new product because of the advertising campaigns and sales promotions, the employee training, and any required changes to the facility. At first, there are negative profits due to fixed start-up costs and inventories, and little revenue. It may take a good deal of time for the new product to be accepted and build market share. During this period, the firm must monitor the results and make any necessary changes in **marketing strategy**. Once the product is successfully launched, it is monitored and managed through the rest of its product life cycle.

Market introduction

The final stage in the new product development process is to introduce the new product to the entire market, or to roll it out market by market.

Marketing strategy

Marketing strategy encompasses the overall plan for achieving marketing objectives.

IDENTIFYING PRODUCTS AND SERVICES

Hospitality and tourism firms may offer more than one service or product line that is targeted at different market segments. It is often necessary to distinguish these offerings from one another if they are to hold different positions in the marketplace. Therefore, branding is a critical component of the marketing strategy for hospitality and tourism firms. The following section defines the terms related to branding and their use in the positioning of products.

The Importance of Branding

Brands are a very powerful marketing tool, and if properly managed, they have the potential of increasing sales, increasing profitability, and increasing customer satisfaction. Definitions of important terms follow:

Brand

The name, sign, symbol, design, or any combination of these items that is used to identify the product and establish an identity that is separate and unique from competitors.

Brand name

A part of the brand consisting of the words or letters that can be used to identify the firm.

Brand mark

The symbol or logo design used to identify the product.

Trademark

A trademark is the brand that has been given legal protection and is protected for exclusive use by the owner of the trademark.

- **Brand.** A brand is the name, sign, symbol, design, or any combination of these items that is used to identify the product and establish an identity that is separate and unique from competitors. Consider the impact that various brands have within the hospitality and tourism industry. Are brands more recognizable than the golden arches of McDonald's or the green circle of Starbucks Coffee?

- **Brand name.** The brand name is the part of the brand consisting of the words or letters that can be used to identify the firm.

- **Brand mark.** A brand mark is the symbol or logo design that is used to identify the product. Consider the stylized *M* and *H* that represent Marriott International and Hilton, respectively. When we see this brand symbol on the side of the hotel, we instantly know which brand the hotel represents.

- **Trademark.** A trademark is a brand that has been given legal protection and is restricted for exclusive use by the owner of the trademark.

The following example illustrates the importance of branding and its impact on sales and customer satisfaction. In a university dining services operation, one of the venues that was available on campus was an unbranded pizza operation. It was successful and turned a reasonable profit for dining services and the university. Students could purchase pizzas from the operation à la carte or use part of their meal plan as a credit toward the cost of a

Some brands are recognized worldwide. Coca-Cola is a registered trademark of The Coca-Cola Company, Courtesy of Hilton Hospitality, Inc., Hyatt Hotels Corporation, and Allied Domecq QSR.

pizza. As any professional manager would do, the dining services director of the university was seeking ways to increase student satisfaction with the dining services operations and also increase profitability for the university. One of the options considered was replacing the unbranded pizza operation with a regional or national brand pizza operation. After surveying the student body to determine preference, it was decided that Pizza Hut was the most popular choice among the students. Working with the corporate office of the contract food service company, which had previously negotiated with Pizza Hut for franchises at other universities, they were able to secure a franchise and open the Pizza Hut. In the first year that the Pizza Hut was in operation, sales increased nearly 30 percent. This increased revenue more than offset the franchise fee and other types of royalties that the management services company paid to Pizza Hut, Inc. The results of surveys administered to the students indicated that customer satisfaction had also increased. This is one example of the impact that brands can have.

Characteristics of Effective Branding

Marketers, especially in other fields, have long studied the use of brand names and have established criteria that are believed to make brand names more effective. Within the hospitality and tourism industry, these criteria are not always closely followed. Instead, the names of families or the founders have been used as the basis for the brand name. Consider that McDonald was the family name of the two brothers who first opened a hamburger restaurant in California. J. W. Marriott Sr. opened his first restaurant, a Hot Shoppe, in Washington, D.C. Conrad Hilton opened his first hotel in Texas.

Peripheral services

Additional goods and services that expand the core offering and can be used to obtain competitive advantage. Peripheral services consist of facilitating products and supporting products.

Facilitating products

Facilitating products are services that enable the customer to consume the core product. They must be present to make the product available where and when the customer wants it.

Supporting products

Supporting products are additional goods and services that can be bundled with the core service in an attempt to increase the overall utility or value for consumers (e.g., concierge service, multilingual staff, 24-hour room service, and complimentary newspapers for business travelers).

Augmented product

The augmented product is the core product and peripheral services that combine to form the package of benefits offered by a product or service. It encompasses everything surrounding the service and its delivery, including intangible attributes such as accessibility and atmosphere.

Supporting services such as a hotel gym are becoming increasingly important to guests. Courtesy of Wyndham Worldwide.

The **augmented product** is the core product and peripheral services that combine to form the package of benefits offered by a product or service. In addition, the augmented product includes how the service is delivered. In other words, the augmented product encompasses everything surrounding the service and its delivery, including intangible attributes such as accessibility and atmosphere. For example, Las Vegas hotels and casinos have augmented the core product to include extravagant design, in an attempt to attract visitors and gain a competitive advantage over other hotels and casinos. The basic hotel service is augmented with casinos, shows, high-quality restaurants, and incredible atmospheres. Also, the hotels make themselves very accessible, with good deals and special packages.

PRODUCT LIFE CYCLE

The product life cycle theory describes how a product progresses from its infancy as a new product in development through a growth phase to a maturity phase and then eventually into decline. Each stage of the product life cycle will be discussed in detail, followed by a discussion of the uses of the theory. Figure 8.1 illustrates the general shape of a typical product life cycle and its four stages.

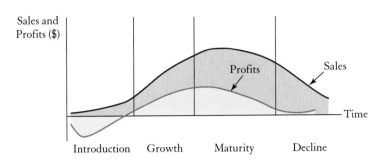

FIGURE 8.1 • *The product life cycle.*

Introduction Stage

The first stage of the product life cycle is called the **introduction stage**. At this point, the product has been through the new product development process presented in Chapter 7. It has survived analysis and testing, and it was deemed worthy of market introduction. The product represents a new concept, so there are no competitors offering the same product, and if the product is unique, there aren't even similar products in the market. Therefore, the goals for the firm are to develop product awareness and stimulate trial and adoption. To accomplish these goals, the firm must make a sizable investment even though sales will initially be low, leading to negative profits. The investment is in the form of capital expenditures on facilities and inventories, and a promotional campaign to attract customers. However, even though the cost per unit of manufacturing the product or providing the service is high, it is often necessary to offer discounts and other promotions to induce potential customers to try it. The pricing decision is usually based on the estimated costs and demand for the product because there are no direct competitors. During the introductory phase, customers tend to be innovators who are willing to take risks to try new products and services. The distribution of the product is selective in an attempt to build a customer base before adding new units or distributors. Many of the large hotel and restaurant chains started with one unit and eventually grew to become a large chain or franchise. For example, Holiday Inn started with a single property in Memphis, Tennessee, in 1952, and Wendy's restaurant chain started with a single unit in Columbus, Ohio, in 1969. Some hotels may start with a test-market property, but many recent concepts were started with more than one property. For instance, Wyndham's Garden Hotels were opened with multiple units in an attempt to generate more awareness and interest than could have been attained with a single property. It is more common for restaurants to begin as single-unit operations and add more units as they become successful and generate cash flow. This is due to the fact that repeat business can be generated from the local market, whereas hotels are dependent on a more transient market.

Introduction stage

The first stage of the product life cycle is called the introduction stage. At this point, the product has been through the new product development process. It has survived analysis and testing, and it was deemed worthy of market introduction.

Growth Stage

If the firm is able to accomplish its goals in the introductory stage and the product builds an adequate customer base, the product will move into a growth stage. The **growth stage** is evidenced by rapidly rising sales and profits, and a decreasing cost per unit for providing the product or service. This positive outlook attracts competitors who are willing to take the risk because of customer acceptance and increasing profit margins. In this stage, the profits being generated by the product allow the firm to consider product extensions, new markets, and organizational expansion in the form of additional properties or units. Minor changes may be made in the unit design and concept, but normally the owners attempt to standardize the physical plant, thereby reducing developmental costs. The owners' rationalization is that if the original unit is successful, additional units will also be successful. During the growth stage, the organization typically expands its distribution by adding new units. These units are often located in clusters within geographic regions.

It is during the growth stage that the second group of consumers, known as early adopters, begins to enter the market as they obtain feedback from the innovators. The increase in competitors during this stage and the need to build market share put downward pressure on price. The use of the intensive distribution strategy helps the firm build its customer base and market share by creating more awareness and interest in the product. The goal is that the firm penetrates the market and develops loyal customers, while gradually reducing the amount of sales promotions and discounts. Instead, more emphasis can be placed on other forms of promotion, such as personal selling and advertising. The restaurant industry is a good example where new concepts enter the market every year, and those that are successful become larger chains and franchises. It is important to note that there is no standard length of time that a product remains in the growth stage. Some products experience strong growth over a short period of time, and then sales level off quickly, while others maintain a lengthy period of growth.

Maturity Stage

If an organization is able to achieve the desired success in the growth stage, it will eventually move to the **maturity stage**. At this point, the organization has expanded as much as the market will allow, and volume, measured in annual gross sales, will level off. Companies in this stage of the product life cycle find that the market is often saturated and competition is increasing from alternative options. Industry profits tend to peak near the end of the

Growth stage

The growth stage is evidenced by rapidly rising sales and profits and a decreasing cost per unit for providing the product or service.

Maturity stage

A stage within the product life cycle where the organization has expanded as much as the market will allow, and volume, measured in annual gross sales, will level off. Companies in this stage find that the market is often saturated and competition is increasing from alternative options.

growth stage as the product moves into maturity. However, there are still high profits due to the large volume and the beginning of a decline in the number of competitors. In other words, the weaker competitors leave as the market reaches equilibrium and stronger competitors are left to battle for market share. A common strategy is for firms to standardize products and remove some of the less-valued attributes. This streamlining will enable the firm to take advantage of the **economies of scale** associated with higher volume, thereby widening the profit margin. For example, Delta Airlines introduced box lunches that passengers received as they boarded the plane. A couple of years later, the airline announced that it would no longer include sandwiches in the box lunches, a move expected to save tens of millions of dollars. Finally, the airline eliminated lunches and snacks entirely on most of its flights.

Economies of scale
Cost efficiencies derived from operating at high volumes.

There may also be changes in consumer preference as the consumer turns toward newer and more innovative concepts. For example, some pizza restaurants like Bertucci's Brick Oven Pizzeria and California Pizza Kitchen emphasize the method of preparation as being unique in comparison to traditional pizza restaurants. The advertising and promotions during this stage focus on differentiating the product, although it can be difficult because the core products tend to be very similar. This product homogeneity increases the consumer's price sensitivity and firms are forced to price at the market. At this point, the market may fragment into more segments with different needs and price sensitivities. Most hotel chains offer more than one brand in an attempt to attract consumers from various market segments. For example, Holiday Inns have limited service hotels (i.e., Holiday Inn Express), full service hotels (i.e., Holiday Inn), business hotels (i.e., Crowne Plaza), and luxury hotels (i.e., InterContinental).

In this stage, the distribution of the product becomes even more intensive to ensure consumer convenience and accessibility. This expansion can be developed internally, or it can be the result of mergers and acquisitions. Weaker competitors may be acquired by stronger—and often larger—competitors who wish to gain access to new markets. Most of the products in the United States are in the maturity stage, which can last indefinitely. At this stage, the product adoption cycle has progressed to the point of including the majority segment of consumers, leaving little room for growth in the sales for the product category. As a result, individual brands can only increase sales at the expense of their competitors, rather than rely on new consumers in the market. The quick-service (i.e., fast-food) industry is notorious for its fierce competition in advertising and pricing. For example, Subway is being attacked by competitors such as Quiznos that refer to the brand as "wrong way."

Decline Stage

Decline stage

During the decline stage, the last stage in the product life cycle, industry sales and profits decline more rapidly, and the number of competitors gets reduced to those with strong positions.

The last stage in the product life cycle is decline. During the **decline stage**, industry sales and profits are dropping more rapidly, and the number of competitors is reduced to those with very strong positions. The only new consumers entering the market are the laggards, and prices are often cut even further. Firms have progressed through the experience curve and the cost per unit has been driven down with accumulated volume. At this point, firms have phased out the weaker brands and focus more on the strong brands. The product consists of the core product and only those peripheral services that are of real value to the consumer. Distribution is selective as weaker outlets are closed. Hospitality firms will sell or close their properties in markets that aren't performing well in an attempt to free up resources for the more successful properties. For example, Planet Hollywood started its decline stage by closing restaurants that were not profitable in an attempt to remain viable, but the company eventually went bankrupt and decided to go out of business completely.

The major objective during the decline stage is to reduce overall marketing expenditures and increase cash flow. This strategy is referred to as "milking the brand" because you are trying to get as much profit from it as possible.

The decrease in marketing expenditures comes in the form of reduced customer service, reduced quality and variety, reduced distribution, and reduced promotion and advertising. Firms are left with a group of loyal customers that may or may not be large enough to continue with a profitable operation. It is critical that firms are relatively certain about the product's status in the product life cycle because these actions may force the product into decline prematurely. Many independent hospitality and tourism firms are finding themselves in the decline stage as large chains and franchises take advantage of their lower costs and engage in price wars that force the weaker firms out of the market.

APPLYING THE PRODUCT LIFE CYCLE

McDonald's serves as an excellent example of the way a corporation progresses through the organizational life cycle. McDonald's, under the direction of Ray Kroc, began with a few units in the mid-1950s. The corporation quickly achieved a sound financial base and rapidly moved into the growth stage of the life cycle. New units were continually being constructed, and soon the familiar red-and-white buildings with the golden arches could be found throughout the country. However, an important decision was made as McDonald's was nearing the end of the maturity stage. The upper-level management felt that the red-and-white buildings with the golden arches had outlived their useful life and that a new image was needed.

With this in mind, the corporation began to rethink the design and décor of both new units and the vast majority of existing units. They determined that a more subdued appeal was needed to attract different target markets. The term *fast food* was not used in any promotional or corporate literature. Instead, emphasis was placed on the image of McDonald's as a restaurant. Instead of seeing its sales level off, McDonald's was able to inject new life into its concept and therefore continued to expand and increase the number of units, total sales, and bottom-line profits. Later in McDonald's history, when sales growth had begun to slow, the corporation's leaders launched a breakfast program (McDonald's had previously served meals only during lunch and dinner). By serving breakfast, the company was able to increase sales without adding new units or franchisees. After that, they added another feature that is very common today—the drive-through window.

More recently, McDonald's has developed units in nontraditional locations as a means of increasing sales. These new locations include gas stations and convenience stores, as well as retail locations such as Wal-Mart. Another way McDonald's expanded its product life cycle was through entering international markets in an attempt to increase its growth potential. However, the future is unsure for the fast-food giant. The beginning of the twenty-first century marked the first time McDonald's was forced to close some of its less profitable units since the company was formed.

Developing Strategies for the Product Life Cycle

A number of strategies have been used for the various stages in the product life cycle. To develop strategies, however, management must first analyze the life cycle. This can be done in a seven-step process:

1. **Compile historical data.** It is imperative that hospitality firms compile historical sales data. Ideally, the data should be available for the entire history of the organization. The specific type of data needed include sales volume (in units), prices, total sales revenue, costs, and profits.

2. **Identify competitive trends.** Recent activities of major competitors should be monitored closely to determine changes in market share and position, as well as changes in quality of the product-service mix. Additionally, the

other elements of the marketing mix should be monitored for significant changes.

3. **Determine changes in product-service mix.** The marketplace must be monitored to learn about new products and services that other hospitality organizations are introducing and to anticipate the potential effects on your operation.

4. **Study the product life cycles of similar products.** It is helpful to study the life cycle of similar products or services to determine whether a pattern exists. Rarely is a product or service so new and unusual that it is not possible to compare it with a previous one.

5. **Project sales.** Based on the data collected, sales for a two- to three-year period should be projected. Applying computerized statistical techniques may be particularly beneficial at this stage. Specialized software packages are available that will allow a marketing manager to develop sophisticated sales forecasts. However, for many business decisions, the statistical procedures and techniques that are part of spreadsheet software, such as Microsoft Excel, will suffice. The software will permit the development of multiple scenarios or what-if scenarios by altering the levels of the decision variables. In addition to projecting sales, management should examine key financial ratios and other indicators of financial performance.

6. **Locate the current position on the life cycle.** Based on the historical data as well as the projections, it should now be possible to locate the product's position on the life cycle. This position is used to determine the most appropriate baseline marketing strategies.

7. **Develop strategies.** Once the position is located on the product life cycle, strategy formulation begins. Table 8.1 illustrates the characteristics and strategies that apply to different stages in the product life cycle. These strategies should not be viewed as being absolutely firm, but they do represent the most widely accepted ideas in the marketing community.

Ways to Extend the Product Life Cycle

One of the marketing manager's goals is to extend the product life cycle as long as possible. By doing this, cash flow can be extended and greater long-term profitability will result. There are several techniques that can be used to accomplish this.

INCREASING SALES TO EXISTING CUSTOMERS. During the maturity stage of the product life cycle, the rate of sales growth begins to decrease and eventually

	STAGE I INTRODUCTION	STAGE II GROWTH	STAGE III MATURITY	STAGE IV DECLINE
CHARACTERISTICS				
Sales	Low	Rapidly rising	Peak	Declining
Profits	Negative	Positive and increasing	High, starting to decline	Declining
Cash flow	Negligible	Moderate	High	Low
Customers	Innovators and some early adopters	Remaining early adopters and some early majority	Remaining early majority and late majority	Laggards
Competitors	Few increasing in number and strength	Many	Declining in number	
STRATEGIES				
Marketing objective	Create trial and awareness.	Increase sales and maximize market share.	Increase profits and maintain market share.	Decrease market expenditures and maximize short-term profits.
Product	Core product with some basic peripheral services.	Minor product changes and extensions.	Add attributes with positive differentiation.	Core product and key attributes.
Distribution	Selective	Becoming intensive	Intensive	Selective
Price	Set initial price based on costs and estimated demand.	Price to penetrate market based on actual demand.	Lower price to increase market share.	Reduce price to maintain volume.
Promotion	Create trial and awareness through sales promotions.	Build awareness and interest and reduce sales promotions.	Use to differentiate among major competitors.	Reduce expenditures and focus on loyal customers.

TABLE 8.1 • *Characteristics and Strategies for Stages of the Product Life Cycle.*

INTRODUCTION

Distribution is an important element of the marketing mix, but it is often difficult to understand its role in services marketing. Service channels are usually not traditional in the sense that there is a manufacturer, a wholesaler, and a retailer. Often, one firm performs all of the channel functions because there is no physical transportation of a product, and the production and consumption of the service occur simultaneously. However, service firms in industries like hospitality and tourism must still make decisions regarding channel organization and channel management.

One of the decisions that must be made by hotel and tourism firms concerns the use of **intermediaries**. Intermediaries, like wholesalers and retailers, may be valuable to service firms because of their expertise and ability to specialize in certain channel functions. Also, government organizations such as travel bureaus exist to help promote and distribute travel services to individuals and groups for their constituents.

The fastest-growing distribution alternative involves **electronic commerce** over the Internet. Hospitality and tourism firms use this outlet to promote their services and offer a direct channel to consumers. This form of commerce is efficient and provides other advantages that will be discussed in this chapter.

Intermediaries

Intermediaries specialize in certain functions in the service delivery process and can add value to the service with their knowledge and expertise (e.g., travel agents, meeting planners, tour wholesalers and operators, and travel bureaus).

Electronic commerce (e-commerce)

A term used to describe the buying and selling process obtained through electronic means such as the Internet.

CHANNEL STRATEGY

A firm's channel strategy must be consistent with the other elements of its marketing mix in order to be successful. The overall position of the firm in the marketplace is established by many factors, including price levels, product–service mix characteristics, and distribution. The promotion strategy is used to convey this positioning strategy to potential users of the firm's product or service. The delivery of products or services is intertwined with these other decisions.

For example, consumers would not associate gourmet-quality food with an establishment that is part of a food court in a shopping mall. Similarly, consumers would not expect to pay high prices for food purchased through this type of outlet.

The main objective of the distribution function is to get products and services to consumers where, when, and how they prefer them. A good distribution system will result in a smooth flow of products and services to consumers while at the same time achieving the firm's goals concerning market coverage, sales, and profitability. Firms have limited resources and must determine the most efficient and effective way to distribute their products and services. Some of the necessary activities associated with distribution include:

- Communicating and negotiating

- Facilitating transactions

- Storing and moving physical goods

- Installing products and providing service

Channel Organization

Channel design decisions must be made with regard to channel width (i.e., desired market coverage) and channel length (i.e., number of intermediaries). It is also possible to use a single channel to distribute a firm's products and services or multiple channels of various widths and lengths. Channel decisions are affected by product–service mix characteristics, market characteristics, and environmental characteristics. Obviously, the intangible nature of services tends to minimize the length of the channel of distribution. As discussed earlier, the service delivery process often requires consumers to be present during the production process. This eliminates the need for the storage and movement of a physical product. However, distribution is still an important consideration in the delivery of services. Some firms use a variety of channels depending upon the desired market coverage, the positioning of different services or brands, and the existence of different markets.

CHANNEL WIDTH. The **channel width** decision is based on the desired amount of market coverage. In other words, larger widths would be associated with more market coverage. Basically, three channel-width strategies are employed by firms: (1) exclusive distribution, (2) selective distribution, and (3) intensive distribution. The width of the channel ranges from exclusive distribution (one outlet) to intensive distribution (as many outlets as possible). As mentioned earlier, this decision must be consistent with the firm's other marketing mix strategies.

The narrowest channel width is **exclusive distribution**, where a firm limits the availability of its products or services to a particular outlet. This is common among independent operators in the hospitality industry. Le Cirque 2000 restaurant in New York City is a single-unit operation, and it is the only place consumers can purchase and experience this firm's product. This is also true of independent hotels such as the Palace Hotel in New York City and resorts such as The Greenbrier in West Virginia or The Homestead in Virginia.

Channel width

Channel width represents the number of distribution channel partners required to provide the desired market coverage.

Exclusive distribution

The narrowest channel width where a firm limits the availability of its products or services to a particular outlet. This is common among independent operators in the hospitality industry.

Foxwoods Resort Casino uses an exclusive distribution strategy by having only one location. Courtesy of Foxwoods Resort Casino.

Selective distribution

Selective distribution refers to the middle channel width, where a firm uses more than one outlet but restricts availability of the product or service to a limited number of outlets.

Intensive distribution

The widest channel strategy is intensive distribution, where firms attempt to make products and services available through as many outlets as possible. This is a common approach among franchise operations that use mass advertising and realize economies of scale.

Many single-unit restaurants and lodging facilities offer a personal touch and a one-of-a-kind experience. However, this individual attention comes at the expense of market coverage and the cost economies associated with high-volume business.

The middle channel width is referred to as **selective distribution**, where a firm uses more than one outlet but restricts availability of the product or service to a limited number of outlets. In the hospitality industry, many firms limit market coverage based on geographic segmentation. Some multiunit operations are strictly local, but some are regional or national with a limited number of outlets. Restaurant chains such as Hard Rock Cafe and ESPN Zone limit themselves to large cities. In contrast, Bertucci's Brick Oven Pizzeria, based in Somerville, Massachusetts, limits itself to the Northeast and recently expanded to the mid-Atlantic region. Many other multiunit restaurant operations are family-owned and stay within a very confined area. Some hotel chains, such as Omni Hotels and Four Seasons, have a limited number of hotels that are found in large cities, while others operate in limited regions. This distribution strategy is also popular among many travel agents, noncommercial foodservice firms, and certain airlines, such as Jet Blue.

Finally, the widest channel strategy is **intensive distribution**, where firms attempt to make products and services available through as many outlets as possible. This is a common approach among franchise operations that use mass advertising and realize economies of scale. These firms, such as McDonald's and Marriott International, try to standardize their services so that consumers can expect a consistent experience at any of the firm's outlets. Corporate-owned chains like Applebee's also use an intensive distribution strategy by adding units in as many suitable locations as possible. Consumers are more concerned with familiarity and consistency than with a one-of-a-kind experience. However, these firms do their best to provide consumers with a personal touch. Most airlines and car rental agencies use this distribution strategy as well.

CHANNEL LENGTH. The **channel length** decision is based on the number of intermediaries between the manufacturer and the final consumer. In the case of services, the channel is usually very short because of simultaneous production and consumption. In other words, consumers must be present to consume a service such as airline transportation, a meal, or an overnight stay in a hotel. A channel can be either direct, from the manufacturer to the consumer, or indirect, with intermediaries performing some of the necessary channel functions (see Figure 9.1).

A **direct channel** is the most popular for hospitality and tourism firms, as well as for most other service industries. The manufacturer sells directly to the consumer, and the manufacturer performs all of the channel functions. In product firms, this choice is made either because there are no qualified intermediaries or because the manufacturer feels it can do a better job. In service firms, there is often no choice because the service must be performed while the consumer is present. The direct channel enables the firm to have close contact with the final consumer and the ability to react quickly to changes in the market. For example, hotels use **central reservation systems (CRS)** and call centers to make the direct channel more accessible and to operate more efficiently.

Channel length

The channel length equals the number of intermediaries between the manufacturer and the final consumer.

Direct channel

The manufacturer sells directly to the consumer, and the manufacturer performs all of the channel functions.

Central reservation systems (CRS)

These are systems designed to improve the efficiency and effectiveness of the reservations function by providing a central point of contact for handling customers' requests in a timely fashion.

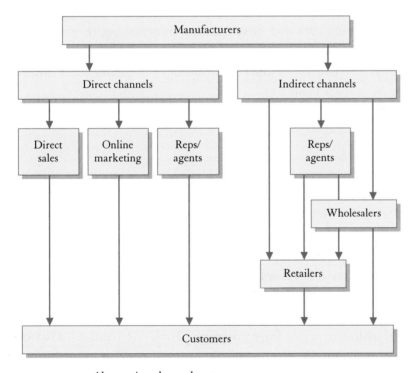

FIGURE 9.1 • *Alternative channel systems.*

Indirect channel

An indirect channel involves at least one intermediary that is responsible for one or more channel functions. This type of channel can exist in many forms, but it is not as common in service industries.

Hotels allow direct assess to booking rooms through the property, call centers, hotel Web site, or property-to-property. An **indirect channel** involves at least one intermediary that is responsible for one or more channel functions. This type of channel can exist in many forms, but it is not very common in service industries. Service firms are normally both producers and retailers.

There are a few indirect channels in the hospitality and tourism industries, but they seem to be more prevalent in the travel industry or in business markets that involve large-volume purchases. For example, tour operators (i.e., wholesalers) work directly with travel service firms such as hotels and airlines to combine services to market as a package to travel agents, who, in turn, market to the final consumers. Another example of an indirect channel is the meetings market. Hotel salespeople market their properties to meeting planners who purchase the hotel product on behalf of a group of final consumers. The various intermediaries will be discussed in more detail in the next section.

Global distribution systems (GDS)

Systems used by hospitality and travel firms to facilitate transactions within the distribution channel.

Most hospitality and travel firms use a combination of direct and indirect channels to reach as many consumers as possible. **Global distribution systems (GDS)** are used by airlines and hotels to coordinate their distribution activities and provide linkages to intermediaries. A GDS provides distribution channels that give customers the ability to easily search for hospitality and travel services and to conduct the transaction immediately. The system serves many roles, ranging from those that are transaction-based to those that are strategic in nature. In other words, a GDS is used for inventory control and rate management, storing data and disseminating information, revenue generation, and strategic positioning. Nyheim, McFadden, and Connolly (2005) provide a thorough discussion of global distribution systems and other hospitality technologies in their book.[1]

Intermediaries

Many of the distribution channels in service industries tend to be direct in nature, eliminating the need for intermediaries. However, the hospitality and tourism industries do have their share of valuable intermediaries that are responsible for volume business for hotels, airlines, and cruise ships. Intermediaries specialize in certain functions in the service delivery process, and they can add value to the service with their knowledge and expertise. This specialization results in more efficient production and distribution of services, as well as lower prices for consumers. Table 9.1 contains a list of the most common intermediaries in hospitality and tourism distribution channels.

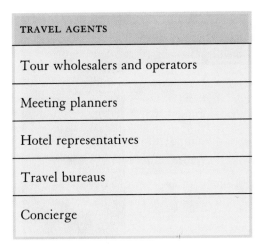

TRAVEL AGENTS
Tour wholesalers and operators
Meeting planners
Hotel representatives
Travel bureaus
Concierge

TABLE 9.1 • *Most Common Intermediaries in Hospitality and Tourism.*

TRAVEL AGENTS. Travel agents are responsible for a large volume of bookings for airlines, hotels, car rentals, and cruises. In addition, travel agents sell admissions to tourist attractions and special events. Although most of this volume comes from leisure travelers, corporate travelers can also account for a sizable amount of a travel agent's business. Some firms choose to use travel agents who specialize in corporate business rather than operate their own corporate travel departments. The benefit of using a travel agent is that agents specialize in finding and securing good rates for their customers. Another reason that travelers use travel agents is because of their extensive knowledge regarding travel products. Most agents have traveled to many popular cities and destinations, and they have access to informative promotional materials. It is important for travel agents to provide some additional value or they will cease to exist. Consumers will make their own travel arrangements via the Internet or through direct contact with the service providers.

The travel agent's expertise and access to valuable markets can be useful to hotels, car rental agencies, airlines, and cruise operators. It is virtually impossible for any of these firms to operate their normal business while keeping abreast of the many market segments and having access to all of their potential customers' preferred methods for purchasing travel products. Travel agents and hospitality and tourism firms seek to form relationships that will be mutually beneficial. Hospitality and tourism firms are looking for more volume, but they want consumers who will fit their overall customer mix. The current trend is for consumers to use Internet travel agencies like Expedia, Travelocity, and Orbitz. This process is more cost-effective for the agency and the consumers because much of the process is automated and consumers take part in the search process. Some of the online travel

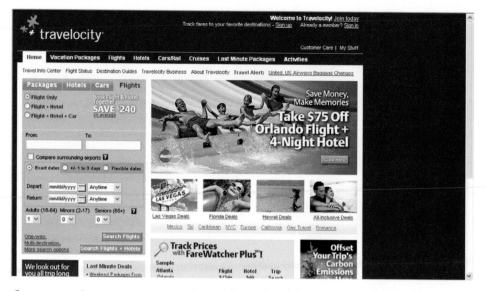

Consumers often use Internet travel agencies such as Travelocity to plan their trips. Courtesy of Travelocity.

agencies like Priceline offer an "opaque" service where consumers bid on travel products like in an auction without knowing the brand in order to get a lower price.

TOUR WHOLESALERS AND OPERATORS. Tour wholesalers and operators contract with hospitality and tourism firms to obtain services that can be combined in a package and offered to the leisure market. These packages can contain any combination of lodging, transportation, event or attraction tickets, and meals. These packages are marketed to travel agents and sometimes to consumers via the Internet or some other direct source. Tour wholesalers exist because they have access to the various suppliers and they specialize in packaging travel products, but they rely on travel agents to get the product to the mass market. This packaging concept appeals to consumers because of the convenience and the idea that the package can be purchased for a lower price than the components purchased individually. Once again, there is some value added to the services.

The package concept is particularly appealing to people engaged in international travel, senior citizens, groups, and novice travelers. There is some degree of risk associated with traveling to a new or foreign destination, but it is reduced by intermediaries such as tour wholesalers and travel agents. Tour wholesalers are able to sort services from suppliers into like grade and quality, package them, and offer them to retailers. This is a more efficient way to sell travel products to large volumes of leisure customers. Each of the channel members has a specialty that improves the service delivery process as well as the overall value of the final product.

MEETING PLANNERS. Large organizations such as corporations and trade associations have individuals or departments that are responsible for the travel plans of its members. These meeting planners negotiate with hotels, airlines, and other travel firms on behalf of their members for guest rooms and meeting space. There are also independent meeting planners and event planners who will work for organizations on a contract basis. As organizations seek to reduce overhead, outsourcing services such as meeting planning will become more common. Meeting planners are similar to travel agents in that they are familiar with many popular destinations. They have some expertise in areas such as negotiating, site selection, budgeting, and promotion, but it varies depending on whether they plan meetings for corporations, associations, or incentive groups. Each of these markets will be explained in more detail in Chapter 14, "Personal Selling."

HOTEL REPRESENTATIVES. Large hotels have sales staffs that are responsible for selling guest rooms and meeting space to groups. These salespeople negotiate with meeting planners, tour operators, and travel agents in an effort to fill the hotel. Unfortunately, smaller hotels may not be able to justify the hiring of full-time salespeople, either because they don't have enough demand for the service or because they cannot afford to hire them. In this case, it may be in the hotel's best interest to hire an independent hotel representative to market the hotel to chosen market segments. Even large hotels may hire these independent representatives to take advantage of their access to certain markets. Much like travel agents, hotel representatives are able to deal with a wide array of consumers. Hotel representatives may not be as familiar with the hotel product as an in-house sales staff, but they may have more knowledge regarding the consumers that the hotel is targeting. Also, the hotel representatives may have better access to the targeted consumers.

DESTINATION MARKETING ORGANIZATIONS. Each tourism city, state, or region has some form of **destination marketing organization (DMO)** that is responsible for promoting the long-term development and marketing of a destination, focusing on convention sales, tourism marketing, and service. In the United States, each state has its own office for travel and tourism. These agencies, or bureaus, are responsible for promoting the state as a travel destination and securing major events. They are funded by the government and work in cooperation with the state's hospitality and tourism firms. In addition, each major city or region within a state will have a **convention and visitors bureau (CVB)** that is responsible for promoting that city or region. Convention and visitors bureaus work with local hospitality and travel firms to secure conventions, meetings, and special events for the region. Convention and visitors bureaus can receive funding from various sources such as the government,

Destination marketing organization (DMO)

An organization that promotes the long-term development and marketing of a destination, focusing on convention sales, tourism marketing and service.

Convention and visitors bureau (CVB)

Each major city or region within a state has a convention and visitors bureau (CVB) that is responsible for promoting that city or region. Convention and visitors bureaus work with local hospitality and tourism firms to secure conventions, meetings, and special events for the city or region.

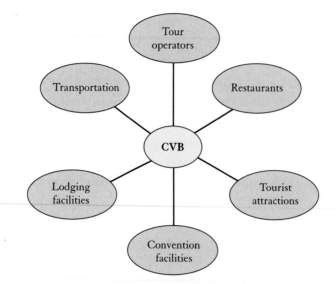

FIGURE 9.2 • *Convention and visitors bureau constituencies.*

membership fees, hotel taxes, and fees for services. CVBs also promote leisure travel to tour operators and travel agents, as well as the mass market of potential travelers. A CVB serves as a cooperative, representing hotels, motels, restaurants, convention facilities, tour operators, tourist attractions, transportation carriers, and other retail establishments that support tourists (see Figure 9.2). Most countries have a similar system focusing on regional, state, province, and city tourism destinations. These organizations are discussed in more detail in Chapter 16.

DESTINATION MANAGEMENT COMPANIES. These companies specialize in the organization of meetings, incentives, and events. In addition, **destination management companies (DMCs)** arrange social activities and programs for meeting attendees and their companions. Other special services include catering, dinners, and entertainment. Finally, a DMC can also make hotel reservations, arrange transportation and provide travel management, guides and hostesses. Destination Management Companies remain behind the scenes while ensuring that everything runs according to plan. DMCs are able to tailor their services to meet an organization's particular needs by using their many contacts and partners in the destination area. A list of destination management companies and suppliers/vendors is often available through destination marketing organizations on their Web sites.

CONCIERGE. Many full-service hotels employ an individual to help guests with local arrangements for restaurants and visitor attractions. In this sense, the concierge is an intermediary for the restaurants and local attractions. She will send business to retail operators with whom she has a good working

Destination management company (DMC)

A local firm that arranges activities and programs for meeting and event planners who are not familiar with the specific location or the local suppliers.

relationship. As a result, it is in the best interest of the local restaurants and visitor attractions to introduce themselves to the hotel concierge and give her a tour of the facility. The quality of the guest's experience with the recommended restaurant or visitor attraction will reflect directly on the concierge and the hotel. Therefore, the retail establishments must assure the concierge that the consumer will be satisfied.

Channel Management

Once a channel is developed, it becomes an ongoing task to manage it over time. Many conflicts and problems can occur that will require the cooperation of the members of the channel. It is also important to note that the same company can be a part of more than one channel and occupy a different position in each channel. For example, a restaurant would be a consumer in the channel for bulk food items and napkins, but a producer in the market for meals and dining. Similarly, hotels purchase many products and services, ranging from pens and soap to linens and pool chemicals. Therefore, a problem in one channel will affect the performance of the other channels in which the firm is a member. The Ritz-Carlton chain, a past recipient of the Malcolm Baldrige National Quality Award, recognizes the critical nature of these relationships and makes a special effort to recruit suppliers who understand and agree with its philosophy of customer service and quality.

There will always be conflicts between parties engaged in some form of negotiation over issues such as price, quantity, quality, and availability. Rather than attempt to eliminate these conflicts, it is better to find ways to manage them. In competitive markets, it is necessary to create fair exchanges so that both parties are satisfied. This mutual satisfaction can be the cornerstone of a loyal relationship that will benefit both parties in the future. Otherwise, it is in a firm's best interest to find a more equitable arrangement with other suppliers or retailers. Approaches to managing channel conflict can be behavioral (channel power and channel leadership) or contractual (vertical marketing systems).

CHANNEL POWER. This can be defined as the ability of one channel member to influence the behavior of other channel members in such a way as to get them to do things that they normally would not do. The most common forms of **channel power** are reward, coercive, expert, legitimate, and referent.[2] The balance of power depends on which channel member uses the bases of power most effectively. Any one of the channel members could conceivably have access to any of the forms of power.

Channel power
The ability of one channel member to influence the behavior of other channel members in such a way as to get them to do things that they normally would not do. The most common forms of power are reward, coercive, expert, legitimate, and referent.

Reward power

The ability of one channel member to influence the behavior of another member through the use of incentives. These incentives can be in the form of discounts, trade promotions, or some other form of promotional support.

Coercive power

The ability to influence a channel member's behavior through the use of threats. Threats could include restricted availability or access to products, or other unfavorable terms such as price or discounts, for example.

Expert power

Expert power is the result of the superior knowledge of one channel member relative to another. Some hotels agree to pay commissions and employ independent hotel representatives because of their expertise in dealing with certain market segments.

Legitimate power

Legitimate power is obtained through contractual arrangements that specify the members' expected behaviors. The most common form of legitimate power in the hospitality industry is franchising.

Referent power

Referent power occurs when a channel member has a certain prestige or image that would benefit another member as a result of their association.

Reward power is the ability of one channel member to influence the behavior of another member through the use of incentives. These incentives can be in the form of discounts, trade promotions, or some other form of promotional support. Airlines often reward travel agents by offering special commissions on certain flights. A related form of power is **coercive power**, or the ability to influence a channel member's behavior through the use of threats.

These threats could be in the form of restricted availability of products, or other unfavorable terms such as price or discounts. In this case, a travel agency may limit its association with an airline because the commission is too low. **Expert power** is the result of the superior knowledge of one channel member relative to another. Some hotels agree to pay commissions and employ independent hotel representatives because of their expertise in dealing with certain market segments. **Legitimate power** is obtained through contractual arrangements that specify the parties' expected behaviors. The most common form of legitimate power in the hospitality industry is franchising, which will be discussed in detail in the section on franchising. Finally, **referent power** occurs when a channel member has a certain prestige or image that would benefit another member as a result of their association.

CHANNEL LEADERSHIP. At some point, one of the channel members should take a leadership role. The leader can then organize the other channel members and strive toward common goals and objectives. The channel leader can be a manufacturer, an intermediary, or a retailer. However, the leader will normally be large and have a sustainable, competitive advantage in its industry because of financial resources, marketing skills, or some other factor. These competitive advantages will enable firms to obtain channel power and leadership. It is often beneficial for other channel members to associate themselves with successful companies.

Manufacturers can obtain a power base and take on a leadership role if they maintain ample resources or control a product that is in short supply and in great demand among consumers. For example, a popular resort such as Walt Disney World can exercise power and leadership over travel agents, car rental companies, and airlines. Intermediaries such as wholesalers and retailers can gain control over a channel if they have the ability to group components from various manufacturers and create an attractive product or if they have access to important markets. Tour wholesalers combine travel products into packages that are marketed to travel agents, who are retailers that have access to important markets and specialize in dealing with the various market segments.

VERTICAL MARKETING SYSTEMS. One approach to reducing channel conflict and uncertainty is the **vertical marketing system**. In a vertical marketing system, channel members work together as if they were one organization. Channel members work together to achieve a higher degree of efficiency, thereby reducing the overall costs of providing products and services. Vertical marketing systems offer a unified approach to channel management and can be corporate, administered, or contractual.

In a **corporate vertical marketing system**, all of the participants are actually members of the same organization. In this case, the original firm either develops or purchases other firms at the various levels in the channel. McDonald's operates its own food distributors in an effort to control price fluctuations and availability of its food supplies. A corporate system can be developed through backward integration (toward the manufacturer or supplier) or forward integration (toward the retailer or distributor). An example of forward integration would be a food distributor that decides to start a catering operation.

An **administered vertical marketing system** is one in which a manufacturer or supplier attempts to control the flow of goods or services through the channel. This is usually associated with expert power in that distributors and retailers are willing to relinquish some of their control in order to benefit from the producer's knowledge and background. Event management companies may have this type of arrangement with ticket agents who market and sell their events. This arrangement is similar to a conventional channel, but a greater degree of cooperation and sharing of information is necessary for a successful operation.

A **contractual vertical marketing system** unifies the channel members by means of a legal and binding contract. The firms agree to abide by the terms of the contract, the goal of which is to realize cost economies that would not be possible if the firms operated independently. This approach is similar to a corporate system, but it may be preferable when firms do not have the resources or expertise to develop operations at all channel levels. The firms benefit from pooling resources for functions such as advertising and research. Franchising is one example of a contractual distribution system.

CHANNEL MEMBER SELECTION AND RETENTION. It is important that firms exercise good judgment when choosing channel members. Intermediaries must demonstrate the ability and willingness to perform the desired tasks. In addition, prospective channel members must buy in to the philosophy of the service provider. The service provider should determine the characteristics that it feels are critical in a channel member and then evaluate potential members on the basis of these characteristics. Once a firm is selected, it is necessary to retain the firm through the use of financial and nonfinancial motivators.

Vertical marketing system

In a vertical marketing system, channel members work together as if they were one organization. Channel members work together to achieve a higher degree of efficiency, thereby reducing the overall costs of providing products and services.

Corporate vertical marketing system

All of the participants are actually members of the same organization. The original firm either develops or purchases other firms at the various levels in the channel.

Administered vertical marketing system

A manufacturer or supplier attempts to control the flow of goods or services through the channel. This is usually associated with expert power in that distributors and retailers are willing to relinquish some of their control in order to benefit from the producer's knowledge and background.

Contractual vertical marketing system

A contractual vertical marketing system unifies the channel members by means of a legal and binding contract. The firms agree to abide by the terms of the agreement, the goal of which is to realize cost economies that would not be possible if the firms operated independently.

Financial motivators are aimed at improving the channel member's profit. A service provider can improve a channel member's profit by offering more discounts or promotions related to desired outcomes, reducing prices, or increasing promotional support. Although financial motivators are effective, nonfinancial motivators should also be considered. Some nonfinancial motivators that could be used are training or improving products and services. For example, tour operators and tourism bureaus often invite travel agents on trips to the destination in order to familiarize the agents with the product. These trips are free of charge and allow travel agents to get a firsthand look at the destination so that they can relay the information to their customers. Hotels use a similar practice with meeting planners considering properties for their groups.

Building Customer Value in Channel Systems

When choosing a channel system to reach target customers, it is important for a firm to enhance customer value by increasing customer benefits (i.e., improve quality) and/or decreasing the customer's cost of purchase (i.e., lower the price).[3]

INCREASING CUSTOMER BENEFITS. Customer benefits can be increased by choosing a channel system that delivers more product benefits, delivers more service benefits, builds brand image, and/or builds company benefits:

- **Delivering product benefits.** Product benefits can come in the form of product quality, product assortment, and product form. In hospitality and tourism, it is critical to meet customer quality expectations and provide consistent service. Direct channels provide the firm with the best opportunity to control quality, while indirect channels require a firm to place its trust in an intermediary. For example, tour operators rely on travel agents to sell their products to the final consumer. The channel system must also provide the range of products necessary to achieve a desired level of customer appeal. Travel bureaus need the full support of all businesses in the region to promote their tourism products to travelers.

- **Delivering service benefits.** Service benefits can come in the form of after-sale service, availability and delivery, and transaction services. After-sale service can be crucial in achieving customer satisfaction in the event of a service failure. For example, there are many stories of students going through tour operators or travel agents to purchase spring break package vacations, only to arrive in foreign cities and not have a room. Then when they try to contact the company that sold them the trip, it is often impossible to get through to someone. This reflects on all of the brands involved in the package, as well as the destination. Intermediaries are also used in indirect channels to make products more readily available. Internet travel companies such as Priceline and Expedia exist for this purpose. Customers get the best prices in a short period of time without having to search the alternatives. These intermediaries also facilitate the transaction and delivery of the hospitality or travel product. For example, tour wholesalers or operators can package the hospitality products and obtain one payment from the customer.

- **Building brand image.** One of the major issues facing hotels is the image that using Internet travel firms may convey. These companies tend to be viewed as discounters offering great values (i.e., low prices). It is relatively easy for hotels in the economy and budget categories to choose this channel, but higher-priced hotels have a much more difficult decision. Upscale and luxury hotels may diminish their brands by using Internet travel companies. Another problem is that some Internet travel companies sell hotel rooms at higher prices than the customer could get by going directly through the hotel. When customers become aware of this, it will reflect poorly on the hotel. Another common intermediary for hotels is the hotel sales representative who sells to groups and represents the hotel. The hotel loses some control over the message and the way the property is conveyed. Finally, building brand image is also an issue when franchising—the franchisor loses some control over brand image and must rely on the franchisees to adhere to the business system.

- **Building company benefits.** This form of benefit is related to brand image. The use of intermediaries such as hotel representatives and travel agents can actually benefit the firm because of the personal attention that customers get from qualified professionals. These types of intermediaries have good product knowledge and experience. They are experts in dealing with their respective target markets and provide a valuable asset in their use of relationship marketing with customers. Franchising is also a way to benefit from the relationships local owners already have with customers in the area, rather than opening a new restaurant without having any previous ties in the community.

IMPROVING COST EFFICIENCY. One of the other ways to increase customer value is to lower the cost of purchase, both actual and perceived. For instance, the cost of planning and purchasing a vacation may be higher when the customer has to contact hotels, car rental agencies, airlines, and tourist attractions to purchase each component separately. Meanwhile, tour operators package these same vacation components and offer them directly, or through

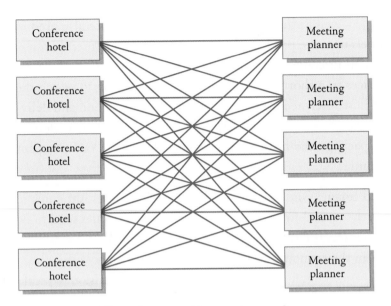

FIGURE 9.3A • *Channel system without an intermediary.*

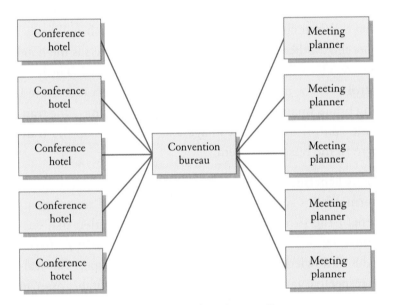

FIGURE 9.3B • *Channel system with an intermediary.*

travel agents for one price that is lower, or at least perceived to be lower, than if purchased separately. Convention and visitors bureaus serve as clearinghouses for travelers and reduce the number of transactions. Figures 9.3a and 9.3b illustrate the importance of this function in regard to meetings and conventions.

Assume there are five different meeting planners looking for a conference hotel in which to hold a meeting. If there are five conference hotels in a city, each of the meeting planners would have to contact all five hotels and send requests for proposal (RFP). With five hotels and five meeting planners, this would result in a total of 25 contacts or communications (see Figure 9.3a).

Consider this same situation with a convention bureau to act as an intermediary, or clearinghouse for the two groups. Each of the meeting planners would send an RFP to the CVB, which would then forward the RFP to the conference hotels. This would result in a total of ten contacts or communications between the meeting planners and the conference hotels (see Figure 9.3b). This example is simplistic; however, it does demonstrate the value of using an indirect channel system with an intermediary. The number of contacts was reduced from 25 to 10 with just five customers (i.e., meeting planners) and five service providers (i.e., hotels). As the number of customers and service providers increases, the number of contacts or transactions will increase exponentially. Therefore, it is necessary to weigh the benefits and costs of adding channel members and make a decision that is best for a particular service provider.

FRANCHISING

Franchising is a contractual arrangement whereby one firm (the **franchisor**) licenses a number of other firms (each firm is a **franchisee**) to use the franchisor's name and business practices. In other words, franchising is a network of interdependent business relationships that allows a number of operators to share a brand identification and a successful method of doing business (i.e., a proven marketing and distribution system). As a franchisee, you own the assets of your company, but you are licensed to operate someone else's business system. In 2003, there were over 2,500 franchise systems in the United States with more than 534,000 franchise units. This represents 3.2 percent of all businesses, controlling over 35 percent of all retail and service revenue in the U.S. economy.[4] Franchising opportunities can be found for a variety of industries, including hospitality and travel, through Internet sites like Franchising.com, FranchisingOpportunities.com, and Entrepreneur.com.

As a method of distribution, franchising provides many opportunities for growth and profitability. However, when considering a franchising relationship, both parties should carefully evaluate the alternative forms of ownership and operation. The individual goals and objectives of each party have to be weighed against the trade-offs of a franchisor-franchisee relationship. In essence, franchising is a strategic alliance between groups of people who have contractual responsibilities and a common goal. By choosing to invest in a franchise operation, an owner is expressing the belief that he or she will be

Franchising

A contractual arrangement whereby one firm licenses a number of other firms to use the franchisor's name and business practices.

Franchisor

The firm that licenses other firms to use its name and business practices.

Franchisee

A firm that obtains a license from another firm to use its name and business practices.

	ADVANTAGES	DISADVANTAGES
FRANCHISEE	Established product/service Technical/managerial assistance Quality standards Less operating capital Opportunities for growth Cooperative advertising	Additional fees/expenses Loss of control Difficult to terminate Pooled performance
FRANCHISOR	Rapid expansion Diversified risk Cost economics Cooperative advertising Employee issues	Loss of control Reduced profits Legal issues Recruitment

TABLE 9.2 • *Franchising advantages and disadvantages.*

more successful using someone else's business system rather than investing his or her money in an independent operation and developing his or her own business system. Table 9.2 summarizes the advantages and disadvantages associated with franchising.

Franchisee

ADVANTAGES. There are many advantages to joining an existing operation rather than starting from the beginning. First, there is an established product or service with a brand name and an identity in the marketplace. It is normally very costly and time consuming to build a brand image. Trying to start a new pizza business would be much more cumbersome than opening a Domino's Pizza. Second, franchisees receive technical and managerial assistance from the franchisor. This assistance could be in the form of recruitment and training of employees, or in the design of the facility. Franchisors transfer the knowledge they have accumulated as they progressed through the learning curve, thereby accelerating the process for franchisees. Third, the franchisee benefits from the quality standards that are already in place for the franchise. There is a system of controls that guide the operations and provide for a certain level of quality and consistency. Fourth, there is often less of a capital requirement for opening a franchise unit relative to the start-up costs for an independent operation. Franchises have a track record that can be used to estimate demand, design the facility, schedule employees, and order inventory. Fifth, there are opportunities to expand the business within the operating region. Franchisees are usually given some form of territorial rights to add units based on demand. Finally, the sixth advantage is that the franchisee benefits from the pooled resources of the many participants in advertising and promoting the product. The use of cooperative advertising results in a more efficient and effective means of communicating with customers. An independent restaurant would not be able to afford to place advertisements in major magazines or during prime-time television shows.

DISADVANTAGES. There are also some disadvantages to becoming a franchisee. First, there are franchise fees and royalties that must be borne by the franchisee in return for the benefits just described. These expenses are normally a percentage of sales and result in a decrease in the profit margin. Second, the franchisee must adhere to the standards and procedures as set forth in the agreement. This restricts the franchisee's ability to control the entire operation in that certain requirements regarding products, price ranges, and expansion are imposed by the franchisor. Third, it may be difficult to terminate the agreement if the franchisee would like to change brands or sell the business. Finally, the brand image is the result of the pooled performance of all corporate-owned and franchised units. The franchise's reputation and image can be negatively affected by the performance of individual units.

Franchisor

ADVANTAGES. Many companies are choosing to expand their operations using the franchise approach because of its advantages. Companies can experience more rapid expansion, since franchisees provide additional investment capital and access to untapped markets. By limiting the investment and adding "partners," the franchisor is able to diversify the risk of doing business. A byproduct of this rapid expansion is the realization of cost economies from operating at a higher level of volume. The organization will get better prices on supplies and be able to allocate fixed costs over a larger number of units, bringing down the cost per unit. A related issue is the use of cooperative advertising. As mentioned before, this is an advantage for both the franchisor and the franchisees. Finally, certain human resources and management tasks are simplified by franchising. The franchisees play an important role in the selection and retention of employees. Plus, owners are very careful to monitor the performance of the franchise because they benefit directly from the profitability of the unit.

DISADVANTAGES.   There are also a few disadvantages associated with being a franchisor. First, there is a reduction in control of the operation. Having many owners or managers will have an effect on the overall performance of the franchise. Even though operating standards and procedures are written into the agreement, they are not always followed. Second, there is a trade-off between risk and return. The sharing of risk and ownership results in the sharing of profits as well. Third, the size and visibility of franchises exposes them to more potential litigation. They are easy targets for legal actions such as antitrust suits and class-action suits. Also, injury claims are prevalent in many service industries.

For example, McDonald's was once sued by an elderly woman who spilled coffee in her lap while driving her car, and has been sued by obese people who accused the fast-food restaurant of causing their weight problems. Finally, it is difficult to find qualified prospects to be franchisees. Although many investors have the necessary capital, they may lack the necessary knowledge and experience to run a successful franchise unit in the product or service category.

Summary of Chapter Objectives

This chapter discussed the role of marketing channels in planning the marketing strategy for hospitality and tourism services. Decisions must be made regarding channel width (how many outlets) and channel length (number and type of intermediaries). If the decision is made to use an indirect channel (at least one intermediary), then the firm must examine channel management issues such as channel leadership and channel power. Finally, the extent of the relationships with other channel members will need to be considered.

Some type of vertical marketing system can be used to provide more certainty in the relationships. Franchising is probably the most common form of vertical marketing system.

Intermediaries exist in channels because they perform certain channel functions more effectively than the other channel members. One advantage of using intermediaries is the fact that they often have access to markets that are desired by a manufacturer or producer. Travel agents and tour operators specialize in packaging trips and selling them to groups and individuals for pleasure travel, and meeting planners and travel bureaus work more with business groups for conferences and conventions.

Key Terms and Concepts

Administered vertical marketing system

Central reservation systems (CRS)

Channel length

Channel power

Channel width

Coercive power

Contractual vertical marketing system

Convention and visitors bureau (CVB)

Corporate vertical marketing system

Destination management company (DMC)

Destination marketing organization (DMO)

Direct channel

Electronic commerce

Exclusive distribution

Expert power

Franchisee

Franchising

Franchisor

Global distribution system (GDS)

Indirect channel

Intensive distribution

Intermediaries

Legitimate power

Referent power

Reward power

Selective distribution

Vertical marketing system

Questions for Review and Discussion

1. What factors are considered in determining a firm's channel width and channel length?

2. List and give examples of the intermediaries that exist in the hospitality and tourism industry.

3. List and describe the five forms of channel power.

4. Explain the three types of vertical marketing systems.

5. What are the ways a firm can enhance customer value through channel systems?

6. What is franchising? Why would firms or individuals choose to enter this type of arrangement?

7. If you have ten tour operators and 100 customers, what is the difference in the number of transactions with, and without, a travel agent acting as an intermediary?

8. Internet exercise: Use the Internet resources for identifying franchise opportunities and put together a proposal for a group of investors who want to start a restaurant operation in the Midwest. The investors are looking to

chapter review

become franchisees with an existing casual dining restaurant chain that will have a good potential for success. The investors are starting a management company and pooling their resources, so there shouldn't be any capital or net worth restrictions. Choose a franchise operation and justify your decision based on the Midwest market and the restaurant concept's potential appeal.

Notes

[1] Peter D. Nyheim, Francis M. McFadden, and Daniel J. Connolly, *Technology Strategies for the Hospitality Industry* (Upper Saddle River, NJ: Prentice-Hall, 2005), pp. 153-186.

[2] Jack J. Kasulis and Robert E. Spekman, "A Framework for the Use of Power," *European Journal of Marketing* 14 (1980): 183.

[3] Roger J. Best, *Market-Based Management: Strategies for Growing Customer Value and Profitability*, 2nd ed. (Upper Saddle River, NJ: Prentice-Hall, 2000), pp. 204-207.

[4] Robert Gappa, "What Is Franchising?" (2003), available at www.franchising.com.

chapter review

Case Study

The Wing Shack

A couple of college students decided to start a business together after graduating. The two friends traveled the region in search of the ultimate buffalo chicken wings. After researching these other operations, the two returned to their town and started to put the wheels in motion to find a location and develop a business system. The idea was to open a small restaurant and focus on delivery within the local area, including the college campus. As luck would have it, a restaurant recently had gone out of business in a high-traffic area. The two young men found themselves meeting with realtors, bankers, accountants, lawyers, and town officials in an attempt to achieve their dream of opening a restaurant. After many negotiations, the two began planning for the opening of their restaurant. They decided to call it the Wing Shack and cater to the college crowd.

The restaurant had a small bar area, a pool table, a few televisions, a juke box, and 12 tables for dining. The menu consisted of chicken wings (including boneless), chicken sandwiches, a few appetizers, and a few sides (e.g., french fries). The chicken wings were meatier than those of most restaurants, and there were 20 flavors to choose from. For beverages, the owners decided to put 20 beers on tap, showcasing the regional microbrews. Business was slow at first, but word of mouth quickly spread and the restaurant started to get more and more customers. One of the early strategies employed by the owners was to have all-you-can-eat wings on the slower nights of the week (Sunday to Wednesday). Eventually, the restaurant had people waiting in line to get a table, and the sit-down business was as good as the delivery business.

After three years of successfully running the business and seeing increased profits, the owners considered expanding. The business system was solid and the restaurant benefited from a good marketing strategy, including being a sponsor of the college's athletic programs. Initially, the owners decided to open another restaurant in a city about one hour away. This required the owners to commute on a regular basis and put a strain on their partnership and relationships. They felt they were spread too thin, and in hindsight they weren't sure if this was the best idea. This led the young entrepreneurs to investigate the possibility of franchising. The profit after taxes for the original restaurant was approximately 28 percent of revenue. Franchise fees for restaurants in this category usually run around 3 to 4 percent.

Case Study Questions and Issues

1. What issues must the owners consider before deciding whether to open more restaurants on their own or to franchise?

2. Assuming the original restaurant is in the Northeast, what cities or towns would you suggest for the next five restaurants?

3. How many franchised units would they have to contract to make the same profit as they do in the original unit (assuming the revenue will be similar for all units)?

case study

5. **What role does marketing play within your company?**

Marketing's primary role is to build and manage the most profitable portfolio of customers to drive preference, premiums and profits for our brands.

6. **If you could offer one piece of advice to an individual preparing for a career in the hospitality and tourism industry, what would you suggest?**

The individual should take all opportunities to get hands-on experience in different departments of a hotel (e.g., housekeeping, front desk, sales) to better understand all the customer touch points and all the business processes that drive revenue and profit for the hotel. With this foundation, you are better prepared to take on a broader, more senior role in developing and executing strategies that achieve a balanced scorecard (excellent guest satisfaction, superior associate satisfaction, and outstanding financial results).

industry profile

INTRODUCTION

Electronic commerce, or *e-commerce,* refers to the practice of carrying out business transactions over computer networks in an effort to generate sales and improve organizational performance. Previous forms of electronic business included electronic data interchange (EDI) by businesses and the use of automated teller machines (ATMs) by consumers. These applications were limited to one-to-one or one-to-many, whereas the new form of electronic business application (the Internet) allows many-to-many communications. The number of companies engaging in electronic commerce on the Internet's World Wide Web (the Web) has been growing at a rapid rate since its global consumer introduction in the early 1990s. Organizations can communicate with all of their stakeholders through this form of electronic commerce. Investors can obtain information about the company, consumers can obtain information about products or complain about customer service, and suppliers can communicate with their business partners. In addition, firms can gather information about their customers with online surveys and sales promotions.

One of the major reasons for the popularity of electronic commerce is the ability of manufacturers, retailers and service providers to sell directly to consumers at retail or near-retail profit margins without sharing the revenue with other channel members. Firms are able to increase profitability, gain market share, improve customer service, and deliver products more quickly as a result of this direct channel to the consumer. Before discussing the details of electronic commerce, it is necessary to provide some background on the Internet and the World Wide Web.

> **Electronic commerce (e-commerce)**
>
> A term used to describe the buying and selling process obtained through electronic means such as the Internet.

What Is the Internet?

The precursor of the Internet was first introduced by the Rand Corporation in 1964 as a method for secure contact between the Pentagon and units of the U.S. armed forces.[1] It was a decentralized computer communications network with no central computer or governing authority. In the event that one or more computers on the network were destroyed, it would still be possible to send information between the remaining computers. In other words, the Internet is simply a network of networks. Its use was expanded to university faculty and other researchers in the early 1970s, and it was improved with the National Science Foundation's creation of a high-speed long-distance telecommunications network in the mid-1980s. The government restricted the use of the Internet to nonprofit, educational, and government organizations until 1991, at which time commercial sites were allowed to participate.

Since the early 1990s, the Internet has become an avenue for sharing information, obtaining software, selling products and services, retrieving data, exchanging messages via e-mail, allowing interactive discussion groups, and displaying video and audio files. The Web was first developed in 1989 at the European Organization for Nuclear Research (CERN) in Geneva, Switzerland, as a means of communication that could be used while simultaneously working on another project. This was made possible by the use of **hypertext**, which is a method of linking related information without a hierarchy or menu system. An example of this concept is the use of help screens in software applications. The software that is used to access the documents stored on servers located throughout the world is called a **browser**. Several browsers are available for both the Windows and Apple operating systems, including Internet Explorer, Firefox, and Safari. The actual link to the Internet is made through a commercial service or Internet service provider (ISP) that sells services that connect individuals and organizations to the Internet.

Hypertext

A method of linking related information without a hierarchy or menu system.

Browser

An application program that allows users to display HTML files obtained from the World Wide Web. Popular browsers include Internet Explorer, Firefox, Safari, and Netscape.

THE CYBERSPACE COMMUNITY. *Cyberspace* is a term coined by William Gibson in his novel *Neuromancer* to describe the electronic communities that formed on the Internet. These communities are similar to normal communities in that members do not like being bothered by salespeople, and they have formed their own rules of "netiquette" concerning such actions.

Therefore, most marketing of products and services has been restricted to the World Wide Web. The Web offers the greatest flexibility regarding the use of graphics and interactive communication, and it is the easiest area of the Internet to navigate. Also, as mentioned before, the ability to use many-to-many communication allows firms to mass-market their products and services within these electronic communities. In addition to mass marketing, the use of personalized content management allows companies to tailor Web content based on a user's Web behavior and preferences. Amazon.com was among the first to offer personalized Web content based on past purchase behavior and online browsing behavior.

SECURITY ISSUES. One of the appealing features of the Internet is the fact that there is open access without a governing body. This lack of governance or authority has left many to question the security and safety of the Internet. Some potential applications have been slow to develop because of the hysteria surrounding Internet security. Online banking, investing, and travel reservations were initially slow to gain volume due to consumers' concerns about security. Initially, firms promoted products and services online but provided a toll-free number consumers could call to place orders. More recently, more consumers are placing their orders online, but companies still provide toll-free numbers for those who are hesitant to provide confidential information, such as credit card numbers, online. Airlines were among the first providers to provide a financial incentive to purchase online. Later, they shifted to an additional financial cost if toll-free numbers of support personnel were accessed to make a purchase.

Concerns about Internet security have been blown out of proportion. Although online business transactions are not perfectly secure, they are no riskier than ordering via telephone or fax. Computer hackers are similar to everyday criminals who try to find ways to circumvent security systems and procedures, although there are some additional security issues associated with electronic commerce. First, the Internet is an open network without any physical barriers to prevent theft (e.g., hidden cameras, safes, security guards). Second, the same technologies that are being used for commerce can be used to breach security (e.g., computer software used to search for passwords).

Several methods can be used to restrict access and improve security in electronic commerce. First, a form of **authentication** can be required through the use of some combination of account numbers, passwords, and IP (Internet protocol) addresses. Second, a **firewall** can be used to monitor traffic between an organization's network and the Internet. This barrier can restrict access to certain IP addresses or applications. A third method is to use coding or **encryption** techniques to transform data to protect their meaning. These security methods can be used individually or together depending on the level of security desired. For instance, firms that are transmitting payment information will be more inclined to use all three levels of defense. This next section covers four topics: the traits of a networked economy, the definition and scope of electronic commerce, the use of electronic marketing, and the beginning of electronic commerce.

Traits of a Networked Economy

Some people view electronic commerce as a boom-and-bust cycle, but that is really not true. In the mid-1990s, there was a dramatic increase in activity in the broad field of e-commerce. Companies such as eBay, Amazon, and Expedia provide tangible evidence of the impact that e-commerce has had on the business world. These companies, and hundreds like them, created an economic boom unlike anything seen before. It began to unravel in 2000, with the dot-com bust." The impacts are still being felt. Most traditional companies, including those in the hospitality and tourism industry, were forced to

Authentication

Verifying the appropriate access by a user through the use of some combination of account numbers, passwords, and IP (Internet protocol) addresses.

Firewall

A filter is used to monitor traffic between an organization's network and the Internet. This barrier can restrict access to certain IP addresses, applications or content.

Encryption

Transmitted data are scrambled to prevent unauthorized access by users or hackers.

change their business practices and business models. Online reservations for hotels, airlines, and restaurants, online check-in for airlines and hotels, and other forms of electronic exchanges are now quite common. In the airline industry, these transactions are ubiquitous.

Those who follow the evolution of electronic commerce agree that a networked economy, based on firms that have an Internet presence and conduct business online (at least in part), has several important traits:[2]

- **It creates value largely or exclusively through the gathering, synthesizing, and distribution of information.** Firms that engage in e-commerce activities can collect significant data about their customers. They can more easily determine consumers' likes, dislikes, and responses to various marketing stimuli. The wealth of data, which is readily analyzed, allows marketing managers to make better-informed decisions.

- **It formulates strategy in ways that result in a convergence of management of the business and management of various technologies.** The management of technology is viewed not as a separate function, but as a core business competency. The development of e-commerce applications is viewed not as a parallel activity, but as part of the core set of activities within the firm.

- **It allows firms to compete in real time, not in cycle time or in asynchronous time.** Historically, businesses made changes on an intermittent basis, as a result of data about, for instance, financial performance or guest response. With the increasing use of technology, this lag time can be nearly eliminated. For example, an airline can post price changes to an e-commerce Web site and then monitor site transactions to determine within a very short time whether the price change has resulted in the desired change in buyer behavior.

- **It operates in business environments in which there are low barriers to entry and extremely low variable costs.** This trait is applicable to pure electronic commerce companies, but less so to companies in the hospitality and tourism industry. Hospitality and tourism firms have higher capital costs for buildings, fixtures, and equipment than do firms that are pure electronic commerce companies.

- **It organizes resources around the demand side of the business (i.e., the level of demand from potential buyers of the products and services).** Demand from potential customers is constantly monitored to determine changes in demand. These firms then attempt to influence demand by changing marketing variables such as price and availability.

- **It examines relationships with customers in "screen-to-face" interfaces in which technology is used to manage and customize customers' experiences.** In order to increase relationship-building interactions and reduce labor costs at the same time, technology is used to "push" customized information to the consumer. This can take many forms, including e-mail and web site information that is customized to match the interests and past behavior of individual consumers.

- **It uses technology-mediated methods to measure and track customer behavior and interaction patterns.** These data are then used to customize future interaction with individual customers and customer groups with similar buyer behavior.

Definition and Scope of Electronic Commerce

The use of digital technology has dramatically shifted the business paradigm, both domestically and internationally. Digital technology has created entire new industries, shifted others, and forced managers and leaders of firms to look at their customers, markets, and competitors in entirely new ways. The size and scope of e-commerce has changed dramatically in the past ten years. Numerous industry publications and research organizations report on these trends. Among the most notable are www.emarketer.com, www.cnet.com, and www.forester.com. Table 10.1 provides several facts and figures that characterize the development of the Internet within the hospitality and tourism industry.

Electronic commerce can be characterized by several attributes.[3] First and foremost, e-commerce is about exchanges:

- **Exchange of digitized information.** The foundation of e-commerce includes exchange of digitized information. These exchanges can involve information or communications, or they can be related to the purchase of goods or services in a digital format. The exchanges occur between organizations or individuals.

- **Technology-enabled transactions.** E-commerce is about technology-enabled transactions. Use of Web browsers is the most common form of e-commerce, but there are others. When banks use ATM machines or companies use phone or personal digital assistant (PDA) interfaces to create exchanges, these are part of e-commerce as well. Years ago, companies managed these exchanges through human interaction, but technology is used more frequently today. The result is normally better response to customer needs and a reduction in the cost of the exchange. Perhaps the best

INTERNET AND ELECTRONIC COMMERCE TREND SUMMARY	SOURCE
Click-through rates for U.S. e-mail marketing campaigns is very high for restaurants (57.5%) and high for travel and hospitality (23.4%), both ranking in the top five among all industries.	Harte-Hanks Postfuture, August 2006, emarketer.com
Hospitality and travel ranks fourth among all industries for profitable e-commerce operations, with 75% of responding firms reporting profitability.	Information Week, September 2002, emarketer.com
Broadband access in worldwide hotel properties will increase from 14,300 in 2004 to 54,000 in 2009.	In-Stat, October 2005, emarketer.com
TravelCLICK reports reservations made through the Internet to central reservation offices (CROs) of 30 major hotel brands in 2003 rose by 34% over 2002.	TravelCLICK www.emarketer.com April 2, 2004
According to Nielsen/NetRatings, the top travel Web sites are MapQuest, Expedia, Travelocity, Orbitz, and AOL Travel. They attract between 1,155 and 4,790 unique at-home users per week.	Nielsen/NetRatings www.emarketer.com September 2003
The average annual amount spent online by U.S. Internet buyers ages 14+ increased from $563.99 in 2000 to $677.76 in 2003. This spending level is projected to increase to $928 by 2005.	www.emarketer.com September 2003
According to the U.S. Department of Commerce, U.S. online retail sales are projected to increase from $28.15 billion in 2000 to $88.1 billion in 2005.	U.S. Department of Commerce www.emarketer.com September 2003
Online advertising spending is projected to increase from $6.0 billion in 2002 to $9.9 billion in 2007. The previous high was $8.1 billion in 2000, the last year of the dot-com boom.	www.emarketer.com December 2003
U.S. online advertising by travel and hotel companies increased by 7% in 2000, 10% in 2001, and 14% in 2002.	Interactive Advertising Bureau (IAB)/ PricewaterhouseCoopers www.emarketer.com June 2003
A recent study by Ipsos-Reid determined that 35% of Canadians say their primary source of information for upcoming travel is the Internet, whereas only 14% say the same for travel agents. Only 6% use brochures for information.	www.emarketer.com August 2004

TABLE 10.1 • *Electronic Commerce Trends*

INTERNET AND ELECTRONIC COMMERCE TREND SUMMARY	SOURCE
According to Harris Interactive, the percentage of adults with broadband access in December 2003 was 37%, up from 27% a year earlier.	HarrisInteractive www.emarketer.com January 2004
Broadband access for US households is predicted to increase: 2005 – 13% 2006 – 23% 2007 – 35% 2008 – 51% 2009 – 69%	Park Associates, June 2005, emarketer.com
Internet access by the U.S. population increased from 9% in November 1995 to 69% in October/December 2003. 1. Airline tickets, hotel reservations, or travel packages: 71% of users 2. Software for a personal computer: 46% of users 3. Tickets for an entertainment event: 44% of users 4. A personal computer or hardware for a personal computer: 40% of users 5. A book: 39% of users	Wall Street Journal Online January 14, 2004 HarrisInteractive www.emarketer.com January 2004 America Online/ RoperASW www.emarketer.com April 2003
The top reasons why U.S. business travelers prefer video, audio, and Web conferencing to traveling to meetings: 1. Saves time and is more efficient: 69% 2. Reduces corporate travel budgets: 37% 3. Company policy: 36% 4. Promotes better work-life balance: 29% 5. Increases productivity: 28% 6. Concern about travel safety: 12%	MCI/Impulse Research Corporation www.emarketer.com October 2003
Use of audio, video, and Web conferencing among U.S. senior management professionals in the past year: 1. Audio conferencing: 89% 2. Web conferencing: 64% 3. Video conferencing: 57%	MCI/Impulse Research Corporation www.emarketer.com October 2003
Web conferencing revenues worldwide (in billions): 2001: $0.27 2008: $2.0 (projected)	Frost & Sullivan www.emarketer.com April 2002

TABLE 10.1 • (*continued*)

example of an effective technology-enabled exchange is the use of online reservations for airlines and hotels. Consumers are able to access vastly more information than would be possible through a voice-only interaction with the airline or hotel company. The company is able to provide the information and make a sale less expensively using an e-commerce exchange.

- **Technology-mediated transactions.** With each passing year, e-commerce is moving beyond technology-enabled transactions to technology-mediated transactions. For example, when a customer makes a transaction at a large discount retail chain and the individual items are scanned, they are subtracted from the store inventory. When a predetermined inventory level is reached, this will automatically trigger a reorder from the manufacturer. Orders from hundreds of stores are automatically combined and placed as a single daily order with the manufacturer. Similar mediation is occurring within the hospitality and tourism industry. For example, when a guest checks out of a room via the interactive video services in the room, the now vacant room is added to the inventory of those that need to be serviced by housekeeping. Once the room is cleaned, it is automatically added back into the available room inventory. Similarly, when items are sold in a fast-food restaurant, this inventory can be tracked and reorder points established so that managers can spend more time interacting with customers and employees instead of tracking and ordering inventory.

- **Intra- and interorganizational activities.** Within hospitality and tourism organizations, there are many electronically based activities both within the organizations and between organizations and individuals. All of these activities are considered part of electronic commerce. Any electronic activity that directly or indirectly supports exchanges is part of the world of e-commerce.

Why Use Electronic Marketing?

Pure e-commerce companies
Refers to firms that operate solely on the Internet. They do not operate any physical facilities.

The use of electronic commerce is a multifaceted industry. There are **pure e-commerce companies**, such as Expedia, Hotels.com or Kayak.com as well as established firms like Marriott International or Hilton Hotels and Resorts that use e-commerce as an addition to their other forms of marketing. All are correct approaches and are designed to be an important part of a firm's overall marketing strategy. Any hospitality or tourism firm should carefully consider how the use of the World Wide Web and electronic commerce fits with the balance of the marketing strategy before investing significant time, effort, and resources in an e-commerce strategy. A decision about entering the e-commerce space is a critical one and should not be taken lightly. Managers should fully consider broad perspectives before making decisions and moving forward. The following are some of the specific questions that should be addressed before action is taken:[4]

- What is the firm's purpose for engaging in online communications?

- What are the firm's goals and specific objectives? What outcome is the firm seeking to achieve?

- Why should the firm want to go online? Is it to introduce new products and services? Is cost reduction one of the goals? Are enhanced relations with current customers an objective?

- What online expectations does the firm have? Are there different objectives for different divisions of the firm, such as marketing, human resources, or finance?

- How will electronic commerce efforts be integrated with other forms of communication? How will consistency of branding and identity be maintained?

- Who will be in charge of Web site creation, maintenance, and evaluation?

It's increasingly common for businesses of all sorts to have Web sites. Reprinted with permission of John Wiley & Sons, Inc.

in the hospitality and tourism industry. There are two critical components for all e-commerce business models: the revenue model and the value proposition.

REVENUE MODEL. A **revenue model** simply shows how the firm will generate revenue or income. Without some income stream that exceeds the level of expenses, the business model is not going to be successful and the company will not be able to sustain itself. There are five primary revenue models.[6]

Revenue model

This shows how the firm will generate revenue or income. Without some income stream that exceeds the level of expenses, the business model is not going to be successful and the company will not be able to sustain itself.

1. **Sales.** Firms generate revenue from the sales of products or services on their Web sites. An example is Marriott.com or Hilton.com.

2. **Transaction fees.** Firms generate revenue based on commissions or fees on each transaction. Expedia.com is an example of a hospitality and tourism firm that uses this model. Expedia generates revenue each time a reservation is made, and it also collects commissions on some transactions on its Web site.

3. **Subscription fees.** Customers pay a fixed fee, either monthly or yearly, to subscribe to the service. Perhaps the most well known is America Online. In the hospitality industry, hotels subscribe to convention and visitors bureau sites to obtain requests for proposals (RFPs) electronically.

4. **Advertising fees.** Firms charge for placing banner advertisements and other forms of advertising on their Web sites. Kayak.com is an example of such a Web site.

5. **Affiliate fees and other sources of revenue.** Firms receive commissions and other forms of compensation for referring customers to other Web sites. They may receive a small fee for those who click through to the second Web site and a larger commission based on the purchases made on the second site. Amazon.com was among the first companies to offer this type of financial arrangement. One of its goals was to increase the number of visitors to its Web site.

Value proposition

How will the firm create value for the buyer? The value proposition defines how the firm will fulfill the needs of the consumer.

VALUE PROPOSITION. Any business plan for a firm engaged in electronic commerce should include a **value proposition** for the business model. How will the firm create value for the buyer? The value proposition defines how the firm will fulfill the needs of the consumer. Amit and Zott identified four primary ways that firms create successful value propositions:[7]

1. **Search and transaction cost efficiency.** This value proposition allows for faster and more informed decision making by providing a wider selection of products and services, as well as economies of scale. Marriott International and

Hilton have been leaders in developing Web sites that set the standard for the hospitality and tourism industry in this regard.

2. **Complementarities.** This involves bundling products and services together to provide more value than if purchased separately. Expedia.com and Travelocity.com were among the early leaders in bundling the services of a travel agent together in an e-commerce business model. Many Web sites now provide bundled services such as airfare, lodging, rental car, and tourist attraction admission fees for a bundled price that is significantly less than purchasing the same services separately.

3. **Lock-in.** The high cost of switching will keep customers from changing suppliers. Many hospitality and tourism firms, including the airlines and major hotel chains, use frequent flyer and guest programs to lock in customers.

4. **Novelty.** This approach creates value by using innovative ways to structure transactions, connect business partners, and open new markets.

Electronic Commerce Business Models

Numerous researchers have developed and identified many different forms of business models. Turban, King, Lee, and Viehland summarized these in several models, which encompass the vast majority of models used by electronic commerce firms:[8]

- **Online direct marketing.**

- **Electronic tendering systems.**

- **Name your own price.** Consumers are able to set a price at which they will buy the product or service. When that price becomes available, the transaction is made.

- **Find the best price.** Online services such as Hotels.com™ and Expedia.com allow consumers to compare prices and find the lowest-cost providers.

- **Viral marketing.** This emulates word-of-mouth advertising by spreading the word electronically. With the use of message board, instant messaging, and e-mail, news of an excellent "deal" spreads rapidly.

- **Online auctions.** These provide a venue for buyers and sellers to come together to exchange products and services. The best-known online auction is ebay.com™.

Internet Strategies

Not all firms use the Internet for the same purpose. Some firms take orders through their Web sites, while others simply use the sites to provide information to consumers and other stakeholders. The following is a list of some of the more popular uses of Web sites:

- Providing customer service

- Selling products or services

- Educating and informing potential customers

- Offering discounts

- Promoting products and improving brand image

- Obtaining customer information and building a database

It is incumbent upon the firm to determine how its Web site will fit into the overall marketing plan. Strategies can then be formulated to attain the firm's goals and objectives.

Customer service has played an important role in the quest for product or service quality. Ritz-Carlton introduced the concept of total quality management to the hotel industry, and a main component of the quality formula was customer service. As the number of Internet users continues to grow, Web sites become more attractive as outlets for customer service. This approach has proven to be more efficient than the telephone call centers. Firms can list answers to commonly asked questions and guide inquiries or complaints through the proper channels. Customers can go directly to the needed information rather than wait for service via a call center. Customers' concerns can be expressed via e-mail or live-chat.

Another reason for having a Web site would be to sell products and services. Most hotel and resort sites have a link to reservations so that consumers can easily purchase the product after browsing the site. Airlines and rental car agencies provide similar services as well. The easier it is for consumers to find your product and complete a transaction, the more successful you will be in selling your product. Many Internet users value the convenience associated with electronic commerce. For example, consumers have 24-hour, 7-day-a-week (24/7) access to the Web site. They are not bound by the normal hours of operation that a firm chooses, and can shop whenever they wish. Web sites can be used to educate and inform consumers about a firm's products or services. Information search is the step after problem recognition in the consumer decision-making process. In the past, this information was obtained through

Most companies use their Web sites for many purposes, including providing product information, customer service, and promoting brand recognition. Courtesy of Hobart Corporation.

word of mouth, past experience, an on-site visit, speaking with salespeople over the telephone, or reviewing printed brochures. Now it is possible to provide basic information regarding a hotel or restaurant over the Internet. Consumers can get prices, availability, hours of operation, directions, and menus. Hotels can provide materials for meeting planners at a fraction of the cost of producing and mailing brochures, planning guides, and videos. Travel agents also find Web sites to be valuable resources that can be accessed easily and are more convenient than maintaining large inventories of brochures and pamphlets that become outdated.

The Internet has become a useful outlet for reaching price-sensitive consumers. Firms offer reduced prices to attract bargain hunters who are familiar with normal price ranges for products and services. These consumers are aware that many firms offer discount prices through their Internet sites, and they take the time and effort to search for deals. For example, airlines use the Internet to sell unused capacity to consumers who are willing to make their arrangements on short notice. The participating airports and routes are announced midweek for travel originating Friday or Saturday and returning on Monday or Tuesday. International flights are even included in this service, as well as hotel rooms and rental cars from the airline's partners. The discounts are normally for periods of slow demand or packages of services and are often accompanied by certain restrictions involving time or quantity.

Some firms categorize their use of the Internet as a component of the promotional mix. In some ways, it is a form of advertising, but it can also be used for sales promotions. Therefore, the firm's Web site should be integrated with the other components of the promotion mix in an effort to position the firm in the marketplace and improve its brand image. It is imperative that a hospitality and tourism company develop a Web strategy that is consistent with and integrated with all other elements of the promotional strategy. Marriott International™ has developed its Web strategy to drive traffic to the Web site. Marriott customers can make reservations at the guaranteed lowest rate, check frequent-guest program points, redeem points, and fully manage their relationship with Marriott branded hotels. When customers visit the Web site, Marriott is able to draw upon vast quantities of personal purchase behavior to personalize the purchase experience for guests. Their approach integrates Web browsing behavior with prior purchase behavior to target the specific needs of the individual.

As a part of the strategy development, sales promotions such as contests and sweepstakes can be used to attract customers and create an awareness of and interest in the brand. These promotions should be creative and entertaining so that consumers become involved with the brand while trying to win free services and merchandise.

Finally, most of the aforementioned Internet uses have the added advantage of gaining access to customer information. Firms can build databases filled with customers' names, addresses (including e-mail addresses), telephone numbers, and purchase histories. These databases can be used for future mailings and promotions. One popular use of these databases is to survey customers and prospects about their behaviors, perceptions, and backgrounds. This information can be used to design products and services, promotions, and competitive strategies. In fact, surveys can be placed on the Web site, resulting in an efficient data collection process.

SITE DESIGN AND LAYOUT. A firm's Web site needs to be creative and to catch the attention of visitors to the site. However, it is important to avoid overly complex layouts with hard-to-find links that slow movement between areas of the site. There should be a balance regarding the use of graphics and the speed of movement. The following are some useful tips regarding page layout:

- Include the corporate logo at the top of every page as if it were a letterhead.

- Use graphic links for effect, but make sure there are also text links.

- Code pages so that the text is displayed before graphics are downloaded.

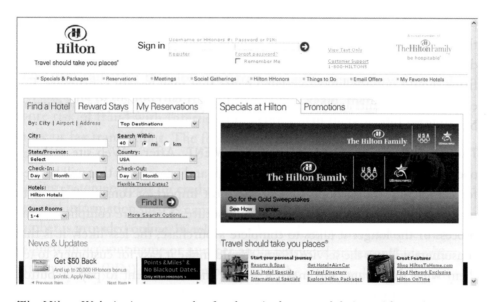

The Hilton Web site is an example of a clear site layout and design with consistent use of the corporate brand. Courtesy of Hilton Hospitality, Inc.

- Use a common style on every page and provide a link to the home page (and other pages if possible) through the use of frames or tables, which can keep important links constantly available throughout a Web site.

The rest of the content included on the site depends on the type of product or service that is being marketed. There are not many graphics that would need to accompany an airline's product information. However, hotels can give visitors a "tour" of the facility using photos or a video file. To conserve space, the hotel could use a thumbnail gallery with small pictures visitors can click on if they want to see a larger version. It is important to remember that consumers will access Web sites using a wide array of Internet connections, some of which are quite fast, while others will be quite slow. At present, the fastest Internet connection is 15 to 20 times faster than the slowest connection commonly used today. Currently, 35 percent of U.S. households have broadband Internet access, contrasted with 13 percent in 2005. This figure is projected to increase to 69 percent by 2009.[9] It is important to design the content of the Web site in such a way that an individual with a slower connection will not become discouraged and disconnect due to long download times.

Tourism bureaus and convention and visitors bureaus provide users with many useful links to related sites. Travelers can go to a state's Web site and find general information regarding that state. From there, they can narrow their search to a city or region, where they can find more detailed information. Finally, they can follow links to hospitality and tourism firms such as hotels, restaurants, and tourist attractions and obtain very detailed information on a specific firm. Similarly, most of the search engines have links to

the United States, the percentage of the population that uses e-mail will increase from 55.3 percent in 2005 to 64.9 percent in 2011.[11]

E-mail marketing is a very effective and inexpensive means of communicating with customers or prospective customers. In 2006, U.S. marketers are expected to spend $338 million on e-mail advertising and $1.425 billion on total e-mail marketing. These figures are expected to increase to $616 million and $1.65 billion, respectively, by 2011.[12] Much of the expense is associated with purchasing or developing the lists that are used to generate the e-mail blasts. However, e-mail marketing does present challenges. Marketers express several reservations about the use of e-mail, including:[13]

Reservations about E-mail	Percentage of respondents
Recipient e-mail boxes are swamped and all e-mail suffers	36%
Spam is eroding trust in e-mail	21%
E-mail doesn't get the budget or attention it deserves	11%
Willingness of people to opt-in to new e-mail lists	11%
Lack of accountability or measurement	6%
Difficulty with effective e-mail creative due to image blocking	5%
Deliverability	2%

Budgeting for e-mail varies widely among firms. A recent study indicated that fully one-third of firms don't have any specific budget for e-mail. Perhaps this is because e-mail is often used for a variety of purposes, including lead generation, on-going interactive marketing, or as part of the customer service strategy of the firm. The greatest challenge facing e-mail marketers is how to deal with spam filters. In some instances, as much as half of the e-mail is caught by the spam filters employed by firms, Internet Service Providers, or free e-mail companies.[14]

E-mail can be considered both a mass-market methodology and also a target market methodology. When many companies began using e-mail as a marketing tool, they sent messages to large lists, either purchased from outside sources, or developed internally from customer lists. Over time, this approach has become less effective. More recently, successful firms use e-mail messages in much more targeted fashion. Using market segmentation strategies discussed earlier, successful companies use e-mail messaging to deliver a specific message to a narrowly defined target market. The results are much greater impact, acceptance and success.

Companies continue to rely on e-mail marketing because it works. The return on investment (ROI) for e-mail marketing is impressive. According to the Direct Marketing Association, for each dollar spent on e-mail marketing in 2005, $57.25 was generated. This compares with $22.52 of revenue for each dollar spent on non-e-mail online marketing. More than 80 percent of firms surveyed indicated that the return on investment for e-mail marketing is increasing, indicating that firms are becoming more sophisticated in targeting customers and refining their strategies and tactics.[15]

E-mail marketing is used to acquire and retain customers. The average cost of acquiring customers using selected electronic and traditional methods is shown below.[16]

Internet Search	$8.50
Yellow pages	$20.00
Online display ads	$50.00
E-mail	$60.00
Direct mail	$70.00

Consumers have varying reactions to e-mail marketing. If consumers have an established relationship with a firm and the firm does e-mail marketing in a professional manner, fully 74 percent of the customers view the e-mail messages as valuable. Conversely, if there is no relationship with a firm, only 17 percent of consumers view the e-mail messages as valuable. There are a number of best practices which will increase the acceptance of e-mail and increase customer satisfaction with received e-mail.[17] Specific strategies include:

- Requiring a name to sign up for opt-in e-mails, in addition to an e-mail address.

- Offering a link to the company privacy policy on the registration page

- Offering one-click sign up from the home page.

- Offering content tailored to the specific interest, products or services desired by the e-mail recipient.

- Requesting that the company domain or e-mail address be added to the recipient's address book to reduce the impact of spam filters.

- Offering a text only delivery option.

- Requiring subscribers to confirm their opt-in registration by responding positively to the first e-mail.

- Featuring the company name in the e-mail subject line or the "from" line.

- Featuring the privacy policy or **opt-out** mechanism within each message.

- Placing key points of content in the first two paragraphs of the e-mail message.

- Having a mixture of graphics and text content.

One of the issues that e-mail marketers must address is how frequently to send messages. The frequency with which consumers wish to receive e-mail messages from companies is shown below.[18]

Frequency of e-mail	Percentage of Respondents
Daily	1%
Few times per week	2%
Weekly	17%
Every other week	21%
Monthly	36%
Quarterly	10%
Seasonally	13%

Getting found Online: Search Engine Optimization

Being found by individuals doing online searches is driven to a large extent by successfully being recognized by the major search engines. Google and Yahoo! are the dominate search engines used by individuals. The following table shows the share of online searches in the U.S. during the July 2006 to January 2007 period.[19]

Search Engine	Market Share
Google sites	47.5%
Yahoo sites	28.1%
MSN-Microsoft sites	10.6%
Ask network	5.2%
Time Warner network	5.0%

There are a variety of techniques and best practices that will lead to success in search marketing. These approaches are divided into three areas: (1) natural or organic search optimization or search engine optimization; (2) paid keyword search; and (3) search feeds:

1. **Natural or organic search optimization.** This approach is sometimes called free or unpaid search because it is based on developing Web pages so that the search engines will successfully find your content and position it prominently on search results. This approach normally requires considerable up-front work, but does not incur ongoing per-click-through fees.

2. **Paid keyword search.** As the name implies, this approach involves paying the search engine companies to show advertisements for your site when users initiate relevant searches. Most search engines charges on a pay-per-click basis; that is, every time a user clicks on the advertising link, a fee is incurred.

3. **Search feeds.** This approach is used when data describing your Web site are sent to the search engines and a fee is charged to ensure that your pages are part of the site engine's index.[20]

According to MarketingSherpa, a highly regarded source for evaluating online marketing practices, the following provide the best return on investment to the online marketer.

Best Return on Investment for Product Marketing, Spring 2006.[21]

Best Return on Investment	Percentage of Respondents, Top Two Responses
Search engine optimization	68.7%
House e-mail marketing	56.4%
Paid search marketing, pay per click	52.5%
Public relations	41.9%
Direct postal mail	41.1%
Online advertising (banners, etc.)	31.2%

One of the issues that electronic marketers must address is whether to do the work in-house or outsource the work to a third party. There are advantages to both approaches. If the firm is developing and hosting its own Web site, it makes sense to develop the search engine optimization in-house. This is especially true if the number of keywords that are part of a paid search is small. Conversely, if the size and scope of the project are beyond the skills, talents, and capacity of the firm, outsourcing is a good decision. As a general rule, if any of the following are true, outsourcing is a desired approach.[22]

- The monthly paid key word search advertising expense exceeds $10,000.

- The terms list exceeds 2,000 terms.

- Your firm competes in a highly competitive market in which the cost-per-click is above 60 cents.

- The in-house staff spends more than 20 hours per week managing your program.

- The firm changes more than 20 percent of the ad copy monthly.

- The term list changes more than 20 percent per quarter.

- You are frustrated or dissatisfied with the services provided by the in-house operation.

If the firm decides to outsource, the decision about which firm to select is similar to any outsourcing decision. Among the questions and issues that all potential bidders should address are:[23]

- How many years has the company been providing search marketing services? The field of search marketing has evolved very quickly and is changing very rapidly. You want to have a firm that is both experienced and at the same time is nimble enough to be current with technology and technique.

- What is the range of services that the firm provides?

- What percentage of the firm's revenue is provided by search marketing services? A firm that specializes in search marketing may be more desirable than one that is more general, with only a limited scope of business in the search marketing specialty.

- What firms similar to your firm have they provided services for? Check these references.

Whether the firm decides to do the work in-house or outsource, there are two primary approaches to increasing the probability of a potential customer finding your Web site based on a search—natural or organic search optimization and paid search advertising, or **pay-per-click**.

Pay-per-click

When online advertising is used, each time a user clicks on the advertisement and opens the advertiser's Web page, the advertiser pays the host of the advertisement. The cost of pay-per-click varies depending on the competitiveness of the Web site.

Search optimization is based on processes that increases the chances that your Web site will rank well with the dominant search engines, Google and Yahoo!. These processes are based on putting the keywords in the right place on the Web site and having Web content that is sufficient. Search engines use *spiders* to find and review Web sites. These spiders, often called robots, crawl from Web page to Web page, reviewing and indexing content, following links to other Web sites and Web pages.

One of the most important beginning steps to increase search engine effectiveness is to be sure that your Web site is linked to other sites. Without such links, a spider might not even find your Web site. Consider links to your site as votes. Each time another site links to your Web site, it increases the probability of your site being listed higher on search engine results. Links to highly regarded sites are even more valuable. You can easily check which sites are linked to your site by typing "Link: yourdomainname.com" into any of the major search engines.

Keywords are used by search engines to identify content and then rank the content in order of relevancy for users. For example, instead of using the keyword, "coffee" it would be more desirable to use "Nicaraguan coffee." Individuals within your own firm could be used to brainstorm keywords. In addition, Google, the leading search engine provides free online assistance. The following URL provides a free tool that is used to identify keywords and provides a ranking of how well each word would work in a Google search. https://adwords.google.com/select/KeywordToolExternal

It is easy to study the keywords of other sites including competitors. Simply open the site, select "view" and "source," and the listing of keywords will appear. For example, the Web site of two international hotel chains included the following:

meta name="description" content="Hotel and resort information, make reservations and book events, or find special offers at XYZ.com."

meta name="Description" content="ABC Hotels online reservations for leisure and business travel at leading airport, resort, and business hotels worldwide. ABC Hotels is a member of the ABC Family."

Once the keywords are identified, it is important to place them in the titles, headings, and subheadings on each page. The title of each page should be directly tied to the content of the page. Search engines will use these titles to index the content of the particular page.

Meta description tags are used to determine how the author wants the page to be described when a search engine views the page. Meta tags are normally between 50 and 200 characters. Best practice is that a single word not be repeated more than four times, nor any keyword phrase more than once.

Meta keywords are not visible when the page is viewed, but are viewable when the source code is revealed. Words should be inserted that are relevant to the content of the particular page. Limit the number of characters to 75 to 120. An example from two major hotel chains follows:

meta name="keywords" content="hotel, hotel reservations, hotel rates, XYZ, XYZ hotels"

meta name="Keywords" content="ABC hotels, airport hotels, ABC hotels worldwide, ABC international, resort hotels, business travel, vacation travel, holiday travel, hotel reservations, online hotel booking, ABC, family vacation"

Each page should contain 200 to 600 words of actual content. Among this content, the use of keywords should be used four to six times, to increase search engine effectiveness.

Once the site is up and running, it is important to track results. How many visitors does the site attract? How many click-throughs from other sites or pay-per-click advertising click-throughs does the site receive? What are the visitors doing? How many seek more information? How many make purchases? Google offers a free analytics tool, http://www.google.com/analytics/ that can provide very useful information to the marketer.

Budgeting for Online Marketing

How should companies budget for online marketing? How should they allocate resources? A 2007 study published by Hospitality eBusiness Strategies and the New York University Tisch Center Hospitality, Tourism and Sports Management provides insight into current practices.[24] The study reported allocated costs as follows for U.S.-based properties, as a percentage of the online marketing budget.

Activity	Percent of budget
Web site redesign	12.2%
Web site optimization	10.9%
Pay-per-click/paid inclusion	18.5%
E-mail marketing	11.4%
Search engine optimization	12.4%
Strategic linking	7.2%
Consulting fees	7.0%
Display advertising (Banners)	5.0%
Meta search such as Kayak	4.2%
New media formats such as blogs	2.3%
Local search	4.9%

There is no simple answer concerning how much to budget for online advertising, search and e-mail. The correct proportion will vary by company, market, and a host of other variables. A consistent trend is that online advertising contributes more to total media spending each year. According to eMarketer projections, online advertising will account for 7.4 percent of total media spending in 2007 and will increase to 13.3 percent of media spending by 2011.[25]

Summary of Chapter Objectives

This chapter discusses the dynamic marketing specialty of electronic commerce. A relatively recent phenomenon, e-commerce, has had a dramatic and fundamental impact on the methods used by hospitality and tourism firms to market products and services. Electronic commerce is the logical extension of bringing commercial transactions and business processes to the Internet.

The chapter explored key traits of a networked economy and the scope of electronic commerce. Numerous trends were presented that illustrated the worldwide impact of electronic commerce and the growth of the entire sub-discipline of marketing. Electronic commerce is characterized by four primary attributes: exchange of digital information, technology-enabled transactions, technology-mediated transactions, and intra- and inter-organizational activities.

The historical roots of electronic commerce were discussed and the four classifications of electronic commerce were presented. These include business-to-business (B2B), business-to-consumer (B2C), consumer-to-business (C2B), and consumer-to-consumer (C2C).

Several management issues related to electronic commerce were presented, including the structure of business models. The foundation for these models includes the revenue model and the value proposition. Finally, design and implementation issues related to electronic commerce were discussed and the benefits of electronic commerce were explored.

E-mail marketing is becoming increasingly important. Spending on e-mail is increasing, and is especially effective for retaining current customers. Spam continues to be a challenge for marketers, as up to 50 percent of the e-mail sent is seen as spam by the recipients. There are numerous best practices for e-mail marketers that will significantly increase the effectiveness of e-mail.

Search engine optimization is also an important component of a firm's Internet strategy. This optimization, whether done in-house or outsourced, relies on effective use of key word search in the form of meta descriptions and meta words.

chapter review

chapter review

Key Terms and Concepts

Authentication

Browser

Business-to-business (B2B)

Business-to-consumer (B2C)

Consumer-to-business (C2B)

Consumer-to-consumer (C2C)

Domain name system (DNS)

Electronic commerce

Encryption

Firewall

Hypertext

Opt-in and opt-out

Pay-per-click

Revenue model

Pure e-commerce companies

Spam

Value proposition

Questions for Review and Discussion

1. What are the pros and cons of the openness and interconnectedness of the Internet?

2. Why are security issues of such importance in developing an Internet strategy and business plan?

3. What are the traits of a networked economy? Which trait do you believe is the most significant? Why?

4. Which of the electronic commerce trends discussed in the chapter will have the most impact on the hospitality and tourism industry? Why? What specific actions must a hospitality and tourism marketing manager make in order to take advantage of this trend?

5. Review two or three well-known hospitality and tourism company Web sites. Based on your review, prepare the responses to the following questions for class discussion:
   a. What is the firm's purpose for engaging in online communications?
   b. What is the firm's Web strategy? What are the goals and specific objectives? What outcomes do you believe the firm is seeking to achieve?
   c. How are the electronic commerce efforts being integrated with other forms of communication? How will consistency of branding and identity be maintained?

6. What are the four primary classifications of electronic commerce? Which is the most common in the hospitality and tourism industry?

7. What revenue models are most common in electronic commerce? Which one(s) are most applicable to the hospitality and tourism industry? Why?

Notes

1 Herschell Gordon Lewis and Robert D. Lewis, *Selling on the Net: The Complete Guide* (Lincolnwood, IL: NTC Business Books, 1997).

2 Jeffrey F. Rayport and Bernard J. Jaworski, *Introduction to E-Commerce*, 2nd edition (Boston: McGraw-Hill Irwin marketspaceU, 2004), p. 2.

3 Ibid., p. 3.

4 Joel Reedy and Shauna Schullo, *Electronic Marketing*, 2nd edition (Mason, OH: Thompson Southwestern, 2004), p. 30.

5 Efrain Turban, David King, Jae Lee, and Dennis Viehland, *Electronic Commerce 2004* (Upper Saddle River, NJ: Pearson Prentice Hall, 2004), p. 7.

6 Ibid., p. 12.

7 Ibid., p. 13.

8 Ibid., pp. 14–16.

9 Park Associates, 2005, Reported on www.eMarketer.com.

10 Jupiter Research, 2008, Reported on eMarketer.com.

11 David Hallerman, "E-mail Marketing: Getting Through to Customers," eMarketer.com, 2007, p. 12.

12 Ibid., p. 2.

13 MarketingSherpa. E-mail Marketing: Benchmark Guide 2008, p. 5.

14 Ibid., p. 6.

15 David Hallerman, "E-mail Marketing: Getting Through to Customers," eMarketer.com, 2007, p. 9.

16 Ibid., p. 10.

17 Ibid., p. 17–18.

18 Ibid., p. 19.

19 David Hallerman, "Search Marketing: Counting Dollars and Clicks," eMarketer.com, 2007, p. 18.

20 Alan Rimm-Kaufman, *Search Marketing Firms: A MarketingProfs Shopper's Handbook*, 2005, pp. 5–7.

[21]   David Hallerman, "Search Marketing: Counting Dollars and Clicks," eMarketer.com, 2007, p. 20.

[22]   Alan Rimm-Kaufman, *Search Marketing Firms: A MarketingProfs Shopper's Handbook*, 2005, pp. 9–11.

[23]   Ibid., pp. 11–12.

[24]   Hospitality eBusiness Strategies (HeBS) and New York University Tisch Center for Hospitality, Tourism, and Sports Management, March 2007, eMarketer.com.

[25]   "Online Ads Nip at Traditional Media," eMarketer.com, November 13, 2007.

chapter review

Case Study

Electronic Commerce Strategy at Malone Golf Club

Derek Sprague, general manager of the Malone Golf Club, pondered changes in the marketing and distribution strategy for his club for the upcoming season. The Malone Golf Club had made significant progress in the past three years. The club completed the construction of a new clubhouse, made minor design changes to several of the 36 holes that make up the two golf courses, and upgraded the food and beverage offerings of the club.

The Malone Golf Club operates as a semiprivate club, offering both annual memberships and daily greens fee access. Many of the daily fee players come to the club, located in Malone, New York, from Canada—Montreal is only a 90-minute drive from the club. The club has used a Web site for several years to promote the golf, golf packages, food and beverage service, and other amenities. The club's approach to the Web site (www.malonegolfclub.com) has been primarily "brochure-ware," that is, it is used as an addition to the printed brochures. Derek is thinking of taking a more aggressive approach to electronic commerce. He is considering a number of options, including accepting reservations online; developing a chat room where members and players could discuss the course, trade stories, and stay in touch with each other; and developing an online push e-mail and promotional strategy for frequent daily fee players and members of the club.

You have been retained as a consultant to the club. Derek has asked you to research the following questions and then meet with him next week. He wants to review your early research before proceeding further or retaining additional consulting assistance.

Case Study Questions and Issues

1. What are the pros and cons of accepting tee time reservations online?
2. Will online reservations impact the staffing of the pro shop?
3. What electronic commerce business model should Malone Golf Club adopt? Should it auction off tee times at low-demand periods or keep the traditional pricing model in place? What are the financial implications of these options?

4. Should the club consider developing its own online reservation system or outsource this to another company that provides the service for other golf clubs?

5. What increase in greens fee and membership revenue will be required to offset the costs of an online reservation system?

6. How will potential online systems integrate with the current tee time system?

7. How might the members and frequent players react to online reservations? Will it be viewed positively or negatively?

Additional Digital Case Studies

PRICELINE.COM • Visit **http://digitalenterprise.org/cases/priceline.html** to explore a second case study.

ORBITZ • Visit **http://digitalenterprise.org/cases/orbitz.html** to explore a third case study.

case study

part 5

Courtesy of Artex International.

Courtesy of ImageState.

chapter

11

Promotion and Advertising

Chapter Objectives

After studying this chapter, you should be able to:

1. List the elements of the promotional mix.

2. Explain the difference between advertising and sales promotion.

3. Describe the roles of advertising and promotion within a larger marketing program.

4. Outline effective promoting over the four stages of the product life cycle.

5. Describe methods for establishing promotional budgets.

6. Explain the key points of advertising positioning and strategy.

7. Plan an advertising campaign.

8. Evaluate an advertising campaign.

9. Manage relationships with advertising agencies.

10. Identify the social and ethical criticisms of advertising.

11. Outline the economic effects of advertising.

Chapter Outline

David Melton *Franchisee*

Domino's Pizza • New York, New York

1. What are the major components or duties associated with your current position?

I'm a Domino's Pizza franchisee. My job is to find exceptional people who will join me on my mission to be the best pizza delivery company in my market. I recruit, hire, train, and manage store managers, who then do the same for the assistant managers and delivery teams at their stores. As a small-business person, I'm also an administrator, marketer, manager, repairman, mentor, mediator, banker, financial analyst, negotiator, motivator, innovator, and medium- and long-range planner.

2. What are the components of your position that bring you the most satisfaction? What about your position causes you frustration?

I love helping people develop, gain experience, and succeed. I've watched people come into our door scared of their own shadow and practically unable to speak to other people. Several months later they are buzzing around handling everything like the expert they've become. I've sponsored five of my managers who came into Domino's that way and have gone on to become Domino's franchisees themselves, and they own over 20 stores among them. I love getting great performance results in sales, profits, and operations. I love finishing a 400-order day with 10 insiders and 20 delivery people and averaging 12 minutes out the door and 20-minute delivery times. That feels great when you know your team is trained enough, motivated enough, and performs well enough to do that with no mistakes and have 100 percent completely delighted customers.

Keeping up with the administration required by government bureaucracy causes frustration. I'm also frustrated by people who don't think they have to work to get something.

3. What are the most challenging aspects that you're facing?

Staying motivated and sharp for years. It's a goal to get all of the functions of a business into a routine so they are all properly handled, but routine also runs against the instincts of someone with an entrepreneurial spirit.

4. What major trends do you see for your segment of the hospitality and tourism industry?

A move to more convenience and less tolerance for bad service and mistakes. More competitors will do anything for market share, and more competition gives the customer more choices. Customers are less loyal to a brand than ever. They will switch for a price just a few pennies lower.

5. What role does marketing play within your company?

As a Domino's franchisee, we're required to pay a percentage of sales into a national TV advertising fund. We consider TV a vehicle to generate calls from new customers and lapsed customers for an attractive low-price-point offer. TV is important to create and maintain top-of-mind awareness. As a delivery company, we know exactly where our customers live! So a major part of our marketing is database marketing to our existing customers with bulk mailings. We can tailor offers to these customers based on their order history, frequency, and average ticket. We expect our order takers to answer the phone with a higher-ticket offer combo and work their way down in price points.

6. If you could offer one piece of advice to an individual preparing for a career in the hospitality and tourism industry, what would you suggest?

Be prepared to live with a "the customer is always right" attitude. Rule number one, the customer is always right. Rule number two, if the customer is ever wrong, reread rule number one. It's the customers' money that you're after, and if customers leave, so does their money. Marketing to customers is expensive. Each customer costs a lot of money to just get him or her to try your product. Taking care of an existing customer is inexpensive compared to generating a new one. And a customer that has a problem that you take care of will be more loyal to you than a customer who never had a problem. Even if the customer is wrong, if you "win" an argument with a "wrong" customer, they'll still leave. Did you win?

industry profile

INTRODUCTION

Hospitality and tourism firms engage in a good deal of advertising and promotion. In fact, these firms are often at the forefront in terms of creativity and spending. For example, national restaurants are at the top of the list in terms of dollars spent in all forms of television advertising, based on figures from Competitive Media Reporting.[1] As the marketing environment in which hospitality and tourism organizations operate becomes more competitive, the importance of advertising and other forms of promotion increases. This chapter focuses on advertising management and lays the foundation for the next chapter, which focuses on advertising media. Emphasis here is on defining commonly used advertising terms, relations with an advertising agency, advertising budgets, positioning and strategy, and planning and evaluating advertising campaigns.

The Promotional Mix

The more visible forms of advertising are often used to help increase sales and profits. However, all of the elements of the **promotional mix** are equally important. The promotional mix elements include advertising, personal selling, sales promotion, and public relations. This chapter focuses on the last two but will define all four:

1. **Advertising** is any paid form of nonpersonal presentation of ideas and promotion of ideas, goods, or services by an identified sponsor.

2. **Personal selling** is an oral presentation in a conversation with prospective consumers for the purpose of making a sale.

3. **Sales promotion** includes marketing activities other than advertising, personal selling, and public relations that attempt to stimulate consumer demand and increase sales. Commonly, sales promotion is a direct inducement offering an extra incentive to take action, be it to buy the product or service or to obtain further information.

4. **Public relations** is a nonpersonal stimulation of demand for a product or service by providing commercially significant news about the product or service in a published medium or obtaining favorable presentation in a medium that is not paid for by the sponsor.

Promotional mix

The basic elements include advertising, personal selling, sales promotion, and public relations. All of the elements are equally important.

Advertising

Advertising consists of any paid form of nonpersonal presentation of ideas and promotion of ideas, goods, or services by an identified sponsor.

Personal selling

Personal selling is an interpersonal process whereby the seller ascertains, activates, and satisfies the needs and wants of the buyer so that both the seller and the buyer benefit.

Sales promotion

Sales promotion includes marketing activities other than advertising, personal selling, and public relations that attempt to stimulate consumer demand and increase sales. Sales promotions seek to accomplish several broad objectives and can be used for several reasons: to increase consumer awareness, to introduce new products and services, to increase guest occupancy and customer counts, to combat competitors actions, to encourage present guests to purchase more, and to stimulate demand in nonpeak periods.

Public relations

Public relations is a nonpersonal stimulation of demand for a product or service by providing commercially significant news about the product or service in a published medium or obtaining favorable presentation in a medium that is not paid for by the sponsor.

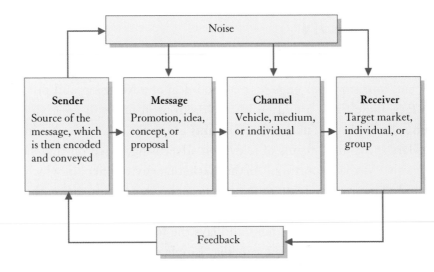

FIGURE 11.1 • *Communications model.*

In all forms of the promotional mix, it remains critical that the intended message be delivered to the potential target markets. A model of communication is shown in Figure 11.1 to illustrate how this process takes place.

Remember that both the sender and the receiver are humans and are subject to the failings common to everyone. No one communicates as well as he or she would like. We simply do not speak as clearly and understandably as we would prefer to do. In addition, we do not listen as well as we should. With this in mind, all communication attempts with target markets should be as clear and concise as possible. In addition to the human failings, potential difficulties arise with the message, the channels that are used, and the noise level in the environment, so efforts must be made to overcome these difficulties. When management designs a new form of promotion, it is sometimes expected that the entire target market can be reached with a limited number of contacts. This is simply not possible, because the target market is being bombarded with other messages; as a result, sometimes the intended message is not received and retained above the noise in the environment. It is important to keep this communications model in mind when designing any type of communications with target markets. It serves as a reminder of how great the challenge really is. It is also critical to review the feedback received, study it carefully, and look for ways to improve the identified weakness.

The Functions of Promotion and Advertising

The terms *promotion* and *advertising* evoke many different responses from hospitality managers. Some smile, remembering a successful advertising campaign from the past. Others view advertising as a waste of time, claiming that advertising and promotion are things that should be used to sell automobiles or computers but not hospitality operations. Those individuals usually champion word of mouth, claiming that good food and service will produce satisfied consumers, who, in turn, will recommend the operation to more consumers, but this is not advertising; rather, it is a form of public relations.

Advertising is not something limited to chain operations, such as McDonald's and Wendy's. Many independent operations, especially those in the foodservice segment, are being squeezed by larger national and regional chain advertising, and managers sometimes mistakenly withdraw from all advertising, rationalizing that they cannot compete with the big chains. This often leads to decline and the eventual demise of the operation. Nor is advertising something a manager does only when business weakens and needs improvement. Managers who fail to engage in a significant advertising program may miss a unique opportunity to increase both customer counts and total sales.

Advertising and promotion are marketing functions that need to be managed along with other functions. They demand management's time and attention if they are to be successful, for advertising must be planned, implemented, and evaluated with care if it is to achieve increased sales. What can advertising and promotion do? First, advertising and promotion present information to the consumer about new products, new services, new décor, and other items of interest. Second, they reinforce consumer behavior by communicating with individuals who have patronized a particular hotel or restaurant in the past. Exposing these consumers to a continuous flow of advertising is likely to induce repeat patronage by reinforcing their positive experiences. Brand loyalty is very difficult to establish, but advertising is one method to use in this effort. Third, advertising induces first-time patronage. When consumers are exposed to a continual flow of advertising, their curiosity is aroused, and this often results in patronage. If a first-time guest is rewarded with a pleasant experience, the foundation for repeat patronage has been successfully established. Fourth, advertising enhances the image of hospitality and tourism operations. Advertising does not always seek to promote a specific product or service; it can instead seek to create and reinforce an image for the consuming public. Words and phrases often contribute to this image building. For example, a slogan used by Westin Hotels and Resorts, "Caring, comfortable, civilized," sought to establish and maintain a specific image in the mind of the consumer.

Advertising and promotion are necessarily a vital part of the marketing program of all types of hospitality and tourism operations. Just what should advertising do? What should it accomplish? Generally speaking, advertising should set out to accomplish three goals: (1) to establish awareness in the minds of consumers, (2) to establish positive value in the minds of consumers, and (3) to promote repeat patronage and brand loyalty among consumers.

Awareness must be created among consumers who have not heard of a particular hotel or restaurant establishment. This awareness should create sufficient interest so that patronage results. Next, to induce both first-time and repeat patronage, a positive perceived value must be established and reinforced in the minds of consumers. All consumers have limited resources for chasing after unlimited wants; hence, only products and services that offer a high level of perceived value will be rewarded with patronage. A hospitality operation might have the very finest to offer in rooms, food, and service in a given market segment, but if it has a low perceived value, the number of consumers served is likely to be small. Finally, advertising should strive to promote brand loyalty and repeat patronage among the highest possible percentage of consumers. Very few hospitality and tourism operations can survive only on one-time patronage. Repeat business must be encouraged and promoted. Even better than repeat patronage is brand loyalty, wherein consumers begin to prefer one brand of hotel or restaurant over and above the direct competition. However, the current competitiveness in the marketplace makes it very difficult to create brand loyalty.

MANAGING THE PROMOTIONAL MIX

It is important for firms to create promotional mixes that will lead to a strong position in the marketplace. Each firm must choose its own mix of advertising, publicity, personal selling, and sales promotions, depending on the firm's positioning and image. However, one marketing tool that is helpful in determining baseline strategies for promotion is the product life cycle.

Promoting over the Product Life Cycle

As discussed in Chapter 7, all hospitality and tourism organizations progress through a distinct life cycle (see Figure 11.2). As an organization moves through the stages of the life cycle, different marketing strategies are recommended. Promotion is one component of the marketing mix that changes over the life cycle of a product.

INTRODUCTION STAGE. Rarely does a new hotel or restaurant open without creating some interest in the local community. The goal of all hospitality

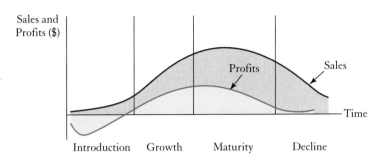

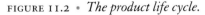

FIGURE 11.2 • *The product life cycle.*

managers should be to capitalize on this natural curiosity and make it work to the advantage of the business. The main focus of the promotional campaign in the introduction stage is to inform consumers in an effort to create awareness. The principal objective during this phase is to build volume within the operation by reaching individuals who are innovators and are most likely to patronize a new operation. This approach is very critical to an independently owned operation. Every effort must be made to reach potential consumers and encourage first-time patronage. All targeted segments should be identified and strategies developed to reach each of these markets.

All elements of the promotional mix are used at this point. Advertising and publicity are used to create awareness and interest in the new operation. Depending on the size of the operation, local, regional, and/or national media are contacted to cover the story surrounding the opening. Personal selling is used to generate awareness and interest among intermediaries. Restaurants will contact hotels, retail businesses, and tourist information sources that are likely to make referrals. In addition, hotels will contact tour operators and travel agents. Finally, sales promotions are used to induce trial. For example, hotels will offer familiarization trips to intermediaries such as travel agents or tour operators, and many hospitality and tourism firms will offer discounted rates to reduce the perceived risk of consuming the service.

It is very desirable to bring all management personnel with marketing responsibilities together to generate ideas for possible promotion. These idea-generating sessions should produce a wealth of potential promotions, leading to a schedule of what is to be done and when it is to be accomplished. The list of possible promotional ideas is endless; a few examples follow:

• Signs can announce "coming soon" for a new hospitality operation and perhaps indicate the number of weeks until the grand opening.

• Press releases can indicate the who, where, what, when, and why of the new operation.

- Mailing lists can be developed from a guest book signed by first-time patrons. This list becomes the foundation for direct-mail campaigns.

- Numerous media can, of course, be used. One rather novel approach involved advertising in the classified section of the newspaper and on radio for high-quality personnel for a new restaurant. The results were not only surprising, but also very successful. Hundreds of individuals applied for jobs, making this particular independently owned restaurant *the* place to work. In addition, the advertisements described in some detail the atmosphere, menu, and image of the restaurant, thereby informing the general public of the existence of the restaurant. The result was high-quality personnel, high guest counts, and very satisfied owners and managers.

- Community opinion leaders, such as doctors, lawyers, and restaurant reviewers, can be invited to preopening events designed to enhance the image of the hospitality operation. The goal, of course, is to present a positive image and influence those who can, in turn, influence others.

- Numerous door prizes, contests, and raffles can be used to encourage patronage. The American consumer seems infinitely willing to take a chance on getting something for little or nothing. Consider the success of Las Vegas and other locations that offer legal gambling. This approach is simply an application of psychologist B. F. Skinner's variable-interval reinforcement schedule. Individuals will continue to take chances, even though the probability of winning is very small.

- Handbills or flyers represent an inexpensive yet effective method for introductory promotion. These are often used as direct-mail pieces, or they may be distributed by other means. One new restaurant located near a large shopping mall and several office complexes distributed handbills offering a variety of discounts and freebies at these locations. In addition, the restaurant invited the administrative assistants of high-ranking management personnel to a complimentary lunch and formed a club that provided incentives and rewards to individuals who provided the restaurant with the largest number of reservations. The results were predictable: very high volume and the satisfaction of all parties involved.

The list of potential introductory advertising and promotional ideas is endless. Each management group must determine a sound strategy for the introductory stage of advertising and promotion.

GROWTH STAGE. During the growth stage, promotion and advertising focus on building name recognition and persuading consumers to purchase the brand. If the introductory stage has been successful, a solid core of consumers has been established. With this core, the promotional objective must be twofold: (1) to reinforce and remind those consumers who have patronized the hospitality establishment, to induce repeat patronage, and (2) to reach those consumers who have not patronized the operation, thereby expanding volume with a significant number of first-time buyers.

During the growth stage, the mention of the name of the hospitality establishment brings a distinct image to the consumer's mind. Therefore, promotion and advertising should seek to reinforce the most positive aspects of this image. The strategies used during this stage include comparative advertising and stressing the special advantages offered by the product–service mix of the operation. In addition, personal selling is still used to build awareness, interest, and desire among intermediaries. However, less emphasis is placed on publicity and sales promotions to build image and persuade consumers to purchase.

MATURITY STAGE. Only the largest and most successful hospitality and tourism organizations progress to this stage of the life cycle. The firms that achieve this level are very well established and have the tremendous advantage of nearly universal name recognition and reinforcement. Foodservice firms that have achieved this level include McDonald's, Wendy's, Chili's, and Taco Bell. Well-known hotel firms include Hilton and Marriott. For example, a McDonald's advertisement need not even mention the product or service to be successful. Simply by using the word *McDonald's,* showing the restaurant and the people who patronize it, or simply the golden arches logo, the advertisement reinforces the image in the minds of consumers. The primary goal of a firm at this stage is to use the organization's size and brand recognition to remind consumers of the product's benefits and continue to differentiate it from the competition. When a company is in the maturity stage, sales growth is usually obtained by taking market share away from competitors, rather than through growth in the overall market. An example of this is the fast-food segment, as each of the largest competitors (McDonald's, Burger King, and Wendy's) attempts to differentiate itself from the others.

In addition to reminder advertising, sales promotions in the form of coupons and discounts are popular. Coupons are normally distributed through a variety of print media or by direct mail. Coupon promotions are generally most effective in increasing consumer counts. Coupons are merely short-term inducements to purchase a brand and are not a means to build long-term loyalty among customers. Rather, the consumer uses coupons as the method to shop for the best deal at any given moment. If a large number of hospitality and tourism operations in a given geographic area offer coupon discounts, consumers can become conditioned to coupons as a way of life, with the result that they will patronize only those operations that offer such discounts. Finally, limited attention is given to personal selling and publicity during this stage.

DECLINE STAGE. The goal of any firm that reaches this stage of its life cycle is to use its competitive advantage to launch new products and services that will further strengthen the organization. By adding to its product–service mix, the firm can attract new consumers and extend its product life cycle. For example, McDonald's has repeatedly used its number-one position in the fast food segment to launch new products and services, most notably a variety of breakfast items, specialty sandwiches, and salads. These products contribute to the sales mix of the organization and serve to broaden the market appeal. All have, of course, been test-marketed prior to being introduced into the system. They are examples of ways an organization can market new products and services from a position of strength and, as a result, become stronger still.

If a firm cannot find ways to extend its product life cycle, then the appropriate strategy is to maximize short-term profit and eventually divest. This strategy calls for the firm to reduce marketing expenditures to the minimum effective level, including a reduction in the promotional budget. At this stage, there is virtually no effort in the areas of personal selling and publicity. In addition, advertising is kept to a minimum and sales promotions are used sparingly. It is assumed that these expenditures will have little effect on consumer purchasing, serving only to decrease the firm's profitability. An example of a firm that went through this phase is Boston Market. Later it emerged from reorganization and continued in operation.

Establishing the Promotional Budget

Promotional expenses should be carefully planned, monitored, and controlled. Compared with major expense items, promotion and advertising may not seem like a large percentage. However, promotional budgets must be set to maximize the use of the sales force and other promotional elements such as advertising, publicity, and sales promotions. Management must carefully establish the promotion budget to maximize the productivity of the dollars spent. Return on investment (ROI) is the key. What has been the return for the dollars invested in promotion?

Some managers promote more when business volume is slow, thereby hoping to increase volume. Others attempt to reduce expenses by cutting back on promotion when a decline in sales volume occurs. Both approaches are subject to error because they are based on intuition rather than on a rational decision-making and budgeting process. **Promotional budgets** serve several useful and important functions: (1) to provide a detailed projection of future expenditures, (2) to provide both short- and long-range planning guides for management, and (3) to provide a method for monitoring and controlling promotional expenses by comparing actual expenses against projections.

Promotional budgets

Promotional budgets serve several useful and important functions: to provide a detailed projection of future expenditures; to provide both short- and long-range planning guides for management; and to provide a method for monitoring and controlling promotional expenses by comparing actual expenses against projections.

ADVANTAGES AND DISADVANTAGES OF ADVERTISING BUDGETS. Numerous executives debate the pros and cons of budgeting promotional expenses. These are the major advantages associated with budgeting:

- **Developing budgets forces management to look into the future.** Although both past and current conditions certainly need to be considered, the future is key. All management personnel must develop the ability to project future trends, revenues, and expenses. Failure to do so can easily lead to "management by crisis."

- **Budgets serve as reference points.** Budget projections need not be financial projections cast in stone. Budgeted figures and media plans are, of course, subject to modification if the marketing situation changes dramatically. The budget, however, is important as a point of reference, a goal, and a standard against which actual performance can be compared.

- **When promotional budgets are established, all management personnel with marketing responsibilities should be involved in their preparation.** This involvement fosters improved communication among individuals. In addition, when all managers have input into the development of the plan, support for the plan increases, as each manager "owns a piece" of the plan. Once individuals identify with the budget as it is developed, this will increase their personal motivation to see that it is implemented successfully.

In addition to the aforementioned advantages, there are also some disadvantages associated with preparing promotional budgets:

- **Time is money.** To prepare a budget properly, managers must invest a considerable amount of time. See Figure 11.3 for a sample of budget items. Because the highest-paid management personnel plan the budget, the cost to the organization can be considerable. Some would argue that this represents time that could be spent more profitably performing other functions. The question to ask is, "How much is it worth to the organization to have well-developed budgets and plans?"

- **What events will shape the future?** The future is always going to be somewhat uncertain, but astute managers should be able to foresee trends and adapt to take full competitive advantage of them. Businesses often fail because management does not foresee changes and, as a result, the firm is unable to adapt in a timely manner. Successful management must develop a proactive rather than reactive posture; it must foresee change before it occurs and adapt to allow the organization to benefit from the change.

Advertising

Print advertising	$250,000
Television advertising	$350,000
Outdoor advertising	$125,000
Internet advertising	$ 35,000
Subtotal	$760,000
Brochures	$ 75,000
Direct mail	$150,000
Total	$985,000

FIGURE 11.3 • *Sample hotel promotional budget.*

BUDGETING METHODS. Promotional budgets are normally either fixed or contingent. Fixed budgets are based on predictions of sales volume and expected levels of advertising. Projected expenditures are normally held firm, even if the assumptions on which the budget was based prove to be incorrect. Conversely, contingent budgets are developed based on several sets of assumptions. This development means that if situation A happens, then implement plan A; if situation B occurs, then implement plan B; and so on. This type of budget draws its name from being based on a number of contingencies, or plans developed to be appropriate for several possible outcomes.

Various methods can be used to develop a promotional budget. Each of these methods falls into one of the four following categories: (1) the percentage-of-sales method, (2) the desired-objective method, (3) the competitive-parity method, and (4) the all-you-can-afford method.

The **percentage-of-sales method** has found very wide use in the hospitality industry. The method offers relative simplicity: a sales forecast is obtained, and a given percentage of this forecast is allocated to advertising. Within the hospitality industry, the amount of money spent for advertising is typically between 2 and 8 percent of gross sales. This method offers the following advantages:

- It is very simple and straightforward.

- Some managers prefer to view all expenses as a percentage of sales, including advertising.

- It works well if sales can be forecasted accurately and market conditions are stable.

Percentage-of-sales method

The method offers relative simplicity; a sales forecast is obtained, and a given percentage of this forecast is allocated to advertising.

However, the percentage-of-sales method also has the following disadvantages:

- If sales decline, so too will advertising expenditures. This is not a valid argument; instead, in this situation it would be wise to increase advertising expenditures.

- Increased advertising should result in increased sales, yet with this method an increase in sales results in an increase in the advertising budget.

The **desired-objective method** involves developing a budget based on well-defined objectives. Management must plan precisely what it wishes to accomplish through promotion and advertising. Based on these objectives, management must then decide what type and what amount of promotion and advertising will be necessary to achieve the objectives. Many factors are considered, including projected sales, previous promotion and advertising, financial position of the firm, and competition within the marketplace. This method has several advantages:

Desired-objective method
The desired-objective method involves developing a budget based on well-defined objectives.

- Rather than simply allocating a fixed percentage of sales for each budget period, management must critically evaluate promotion and advertising expenditures in accordance with objectives.

- Advertising efforts are tied to specific measurable objectives, thereby making evaluation easier.

- Several variable factors, such as competition within the marketplace, are considered.

However, two major disadvantages must also be considered:

- It is difficult to determine the precise mix of promotion and advertising that will accomplish the objectives satisfactorily.

- Engaging in this type of budget preparation is very time-consuming, especially when one considers that advertising and promotion represent only one area on an income statement and only one aspect of the marketing mix.

The **competitive-parity method** for establishing a budget involves direct comparison with the promotion and advertising efforts of major competitors. Based on the type and amount of promotion done by the competition, management then establishes a budget that will roughly match the activities of the major competition. The following advantages are associated with the competitive-parity method:

Competitive-parity method
The competitive-parity method for establishing a budget involves direct comparison with the promotion and advertising efforts of major competitors.

- A relative level of equilibrium is established with regard to the competition.

- The method is simple and straightforward, especially if an industry average is used.

The disadvantages of the competitive-parity method include the following:

- Relative promotion and advertising budgets and media decisions made by one firm usually are not applicable to other firms. For example, how can management be assured that the competition's advertising is appropriate for its hotel or restaurant?

- Basing future plans on the past performance of others is reactive rather than proactive.

All-you-can-afford method

The all-you-can-afford method is usually a last resort practiced by small firms that do not have the luxury of setting aside resources for promotion and advertising.

The **all-you-can-afford method** is usually a last resort practiced by small firms that do not have the luxury of setting resources aside for promotion and advertising. For example, independent restaurants and lodging companies that operate on very tight cash flows must meet their expenses such as payroll and inventory before they can consider the allocation of resources to promotion and advertising. If a small restaurant has only $2,000 to allocate, then the manager or owner must determine the most effective use of the funds.

The all-you-can-afford method is often a reality for small firms, but it is not a sound method to use in determining the promotional budget. Once again, as sales decrease and profits are down, the firm will allocate less money for promotion and advertising at a time when it would be most beneficial. Conversely, when business is good, the firm will have more money to spend on promotion. This is counter to what would make sense from a logical perspective. The main advantage associated with this method is its simplicity; it does not require managers to perform any formal budgeting for promotion, and spending is not related to goals and objectives.

A BUDGETING PROCESS. Those exposed to the budget preparation process for the first time can be overwhelmed. The process is often associated with internal corporate processes that can seem bureaucratic. Figure 11.4 illustrates the budget process in a manner that encapsulates the process in an easily understood format. Initially, senior management must determine future objectives. At the same time, the desired future performance for advertising is projected by taking into consideration trends, future influential factors, past performance, and input from subordinates. A preliminary budget is prepared and then compared with the short- and long-range objectives of senior management. If the budget appears to have a high probability of satisfying the objectives, it is adopted, and controls are established. If the budget fails to meet the objectives, then the objectives and/or the budget must be revised to bring the two into harmony.

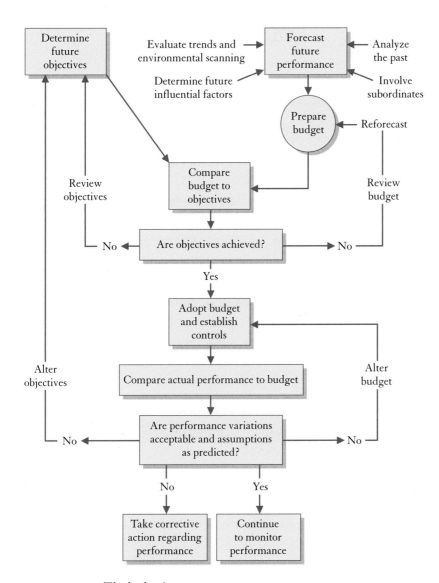

FIGURE 11.4 · *The budgeting process.*

Once management implements the budget, it uses a simple control process. If the promotional mix performs as planned, the monitoring process continues. If, however, evaluation shows that the promotional mix is not successful, several avenues exist:

- The promotional mix can be changed to increase the probability of satisfying evaluation standards.

- The budget can be modified based on changing market conditions.

- The short- and long-range objectives can be changed based on new available information.

ADVERTISING MANAGEMENT

The American Marketing Association defines advertising as "any paid form of nonpersonal presentation and promotion of ideas, goods, or services by an identified sponsor." This definition is accepted throughout the business community. It can be broken down into four components:

Publicity

Any promotion that is not paid for is called publicity. Because the individual or group is not paying for the time or space, those involved do not have complete control and are at the mercy of the writer or producer.

1. **Paid form.** Advertising is paid for and controlled by the individual or group that is the sponsor. Because someone is paying for the space (newspaper, outdoor) or time (radio, television), this individual or group has complete control over what is said, printed, or shown. Any promotion that is not paid for is called **publicity**. Because the individual or group is not paying for the time or space, those involved do not have complete control and are at the mercy of the writer or producer. A common form of publicity is a review of a restaurant in a dining or food section of a local newspaper. Publicity can obviously be either favorable or unfavorable.

2. **Nonpersonal.** Advertising is done through the mass media without personal contact or interaction between the seller and the potential buyer. Advertising relies strictly on nonpersonal promotion of goods, services, or ideas.

3. **Promotion related to ideas, goods, or services.** Advertising need not be restricted to the promotion of a tangible physical product or good. It may try to influence individuals to change their way of thinking or their behavior.

4. **Identified sponsor.** All advertising has an identified sponsor. Promotion is a broader-based term denoting efforts undertaken to induce patronage. It includes personal selling that involves face-to-face communication between the seller and the prospective buyer as well as other efforts designed to increase sales. Simply stated, advertising is a form of promotion, but all forms of promotion are not necessarily advertising.

Forms of Advertising

National advertising

National advertising is aimed at a national audience by using network television and radio, or national print media such as magazines or newspapers. This form of advertising normally promotes the general name of the chain, not individual locations or stores.

Advertising can be divided into two broad categories, national and local. **National advertising** is aimed at a national audience by using network television and radio or national print media such as magazines or newspapers. This form of advertising normally promotes the general name of the chain, not individual locations or stores.

Local advertising is used not only by the major hospitality and tourism chains but also by second-tier chains, regional chains, and independent operations. Local advertising, including television, radio, print, and other media, is used extensively in the hospitality and tourism industry. This is where the action is, and to coin a phrase, the battle of market share is won or lost in the trenches of local advertising.

A simple fact of business life for many managers is that specific advertising media are too expensive for the organization to use. For many managers, cooperative advertising is an excellent alternative. **Cooperative advertising**, as the name implies, involves two or more firms working together to sponsor an advertisement that provides benefit to all parties involved. For example, a group of restaurants located in a given geographic area may join together and promote dining in the area without promoting any one operation specifically. By joining together and sharing the expenses, managers are able to advertise in more expensive media and reach new audiences. Cooperative advertising is an area of tremendous promise because it allows a manager to expand the advertising media selection.

Local advertising

Local advertising includes television, radio, print, and other media.

Cooperative advertising

Cooperative advertising involves two or more firms, one of which is often a national or regional chain, working together to sponsor an advertisement that provides benefit to all parties involved. Franchisees often participate as a second firm.

Advertising Positioning and Strategy

Advertising terms and jargon often sound like the language of war—campaigns are launched and advertisements are aimed at target markets. Advertising need not be anything like war, but successful advertising is the result of carefully planned strategy.

A manager must first decide how to position the product–service mix. Positioning is the manner in which the consumer views the product–service mix, and each hospitality and tourism operation is positioned differently. Before owners or managers make any advertising decisions or plot strategy, they must determine the proper market position.

A successful advertising campaign does not result from haphazard planning and execution. A single advertisement may be very good, but prosperous companies produce consistently superior advertising. Advertising succeeds when good strategy is developed. Strategy is not a magic, secret formula. According to advertising experts Kenneth Roman and Jane Maas, strategy development revolves around five key points:[2]

1. **Objectives.** What should the advertising do? What goals does management want to achieve? For example, a new hospitality operation may set recognition among local residents as an objective, while another hospitality operation might seek to increase sales on slow nights. For the latter

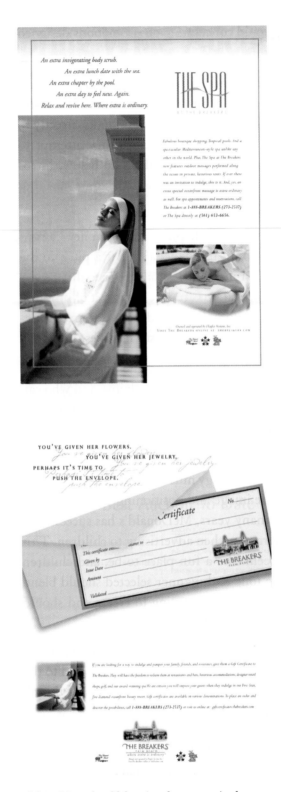

Advertising should be aimed at a particular target market.
Courtesy of The Breakers, Palm Beach, Florida.

- **The appeal must be distinctive.** All advertising must compete not only with all other hospitality and tourism organizations but with advertising for everything from automobiles to washing machines. For the advertising to be effective, the appeal must offer something that separates it from everything else. Distinctive and unusual appeals are needed.

- **The appeal must be believable.** Claims made for the product–service mix must be backed up if the appeal is to have credibility. Because some consumers are more skeptical than others, the appeal should be believable to those who might at first have doubts.

- **The appeal should be simple.** Consumers are confronted each day with hundreds of advertising stimuli, and if one is to be recalled, it must be simple and straightforward. Effective and simple appeals that have been used successfully include "We do it all for you," "You, you're the one," "It's a good time for the great taste" (McDonald's), and "America's business address" "Travel should take you places" (Hilton).

KEYS TO SUCCESSFUL ADVERTISING. To be successful, advertising needs to be approached in a systematic manner. The following are several suggestions on how to improve advertising efficiency:[3]

- **Time.** Advertising should not be considered a necessary evil. Sales and operations are equally important and require time for an advertising program to generate satisfactory results. In order to be effective, advertising must normally be repeated. Frequent exposure to targeted markets will increase the impact of advertising.

- **Budgets.** Budgets should be developed for the needs of each operation. It makes little sense to base an advertising budget on figures and percentages that represent the national average. Generally, a manager must have the courage to spend enough to produce successful results.

- **Study.** A manager needs to analyze the operation and determine the operation's advantages as compared with those of the competition. Disadvantages also need to be identified so that they can be minimized or eliminated completely. The evaluation must be done constantly so that any changes in the competitive situation are noted and adjustments are made quickly.

- **Analysis of market segments.** Each year, many people change jobs and move, and as they do their lifestyles change, too. No market segment is

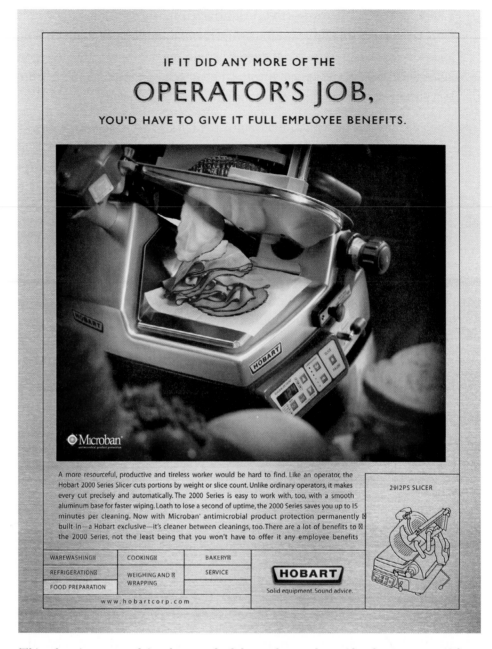

This advertisement explains the appeal of the product and provides the customer with specific information. Courtesy of Hobart Corporation.

constant; they are always changing. For this reason, management must know the patrons of the hospitality operation. By doing this, management can modify the operation to meet changing consumer demands.

- **Media.** Media must be selected very carefully to be effective. Media used must match the intended targeted markets. Each type of medium offers advantages and drawbacks, which are discussed in Chapter 12.

- **Formation of a plan.** Advertising cannot be successful if it is approached in a haphazard manner. It is important that continuity be established among all forms of advertising so that it gains momentum. Continuity can be established through the consistent use of logos, distinctive type styles, music, or creative touches to make the advertising stand out from other advertisements. Managers should not be afraid of advertising and should draw up plans designed to produce results. Nothing is worse than spending too little money on advertising, so advertising expenditures should not be cut. To be successful, advertising must be used regularly, not intermittently. Successful advertising is based on repetition.

PLANNING AND EVALUATING ADVERTISING CAMPAIGNS

Single advertisements may be creative or humorous and may convey a message, but by themselves they are not able to achieve the necessary degree of advertising effectiveness. Many independent hospitality advertisers purchase print advertising or a few radio spots during certain times of the year, particularly when business is slow. This type of advertising is not likely to be as effective as it could be, because continuity between the advertisements is lost. Such advertisements are not packaged as a campaign but are instead a hit-or-miss approach. An **advertising campaign** includes all forms of advertising held together by a single message or overall theme. A campaign is the overall plan or strategy that guides the development of all forms of advertising.

Campaign planning is initiated by considering the competitive situation, currently targeted markets, potentially targeted markets, and market positioning. An astute manager should always be aware of the advertising activities of major competitors. This, of course, is not to say that the competition should dictate advertising activities, but awareness of competitors' activities may indicate trends. For example, what product–service attributes is the competition stressing? Is it food quality, service quality, physical facilities, extra amenities, room atmosphere, or something else? Awareness of the efforts of direct competition may allow a manager to counter the competition's benefits and gain a competitive advantage.

Both the current target markets and the potential new markets must be evaluated. How can management best reinforce current markets to promote repeat patronage? What type of message will reach these markets most effectively? In addition, what new markets should be explored? What is the best

Advertising campaign

An advertising campaign includes all forms of advertising held together by a single message or overall theme. A campaign is the overall plan or strategy that guides the development of all forms of advertising.

Fourth, the advertising plan is implemented. This component includes working with each of the selected advertising vehicles, determining the advertising units (e.g., half-page print advertisements or 30-second radio spots), allocating resources to pay for the advertising time and space, and ordering and scheduling the time and space with each individual vehicle.

The fifth and final component is evaluation of advertising effectiveness. Without engaging in some form of evaluation process, how will management know to what degree the advertising efforts have met with success? There are three important explanations of why some form of evaluation procedure should be undertaken:

- **To gain an understanding of the consumer.** This involves learning what consumers want, why they want it, and how best to serve their needs.

- **To avoid costly mistakes.** When advertising effectiveness is tested, errors that might have gone undetected are noted, and adjustments can be made. In this way, both the effectiveness and cost efficiency of advertising are increased.

- **To add structure.** Rather than viewing advertising as a business expense whose impact is impossible to measure, management can measure the impact of advertising. If sales increase by 10 percent, what is the reason for this increase? What types of advertising and promotion have had the greatest impact on sales?[5]

Evaluating an Advertising Campaign

Several years ago, the president of a large retail chain discussed the firm's advertising efforts with a group of businesspeople. When one person posed a question about evaluating advertising, the president responded, "I suspect that half our advertising is wasted. The only problem is that I don't know which half." This story may bring a smile to one's face, but it is often an accurate assessment of the situation. Large hospitality organizations engaged in national and regional campaigns normally have the resources to evaluate advertising effectively. Smaller advertisers and local advertisers often are not able to evaluate advertising effectiveness.

Advertising effectiveness can be measured for both short- and long-term impact. Short-term measurements are usually given most attention because they directly reflect the income statement and the financial position of the organization. In addition, managers' tenure and bonuses are normally based on short-term performance. The long-term effects of advertising, however, should not be overlooked. Repeat patronage, brand loyalty, and an asset called goodwill reflect long-term effects. Nevertheless, it is difficult to measure the long-term residual effects of advertising within a reasonable margin for error, though in the last several years, econometric techniques have advanced to the point where measuring advertising effectiveness is more precise.

The management of a hospitality operation can evaluate advertising subjectively, either alone or in conjunction with an advertising agency. Experienced management plays a key role in this type of evaluation. If management has successfully directed advertising campaigns, subjective evaluation may indeed be adequate. This is especially true of agency executives, as they often have a wealth of experience that allows them to gauge the overall effectiveness of advertising efforts.

It is also wise to maintain a file of all advertisements. These can then be available for easy reference and reviewed periodically for winners and losers. Subjectivity does have a place in the overall evaluation of advertising effectiveness. The experience and expertise of agency personnel and hospitality managers should not be discounted. These resources are best used in combination with objective methods.

It is almost impossible to measure advertising effectiveness objectively unless well-defined objectives have been formulated prior to initiating a campaign. How would management know whether advertising has been successful if they were not able to compare actual performance with specific objectives? As stressed in Chapter 5, clearly defined, quantifiable objectives are very important. Variances between actual performance and objectives are noted and corrective action taken. In the event that the advertising proves more successful than expected, this too should be evaluated so that the success might be repeated.

Objective testing of advertising is time-consuming and expensive. Not all operations can afford or will want this type of testing. Testing is invaluable if undertaken with care and is cost-effective if used occasionally. Following is a brief review of commonly used techniques, although they are not all suitable for all types of operations:

- **Copy testing.** The process of **copy testing** involves pre-testing the copy of an advertisement prior to running it in the media. Several advertisements are normally shown to a group of consumers, and questions are asked of the group, typically "Which advertisement would interest you most?" "Which advertisement is most convincing?" and "Which advertisement is most likely to cause you to patronize the hospitality establishment?" These questions can be asked of an entire group assembled for review of a series of advertisements, or personal interviews can be conducted.

Copy testing

This involves pretesting the copy of an advertisement prior to running it in the media.

- **Inquiry and sales.** Direct-mail advertising lends itself to the inquiry and sales method. This involves keeping a tally of each inquiry and sale. For example, if a series of advertisements was run to promote banquet business, how many people phoned or contacted the operation? How many of these inquiries were converted into sales? From these tallies, it is easy to compute a cost per inquiry and a cost per sale for this type of advertising.

- **Coupons and split runs.** Coupons can be tallied to evaluate the effectiveness of one promotion against others. For example, did the sundae special sell more than the french fries promotion? Coupons are used extensively by the hospitality and tourism industry because they allow for easy evaluation. Coupons can be carried one step further and used to compare one medium against another. For example, suppose that management had a choice among three print media in which to place advertisements. Which one will reach the target market most effectively? The same advertisements and coupons could be run in the three media, with each coupon coded so that a tally could be made of the number of coupons from media A, B, and C. In this way, a relative ranking of effectiveness is possible.

- **Sales tests.** The level of gross sales or sales of specific items can be monitored following a specific period of advertising aimed at increasing one or the other. It is often difficult to take into account all the variables that affect sales both positively and negatively and thereby establish a cause-and-effect relationship.

- **Consumer testing of awareness, recall, and attitude.** Through assembled groups, telephone surveys, direct mail surveys, and personal interviews, consumers can be tested to determine their relative awareness concerning a specific hospitality operation. Have they heard of the operation? Do they patronize it? If so, how frequently do they visit? Do they recall seeing any advertisements? Which ones do they recall? When shown certain advertisements, do they recall seeing these? This is known as *aided recall.*

Relations with an Advertising Agency

Advertising agency

An independent firm that works for the client to produce creative work and media scheduling.

Should a hospitality organization hire an **advertising agency**? With the exception of small motels or restaurants that do not have large budgets, all larger operations should consider the use of an agency. The final decision is certainly for each organization to make, but agencies offer several advantages. First, an agency can increase the effectiveness of advertising; its work is more professional, and its use of media is better. Second, agencies can be especially helpful in dealing with the special production requirements of radio and television advertising. Third, using an advertising agency is like maintaining a staff of part-time specialists—copywriters, artists, and layout professionals. Fourth, agencies are able to maintain closer contacts with media representatives versus a single advertiser. Finally, some advertising agencies are able to offer consultative services related to such advertising and marketing projects as test marketing.

Management must, however, consider the disadvantages of using an agency. First is, of course, the question of money. There is no such thing as a free lunch, and top-quality professional assistance will cost money. Furthermore, if the hospitality organization has access to adequate freelance talent and assistance, the services of an agency may not be required.

Managers have to make decisions about how advertising will be handled. These decisions should be based on the following factors:

- The amount of available time to devote to advertising

- The sizes of the target market segments

- The specific media that are being considered or have been selected

- Management's knowledge of and experience in advertising

- The amount of money to be spent on advertising

THE ROLE OF AN AGENCY. An advertising agency is an independent business that works for the client who is purchasing the advertising. Agencies come in all shapes and sizes, from one-person operations to large agencies employing hundreds of individuals. Generally, a small advertiser should avoid the very large agencies because these often are not able to give the personal attention that the small advertiser needs and wants. Agencies that push out advertising in huge quantities may lack creativity and may resort to a production-line approach.

Both creative and business professionals who are specialists in various areas staff the agency. First, they apply both art and science to advertising. An agency develops and implements an advertising plan tailored to the needs of the individual client. Second, they coordinate the various functions that must take place if an advertising campaign is to be successful. They do this by coordinating the creative staff, which develops the advertisements, and the business staff, which secures the advertising time and space in the various media. An agency can actually save the client money because the fees earned by the agency are paid as commissions by the medium in which the advertisements are placed.

TYPES OF ADVERTISING AGENCIES. There are several types of advertising agencies. They are classified based on two criteria: the type of business they handle and the range of services they offer. Agencies may serve a broad range of consumer products, or they may specialize in one field such as consumer goods, industrial products, financial services, retail sales, or real estate. It is wise to select an agency with a proven track record in working with service or hospitality industry clients. An advertising agency may offer specific functions such as media buying services or creative services, or it may be a full-service agency. Full-service agencies will handle not only the advertising that the client elects to purchase, but also nonadvertising activities such as sales promotional materials, trade show exhibits, publicity, and public relations.

Advertising agencies provide a wide variety of professional services, including campaign planning, market research, media selection and production, public relations, and campaign evaluations. The following list represents most of the services that an agency should be able to provide:

- Studying the client's product–service mix to determine strengths and weaknesses and the client's relation to the competition

- Conducting an analysis of the current and potential market segments to determine future potential

- Providing direction and leadership with regard to selecting available media and the best method to advertise and promote the product–service mix

- Formulating a detailed plan to reach the stated advertising and promotional objectives

- Executing the plan by coordinating the creative process (writing and designing the advertisements) and the business process (securing the desired advertising time and space)

- Verifying that the desired advertisements have been run in the media selected

- Evaluating the effectiveness of the advertising campaign and submitting a report to the client

SELECTING AN ADVERTISING AGENCY. The agency-client relationship is very important, so the agency should be selected with great care. How should a hospitality or tourism firm go about selecting an agency? Entering into an agency-client relationship is not a move to be taken lightly, but it can be based on a rational process. A few recommendations follow.

First, make a list of the needs that an agency must satisfy. It is also wise to make a list of the major problems or symptoms unique to the character of the specific hospitality or tourism client. Begin a list of questions to ask in selecting an agency, such as "What is the reputation of the agency?" "What experience does the agency have with hospitality or tourism accounts?" and "How much depth of talent does the agency have?" Other needs and criteria should be listed, but these will depend on the needs of an individual hospitality or tourism organization.

Second, make a list of prospective agencies. This will involve checking the track records of several agencies as well as informing them of the organization's interest. Some managers prefer to use an agency questionnaire to gather preliminary data from prospective agencies. Using this type of questionnaire offers both pros and cons. It allows management to gather information from a variety of agencies and then use that information during initial screening. It does, however, occasionally turn off an agency, making the agency feel that the prospective client is asking for too much information before the agency-client relationship has been established.

Third, after a list of prospective agencies has been developed, it must be narrowed to a few viable agencies. At this point management should be prepared to meet with agency representatives, review samples of their work, listen to ideas, and evaluate the agency against the organization's needs and criteria.

Finally, it is always wise to check references. Ask the agency for a list of prior clients and talk with them about such issues as building a working relationship with the agency, timeliness of work completion, accuracy of work, positives and negatives of working with the agency and/or account executive, or other attributes that are of importance.

AGENCY COMPENSATION. How are advertising agencies compensated? Typically, agencies receive payment in several ways: (1) commissions from media, (2) fees or retainers paid by the client, (3) service charges for creative and production work, (4) markups on outside purchases, and (5) tradeouts. Commissions of 15 percent are normally paid to the agency by the media. For example, if an advertisement costs $5,000, the agency would collect $5,000 from the client but would pay the medium $5,000 minus $750 (15 percent), or a total of $4,250. Agencies often do not generate sufficient revenue from small advertisers to cover production and creative costs, and therefore they charge other fees, such as monthly retainers or hourly charges for creative work.

Charges are also levied for such production work as photography and graphics. These are usually billed at cost plus 17.65 percent. If services are performed for the agency by a third party, the agency may add a markup to the amount billed by the third party. This markup would cover the costs of securing the services and coordinating the services of several third-party providers. Charges are made for advertising on which commissions are not paid, such as direct mail and local newspaper advertising.

Trade-outs

When firms trade services in lieu of cash.

Agencies may also accept trade-outs as a form of compensation. **Trade-outs** consist of trading services for services. The agency performs services for the hotel or restaurant in exchange for services in the form of food and beverages or guest rooms that are provided on a complimentary basis up to the retail value of the services provided by the advertising agency. This method is widely used by hotels and restaurants, for it increases the purchasing power of each dollar spent.

Establishing a positive agency-client relationship is of critical importance. Management should be willing to work closely with the agency and be honest and open in communication. A manager should be critical of the agency's work without being overly critical of every advertisement, focusing instead on the broader overall strategy. Taking an active interest in the relationship is a very positive step in making the relationship a good one.

EFFECTS OF ADVERTISING

Advertising is a common practice by firms selling products and services in our society. Consumers are often amused and entertained by advertisements during special events such as the Super Bowl. Every year, the nation is astonished at the cost of advertising for 30 seconds during such major events. In addition, advertisers are given awards for their creativity and special effects, and celebrities receive large sums of money to participate in advertisements. Therefore, it is no wonder that economists and consumer advocates debate the overall impact of advertising on our society.

Social and Ethical Criticisms of Advertising

Many critics of advertising raise questions about the social and ethical issues surrounding the use of advertising and other forms of promotion. The following is a list of the most common criticisms regarding advertising.[6]

ADVERTISING IS MISLEADING OR DECEPTIVE. Originally, advertising was a practice used to inform consumers about products and product uses. It was a way for firms to convey their messages to consumers so that consumers could make informed purchase decisions. Over the years, as the country prospered and firms sold more products to more consumers with more discretionary income, advertising has become a major strategic tool used to differentiate products and services. Unfortunately, in the heat of competition, some firms choose to stretch the truth in an attempt to gain a competitive advantage.

Advertising is indeed a powerful force in the marketplace, and occasionally, it may be used to deceive consumers. The government has gone to great lengths to protect the consumer. Many other groups, including the Better Business Bureau and the National Advertising Review Council, strive to limit the amount of false and misleading advertising. Also, it simply is not in the long-term interests of any hospitality or tourism operation to deceive its consumers. Advertising seeks to induce first-time and repeat patronage by making promises to consumers about specific products and services. Failure to deliver as promised hurts the advertiser's credibility and sales.

ADVERTISING IS OFFENSIVE OR IN POOR TASTE. As mentioned before, the increase in competition has resulted in some firms engaging in questionable advertising practices in an attempt to gain market share. In addition to being misleading or deceptive, some critics have also argued, some advertising is offensive or in poor taste. For example, insurance firms may use "fear appeal" to sell their products, automobile manufacturers may use sex to sell cars, and marketers of children's products target children directly. Firms may argue their First Amendment rights to free speech, but many critics feel that advertisers have crossed the line. Advertising has also been accused of creating and perpetuating stereotypes based on its depiction of certain groups of people. Proponents might argue that art imitates life.

ADVERTISING ENCOURAGES MATERIALISM. Rather than merely informing and educating consumers about product benefits, much advertising focuses on creating needs and promoting materialism. Products and services are being promoted as symbols of status and accomplishment, to the detriment of basic values. Celebrities are used in ads in an attempt to influence consumers and act as a point of reference. Another common practice in advertising is to seek product placement in popular movies, many of which target impressionable youths. For example, the boy in *Home Alone 2* spent some time alone at the Plaza Hotel in New York, indulging himself with the many amenities that the hotel offers. Also, cruises are advertised to people as a reward for working hard and a symbol of accomplishment, as are many tourist destinations and resorts.

difficult. How do you get more local residents to frequent the restaurant in the off-season? With almost 150,000 residents living approximately 10 miles away, and another populated area of 200,000 people approximately 35 miles away, how do you get them to be part of your off-season market? There are no comparable restaurants within a 20-mile radius. The city 35 miles away has a couple of full-service restaurants with quality food and atmosphere, but they do not have the regional reputation that the resort restaurant has.

The restaurant is active in the local community. The Rotary and Lions Clubs hold their weekly luncheon meetings at the restaurant. The restaurant occasionally does outside catering, but demand is minimal. Special functions at the restaurant can be accommodated in the off-season, but the dining rooms are contiguous and relatively intimate, making it difficult to rearrange and close one off from the rest of the restaurant.

The restaurant benefits from billboard advertising and the positive reputation of the chain's five other restaurants. The closest of the other five chain restaurants are 80 miles and 120 miles away. The restaurant has just hired a part-time person as public relations director to help pump up community involvement and increase the restaurant's profile.

Case Study Questions and Issues

1. How can Mike and his new public relations employee generate more local customer business in the off-season?

2. What can they do to entice residents of neighboring communities to drive 10 to 35 miles for an upscale dinner?

3. What type of advertising and promotions might increase local community traffic?

4. What other information is necessary to make advertising and promotion decisions?

case study

Case Study

Mr. C's Sandwich Shoppes

You've been working for Mr. C's Sandwich Shoppes for nearly a year as a manager of one of the five stores operated within a medium-sized city. Edward Callahan, "Mr. C," opened his first store nearly 20 years ago and has steadily expanded since that time. The restaurants feature both eat-in and take-out dining, and are open from 6 A.M. until 10 P.M. every day. In addition to freshly prepared sandwiches and salads, the restaurants feature a variety of baked goods, prepared in a central commissary on a daily basis. The specialty bakery items include bagels, muffins, and other breakfast items, along with exceptional breads in a wide variety of forms. In recent years, same-store sales have flattened somewhat, with the increased completion from larger companies such as Panera Bread™, Chipotle, and Atlanta Bread Company. These chains have each opened a store in the city and have gained customers and market share in the past three years. Each of these competitors advertises and promotes frequently in the local area, using a variety of methods.

For the past two months, you've been encouraging Mr. C to begin advertising and promoting the restaurants. He has responded consistently that word-of-mouth referrals have built the restaurants for many years. He sees no reason to change now. You believe that more aggressive use of advertising and promotions would result in increased sales and market share. In a conversation yesterday with Mr. C, he asked you to develop an analysis of the advantages and disadvantages of increasing advertising and promotion within the local trading area. He asked you to prepare a summary for his review in seven days. Now that he's agreed to let you proceed, how can you best prepare the requested summary?

Chapter Outline *(continued)*

Nick DiMeglio *General Manager*

Ritz-Carlton Aspen Highlands Club • Aspen Colorado

1. What are the major components or duties associated with your current position?

I am charged with leading the Ritz-Carlton Club Aspen Highlands. My focus is to provide exceptional service to our Club Members. The Ritz-Carlton Gold Standards clearly define the expectations for the team. I create the environment where the standards are met though an inspirational leadership style. Building strong relationships with the Aspen community is also a major component of this job. I serve on three local Boards for the Aspen Highlands Community and report to a board of directors as well.

2. What are the components of your position that bring you the most satisfaction? What about your position causes you frustration?

Satisfaction: Building relationships with the board, community, and associates; creating an environment where staff members can grow professionally and personally; quality, leadership and business scores that lead the company or industry.

Frustrations: Poor service to members, business partners, and corporate initiatives.

3. What are the most challenging aspects you're facing?

Staffing, global security problems, weather dependency, and training.

4. What major trends do you see in your segment of the hospitality and tourism?

The fractional ownership is just starting to take off as an industry. More competition will enter the market due to the baby boomer's retiring. Reward programs and brand loyalty will increase dramatically as the competition increases. Service demands will increase, which will place even more pressure in the market for staff members. The consumer will eventually have to pay more for exceptional service. Software technology will help our industry identify our guest/member preferences even further.

industry profile

5. What role does marketing play within your company?

Marketing has helped create the Ritz-Carlton mystique. Market research has helped us understand our member's and guest's preferences. We have used this information to create unique opportunities for the member experience. Our current marketing campaign involves creating energy around our member's engagement. Membership referrals is the best way to grow the brand.

6. If you could offer one piece of advice to an individual preparing for a career in the hospitality and tourism industry, what would you suggest?

Market research is the key to writing and implementing an effective marketing plan. You never have enough information. Study the market as much as you can; when the market changes, be ready to change. The road to perfection is always under construction!

industry profile

INTRODUCTION

No one questions that advertising remains an extremely powerful force in the hospitality and tourism industry. Advertising programs must be managed with care and used to the maximum advantage of the organization. External advertising and promotion constitute a major area of marketing effort for most hospitality and tourism organizations since numerous media are employed in an effort to communicate with selected target markets. The success of these advertising efforts rests to a large degree on the media and the manner in which they are used. Many times, advertisers spend large amounts of money without achieving the desired results. In other cases, advertisers spend only a relatively small amount, yet the results are dramatic. It is useful to remember that it is not how much is invested but how it is invested. Dollars allocated to advertising are expected to increase sales.

Media Selection

Advertising is important because it can make the difference between success and failure. Management must ask three questions when planning and selecting initial advertising:

1. **To whom should the advertising be directed?** Specifically, what target markets have been identified as primary and secondary markets? Which individuals represent opinion leaders and reference group leaders? Opinion leaders are those individuals to which others look for information and confirmation of purchase choices. Reference group leaders are similar, except that they serve as opinion leaders for a group of individuals who have similar interests or backgrounds. Recall that this topic was covered in depth in Chapter 3. Firms should collect market segmentation data and analyze it to determine the heavy users of the product or service.

2. **Where do these people live?** Once firms have identified the large markets, they should find out where these individuals live and work. What are the best methods to reach them through advertising? In many cases, this will be as easy as determining the leaders of the business community in a small town. In other instances, determining where these individuals live and work will prove quite difficult. For example, suppose that an upscale restaurant serving dinner operates in the suburbs of a major city. Where should the restaurant advertise? How should the target markets be reached? Where do these people live and work? These questions may not have self-evident answers, and a considerable amount of research and discussion may be necessary.

3. **What media should be used?** Would it be best to use print advertising? Should radio or television should play a major role? What about outdoor advertising, direct mail, or supplemental advertising? Should directories, such as the yellow pages, be considered? Should Internet advertising be considered?

Developing Media Plans

Media planning process

The media planning process involves four stages: performing a market analysis to determine the current situation, establishing its media objectives, developing media strategies to use in attaining the objectives, and evaluating the media program on a continual basis and adapting it to fit changing conditions.

The stages in the **media planning process** are similar to the marketing planning process. First, the firm must perform a market analysis to determine the current situation. Second, the firm needs to establish its media objectives. That is, what does the firm want to accomplish with its media program? For example, is the firm focusing on creating awareness or increasing sales? Third, the firm must develop media strategies to use in attaining the objectives. Media strategies would entail developing a media mix, determining the desired coverage in regard to target markets and geographic area(s), and scheduling the specific media. Fourth, the firm must evaluate the media program on a continual basis and adapt it to fit changing conditions. A complete discussion of the four stages in the media planning process follows.

PERFORMING A MARKET ANALYSIS. This stage of the process involves a thorough analysis of the market to identify the target markets that become the focus of the media program. This decision is based on the history of the firm, its competitors, and trends in the general population. Advertising is a key element in the positioning of firms and their products or services. Therefore, it is important to select target markets that offer potential for long-term growth and survival. These market segments then become the focus of the media program in an attempt to communicate the firm's products in a favorable light that is consistent with the overall image of the firm. For example, all advertising might be aimed at men and women between the ages of 25 and 35 with annual incomes above $45,000. Or advertising might be slanted toward women such that a 60-to-40 ratio of female-to-male exposure is achieved.

ESTABLISHING MEDIA OBJECTIVES. Media objectives should be tied to the overall marketing objectives of the firm, as well as the promotion or communications objectives. The media objectives should be focused on the goals associated with the media program and be attainable using media strategies. After determining the target market(s) in the market analysis stage, a firm should establish media objectives for these markets considering the distribution of exposures, the media environment, and budget limitations.[1] Some of the more common objectives for media programs are as follows:

- To increase awareness among consumers in the target markets

- To increase coverage in target markets

- To maintain a positive impact on consumer attitudes and perceptions in regard to the firm's image

Good objectives will (1) be stated in clear and concise language, (2) include a specific time frame in which to accomplish the objective, and (3) include quantifiable terms that can be used as a standard by which to evaluate performance. For example, a local restaurant may want to reach at least 70 percent of its target audience with a direct-mail piece within the next 60 days.

DEVELOPING MEDIA STRATEGIES. Once media objectives are established, it is necessary to develop media strategies that will lead to the attainment of the firm's goals. Selecting the proper media mix, determining the target market and geographic coverage, and scheduling the media achieve this.

SELECTING THE MEDIA MIX. When selecting the media mix, it is important to examine the general nature of the target market segments. Table 12.1 contains a list of possible media vehicles and their unique characteristics. A medium should be selected based on its ability to reach the maximum number of potential consumers at the lowest cost. However, it is also necessary to minimize wasted coverage while trying to maximize reach. Wasted coverage refers to advertising exposures that do not involve members of the target market. For example, if low-income households are exposed to ads for an expensive restaurant, the restaurant is wasting money because it is paying to reach consumers who are not in its target market and would be unlikely to dine at the restaurant. If one million people subscribe to a newspaper, advertisers are charged based on a readership of one million, whether the readers are in the target market or not.

Also, the objectives of the overall campaign must be considered. Is the advertiser seeking maximum impact, or is continuity with previous and future advertising more important? For example, if a well-established restaurant had used a refined and sophisticated approach in newspaper and magazine advertising, it would not make sense for it to advertise using a high-volume, high-energy advertisement, for this would break up the continuity among advertisements in different media.

MEDIA TYPE	ADVANTAGES	DISADVANTAGES
Newspapers	Short lead time for placing ads Low cost Good coveage Can be used for coupons	Short life span Wasted coverage Clutter Poor reproduction quality
Magazines	Quality reproduction Long life span Audience selectivity High information content	Long lead time for ad placement High production costs Lack of flexibility "Pass-along" value
Radio	Personal Low cost Flexibility Low production costs Audience selectivity	Lack of visual appeal Fleeting message Flexibility Clutter
Television	Large audience High impact of message Low cost per exposure High credibility	High absolute cost High production cost Fleeting message Clutter Low selectivity
Direct Mail	High selectiviy/low wasted coverage Easily evaluated High information content Short lead time	Poor image Clutter High cost per contact
Internet advertising	Low cost per exposure Easy to monitor click-through impressions Can be highly targeted Short lead time Indexing optimization	Clutter of banner advertising Low selectivity of some Web sites
Outdoor and Transit	Low cost per exposure High repetition Target location	Wasted coverage Legislation/local restrictions Long lead time Lack of flexibility

TABLE 12.1 • *Media characteristics.*

In addition to these general factors, Howard Heinsius, president of Needham and Grohmann, Inc., suggests several essentials in media selection:[2]

- **Market focus.** Carefully examine your market by product–service mix category or brand and by target market segment. How does your hotel or restaurant fit in? What specific attributes do you want to advance?

- **Media focus.** Keep an open mind and listen to all media sales representatives in your area. Make note of changes, events, new programs, and the opportunities they might offer. Media time and space are perishable; keep an alert eye for special purchase opportunities.

- **Periodic media update.** Make sure that information about rates and other important factors such as cost per thousand and circulation is current. The situation can change rapidly. Be sure to stay on top of it.

- **Establish media effectiveness guidelines.** Keep tangible guidelines in mind as you examine each of the media options. This will help you to make better media selections.

- **Advertising by objective.** If specific advertising objectives have been established, such as sales targets or consumer awareness levels, this will aid in determining the best media combination.

- **Coordinate advertising with marketing campaigns.** Advertising is but one part of the total marketing mix. Be sure that it is coordinated with the other efforts in the areas of personal selling, promotion, and public relations.

- **Develop a sound advertising budget.** Start with an amount that is within your means and then allocate it by target markets. It is important to develop specific action plans to achieve each advertising objective.

- **Plan around media pollution.** All forms of media are oversaturated at times. Try to select the best times to get your message across while rising above the pollution of other advertisements.

- **Coordinate local efforts to match the national advertising efforts.** When a national campaign is being run by the parent chain, try to take advantage of this by running a local campaign that will supplement the national campaign.

- **Use a variety of media.** Within the limits of budgets, try to use different combinations and levels of different media to determine which is most effective.

- **Keep accurate files.** It is important to be able to review the results of each advertising campaign. Maintaining accurate records of budget, media schedules, and sales results is critical.

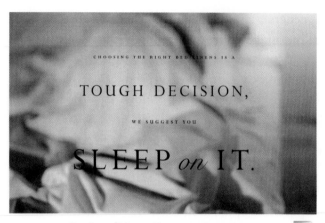

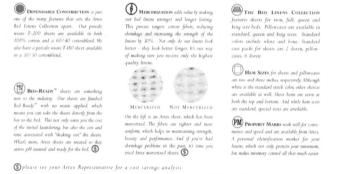

It's important that ads meet the objective determined by the media strategy. Courtesy of Artex International.

The media selection process involves matching available media with the firm's objectives. There may be multiple objectives and many media alternatives from which to choose. Therefore, the process is one of making choices at various levels. For example, once a decision is made to use some form of print media, the decision between newspaper and magazine follows. Then a decision must be made regarding the particular magazines or newspapers that will be used.

DETERMINING TARGET MARKET AND GEOGRAPHIC COVERAGE. Consideration must be given to the amount of coverage desired. The relative costs of the various media must be weighed when decisions are made. The sizes and frequency of advertisements must be carefully analyzed. Hospitality and tourism firms have the option to advertise on an international, national, regional, or local level. Then, at each level, a firm must decide how long or how often to run an ad in a given geographic market.

Scheduling the Media

Each hospitality or tourism organization must tailor the scheduling of media to fit its individual needs. Figure 12.1 illustrates the three most common

Continuous

Flighting

Pulsing

FIGURE 12.1 • *Approaches to media scheduling.*

approaches to media scheduling. **Continuous advertising** refers to the practice of keeping the amount of advertising relatively constant over time. This type is appropriate for hospitality operations with very stable volumes. **Flighting media scheduling** involves a schedule that is set up in spurts and stops. Periods of blitz advertising are used, with no advertising between blitzes. **Pulsing advertising** balances the previous two approaches in that it provides a constant low-level flow of advertising with intermittent periods of blitz advertising. Normally, high levels of continuous advertising are thought to be superior, but economic considerations may necessitate the adoption of either flighting or pulsing media scheduling.

PRINT MEDIA

The two most common forms of print media are newspapers and magazines. Another form of print media is the yellow pages offered by local telephone companies or similar products offered by competing companies. Advertising in the yellow pages can result in immediate action, but it is difficult to differentiate a firm's product and there is little flexibility because the advertisement runs for a 12-month period. However, all of the print media vehicles are popular among hospitality and tourism firms because of their ability to provide detailed information and target specific markets. For example, newspapers offer the following advantages:

- **Short lead time for placing ads.** If a manager decides to run an advertisement on one day's notice, it can normally be scheduled in the next day's newspaper. Also, copy can easily be changed, allowing advertisements to be tailored to fit ever-changing market conditions.

- **Low cost.** An advertisement in a local newspaper is usually lower in both absolute cost and cost per thousand in comparison to other types of media.

Continuous advertising

Continuous advertising refers to the practice of keeping the amount of advertising relatively constant over time. This type is appropriate for hospitality operations with very stable volumes.

Flighting media scheduling

Flighting media scheduling involves a schedule that is set up in spurts and stops. Periods of blitz advertising are used, with no advertising between blitzes.

Pulsing advertising

Constant low-level flow of advertising with intermittent periods of blitz advertising.

- **Good coverage.** Newspapers reach all demographic segments in a geographic area.

- **Can be used for coupons.** Newspapers allow for the use of coupons, which can increase volume and provide the information necessary for evaluating advertising effectiveness.

In general, newspapers are a valuable form of media for local hospitality and tourism firms. Advertisements will reach a broad audience at a relatively low cost. However, newspapers also have the following disadvantages:

- **Short life span of the advertisement.** Newspapers generally have a one-day life span because they are published on a daily basis.

- **Wasted coverage.** Advertisers pay to reach the total number of newspaper subscribers, many of which are not in the target market based on demographics or lifestyles.

- **Clutter.** There is a lot of competition for the reader's attention within the newspaper. It is easy to have an advertisement buried amid other advertisements, decreasing readership and effectiveness.

Magazines offer these advertising advantages:

- **Quality reproduction.** Color photographs reproduce particularly well.

- **Long life span.** Through pass-along readership, magazine advertisements are seen by more people and have a longer life span than that of newspapers and other media.

- **Audience selectivity.** Some magazines are aimed at the general population, but through the use of regional and metropolitan editions as well as selective market magazines, advertisers can pinpoint specific target markets. This is especially true of city magazines.

- **High information content.** Magazines provide ample space to cover detailed topics and supply a good deal of information.

In general, magazines offer better reproduction than newspapers and allow marketers to segment on a regional basis. However, magazines have the following disadvantages as an advertising medium:

- **Long lead time for ad placement.** Magazine publishers require advertisers to adhere to closing dates far in advance of the distribution date. This does not allow for immediate changes of layout and copy if market conditions change rapidly.

- **High production costs.** Costs associated with magazine advertising are generally substantially higher than those for newspapers, including both absolute costs and the cost per thousand.

- **Lack of flexibility.** Magazines are not as well suited for local markets as newspapers, direct mail, or radio. Magazines are generally either regional or national in scope and are often of limited value to localized markets for hospitality and travel firms. Therefore, regional and national chains will normally find more benefit from advertising in magazines. However, city magazines, such as those placed in hotel rooms, do overcome this drawback.

Techniques for Successful Print Advertising

As with all types of advertising, no hard and fast rules exist for print media, but guidelines can aid in management decisions. The following guidelines, developed over time, are generally accepted within the advertising community.

First, every effort should be made to attract the consumer's attention with the headline. Many print advertisements are ineffective because a large percentage of consumers skim through the pages and never read the entire advertisement. The headline must therefore get the attention of the reader and deliver the message.

Second, print advertising is more effective if visual components, such as artwork and photographs, are used. Photographs and artwork are both effective in magazines and newspapers.

Third, every effort should be made to keep the layout and copy simple and straightforward. Print readers are less likely to read an advertisement that looks crowded and contains many ideas. Instead, the advertisement should have one or perhaps two points and no more. Print advertising is an example of where less is more, and this means more effectiveness.

Fourth, print advertising lends itself to the use of coupons. Coupons serve to increase volume and can add value in assessing the effectiveness of print advertising media. Coupons should be designed as mini advertisements with all necessary information so that the consumer does not need to save the rest of the ad. Placement of coupons is important both within the advertisement and on the page on which the advertisement appears. They should be placed at the edge of the advertisement, and the advertisement itself should be at the edge of the page to make it easier to clip the coupon. Simple things such as coupon placement can dramatically increase advertising effectiveness.

Finally, when a given print advertisement has been effective, management should not hesitate to repeat it. The advertisement may seem old hat to the management of the hospitality or tourism firm, but many potential consumers have not seen the advertisement or do not recall it. Therefore, what has proven successful in the past should be repeated.

Developing Copy for Print Advertising

For some individuals, developing advertising copy is simple and easy; for others it is painful and frustrating. This section offers suggestions that make the task easier. Copywriting does not require the brains of a genius or the writing skills of a Pulitzer Prize winner. It simply requires looking closely at the consumer and the product–service mix.

The first step is to examine the product–service mix. What does the organization's product–service mix offer that is appealing to the potential consumer? It is important to avoid generalizations such as "good food" or "luxurious guest rooms." These phrases may be true, but how will consumers perceive them? Consumers will generally discount the adjectives, and they will not have the desired effect. Items that could distinguish the operation from others and give it a real competitive advantage should be listed. Emphasis should be placed on the tangible aspects of the product–service mix, such as the décor or service personnel. It is very important to try to make the intangibles seem more tangible. This will help the consumer remember the advertisement.

Second, it is important to talk directly with the potential consumer and discuss the benefits of purchasing from the hospitality or tourism company. What is the company going to do for the consumer? What specific benefits are offered? What specific needs are being satisfied? For example, an upscale restaurant appealing to the business community might advertise a "lightning lunch" or "express lunch" featuring a selection of menu items that could be served immediately. It is important to back this claim with a guarantee such as, "If your lunch isn't served within 15 minutes, it's free."

It is important for print advertising to attract the attention of the consumer and remain clear. Courtesy of Allied Domecq QSR.

TYPE OF HEADLINE	EXAMPLE
Direct-promise headline	You'll love our 42-item salad bar Your room will be perfect or you won't pay for it
News headline	Grand opening July 1
Curiosity headline	Who says you can't get something for nothing?
Selective headline	To all single women . . .
Emotional headline	Mother's Day—What have you done for your Mom lately?

TABLE 12.2 • *Examples of Print Headlines*

Third, the consumer benefits should be listed in priority order. Perhaps it is best to develop two or three advertisements around the top three benefits and translate them into headlines. Headlines can take many forms, as shown in Table 12.2.

Once the headline is developed, the copy for the remainder of the advertisement is written. It should reflect and support the headline and should be brief. This is not to say that long copy can never be successful. Instead, each word, each sentence, and each paragraph must say exactly what the copywriter wants it to say. All the words must count, driving home and supporting the benefits to the consumer. Writing, rewriting, and further editing are the key elements in developing copy that sells. Copy should be clear; nothing is worse than vague advertising copy. A vague phrase such as "fine food" is meaningless to the consumer. Copy should instead explain what this food will do for the consumer and how it will make the consumer feel. It is important to make the intangibles more tangible and to talk to the consumer in terms of how the product–service mix will provide benefits that are important to the potential buyer.

Print Advertising Terms

The following terms are commonly used in print media, although some apply to other media as well:

- **Agate line** is a measurement by which newspaper and some magazine advertising space is sold, regardless of the actual type size used. There are

14 agate lines to the inch. Therefore, if a manager wanted advertising space two columns wide and three inches deep, the firm would be charged for 84 agate lines (i.e., 3 inches deep × 14 agate lines = 42 for first column + 42 for second column).

- The **base rate** is the lowest rate for advertising in print media. This rate is for run of paper (ROP) and means that the medium, at its discretion, puts advertisements wherever there is space.

- A **bleed advertisement** is an advertisement that extends into all or part of the margin of a page. Rates for bleeds vary with the medium used. Most media charge extra for bleeds.

- The number of copies distributed is the **circulation**. *Primary circulation* includes those who subscribe, while *secondary circulation* includes those who read pass-along copies; secondary circulation is very difficult to measure. Some business publications are provided, often at little or no cost, to those individuals who qualify by engaging in a specific line of business (*qualified circulation*). For example, meeting planners typically receive publications targeted toward individuals who plan meetings. These publications are not available to the general public.

- The **cost per thousand (CPM)** formula is the oldest means for comparing media rates. For print, the cost per 1,000 units of circulation is calculated on the basis of the one-time rate for one black-and-white page.

- The number of times the same audience—listeners, readers, or viewers— is reached is the **frequency**. It is expressed as an average, since some people may see or hear an advertisement only once, while others see it a dozen times. Placing more advertising in the media currently being used, adding more vehicles in a medium currently being used, and/or expanding into other media, such as radio as well as newspapers, can increase frequency.

- The **milline formula** is used to determine the cost per line per million circulation and is used to compare the costs of advertising in different newspapers. The formula is (line rate = 1,000,000) / circulation = milline rate. The reason for multiplying by 1,000,000 is that larger figures are easier to compare. If the rates compared are quoted in column inches, this rate can be used in the formula instead of the line rate. The same rate—baseline or column inch—must be used for all newspapers compared.

- The number or percentage of people exposed to a specific publication is the **reach** and is usually measured throughout publication of a number of issues. It is the net unduplicated audience.

- The **volume rate**, or *bulk rate,* may be for total space, time used, or total dollars expended during a contract period, usually twelve months. As more advertising is done, unit costs decrease. Newspapers generally quote their rates in agate lines or column inches. Rates get progressively lower as the number of lines increases.

BROADCAST MEDIA

Broadcast media—radio and television—are distributed over the airwaves. The level of involvement is lower than with print media and other advertising mediums, as listeners or viewers can be very passive if they choose.

Radio Advertising

Radio advertising finds extensive use in the foodservice segment of the industry, and in most cases, it is extremely effective. Radio is able to develop a distinct personality for a hospitality or tourism operation, and it can reach consumers 24 hours a day. Radio advertising offers these advantages:

- **Personal.** Radio spots can be written so that they speak directly to the consumer.

- **Low relative cost.** The cost of radio is usually quite low for local advertising, especially when a package involving several spots is purchased.

- **Flexibility.** Radio copy can be changed quickly in response to rapid changes in market conditions.

- **Low production costs.** It is relatively inexpensive to create and produce radio advertising, since there is no visual element.

- **Audience selectivity.** Radio stations have specific formats that appeal to certain target markets. The demographics and psychographics of these markets can be matched with the profile of consumers that purchase the firm's product or service.

Radio advertising also offers some disadvantages:

- **Lack of visual appeal.** It is said that people "eat with their eyes," but this is not possible on radio. Extra effort must be made when developing the copy and sound effects for a radio commercial to stretch the listener's imagination. The commercial must "sell the sizzle."

- **Fleeting message.** Once the commercial has aired, it is gone. The listener cannot refer to the advertisement to check the price, phone number, or hours of operation.

- **Clutter.** The airwaves are filled with advertisements for other hospitality or tourism operations and for every consumer product and service imaginable. Given this noise, it is often necessary to maintain higher levels of advertising to achieve the desired effectiveness.

TECHNIQUES FOR SUCCESSFUL RADIO ADVERTISING. It is important to recognize that those listening to the radio are also engaged in other activities. They may be cleaning house, driving cars, working in the office, or playing at the beach, but they are doing something besides listening to the radio. Because listeners are not devoting 100 percent of their attention to the radio, commercials should be kept simple, focusing on one or two major ideas. It is not effective to bombard listeners with several ideas in each commercial; they simply will not remember these points. It is also important to mention the name of the hospitality or tourism operation and the benefit early in the commercial. Many consumers have a tendency to tune out commercials, but advertisers must work hard to make sure they hear at least part of the commercial.

Second, music should be kept simple, and complex lyrics should be avoided. Ideally, a jingle or short composition should trigger name recognition in the consumer's mind. Short and simple music aids in developing this recognition, especially if it is repeated as a musical logo in all radio commercials.

Third, the advertisement should suggest immediate action. Every effort should be made to get the consumer to act. Consumers will quickly forget the radio commercial, and unless the advertiser can encourage almost immediate action, the effectiveness of the advertising will be decreased.

Fourth, the advertisement should talk directly to consumers in a language and a tone that they will understand. The approach should be personal, much as if it were a conversation, albeit a one-way conversation. Many hospitality and tourism establishments, especially on the local level, have had success using live radio remotes. Live remotes are broadcasts from the hospitality or tourism operation. They often include live comments from radio personalities and are a good way to gain attention for the business. Commercials are often part of the live broadcast. These can be particularly effective if a dominant radio personality does the live remote and commercials. These individuals often have loyal listeners and can have a significant influence on them.

Finally, the copy for radio commercials should be written so that it makes the listener visualize the products and services. The use of jingles and sound effects helps give consumers a mental picture of the intended message.

TYPES OF RADIO STATIONS. The variety of choices in radio stations is very broad. Stations are typically classified as progressive; contemporary; middle of the road (MOR); news, information, and sports; talk; light music; classical; and country and western.

Progressive stations, sometimes called album-oriented rock (AOR), appeal to a young audience with contemporary musical tastes. Those who listen to this type of station tend to "think young" and listen to the less conservative music that this type of station offers its listeners. Contemporary stations offer a milder selection of rock music featuring current hits and sometimes specializing in specific types of rock such as light and classic rock. Middle of the road (MOR) offers as close to a mass appeal format as is offered by radio. This segment was at one time dominant, but its popularity has declined. It appeals to the middle demographic segments.

News, information, and sports radio stations have proven to be very popular in the morning hours since they attract those commuting to work. Talk-oriented stations appeal to an older audience and find their listeners in their homes during the day.

Light music stations offer a type of music that is sometimes called "background music." The sound is very relaxing and unobtrusive. This format has grown in popularity with the increase in the average age, which is the result of the aging of the baby boomers. Classical-oriented stations are not numerous, but they do attract a very upscale audience, one that many hospitality industry advertisers would find attractive. Even within major markets, there is usually only one classical station, as the format does not enjoy wide popularity. The country and western format is widely popular in all geographic sections of the country.

It is not possible to provide a detailed demographic profile of the type of listener that each radio format attracts. Rather, it is best for the individual hospitality manager to compare the listener demographics of the available stations with those the hotel or restaurant is seeking to attract. In this way, the best fit between the radio stations' listeners and the potential advertiser's target market segments can be achieved.[3]

SELECTING RADIO SPOTS. Radio spots can be purchased in a wide variety of lengths, ranging from 10 seconds to 1 minute. Special attention should be paid to (1) the number of spots, (2) the days the spots are broadcast, and (3) the times of day the spots are broadcast.

CLASSIFICATIONS	TIME	RELATIVE COST
Class AA—morning drive time	6 A.M. to 10 A.M.	High
Class BB—daytime	10 A.M. to 3 P.M.	Moderate
Class A—afternoon drive time	3 P.M. to 7 P.M.	Moderate to high
Class C—evening	7 P.M. to 12 A.M.	Low to moderate
Class D—night time	12 A.M. to 6 A.M.	Low

TABLE 12.3 • *Radio Time Classifications*

The number of spots purchased is important in achieving effectiveness in radio advertising. Consumers often require several exposures to the message before they begin to retain it. Repetition is critical to success in radio, as it is in all advertising. The days of the week selected are also important, for they suggest when the hospitality advertiser is seeking to promote business. For example, for an upscale restaurant, is early-week advertising more important, or should the focus be on traditional weekend dining?

The time of day must also be considered. Radio should reach the consumer at a time when a decision is being made or when the advertiser is seeking to stimulate demand. Table 12.3 shows the time classifications used by radio stations. The most expensive times are morning and afternoon commuting times. A hospitality advertiser should seriously consider these times, despite the increased cost, because they are likely to prove the most effective, especially for restaurants.

PRODUCING RADIO COMMERCIALS. Figure 12.2 illustrates a time guide for producing a radio commercial. This guide can, of course, be modified, but generally a commercial should consist of introduction, commercial copy, recap of pertinent points, and musical logo. The introduction usually consists of music and copy written to get the listener's attention. It serves the same function as the headline in a print advertisement.

The copy of the commercial is the real heart of the selling proposition. The copy should explain the benefits of purchasing the product to the consumer. The recap of pertinent points should repeat points that the consumer should remember, such as a special price or new hours of operation. Finally,

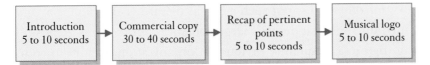

FIGURE 12.2 • *Production guide for a 60-second radio commercial.*

a musical logo is often used to fade out the commercial. Many advertisements allow 5 to 10 seconds at the end for the announcer to read a live segment of the commercial. This segment often calls for immediate action by the listener. Both of these approaches can be very effective.

RADIO ADVERTISING TERMS. As with other forms of media, radio has its own unique terms that are used within the industry. The following are terms commonly used in radio advertising:

- An **advertising spot** is a short advertising message on a participating program or between other radio programs that an advertiser does not sponsor. This is what most people call a *commercial.* Advertising spots may be (1) fixed, broadcast at a time guaranteed by contract; (2) preemptible, broadcast at a certain time unless bumped by an advertiser willing to pay a higher rate; or (3) floating, broadcast when the station decides (run of station, or ROS).

- **Drive time** is the early morning and late afternoon/early evening hours when radio has its largest audiences and highest rates.

- Another way of comparing media vehicles and programs is by referring to **gross rating points**. This rating can be calculated by multiplying the rating points (percentage of households, according to surveys, listening to a program or station at a particular time) by the number of times that program or station is heard or viewed during a given period (usually four weeks). Twenty percent of a potential audience equals 20 rating points.

- **Preemptible rates** are charges for broadcast advertising spots that may be bumped to different time periods by advertisers paying higher rates. They vary in cost by the amount of notice the station must give the advertiser before moving an advertisement; the longer the notice, the higher the rate.

Television Advertising

Each year, more and more hospitality and tourism organizations use television as an advertising medium. For some, the move into television brings

Advertising spot

A short advertising message on a participating program.

Drive time

The early morning and late afternoon/early evening hours when radio has its largest audiences and highest rates.

Gross rating points

Gross rating points compare media vehicles and programs. This rating is calculated by multiplying the rating points (i.e., percentage of households, according to surveys, listening to a program or station at a particular time) by the number of times that program or station is heard or viewed during a given period, usually four weeks.

Preemptible rates

Charges for broadcast advertising spots that may be bumped to different time periods by advertisers paying higher rates. They vary in cost by the amount of notice the station must give the advertiser before moving an advertisement: the longer the notice, the higher the rate.

increased sales; for others, it is not such a bright picture. Television is a very demanding medium, one that delivers large audiences but requires great skill in advertising. Before a hospitality or tourism organization decides to commit resources for television, very careful thought must be given to its impact on the remainder of the organization's advertising efforts. Advantages of television advertising include the following:

- **Large audiences.** Television, even at the local level, is able to deliver large numbers of viewers. It does not allow selectivity of target markets, but market saturation is high.

- **High impact of message.** The combination of sight, sound, and motion holds the potential for tremendous impact on viewers. This combination helps viewers to perceive the hospitality or tourism operation accurately and allows the advertiser to demonstrate the product–service mix.

- **Low cost per exposure.** Even though the absolute cost of television advertising is high, when it is divided by the total audience the cost per exposure is actually very low. In this respect, television is an efficient advertising medium.

- **Credibility.** Consumers perceive claims made in television commercials as credible. Television has had a major impact on society, and consumers assume only successful companies can afford to advertise on television. Also, many of these campaigns include celebrities that enhance the credibility of the commercial.

Television advertising has disadvantages as well:

- **High absolute cost.** For the vast majority of hospitality and tourism organizations, particularly small independent restaurants, the absolute cost of purchasing television time for commercials is simply too high. Venturing into television advertising necessitates such a drastic reduction in other advertising efforts that the final result is often a reduction in overall advertising effectiveness. This single disadvantage should be weighed with great care before television advertising is initiated.

- **High production costs.** To maintain credibility and attract the attention of viewers, firms spend significant money producing television advertisements. Some of the costs involved include celebrities, location and sets, and special effects.

- **Fleeting message.** Much like radio, once a television advertisement is broadcast, it is gone, and a potential consumer cannot refer back to it.

- **Clutter.** Television commercials tend to be grouped together at certain times each hour. This creates a certain amount of competition for the viewer's attention and interest. During prime time less time per hour is devoted to commercials than at other times, but commercial time is more expensive. Digital video recorders, such as TiVo make it possible for consumers to record shows, play them back while skipping commercials. This makes reaching targeted consumers with the advertising message even more challenging.

- **Low selectivity.** It may be difficult to segment the target audience as narrowly as preferred, leading to some amount of wasted coverage.

TECHNIQUES FOR SUCCESSFUL TELEVISION ADVERTISING. First, the visual aspect of the commercial must convey the message to the consumer. The sound should enhance the message, but the message should be able to stand on its visual impact alone. Television is a visual medium; the visual aspect is the key to successful television advertising. Messages that hospitality advertisers try to convey include the luxury and high living of upscale hotels or the fun people have at a restaurant. Showing people in the actual setting, not just showing the facilities or the food and beverages, does this.

Second, television advertising must capture the viewer's attention immediately, or it is doomed to failure. Facing facts, a manager must remember that consumers use commercial time to do other things, such as get snacks in the kitchen. If a commercial does not spark interest, people will not even watch.

Third, the advertisement should stay with one idea and repeat it within the time allocated. Television viewers see many advertisements throughout the day, and they cannot possibly remember all that they see and hear. Therefore, advertisements should focus on one key point. For example, Wendy's, Burger King, and Taco Bell achieved success with campaigns centered on themes that were simple, direct, and memorable. Every effort should be made to trim commercials that talk too much. The adage "A picture is worth a thousand words" should be a guide when evaluating television storyboards.

Fourth, television advertisements should accurately project the image of the hotel or restaurant to consumers. Much time, effort, and money have been invested in staffing and in the physical facilities in order to create an image; advertising should not muddy that image with poor television commercials. For example, one upscale restaurant operating in a major metropolitan area enjoyed a fine reputation and steady clientele. In an effort to increase sales during slow periods, management ventured into television advertising. After work with the creative staff, a storyboard and script were created, and production began. The result was a commercial that featured several still photographs of the restaurant depicting dining situations. These were well done, but the announcer was talking in a hard-sell tone and at a very fast pace. This commercial cheapened the image of the restaurant and, in fact, hurt sales figures.

TYPES OF TELEVISION COMMERCIALS. Advertisements can be creative and may use several different approaches. Television commercials can be categorized into six types:

1. **Demonstration.** Showing an actual part of the operation can be very effective. For example, preparing a certain menu item or banquet service in action within a hotel can help create an image.

2. **Straight announcer.** This involves the use of only one announcer offering the benefit and support.

3. **Testimonial.** This is a form of word-of-mouth promotion in which satisfied consumers talk about elements of the product–service mix.

4. **Problem solving.** This type of commercial offers a problem or series of problems and shows how a given hospitality or tourism operation can be the proper solution. For example, "How can you best celebrate your fortieth birthday? Why of course, come to the famous XYZ restaurant!"

5. **Story line.** Some commercials tell a story in 30 to 60 seconds. For example, imagine a young boy sitting in a classroom at school daydreaming about a hamburger and french fries. The visual pieces and the sound discuss the benefits of the products, and when the commercial concludes, school is out, and the young boy is eating his favorite fast-food meal.

6. **Musical.** Several successful television commercials have used the appealing visual effect of food products backed with appropriate music. If done well, this can be a very effective soft sell. Just as radio stations divide the day into different time classifications, so does television. The television time classifications are shown in Table 12.4.

TELEVISION ADVERTISING TERMS. Many technical terms are used by television stations and advertisers in business negotiations. The following are terms commonly used in television advertising:

- In a **dissolve** one scene fades into the next, with the two showing simultaneously for a moment.

- **Dubbing** refers to recording the sound portion of the commercial separately and then synchronizing it with the visual components.

- With a **fade in/fade out** the screen goes from black to the visual material, or the final visual shot is faded into black.

Dissolve

When one scene fades into the next, with the two showing simultaneously for a moment.

Dubbing

Recording the sound portion of the commercial separately and then synchronizing it with the visual components.

Fade in/fade out

The screen goes from black to the visual material, or the final visual shot is faded into black.

CLASSIFICATION	TIME	RELATIVE COST
Class AA	Daily, 8 P.M. to 11 P.M.	High
Class A	Daily, 7 A.M. to 8 A.M. Sunday, 6 P.M. to 8 P.M.	High to moderate
Class B	Daily, 4 P.M. to 6 P.M. Sunday, 2 P.M. to 5:30 P.M.	High
Class C	Daily, 12 P.M. to 4 P.M. Saturday, 6 P.M. to 4 P.M.	Low to moderate
Class D	Daily, 12 A.M. to 6 A.M.	Low

TABLE 12.4 • *Television Time Classifications*

- The term **fringe time** refers to the periods immediately before and after TV prime time, 4 P.M. to 8 P.M. and after 11 P.M. in all time zones except the Central time zone, where periods run an hour earlier.

- A **network** is a link of many stations by cable or microwave for simultaneous broadcast from a single originating point. The stations may be owned by or affiliated with the network. Major networks are ABC, CBS, NBC, and Fox. However, with the increase in specialized stations because of the growth of cable and satellite television, the importance of the three major networks has declined. Other networks such as CNN, ESPN, Food Network, and more targeted networks have increased their impact on the television market.

- **Prime time** is the time period when television has the largest audiences and highest advertising rates. In the Eastern, Mountain, and Pacific time zones, it is from 8 P.M. to 11 P.M. In the Central time zone, it is from 7 P.M. to 10 P.M.

Fringe time

The periods immediately before and after TV prime time, 4 P.M. to 8 P.M., and after 11 P.M. in all time zones except the Central time zone, where periods run an hour earlier.

DIRECT MAIL

There are those who refer to direct-mail advertising as "junk mail." These individuals believe that direct-mail advertising is of little value and is not appropriate for the hospitality and tourism industry. These beliefs simply are not true. Direct mail can and does work for many hospitality and tourism advertisers. It is used to solicit group and banquet business. Most hotels routinely send direct-mail pieces describing guest room and meeting facilities to potential meeting planners and then follow up with inquiries and personal calls to generate leads from the mailing. Direct mail is also used to promote special events, such as holidays or special packages, and often to offer promotional discounts.

The advantages of direct mail can be summarized as follows:

- **Highly selective, low-waste coverage.** With direct mail, an advertiser can be very selective with the target market segment and can include only the very best potential consumers on the mailing list. Direct mail need not be junk mail addressed to "occupant" or "homeowner." The widespread use of personal computers has allowed even small hotels and restaurants to manage large databases and address lists that can then be merged with personalized letters.

- **Easily evaluated.** It is easy to monitor the effectiveness of direct-mail pieces by looking at inquiries and sales. Many firms include a postage-paid postcard for the prospect to use to inquire about additional information, which can be used to measure exposures and interest.

- **Short lead time.** It is relatively easy to produce and copy direct-mail pieces. Therefore, firms can keep pace with rapid changes in market conditions.

- **High information content.** There are no time or space limits, as is the case with other media. There are the limits of size or shape. Therefore, one can be very creative. The manager who develops the direct-mail piece has a great deal of control over the design, production, and distribution of the direct-mail efforts. Direct-mail pieces can contain detailed explanations and presentations.

The following disadvantages are associated with direct-mail advertising:

- **Poor image.** Direct mail suffers from a poor image in the minds of many consumers. Unless the piece is able to attract immediate attention, most consumers will not read it.

- **Clutter.** In recent years, there has been tremendous growth in the use of direct mail, especially in the area of direct-mail marketing of retail items. As a result, the number of direct-mail pieces that the typical consumer receives each day is increasing, and it is becoming more difficult to get the desired message to the consumer.

- **High cost per contact.** When all the costs associated with direct mail are added up, the total is often surprising to the advertiser. Included in these costs are mailing lists, printing, production of letters, envelope stuffing, and postage.

Techniques for Successful Direct-Mail Advertising

First, any direct-mail piece that achieves success must capture the potential consumer's attention. Many consumers throw out direct-mail advertising without opening it; others open it but do not read it. This is obviously a waste of a firm's money. A tried-and-true approach to direct-mail advertising is based on the AIDA principle (attention, interest, desire, action). If the advertising fails to motivate the consumer to act immediately, chances are that the advertising will be set aside and eventually forgotten. Consumer action is the goal of direct-mail advertising; action leads to inquiries, inquiries lead to prospects, and prospects lead to sales. Examples of copy written to spur action include "Act within 10 days and receive a free gift" or "Call today for reservations; only a limited number will be accepted for this special evening."

Special attention needs to be given to the layout and copywriting of direct-mail pieces. Generally, long paragraphs of copy should be avoided because most people simply will not read them. Research has shown that the more personal the appearance of the direct-mail piece, the greater the likelihood that the recipient will read it. Many firms doing small, selective mailings will personalize them with a regular stamp and/or envelopes that are addressed by hand. Both techniques usually prove to be more effective than using bulk rate postage and peel-off address labels.

If specific direct-mail pieces prove successful, an advertiser should run them again. The piece may seem old to the management of the hospitality or tourism operation, but to consumers, it will be new and different. If something works, there is no reason to change merely for the sake of change.

Finally, direct-mail efforts are often successful because of the creativity on the part of the advertiser. Taking a familiar object and putting it to new use can create dramatic results. For example, one restaurant used brown lunch bags instead of standard envelopes. The phrase "Are you still brown-bagging it?" was printed on the outside of the bag. Another restaurant used pieces that resembled parking tickets and put them on the cars parked in certain areas. Printed on the top of the pseudo-ticket was "Here's your ticket to a great lunch." Although, strictly speaking, this last promotion is not direct mail, it was very successful and used a direct-mail approach.

Artex International direct-mail pieces are successful at capturing the attention of potential customers. Courtesy of Artex International.

The Direct Marketing Association (DMA) offers a wealth of information that will be useful to any hospitality and tourism organization that is developing direct marketing materials. Additional information can be found at www.the-dma.org.

Mailing Lists

Maintaining mailing lists is critical to the cost-effectiveness and success of any direct-mail advertising program. Only names of potential consumers should be included, and names that are duplicated because several lists are used should be avoided. Both of these problems sound simple, but solving them is often easier said than done.

Mailing lists fall into two categories: in-house lists and external lists. The management generates in-house lists internally. These lists should include those who have patronized the hotel, restaurant, or tourist attraction or who have the potential to generate a significant amount of business. Many restaurants use the guest book concept very successfully. They place a guest book at the entrance and ask each individual to sign it. Another approach is to keep a large bowl at the host's stand into which guests may place business cards. The names and addresses provided by the guests become an excellent foundation on which to build a mailing list. Within hotels, it is relatively easy to build a mailing list based on registration information, as well as the contacts that are made by the sales and marketing staff.

External lists are obtained from companies that sell mailing lists based on demographics, socioeconomic levels, geographic areas, and numerous other variables. Costs of these lists vary depending on selectivity and size. Lists purchased externally should be guaranteed to be current. Reputable companies will guarantee lists to be 90 to 95 percent accurate and current. Mailing lists can also be purchased from clubs, associations, and other businesses.

One final word on direct-mail advertising: results may seem discouraging based on the total number of pieces mailed. Typically, the response rate on mail promotions is less than 1 percent. Anything more than 1 percent is very good, and more than 5 percent is outstanding. Consider a restaurant that sent a mailing to 20,000 potential consumers advertising a promotional item. A response rate of 1 percent would be 200, 2 percent would be 400, and 5 percent would be 1,000. As few as 200 extra covers can have a substantial impact on sales.

SUPPORT MEDIA

In addition to the major types of media discussed earlier, other forms of media are used by firms to support, or supplement, the media effort. This section covers three forms of support media: outdoor advertising, brochures and collateral materials, and specialty advertising.

Outdoor Advertising

Outdoor advertising has widespread use among those hospitality operations located near interstate highways, but it can be effective in other locations as well. One hospitality organization in a large northern city allocated a substantial portion of its advertising budget to outdoor advertising. The outdoor displays were both creative and somewhat risky, and the results were very successful. The advantages of outdoor advertising include these characteristics:

- **Low cost per exposure.** When the cost of producing and placing an outdoor advertisement is divided by the total number of exposures, the cost per thousand is extremely low.

- **High repetition.** Consumers who frequent a given route will see the outdoor advertising again and again. This repetition aids in recall and retention.

- **Ability to target location.** Outdoor advertising is particularly useful for hospitality and tourism firms in targeting customers looking for lodging, a restaurant, or some other type of travel service (e.g., car rental, tourist information, etc.) in the immediate area.

Also, the following disadvantages are associated with outdoor advertising:

- **Poor audience selectivity/high wasted coverage.** While the cost per thousand is low, outdoor advertising does not lend itself to reaching small target market segments. It is a mass-market method.

- **Legislation/local restrictions.** Beginning with the Highway Beautification Act in 1965, all levels of government have discussed and often have enacted legislation to limit and tightly control the construction of outdoor billboards and signs. The impact of legislation varies greatly among states and localities. Despite legislative efforts, on average, new billboards are twice as big as they were in 1965, and there are 50 percent more of them than 30 years ago. Today there are an estimated 450,000 billboards on federal-aid highways, compared to the 330,000 billboards that first inspired the act.[4]

- **Long lead time.** It requires considerable planning to use outdoor advertising. It takes time to create and display an outdoor advertisement.

- **Lack of flexibility.** Once outdoor advertising is in place, it is not subject to change without considerable effort and cost.

TECHNIQUES FOR SUCCESSFUL OUTDOOR ADVERTISING. Three simple strategies should govern all outdoor advertising. First, the copy should be kept brief and the print large. Those viewing outdoor advertising will be riding in buses, cabs, and cars or walking down the street. They focus their attention on the advertisement for only a few seconds, so the message must be brief. The message should be a maximum of five to seven words—the fewer, the better. Information such as the telephone number or hours of operation is not likely to be remembered and should not be included.

Second, a picture or illustration is often very helpful in gaining attention. The picture or illustration should convey the message and be used to provide clear name recognition. The best example is the McDonald's golden arches. The arches are used on most outdoor advertising for McDonald's. The visual image is easily recognized.

TYPES OF OUTDOOR ADVERTISING. Standard outdoor advertising consists of posters and painted bulletins. Posters are blank boards on which the printed advertising is mounted. Painted bulletins are more permanent signs on which the message is painted. Electronic signs placed in high traffic interior and exterior locations provide moving, eye-catching images presented in high definition resolution. Posters and painted bulletins and electronic signs are available in a wide variety of sizes. Painted bulletins are sold individually, and posters are sold by showings. A **showing** refers to the coverage of a market within a 30-day period, not the number of posters. A 100 showing is complete coverage of a market, a 50 showing is half of it, and so on. In some communities, ten posters might be a 100 showing, but in much smaller places, two posters could be a 100 showing. An **outdoor advertising plant** is a company that buys or leases real estate (where it erects standard-size boards) or rents walls of buildings. It then sells use of space at these locations to advertisers.

When renting posters, circulation, or the number of people who will see the board, should be considered. The length of time a passerby can see the poster clearly should be considered. Not all locations are good ones. The physical condition of the posters and painted bulletins should also be considered. Nothing will reflect more negatively on an advertiser than a poorly maintained board or one with its lights burned out.

Another type of outdoor advertising is referred to as *transit advertising*. This refers to advertising placed on vehicles used in transporting people or in public places that people encounter in their daily travel routines. For example, most cities sell advertising space on buses, taxis, and subways, as well as on walls in the stations where people wait for these forms of transportation.

Showing

A showing refers to the coverage of a market. A 100 showing is complete coverage of a market; a 50 showing is half of it.

Outdoor advertising plant

A company that buys or leases real estate (where it erects standard-size boards) or rents walls of buildings. It then sells use of space at these locations to advertisers.

Internet and Web Advertising

The use of Internet advertising has increased substantially in the past few years. Using Web sites, which attract tourists, or others that are part of the target market for a hotel, restaurant, or tourist destination, the advertiser is able to reach new potential customers via Internet advertising. The advantages of Internet advertising include the following characteristics:

- **Low cost per exposure.** When the cost of producing and placing an Internet banner advertising is divided by the total number of exposures, the cost per thousand is extremely low. It is important to place banner advertisements on Web sites that receive substantial traffic represented by individuals in the target market.

- **Easy to monitor click-through impressions.** Internet advertising allows advertisers to monitor the number of "hits" that an advertisement receives and then the number of individuals that "click through" to the advertiser's Web site to gather additional information. Normally, a click-through rate of 1 percent is considered a reasonable expectation. "Hits" can be misleading, as each graphic on a page may be counted as a "hit." A more accurate count is obtained by using "page views" or "page impressions." These terms refer to the number of times that a specific Web page has been requested by the server.

- **Can be highly targeted.** By selecting Web sites that have traffic that matches the target market closely, the advertising can be highly targeted.

- **Short lead time.** Once designed, internet banner advertisements can be placed very quickly and can be changed equally quickly.

- **Search engine optimization.** The leading search engines, such as Google or Yahoo use automated crawlers which search web pages for content, that is then reflected when a user does a search. Search engines may charge for this service, or may provide it without charge. Firms that specialize in optimizing your web site for search engines are readily available and represent a good choice for small operators with limited resources.

The following disadvantages are also associated with Internet advertising:

- **Clutter of banner advertising.** Often Web sites have a number of banner advertisements which creates clutter and reduces that effectiveness of any single advertisement. In addition, software which blocks advertising is readily available.

- **Low target market selectivity of some Web sites.** Web sites that attract a broad array of users may provide little selectivity for hospitality companies.

Brochures and Collateral Materials

Brochures are developed and used to supplement other forms of advertising, as well as personal selling efforts. Normally, **brochures** are used in direct-mail campaigns in addition to being placed in hotels, restaurants, tourist attractions, and tourist information centers. Other forms of **collateral materials** include meeting planner guides and video brochures. Hotels, cruises, and resorts use video brochures that provide a quick four- to six-minute tour of the property. However, written brochures are still the most common item for creating awareness and interest among potential consumers.

Brochures play a vital role in the advertising and promotional efforts of hotels, and they can be beneficial to restaurants and travel firms as well. They can be used in a wide variety of situations. It will not be possible to tell the entire story within a brochure, as there are space restrictions. The most important point to remember is to communicate your facility's positioning. It is imperative that you create and maintain an image in the consumer's mind. Once you have determined the type of positioning statement you want to communicate, you can move on to the key benefits and support that the brochure will communicate. The following guidelines will lead to more successful brochures:

- **Brochure cover.** First, the cover design is very critical. It should communicate where your property is located and your positioning statement. The cover is valuable space, and it should be used to convey your primary selling message and the key consumer benefit. The photograph used on the front cover should grab the attention of potential guests, capturing their interest.

- **Photographs.** All photographs should help to stretch potential guests' imagination. They should be able to see themselves in the setting. Photographs of activities are more useful than photographs of just the facilities. If you plan to use food in the photographs, use close-up photos of finished products, not just the ingredients. Avoid the use of standard types of photographs that are all too common in hotel brochures. These include the smiling chef standing beside the buffet table and service personnel serving food in a restaurant. Strive for a fresh approach.

- **Information.** Potential guests need information that will help them to better understand things about your product–service mix. The use of maps

Brochures
Developed and used to supplement other forms of advertising and promotion; used in direct-mail campaigns in addition to being placed in hotels, restaurants, tourist attractions, and information centers.

Collateral materials
Include printed materials such as brochures, meeting planner guides, or other material.

and/or graphics on the brochure helps the reader gain a better understanding of where you are located, as well as some specifics about the types of products and services offered. Basic information such as street address, Web site address, telephone number(s), and chain affiliation should also be included.

- **Copy.** Just as with any type of advertising, the copy used in a brochure must talk to the consumer in his or her own language and must speak directly in terms of important benefits. Here a professional copywriter may be useful. It is important to avoid clichés, as these will actually turn off potential guests.

Specialty Advertising

In addition to the basic media used by hospitality and tourism firms, **specialty advertising** materials bearing the firm's name and logo can be given or sold to a targeted consumer. There are literally thousands of specialty items, including pens, pencils, calendars, rulers, paperweights, jewelry, matches, programs, candy jars, travel bags, and T-shirts.

Here are some of the advantages of specialty advertising:

- **Retention.** If the item is of value or usefulness to the recipient, it is likely to be retained, and the advertising message is seen repeatedly.

- **Selectivity.** Most specialty items are distributed directly to consumers in the firm's target market. For example, hotel pens and children's cups in restaurants are kept by customers, and hotels, restaurants, and airlines all sell shirts and hats bearing the firm's name and logo.

- **Low cost.** When purchased in large quantities, many specialty advertising items can be fairly inexpensive per unit.

Here are some of the disadvantages associated with specialty advertising:

- **Image.** It is important to use items that are consistent in quality with the overall quality perceptions that consumers have of the firm. If the items are cheap, they will have a negative impact on the image of the firm.

- **Clutter.** Many firms distribute items such as pens and key chains. Firms must develop unique items that will be of some value to consumers.

chapter review

Summary of Chapter Objectives

This chapter covers the vast area of external advertising and promotional media. These media constitute an invaluable resource that, if managed properly, can generate increased sales and substantial profits. Managed poorly, these media will drain away advertising resources and leave little or nothing to show in return. As with all investments, management must evaluate advertising for its return on investment. The relationships between a hospitality client and an advertising agency involve both positive and negative aspects. Management should consider several factors when selecting an agency and should consider compensation practices within the industry.

Media selection involves several factors. These include the nature of the target market, the campaign objectives, the desired amount of coverage, and the activities of direct competition. Media plans must be developed to achieve maximum effectiveness. These plans must closely consider the target markets to blend the media to achieve the desired results. Media scheduling includes the following approaches: continuous, flighting, and pulsing advertising.

External advertising media include newspapers, magazines, radio, television, direct mail, outdoor, Internet, and supplemental advertising. Each of these media has its appropriate use, advantages, drawbacks, and techniques that are generally successful. An understanding of advertising terms allows a manager to communicate more intelligently with media and advertising agency personnel.

Key Terms and Concepts

Advertising spot

Agate line

Base rate

Bleed advertisement

Brochures

Circulation

Collateral materials

Continuous advertising

Cost per thousand (CPM)

Dissolve

Drive time

Dubbing

Fade in/fade out

Flighting media scheduling

Frequency

Fringe time

Gross rating points

Media planning process

Milline formula

Outdoor advertising plant

Preemptible rates

Pulsing advertising

Reach

Showing

Specialty advertising

Volume rate

Questions for Review and Discussion

1. What factors affect the selection of advertising media?

2. Discuss the media planning process. What are the steps involved?

3. What are the advantages and disadvantages of each of the major media types?

4. Cite and discuss techniques for successful print advertising and for developing copy for print advertising.

5. What are the methods of media scheduling? Which one do you consider the best? Why?

6. Compare and contrast the various types of media based on their respective characteristics.

7. *Assignment for class discussion:* Every city or town has its share of media that can be used for advertising.

   a. Discuss some of the media vehicles used by hospitality and tourism firms in your area.

   b. What similarities and differences exist among the different types of firms?

   c. How do the characteristics of these vehicles affect the firms' decisions?

   d. Contact some of the local media and ask them how they charge for advertising.

   e. In each medium, how much does it cost to produce a typical advertisement (i.e., the cost range), and what is the lead time to place the ad?

Notes

[1] David W. Nylen, *Marketing Decision-Making Handbook* (Englewood Cliffs, NJ: Prentice-Hall, 1990), p. G-150.

[2] Howard A. Heinsius, "How to Select Advertising Media More Effectively," in *Strategic Marketing Planning in the Hospitality Industry*, ed. Robert L. Blomstrom (East Lansing, MI: Educational Institute of the American Hotel and Motel Association, 1983), pp. 256–258.

[3] Harry A. Egbert, "Advertising for Hotels," ed. Robert L. Blomstrom (East Lansing, MI: Educational Institute of the American Hotel and Motel Association, 1983), pp. 280–284.

[4] The Environmental Working Group, http://www.ewg.org/reports/billboards/billboards.html, 2003.

chapter review

Case Study

Advertising Decisions for the Alexandria Inn

Bill Walker is a co-owner of the Alexandria Inn, an independently owned casual restaurant located in an urban area in the southeastern United States. The city in which the Alexandria Inn is located has a year-round population of 200,000 that increases to nearly 350,000 during the tourist season, which lasts for six months each year, with the peak being in the summer months. The restaurant has seating for 200, divided between three separate dining areas. An additional 45 seats are in the lounge area. There is currently no outside seating, although Bill has considered adding an outside dining area. During the most recent fiscal year, the restaurant had annual sales totaling $2.1 million, of which 70 percent was food, with the remaining 30 percent representing alcoholic beverages. There is a modest amount of offsite catering, which accounts for $125,000 annually.

The Alexandria Inn, which Bill and his co-owners developed as a mid-priced restaurant, competes with several national chains located within a two-mile radius. These chains include Macaroni Grill, Chili's, and TGI Friday's, all of which are quite successful. During the last year, Bill has noticed that each of these national chains has been much more aggressive in advertising and promotions. These and other regional and national chains are running advertisements on a continuous basis, both on radio and in print, as well as pulsating advertising on television. Most of this television advertising is during the period of high tourist demand. In addition to their use of advertising, these chains offer nearly constant promotions of one or more items on their menus, and are again more aggressive during the height of the tourist season.

Bill asserts that the target market for the Alexandria Inn consists of more than 125,000 people who live within an eight-mile radius of the restaurant. About 40 percent of the restaurant's business comes during the lunch period, and the largest demand during lunch is from individuals who work within two miles of the restaurant. Bill has cultivated a strong demand from several corporate office parks located near the restaurant. His strategy asserts that this demand is more consistent than catering to tourists. His goal is to keep a more even demand throughout the entire year, something that focusing on tourists as his primary target market would not allow.

Bill's dilemma is quite clear. Should he start to more aggressively advertise and promote the restaurant? If yes, where and how? The restaurant has an ongoing relationship with a marketing and public relations firm that Bill has worked with for the past three years. This firm creates and produces all of the posters, banners, and similar work used inside the restaurant. In addition, this same firm does all the menu design and production. Bill has been very pleased with their work, and the prices have been quite reasonable.

In recent weeks, Bill has been approached by both another marketing firm and a radio station soliciting his business. The marketing firm has promised a 10 percent discount on all design and production costs. The radio station is offering a commercial package that offers 20 percent more advertising time than regular advertising rates. In order to secure his business, the radio station is willing to tie future advertising rates to documented increases in business at the Alexandria Inn.

Last evening, Bill told his general manager, Chris Williams, that he felt overwhelmed and confused. At times like this he wished that his restaurant were part of a chain so that he could get some help with advertising and promotion. The two of them talked for a while about what to do. They developed the following questions, agreed to think about them, and will meet again in a week to consider options. What should Bill do?

Case Study Questions and Issues

1. As an independent restaurateur, should he start advertising?

2. How should he achieve his goal of increasing dinner volume by 10 to 15 percent?

3. How should he increase his goal of increasing lunchtime off-site catering by 10 percent?

4. He is being given the hard sell by the radio station sales representative; should he consider advertising in other media, such as print or television? Is direct mail an option he should consider?

5. His clientele is quite loyal, with approximately 60 percent of his customers being repeat customers. How can he best attract more business from this group while bringing in first-time guests?

6. Only about 10 percent of his business comes from tourists visiting the area. Should he advertise to attract this market? If so, how?

Courtesy LEGOLAND® California. LEGO, LEGOLAND, the LEGO and LEGOLAND logos and the brick configuration are trademarks of the LEGO Group and are used here with special permission. © 2004 The LEGO Group.

Sales Promotions, Merchandising, and Public Relations

Chapter Objectives

After studying this chapter, you should be able to:

1. Understand the concept of sales promotion and its role in marketing strategy.

2. Compare and contrast the various types of sales promotions and the advantages and disadvantages associated with their use.

3. Explain how to manage sales promotions.

4. Outline the concept of merchandising.

5. Discuss the concept of public relations and its role in marketing strategy.

6. Describe the various public relations techniques.

Chapter Outline

(continues)

5. **What role does marketing play within your company?**

Targeted marketing is critical to the success of the hotel, but only if supported by equally effective customer service. The hotel has a detailed marketing plan and budget designed to create awareness of the hotel's new image and the enhanced food and beverage venues.

6. **If you could offer one piece of advice to an individual preparing for a career in the hospitality and tourism industry, what would you suggest?**

Develop a passion for the industry by gaining a variety of hospitality experiences including a background in business management and marketing. The industry has unlimited potential for creative, enthusiastic individuals with self-motivation and excellent communication skills.

industry profile

INTRODUCTION

The hospitality and tourism industry is a people-oriented business. Hospitality operations promote hospitality, yet hospitality cannot be purchased, cannot be traded, and does not appear on the menu. Hospitality is intangible, yet it is absolutely necessary for success. When service personnel project the spirit of hospitality, the results can be dramatic: increased sales, increased profits, increased consumer satisfaction, and, yes, increased employee satisfaction and motivation. Hospitality and tourism companies also sell atmosphere, convenience, entertainment, escape, and social contact. All of these are related to the spirit of hospitality and are equally intangible. All deserve consideration as promotable items.

SALES PROMOTIONS

Historical Perspective on Promotions

Retail stores first started offering trading stamps to consumers with purchases in the late 1800s. Thomas Sperry and Shelley Hutchinson offered their S&H Green Stamps to various retailers with the idea that they could be redeemed for merchandise at a central distribution point. This concept continued until the use of trading stamps peaked in the 1960s, with many grocery stores, gas stations, and other retail establishments participating. Then, in response to high inflation and the energy crisis in the 1970s, the popularity of trading stamps began to wane. Consumers were more interested in actual cost savings than in sales promotions or premiums such as trading stamps. Trading stamps all but disappeared by the 1980s, until a similar concept was adopted by the airline industry: frequent-flyer programs.

Much like trading stamps, the objective of frequent-flyer programs is to reward consumers in relation to the amount of products or services that they purchase. Trading stamps were distributed based on the amount of money a customer spent, and frequent-flyer miles are currently distributed based on the number of miles a customer travels. This type of nonprice promotion, or premium, has been adopted by other sectors of the hospitality and tourism industry. Hotels offer frequent-guest programs, and restaurants offer frequent-diner programs. In addition, many hospitality and tourism firms have formed relationships around the trading-stamp concept. For example, if you stay at a

WYNDHAM | REWARDS^{SM}

Frequent-customer programs are effective for building repeat business. Courtesy of Wyndham Worldwide.

Marriott hotel or rent a car at Avis, you can earn frequent-flyer miles for United Airlines. Credit card companies, such as American Express, have developed broad-based mileage and merchandise credits in cooperation with airlines, hotels, and retailers. Nearly all credit card providers have adopted some type of mileage program, with American Express Membership Rewards being the most popular.

Frequent-customer programs have become very popular as a means for firms to build repeat business and brand loyalty. However, these programs do have some drawbacks. For instance, frequent-diner programs can be inexpensive to maintain, but the start-up costs can be high.[1] Also, a great deal of time and effort is required to plan the program's structure and benefits. Customers find ways to "cheat" the program, and restaurants risk alienating customers when changes are made to the programs. Finally, customers may get bored with the program, and it could become difficult to track customer visits and points over time. And, in the case of airlines or hotels, customers redeeming points could displace paying customers during periods of high demand.

Role of Sales Promotions

Sales promotions

Sales promotions include marketing activities other than advertising, personal selling, and public relations that attempt to stimulate consumer demand and increase sales. Sales promotions seek to accomplish several broad objectives and can be used for several reasons: to increase consumer awareness, to introduce new products and services, to increase guest occupancy and customer counts, to combat competitors' actions, to encourage present guests to purchase more, and to stimulate demand in nonpeak periods.

In recent years, most companies have devoted an ever-increasing percentage of their budgets to sales promotions and have reduced the percentage devoted solely to advertising. **Sales promotions** seek to accomplish several broad objectives and can be used for several purposes:

- **To increase consumer awareness.** This is the first step in attracting new guests or customers. To attract a guest, one must first stimulate interest and a desire to act. Advertising seeks to increase awareness as well, but sometimes it takes a targeted promotion to turn that awareness into consumer purchasing action.

- **To introduce new products and services.** Every hotel and restaurant launches new products and services. The best way to ensure that the target markets are aware of these products and services is to initiate a special promotion to draw attention to them. When McDonald's or Taco Bell launches a new product, it supports the introduction with extra advertising and special promotions designed to promote trial of the new product. Merely introducing the new product or service to the target markets is not enough; you need to create interest, encourage trial purchases, and stimulate future demand for the new products and services.

- **To increase guest occupancy and customer counts.** With increasing competition in many markets, one of the few avenues for market share growth is to take business away from the direct competition. To accomplish this, it is necessary to feature promotions that offer consumers a better deal or greater value than they can receive elsewhere. Promotions are used to spread the word to potential guests.

- **To combat competitors' actions.** If the direct competition is gaining market share at the expense of your hotel or restaurant, you may be forced to match their promotion or to add one of your own with a new twist. For example, Marriott International was among the first hotel companies to offer a frequent-guest program. This program proved to be so successful that competing hotel chains were forced to offer frequent-traveler programs to compete with Marriott. Each company offered a slightly different program, seeking to gain a competitive advantage and therefore promote brand loyalty.

- **To encourage present guests to purchase more.** Total sales can be increased by packaging (bundling) different products and services at a total price that is less than the cost of purchasing the components separately. Promotions can also be used to encourage guests to trade up to more expensive products and services by offering a discounted price on the more expensive product or service. The primary purpose is to increase sales by encouraging present guests to purchase more.

- **To stimulate demand in nonpeak periods.** All hospitality and tourism operations have periods when demand is weak. Promotions can be used to increase weekend business for a business-oriented hotel or stimulate offseason and shoulder-season business at a resort. Within the food service segment, promotions can be used to increase sales during periods of the day or days of the week when demand is slow. For example, some restaurants stimulate early evening business by offering a discount to senior citizens who dine between 5:00 and 7:00 P.M., when business is often slow. They take advantage of the fact that seniors usually try to dine earlier and are often more conscious of the price–value relationship. Early dining promotions directed at this target market are often quite successful.

The ultimate goal of all forms of promotion is to stimulate attention, interest, desire, and action (AIDA). Sales promotions are most effective as short-term inducements to purchase a particular brand. As such, they can lead to desire and action, but sales promotions are normally not as effective as long-term strategies.

Types of Sales Promotions

Firms use two common strategies within the broad sphere of sales promotion: push promotion and pull promotion. A marketing manager uses the **push promotional strategy** when he or she wants to push the product–service mix through the service delivery system or channels of distribution. This approach encourages increased purchases and increased consumption by consumers. A **pull promotional strategy**, by contrast, is aimed at stimulating consumers' interest and having them pull the product through the channels of distribution. This, in turn, puts additional pressure on the retail outlets or hospitality facilities to supply the products and services most in demand by consumers. Descriptions of some of the more commonly used push and pull techniques follow.

TECHNIQUES FOR PUSH PROMOTIONS

- **Point-of-sale (POS) displays.** The displays usually seen at the counter of fast-food restaurants or as table tents in other types of restaurants, called **point-of-sale (POS) displays**, are designed to stimulate increased sales. Similarly, signs, banners, and table tents are often displayed by hotels in their lobbies, restaurants, and guest rooms.

- **Cooperative advertising.** A national chain normally provides advertising at the national, regional, and local levels to support its outlets. Also, franchisees will often receive financial assistance with local advertising, in addition to the chain's national advertising, as part of the franchise agreement. This practice is called **cooperative advertising**.

- **Advertising materials.** To encourage the local property to run advertising, the national chain will supply camera-ready advertising materials as well as prepared radio commercials.

- **Traditional and electronic collateral material.** Many firms supplement their other promotional efforts with materials such as brochures, flyers, or directories of other outlets within the chain. Beyond the traditional print collateral materials, firms use Web-based promotions to communicate with current and prospective customers.

Push promotional strategy

A marketing manager uses the push promotion when he or she wants to push the product–service mix through the service delivery system or channels of distribution. This approach encourages increased purchases and increased consumption by consumers.

Pull promotional strategy

Pull promotion is aimed at stimulating the interest of consumers and having them pull the product through the channels of distribution. This puts additional pressure on the retail outlets or hospitality facilities to supply the products and services most in demand by consumers.

Point-of-sale (POS) displays

These displays, usually seen at the counter of fast-food restaurants or as table tents in other types of restaurants, are designed to stimulate increased sales.

Cooperative advertising

Cooperative advertising involves two or more firms, one of which is often a national or regional chain, working together to sponsor an advertisement that provides benefit to all parties involved. Franchisees often participate as a second firm.

- **Convention and owners'/managers' meetings.** National chains use these meetings as a method to introduce new products and services to those who will be working in the individual units. These meetings are used for sales and service training.

TECHNIQUES FOR PULL PROMOTIONS

- **Sampling.** This technique can be used very effectively by food service managers. For example, samples of menu items can be distributed in the lobby area of a fast-food restaurant, thereby encouraging customers to try the new product. The goal is to convert this trial into regular use and repeat purchase. Within the lodging field, this technique is common as well. Meeting planners usually visit the potential hotel meeting site to "sample" the product and service before they make a final decision about the host hotel for an upcoming meeting.

- **Price reduction promotions.** Price reductions for a limited time can encourage trial and increase sales. Many business-oriented hotels that are normally busiest Monday through Thursday have used weekend price reductions to increase volume during otherwise slow periods. By promoting getaway weekends at discounted prices, these hotels built weekend business. Chains such as Marriott International, Hyatt Hotels and Resorts, and Hilton have used this approach very successfully. As with all promotions of this type, restrictions should apply and a definite time period should be stated. By contrast, recreation-oriented hotels, such as Great Wolf Lodges, charge higher prices on the weekend and offer discounts during the week.

- **Coupons.** These are certificates that entitle the consumer to receive a discount when presented at the retail outlet. **Coupons** can be distributed in newspapers or magazines, face-to-face, or via direct mail.

- **Combination offers or bundling.** This involves combining two or more products or services and offering them for less than what they would cost if purchased separately.

- **Premiums.** Extra merchandise or gifts that the hotel or restaurant gives away or sells at a very favorable price to guests are **premiums.** Examples include items such as hats, tote bags, glassware, and T-shirts with the logo printed on them. If the hotel or restaurant is able to cover the direct costs of the item, the premium is called *self-liquidating.* Some operations, such as Cheers in Boston or Emeril Lagasse's restaurants, have historically sold a considerable volume of logo merchandise.

Coupons

Certificates that entitle the consumer to receive a discount when presented at the retail outlet. The primary objectives for coupons are to stimulate trial of a firm's products and/or services by reducing the price, encouraging multiple purchases, and generating temporary sales increases.

Premiums

The tactic of giving away something or selling it at reduced cost is used to bring in new guests, to encourage more frequent visits by current guests, and to build positive word of mouth about the operation.

Contests

A contest requires some skill on the part of the participant to win prizes.

Sweepstakes

In sweepstakes, prizes are awarded solely based on chance.

- **Contests and sweepstakes.** The attraction of contests and sweepstakes is the highly desirable prizes that consumers can win. There is one minor difference between a contest and a sweepstakes. **Contests** require some skill on the part of the participant, while **sweepstakes** are based solely on chance. In all states, non-state-run lotteries are illegal. Lotteries consist of three elements: (1) the element of chance; (2) consideration, or giving something in return—for example, having to make a purchase in order to enter the sweepstakes; and (3) a valuable prize. To avoid illegal activities in most localities, it is necessary to eliminate one of these elements. If a purchase is not required to enter the sweepstakes, it is not classified as a lottery and is therefore legal in most localities. Contests, because they require some skill on the part of the participant, are not considered to be lotteries because there is no element of chance involved.

Commonly Used Techniques

The most common sales promotion techniques in the hospitality and tourism industry are coupons, sampling, premiums, and contests or sweepstakes. The following sections provide a complete discussion of these techniques.

COUPONS. The primary objectives for coupons are to stimulate trial of your products and services by reducing the price, encourage multiple purchases, and generate temporary sales increases.

Coupons offer several advantages:

- The coupon represents a tangible inducement, offering a savings or benefit.

- The price reduction is for a limited time and will not affect profit margins in the long term.

- Coupons can be used to accomplish specific objectives, such as boosting business during nonpeak periods.

- The maximum cost of the promotion can be calculated in advance. For example, past experience will allow you to estimate the percentage of the coupons likely to be redeemed.

Coupons have disadvantages as well:

- Some employees will be tempted to defraud the business. It is possible for them to take cash and substitute coupons. The higher the value of the coupon, the more supervision is necessary.

- Redemption rates are not easily predicted. Among the environmental factors that can affect the redemption rate are the value of the coupon, timing, and the activities of direct competitors. This is most common with new promotions because there is no prior history on which to predict future coupon redemption rates.

SAMPLING. Encouraging trial of new products is the primary objective of **sampling**. If consumers will at least try the product, they are more likely to purchase it in the future. Sampling is also an excellent way to persuade consumers to trade up to more expensive products and services. Sampling can be tied in with other types of promotions. For example, airlines routinely offer upgrades to first class for frequent travelers as a reward for their use of the airline. Not only is this a reward, but after flying in first class, travelers may decide to purchase first-class tickets for subsequent flights, thereby increasing sales and profits. Airlines help the traveler to rationalize this additional cost by awarding additional mileage points when the traveler flies in first class.

Sampling offers these advantages:

- Getting consumers to try the product is superior to getting them to look at an advertisement. It provides the consumer with instant feedback.

- It represents value to the consumer. Many consumers like to think that they can get something free. For example, including small portions of entree and appetizer items in the free offerings during "happy hours" is an excellent way to stimulate dining room business.

Some disadvantages of sampling include:

- Giving away products can become a major expense if it is done for an extended period of time.

- Samples of food products must be served when they are freshly prepared. If the products are to be held for any period of time, care must be taken to ensure that the quality can be maintained.

PREMIUMS. Premiums—items that are given away—are used to bring in new guests, to encourage more frequent visits by current guests, and to build positive word of mouth about the operation.

Advantages include the following:

- Most consumers like to get something for nothing or for a good price. It helps to build goodwill for your business, especially if the premium is highly valued by the consumer.

> **Sampling**
> Sampling encourages the trial of new products. If consumers will at least try the product, it is believed that they are more likely to purchase it in the future. Sampling is also an excellent way to persuade consumers to trade up to more expensive products and services.

- If the premium is clever or unique, it will build positive word of mouth as consumers tell others where they found it. When your logo is included on the premium, the message is always in front of the consumer.

Disadvantages of premiums include:

- Storing and handling the premium items can be a challenge if they are large or bulky.

- Employees and others may take the premiums for their own use or for their families and friends.

- The quality of the premium must be equal or superior to the image of the hospitality facility. If the premium does not work properly or breaks, it will diminish the image the consumer has of the facility or organization.

- Anticipating demand for premiums is difficult. If they are to be advertised as being available, it is imperative that a sufficient inventory be maintained so that consumers are not disappointed. Raising expectations and then not delivering will result in negative consumer perceptions.

CONTESTS AND SWEEPSTAKES.   These are being used with increasing frequency, especially within the more competitive segments of the industry such as fast food. They are designed to increase the number of customers and build market share, often at the expense of the competition.

Advantages of contests include the following:

- Consumers are more involved in the process because there is some element of skill and thinking required, thereby presenting an opportunity to create and support a more lasting positive image in the consumer's mind.

- Those who enter have already shown an interest in your products and services and are more likely to purchase them. This eliminates the potential for chance winners who do not usually purchase the product.

Disadvantages of contests include these:

- There can be some difficulty in judging entries because the criteria are often subjective. Those selected to judge must take the responsibility seriously, because the contestants will be serious about the outcome.

- Often the rules and guidelines for the contest are lengthy and may turn off potential participants.

The advantages of sweepstakes include the following:

- Entry is very easy; no purchase is necessary. The names and addresses of those who enter can be stored in a database and used in future direct-mail advertising efforts.

- Because the rules are usually quite simple, attention can be focused on the prizes in advertising.

- Sweepstakes will attract more participants than contests because it is easier to enter. No skill is involved, and it takes little time or effort to complete the entry.

- Selection of the winner is easy and judging is not required.

Disadvantages of sweepstakes include these:

- The entry box may be stuffed. It is possible for a consumer to reproduce the entry blank and enter thousands of times. For this reason, the rules should prohibit mechanical reproduction of the entry forms.

- An individual's chances of winning the large prizes are very small, so people may get discouraged and not enter.

Managing Successful Promotions

When developing a sales promotion campaign, the marketer must consider several major aspects. First, it is necessary to determine the size of the incentive that has to be offered to get consumers to participate. The larger the incentive, the more likely it is to attract attention. Second, the firm must establish the conditions for participation. Hospitality and tourism firms often limit offers to certain times of day or days of the week. In addition, offers may require reservations in advance and depend on availability. Third, the marketer must determine the timing of the promotion, including its duration. Will it be combined with other promotions, such as advertising? Will it be offered during peak or nonpeak periods? How long will the sales promotion be available?

Finally, it is necessary to determine how consumers will be informed of the promotion, and to estimate the total budget for the promotion. Coupons are normally distributed by mail, and other promotions are advertised at the point of purchase or via some other media vehicle. Coupons can also be distributed via the Internet.

The hospitality industry trade journals are filled with terrific ideas for promotions. There is never a need to reinvent the wheel. Rather, simply modify the ideas that others have used successfully before. Like anything else managers do, developing a promotion calls for careful planning, execution of the plan, and evaluation:

1. **Select the target market for the promotion.** Analyze sales records to determine the most likely target markets for a special promotion, as these segments offer the greatest potential for increased sales.

2. **Establish specific objectives for the promotion.** Objectives should be very specific, detailing exactly what the promotion should accomplish. Desired results should be quantified.

3. **Select the promotional technique.** Based on the situation and the advantages and disadvantages of each of the techniques, select the one best suited to the situation.

4. **Brainstorm about the potential offer.** There are hundreds of excellent ideas. Make a list of those being considered and seek input from others. All potential offers should be examined carefully from two perspectives: the potential appeal to the target market and the potential sales increase in light of the projected costs and expenses.

5. **Create the promotional theme.** This is the area where you can be very creative. What will the promotional copy or tag line be? Does it capture the interest of potential guests? Can it be used both internally and externally in the promotion? For a promotion to achieve the maximum potential, it needs to be carried forward both outside and inside the operation. Externally, it should build business. Internally, it should create excitement among the staff and build morale.

6. **Develop the promotional budget.** A projection of the total anticipated costs should be prepared to include all internal and external costs. To be able to evaluate the promotion, all costs, both direct and indirect, must be measured. It is wise to project the impact on costs and revenues at several different levels of consumer participation.

7. **Select the advertising media and vehicles to support the promotion.** Based on your knowledge of the media, those that will best support the total promotional campaign should be contacted. Advertising space and time should be secured.

8. **Develop an implementation timetable.** Promotions require attention to detail so that all phases are integrated and implemented properly. To

accomplish this, a timetable is required. Specific dates should be established for each task. Assigning responsibility to a specific individual or team for the completion of these tasks will increase accountability.

9. **Conduct internal training for the entire staff.** Just prior to the implementation of the program, the entire staff should be briefed so that they are familiar with the details of the promotion. Items of interest are how long the promotion will last and how the details will be handled by the different members of the staff.

10. **Work the plan.** Put the promotional plan into action and follow the timetable.

11. **Monitor results.** Feedback should be followed very carefully and should be compared with the timetable. Are things progressing as planned? Is the level of consumer participation within the projected range? Are the staff members working as planned? Attention to detail is very important. All information collected should be retained for future use in other promotions.

Evaluating the Impact of Sales Promotions

There are several elements of a sales promotion that must be evaluated in order to determine the actual impact of the final promotion. The following is a brief description of the major elements.

ADMINISTRATIVE COSTS ASSOCIATED WITH CONDUCTING A SALES PROMOTION. Some costs are directly related to conducting a sales promotion, such as printing, mailing, and advertising. The firm should estimate these fixed costs prior to launching a sales promotion.

COST OF DISPLACED SALES. A certain number of customers would have consumed the service at the regular price. When these customers participate in a promotion, such as a coupon or some other form of price discount, the firm loses revenue equal to the difference in price multiplied by the number of consumers. For example, some consumers order pizza delivery from the same provider time after time. If the firm offers a $1-off coupon that is redeemed by 200 regular customers, the firm loses $200 in revenue.

ADDITIONAL REVENUE FROM NEW CUSTOMERS. One of the main objectives of sales promotions is to induce trial among new customers, with the eventual goal of having them become repeat customers. Any revenue received from new customers is positive and will offset the administrative costs and losses from displaced sales. For example, the pizza delivery restaurant may have had 200 new customers pay an average of $10 per order, resulting in additional revenue in the amount of $2,000. In that example, after accounting for displaced sales, this would leave $1,800 to cover the administrative costs of offering the promotion.

It is important for firms to consider all of these costs to determine the necessary budget, as well as the viability of a particular sales promotion. The elements listed earlier are short-term in nature and should be evaluated in conjunction with the potential long-term effects of having additional customers. The increase in revenues may be accompanied by a decrease in unit costs as the overall volume increases. In some cases, a hospitality or tourism firm may be content to break even or actually lose some money on a sales promotion in the short run in order to achieve its long-term objectives.

MERCHANDISING

When the consumer comes through the front door of a hospitality operation, management and the service employees should focus on satisfying that customer. Satisfied consumers tell their friends about positive experiences, engage in repeat purchase, and in doing so increase sales and profits. J.W. Marriott, the founder of the corporation that bears his name, believed that his top objective was to take care of his employees, who, in turn, would take care of the customers, resulting in increased sales and profits.

Hospitality is a form of retail business, and adequate effort should be made to merchandise hospitality services to consumers once they enter the establishment. All too often, the service employees show about as much enthusiasm for selling as for changing a flat tire. Instead of performing as professional salespeople, they often serve as little more than order takers. They saunter up to the table with a guest check in hand and ask unsmilingly, "Ya ready to order?" When asked a simple question such as how an item is prepared, the answer might be, "I don't know; I'll ask the chef." When they bring items to the table, they often ask, "Who had the roast beef?" while the plate is passed from one guest to the next. Sound familiar?

Missed Selling Opportunities

Lack of professional selling on the part of a service organization's employees results in lower sales and less-satisfied consumers. All of this is simply a matter of missed opportunities. For example, consider the following situation in which four friends were planning to have dinner at a restaurant. They were seated by the host, following this greeting: "Do you have a reservation?" After they had waited about five minutes for a server to approach the table, Sally appeared, presented each guest with a closed menu, and asked, "Would anyone like anything from the bar?" Each responded no, and Sally said that she would be back in a few minutes to take their dinner orders. She returned in a few minutes, asking, "You ready to order?" When a guest inquired about any special items or recommendations, Sally responded, "There isn't a special today; I guess the chef just wasn't in the mood. Everything on the menu is good. Can I take your order?" The guests then placed their orders, which Sally took without speaking, except to ask about the type of vegetable and salad dressing that each guest would like. What was wrong with this situation, and who is at fault?

Clearly, Sally failed to sell; she merely took the orders. She failed to use **suggestive-selling techniques** to recommend a round of drinks, a bottle of wine, an appetizer, or a specialty of the house. Simply stated, Sally failed to do her job, but the fault is management's, not Sally's. Management has the responsibility to recruit, train, supervise, coach, counsel, and motivate the service personnel. If they fail to do their jobs, management must accept the responsibility. Figure 13.1 summarizes the loss of potential revenue from the table that Sally serviced. The total potential lost revenue is $80 for the party of four. Although they might not have spent the entire $80, they might easily have spent an additional $10, $20, or $30. The point is that service people are salespeople. They must be taught to suggestive-sell, to increase the check averages, to deliver additional profits, and to ensure guests' satisfaction. If employees suggestive-sell, they have a 50/50 chance of being successful. However, if they do not suggestive-sell, the chances of success are nil. Suggestions for ways to effectively suggestive-sell are shown in Figure 13.2.

This example focused on a foodservice operation, but similar examples can be seen in other segments of the hospitality and tourism business. For

Suggestive-selling techniques

Suggestive selling occurs when a service provider actively promotes one product over another to a consumer (e.g., a front desk employee suggests an upgrade to the concierge level over a standard room when a guest checks in at the hotel).

Drink sales	4 @ $6.00	$24.00
Wine sale	1 bottle @ $28	$28.00
Trading up/suggestive selling a more expensive entrée or accompanying item	4 @ 2.00	$ 8.00
Dessert	4 @ 5.00	$20.00
Potential lost revenue		$80.00
Potential lost gratuity @ 15%		$12.00

FIGURE 13.1 • *Potential impact of missed selling opportunities.*

1. Develop a positive mental attitude. Not everyone will accept the suggestions, but all guests will appreciate the desire to serve and attend to their needs.
2. Do not try to manipulate the guest; simply make positive and upbeat suggestions.
3. Suggest favorite items or aspects of the product–service mix with which the employee is most familiar. This makes the suggestion more personal and sincere, increasing the chances of success.
4. Use props to support suggestive selling. For example, it is relatively easy to turn down an offer for dessert, but if a dessert tray is brought to the table and the server offers the right suggestion, sales of desserts will increase. Offering samples of wine will increase the sale of wine by the glass. Some restaurants offer "flights of wine" in which several small samples are provided at about the same cost as a glass of wine. Some guests will merely try the samples, but others will purchase additional wine after trying the samples.
5. Always make positive suggestions; always focus on the positive aspects of the product-service mix. If a guest makes a negative comment, acknowledge the comment, but try to turn the negative into a positive.
6. Always be attentive to guests' needs. Some will be very receptive to suggestive selling, but others will want speedy treatment with a minimum of extra conversation and suggestive selling. Do not use a "canned presentation" to suggestive-sell. Stay tuned to the guests' needs and vary the suggestive-selling presentations.
7. Never make excuses for why suggestive selling will not work or has not worked in the past.

FIGURE 13.2 • *Suggestions for effective suggestive selling.*

instance, cruise lines could encourage passengers to book higher-priced cabins, purchase trip insurance, or buy excursion packages for ports of call. Similarly, car rental agencies could offer promotions that encourage customers to upgrade their vehicles, extend their rental periods, or purchase additional rental services such as GPS navigation systems.

Training Guest-Contact Personnel

Management has the responsibility to recruit, orient, train, supervise, coach, counsel, and motivate service personnel. This is no small task, and it does not happen by accident. When recruiting, it is imperative that management view potential guest-contact employees as the lifeblood of the organization, for they can make or break the hotel or restaurant. Managers should seek to hire individuals who "come alive in front of the guest." Recruiters and interviewers should look for enthusiasm, a high level of empathy, good organizational skills, obvious ambition, high persuasiveness, experience, verbal and communication skills, and a "can do and will do" attitude. An example of a hospitality service firm that does an excellent job of recruiting frontline service staff is Southwest Airlines. In an industry plagued by blandness and sameness, Southwest Airlines has managed to create a unique product–service mix that has made it one of the most profitable airlines. This focus on customer service stems from their mission statement: "The mission of Southwest Airlines is dedication to the highest quality of Customer Service delivered with a sense of warmth, friendliness, individual pride, and Company Spirit."[2]

A wide variety of training methods can be used with guest-contact and service personnel, but the overall focus should be on the following four basics: product–service knowledge (cognitive aspect), physical skills (psychomotor aspect), attitude (affective aspect), and reassurance (affective aspect). Each of these is discussed in the following paragraphs.

PRODUCT–SERVICE KNOWLEDGE (COGNITIVE ASPECT). This refers to learned or memorized job knowledge, such as how specific menu items are prepared or presented, specific attributes related to guest rooms, or other ingredients of the product–service mix.

PHYSICAL SKILLS (PSYCHOMOTOR ASPECT). These are learned physical skills, such as how to prepare a salad tableside or how to present, open, and pour a bottle of wine.

ATTITUDE (AFFECTIVE ASPECT). This is more difficult to teach because it is related to an individual's perceptions and beliefs, which are not easily changed. Attitudes affect the individual's behavior and motivation to provide service to the guest. Even if training in the first two areas results in exceptional employee performance, poor attitudes can and do result in unsatisfied guests. All employees must be trained, coached, counseled, and led by example in displaying the spirit of hospitality in serving guests. Bear in mind that in today's service economy, poor employee attitude is the number-one complaint of consumers. Consumers will tolerate minor problems, but they will not and should not be expected to deal with poor employee attitudes. The focus of training employees should be that the firm is able to tolerate any employee mistake except rudeness to a guest.

REASSURANCE (AFFECTIVE ASPECT). The service person should be trained in how to reassure guests. This can take many forms. For example, if a guest in a dining room orders an item, the server might respond, "That's our most popular item, you'll enjoy it," or, "All of our desserts are freshly baked, but that one is my favorite." Service personnel also need to be trained in how to effectively handle guest complaints. Some guests will complain no matter what you do to please them, but this group represents a very small minority. The vast majority of guests who complain have good reason, and every effort should be made to correct the error and make sure they are satisfied. It is wise to think of a guest's complaint as the tip of the iceberg, because for every complaint you hear, there are likely to be others that you do not hear. It is imperative that employees receive specific training on how to handle guest complaints. Part of the training should also provide guidance on how an employee can get the manager involved in resolving the complaint so that the guest is satisfied.

Training service personnel is of critical importance if internal promotion is to be successful. An employee must be aided in developing product–service knowledge, physical skills, a positive attitude, and the ability to reassure and effectively handle all guest situations.

Entertainment

Entertainment can generate increased sales and more satisfied guests. Entertainment in recent years has taken on new forms, including in-room movies and video games, large-screen television and multiscreen sports bars, various forms of disk jockey and music video entertainment, comedy clubs, Podcasts and Youtube. and other types of media entertainment. Many forms of entertainment are suitable, but live entertainment has long been regarded as the most powerful form.

Live entertainment is not the right choice for all hospitality and tourism operations, but it can be considered for some, based on the following factors:

- What impact will the entertainment have on volume, both in sales and in the number of guests?

- Is the physical layout of the facility suitable for live entertainment?

- How will the costs associated with live entertainment, such as payment to performers and increased advertising, be covered?

First, the impact that entertainment will have on sales volume should be analyzed closely. The break-even point should be calculated. Different methods to cover the costs of entertainment are feasible; these include charging higher prices for food and beverage to offset the increased cost, instituting a cover charge or a cover charge and minimum purchase, and covering costs through increased sales.

Second, the physical layout of the facility must be examined closely. Is the configuration of the facility suitable for live entertainment and perhaps for dancing? Many operators have learned that their facilities were simply too small for live entertainment—but not until after they had made the commitment.

When entertainment of any type is selected, the marketing concept should be the paramount concern. Management should focus on the needs and wants of the guests, not their own likes and dislikes.

Other Merchandising Techniques

Many other techniques should be considered. These include brochures and meeting planner guides, directories, flyers, and in-house signs, and tent cards. All of these techniques offer a great deal of potential when they are used properly and directed toward the appropriate target audience.

Brochures are not as easy to design as one might think. When brochures are placed in a rack with others, it becomes clear how difficult it is to design a brochure that will stand out from the others, capture the potential consumer's interest, and spark further inquiry or action. If a brochure is able to accomplish this, it truly is successful. Nykiel offers several suggestions for designing an effective brochure:[4]

- **Identify the facility, including logo.** It is important to emphasize the chain affiliation if one exists. The consistent use of logos is very important in developing an image.

- **Include descriptive facts on the facility.** Too many brochures use pretty faces and flowery copy and do not provide enough description of the facts related to the facility.

- **Provide map and directions for how to get to the facility.** This is particularly necessary if the facility is more difficult to find than those of direct competitors. A map showing mileage and travel times from major cities or other attractions is also useful.

- **Include basic information.** Be sure to include address, telephone number, Web site address (URL), and other pertinent information, such as hours of operation.

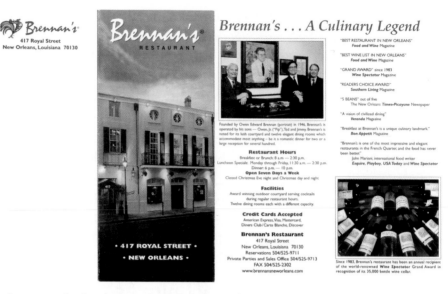

It is important for brochures to include information, not just pretty pictures and a logo. Courtesy of Brennan's Restaurant. The Brennan's logo is a registered trademark.

- **Provide person to contact for further information.** This might be the director of marketing, catering, or another department, depending on the purpose and intended target audience for the brochure.

- **List products, services, and amenities offered by the facility.** It is important to emphasize those aspects of the facility that will help to differentiate it from the competition.

- **List attractions and interesting things for guests to do while they are in the area.** Attract guests to your establishment by listing some of the main tourist attractions and activities in the region.

- **Provide transportation information.** This would include limousine service, car rental companies, airlines, and other forms of transportation that could be used.

PUBLIC RELATIONS

Public relations

Public relations is a nonpersonal stimulation of demand for a product or service by providing commercially significant news about the product or service in a published medium or obtaining favorable presentation in a medium that is not paid for by the sponsor.

The term *public relations* is widely misunderstood and is often misused within business, and the hospitality and tourism business is no exception. Every business interacts with a variety of publics: consumers, the general public, the financial community, the organization's employees, government, the media, suppliers, and many others. **Public relations** is the process by which the relationships with each of these publics is managed. All businesses must realize that the general public is affected by everything that companies say and do. Public relations are most obvious in the event of a disaster, such as a hotel fire, but public relations encompass many other facets, and can and should take a positive tone. The following section will discuss aspects of public relations, offering guidelines for effective public relations, techniques that can be used effectively to manage public relations, and a specific application of public relations: the opening of a hotel.

It requires great skill to effectively manage public relations, which is why many firms use external consultants and agencies to assist them with this effort. Public relations should be an integrated part of the overall marketing plan. Just as objectives, strategies, tactics, action plans, target audiences, implementation schedules, and methods for evaluation are a part of the development of a marketing plan, the same approach should be applied to public relations. Positive and beneficial public relations do not just happen by chance; they must be the result of individuals making it happen according to a plan. One of the basic needs of public relations is for the organization to provide accurate information. The development of a press kit can help to accomplish this goal. Here are the essential components of a press kit:[4]

- **Fact sheet.** This should contain basic information about the facility and the company that owns and operates it. The type of information necessary would include such things as property name, address, telephone number, names of contact personnel, a list of hotel facilities and amenities, and detailed specifications for meeting facilities.

- **Description of the local trading area.** Where is the facility located, and what is the surrounding area like?

- **Special features of the product-service mix.** Are there special aspects of the facility that should be mentioned, such as architecture, type of suites, type of food and beverages, or special services?

- **Specific details about the product-service mix of the facility.** This should provide information about each of the retail outlets.

- **Photographs.** Stock photographs should be maintained of both the exterior and interior of the facility, showing the facilities being used by guests.

- **Biographical sketch of the general manager.** Briefly describe the general manager and his or her background.

The press kit is useful when interacting with members of the media, as well as the other publics. Table 13.1 provides a list of members of the media with whom the public relations personnel should be familiar.

PRINT MEDIA	BROADCAST MEDIA
City editor	Station manager
Food editor	News director
Travel editor	News announcer
Finance editor	Station personalities
Style section editor	
Travel editor	
Business editor	
Feature columnists	

TABLE 13.1 • *Public Relations Media Contacts*

Public Relations Techniques

Public relations can be applied in several ways. Some of the more common techniques include the following:

- **News releases.** These should be routinely sent to the media, providing information about people and events of potential interest. Certainly, not all of the releases will result in positive coverage, but some will.

- **Photographs.** These will be particularly effective if they feature a famous personality or create a human-interest angle.

- **Letters, inserts, and enclosures.** Letters might be sent to government officials urging them to take some type of action. Inserts can be used as envelope stuffers in employee paychecks, or they can be sent as follow-up correspondence to guests or clients.

- **House newsletters.** These can be both internal and external but should be focused on a specific target audience. The purpose is to communicate positive images, increase sales, and influence public opinion.

- **Speeches and public appearances.** Members of the management staff should speak before groups with either professional or civic applications.

Special care should be taken to ensure that the speech is well prepared and delivered.

- **Posters, bulletin boards, and exhibits.** These help draw attention to your organization.

- **Audiovisual materials.** Videotapes, CDs, or DVDs can be distributed to the media and travel professionals.

- **Open houses and tours.** Inviting the media and travel professionals to your property can increase awareness and create interest.

Guidelines for Public Relations

It is difficult to provide a complete list of possible public relations techniques. However, the following guidelines , offer several good ideas for increasing the effectiveness of public relations activities:

- Always identify individual photographs when submitted so that the recipient does not play "editor's bingo" in guessing who's who. Send photos only of people involved, not the person making the announcement. In group shots, identify individuals from left to right, standing, etc.

- Do not fold, staple, crease, or otherwise mutilate photos, or write on the front or back with a heavy hand, thereby damaging the photo.

- Know the publications that you send material to so that you do not waste your company's money or the editor's time. Do not develop a reputation for sending out worthless material, or your important releases may one day be overlooked or discarded.

- Always provide pertinent information such as the company's name and address (not just the public relations or ad agency's name and address), retail price, or cost of the product so that the reader can evaluate its appeal and marketability, and so on. Stick to the facts—no puffery.

- Do not send too many releases at one time and then complain that the publication did not select "the most important one." If one is more important from a marketing standpoint, send it separately or properly identify it. It is really best to space out releases. Few publications maintain files of releases, since they receive hundreds each week.

- Be brief and provide a summary of the release so that it can be judged quickly (and properly) by someone who is not an expert in your field.

Complete information can be briefly stated without reams of company history!

- Do not threaten editors with loss of advertising if they do not run your items or bait them with promises of advertising if they do.

Public relations requires careful planning and attention to detail. Unlike advertising, in which the sponsor controls the content and the timing of the message, public relations requires coordination with many other parties. These parties do not have the interests of the hotel or restaurant as their primary objective. Table 13.2 provides an example of a timetable developed to plan the public relations for the opening of a new hotel. It should be noted that the plans provide a framework around which more specific action plans and responsibilities can be developed. This schedule begins six months before the hotel opens, at which time the announcement of construction plans and the groundbreaking ceremony will have been completed.

Evaluating Public Relations

As with the other promotional program elements previously discussed, it is important to evaluate the effectiveness of the public relations effort. In general, public relations programs are effective because they cost little (in both relative and absolute terms), are not subject to the same clutter as advertising and sales promotions, and have the ability to generate interest in a firm's product or service. Also, when the source is credible, well-managed public relations programs can improve the image of the firm. However, the firm does not determine the message that is sent to consumers because there is no exchange of money, and the publicity can be negative.

The public relations efforts of firms need to be evaluated to ensure an effective long-term program. The following is a list of possible methods that can be used to evaluate these programs:

- **Personal observation.** All members of a firm should take an active interest in the image that is being portrayed by the media. Both positive and negative publicity should be conveyed to proper authorities within the organization. Some companies hire public relations firms or designate employees to be responsible for this task.

- **Public opinion surveys.** Firms can conduct their own studies of public opinion, or purchase the results of syndicated research performed by independent agencies. These studies enable firms to track their progress over time.

150–180 DAYS BEFORE OPENING	60–90 DAYS BEFORE OPENING
1. Hold meeting to define objectives and to coordinate public relations effort with advertising; establish timetable in accordance with scheduled completion data. 2. Prepare media kit. 3. Order photographs and renderings. 4. Begin preparation of mailings and develop media lists. 5. Contact all prospective beneficiaries of opening events. 6. Reserve dates for press conferences at off-site facilities.	1. Launch campaign to local media and other media with a short lead time emphasizing hotel's contribution to the community, announcement of donations and beneficiaries, etc. 2. Send third and final progress bulletin with finished brochure. 3. Commence behind-the-scenes public tours. 4. Hold hard-hat luncheons for travel writers. 5. Set up model units for tours.
120–150 DAYS BEFORE OPENING	**30–60 DAYS BEFORE OPENING**
1. Send announcement with photograph or rendering to all media. 2. Send first progress bulletin to agents and media (as well as corporate clients, if desired). 3. Begin production of permanent brochure. 4. Make final plans for opening events, including commitment to beneficiaries.	1. Send preopening newsletter (to be continued on a quarterly basis). 2. Hold soft opening and ribbon-cutting ceremony. 3. Hold press opening. 4. Establish final plans for opening gala.
90–120 DAYS BEFORE OPENING	**THE MONTH OF OPENING**
1. Launch publicity campaign to national media. 2. Send mailings to media. 3. Send second progress bulletin. 4. Arrange exclusive trade interviews and features in conjunction with ongoing trade campaign. 5. Begin trade announcement.	1. Begin broadside mailing to agents. 2. Hold opening festivities. 3. Conduct orientation press trips.

TABLE 13.2 • *Public Relations Timetable for a Hotel Opening. Source: Jessica Dee Zive, "Public Relations for the Hotel Opening,"* The Cornell Hotel and Restaurant Administration Quarterly, *Vol. 22, No. 1, p. 21. 1984.*

- **Use objective measures.** Firms or their representatives can simply count the number of impressions over a certain time period. More specifically, these impressions can be separated into positive and negative categories. Percentages can be calculated for each category as a percent of the total, and the ratio of positive to negative impressions can be examined as well.

Firms should use a combination of all these types of evaluation techniques. As more companies hire public relations firms and organize public relations departments, more emphasis will be placed on this activity. Public relations is no longer considered a passive practice that cannot be controlled by firms.

chapter review

Summary of Chapter Objectives

This chapter focused on the important aspect of promotions and public relations. The elements of the promotional mix were presented and a communications model was illustrated. The role of sales promotion was discussed, including increasing consumer awareness, introducing new products and services, increasing guest occupancy and customer counts, combating competition, encouraging present guests to purchase more, and stimulating demand in nonpeak periods.

The two basic types of sales promotion strategies are push and pull. Push strategies attempt to push the product–service mix through the service delivery system, while the pull strategy encourages increased purchases and consumption by consumers. Several common techniques were discussed, including coupons, sampling, premiums, and contests and sweepstakes. Recommendations for managing and budgeting for successful promotions were also discussed.

Merchandising techniques were also reviewed. A discussion of the lost revenue potential from missed selling opportunities was presented, as well as suggestions and recommendations for how these missed opportunities could be avoided. Specific material presented included suggestions for training guest-contact employees: product–service knowledge (cognitive aspect), physical skills (psychomotor aspect), attitude (affective aspect), and reassurance (affective aspect). Methods by which guest-contact employees could be trained were presented.

The broad field of public relations was introduced. Public relations involve the management of relationships with the publics with which the firm comes in contact. Specific material presented included the development of a public relations press kit as well as the most commonly used public relations techniques.

Key Terms and Concepts

Contests

Cooperative advertising

Coupons

Point-of-sale displays

Premiums

Public relations

Pull promotional strategy

Push promotional strategy

Sales promotions

Sampling

Suggestive selling techniques

Sweepstakes

Questions for Review and Discussion

1. What is the role of sales promotion?

2. What is AIDA? How is it used as part of the promotion mix?

3. What are several of the objectives of sales promotion? Which of these elements do you believe is the most important for an independent restaurateur? For a mid-priced hotel? Why?

4. What is the difference between push and pull promotional strategies? Use an example to illustrate the difference.

5. When and under what conditions would you recommend push and pull techniques? Why?

6. Cite and discuss the pros and cons of each of the major sales promotional techniques discussed in the chapter.

7. If you were given the job of designing and managing a sales promotion, how might you use the guidelines presented in the chapter? What would you do differently? Why?

8. What are the four skill areas in which guest-contact employees should be trained? Which of these, in your opinion, is the most important? Why?

9. Select a table-service restaurant in your area to visit as a customer. Using the merchandising techniques discussed in the chapter, assess how well the restaurant staff performed. What were their strengths and weaknesses? What could they have done differently?

10. What is public relations? What do public relations personnel do?

chapter review

Notes

[1] Melanie A. Crosby, "Rewarding Regulars: Frequent-Diner Programs Keep Customers Coming Back for More," *Restaurants USA* (September 1998), pp. 12–17.

[2] Southwest Airlines Web site, http://www.iflyswa.com/about_swa/customer_service_commitment/customer_service_commitment.html, December 2003.

[3] Ronald A. Nykiel, *Marketing in the Hospitality Industry* (New York: Van Nostrand Reinhold, 1983), p.130.

[4] Jacques C. Cosse, "Ink and Air Time: A Public Relations Primer," *The Cornell Hotel and Restaurant Administration Quarterly* 21, 1 (1980): 37–40.

chapter review

Case Study

Promotion at Princess Suites

Reginald Jones, director of sales and marketing of the 128-room Indianapolis Princess Suites, strongly subscribes to the 80-20 rule when it comes to marketing. He feels that 80 percent of his business comes from 20 percent of his customers. He has built solid relations with the firms and customers that represent 80 percent of his business. He has established numerous programs and incentives that result in repeat business from these key customers.

The first Princess Suites was built in 1994 outside of Cleveland, Ohio, and the chain has expanded to its current size of 64 hotels. These limited-service hotels offer a queen-size bed or two double beds, two televisions with remote control and 50-channel cable, and a fully equipped kitchen with a two-burner cooking surface, full-size refrigerator, microwave, coffeemaker, and cooking utensils. Also standard for each room is a sofa sleeper, dining table and chairs, and a free local paper. Princess Suites offers free local phone calls, broadband Internet connection, voice mail, access to a fax machine, a 24-hour coin-operated guest laundry facility, an outdoor swimming pool, and a fitness room.

The Indianapolis Princess Suites, located on the south side of Indianapolis, ran a 63.5 percent occupancy last year with a rack rate of $87 single/$92 double. The average daily rate for the past year was $74.21. They generally sell out on Tuesday and Wednesday nights and occasionally on Monday and Thursday. There is little all-suite competition except for a Mickey Suites located across the Interstate. Princess Suites offer the same amenities as Mickey Suites in order to directly compete with them. Princess Suites offers a complimentary breakfast as well as a complimentary beer and wine happy hour to all of its guests. Two full-service hotels, the Pacerd Inn and the Macron Hotel, are close, but Chris does not view them as direct competition. The Pacerd and Macron both have bell service, restaurants serving three meals a day, room service, and meeting facilities that are not available at the Princess Suites. Their rates are significantly higher than the Princess Suites rates, as evidenced by the latest shopping survey.

Reginald takes advantage of co-op advertising dollars offered by Princess Suites by advertising in *USA Today* and *BusinessWeek*. There is a listing in the AAA book, and he takes out a half-page ad in the Indianapolis yellow pages. The local cable channel has been courting him lately, but he feels that television and the local paper are not effective uses of his money. Reginald has been exploring billboard advertising, but he is not familiar with this medium and its effectiveness. The Princess Suites Web site is basic; it is not on par with the competition.

Princess Suites has created a Secretary's Club to reward secretaries when they book the hotel. Every 15 room nights booked at a net rate results in a $15 gift certificate to a local restaurant of their choice. Reginald allows local restaurants to put fliers in the guest rooms in exchange for $45 worth of gift certificates per month. He also purchases additional certificates from the restaurants as needed. Last year alone, he distributed over $1,200 worth of certificates to the Secretary's Club, which he sees as 1,200 room nights he would not have sold without the club.

Chris Wood, the GM of Princess Suites, feels that Princess Suites must develop a promotion which will result in increased sales on Friday through Monday, nights which the hotel rarely sells out and in general has low demand. The business traveler, representing the 80 percent group provides excellent volume during the week. The same is not true on the other days. Chris has challenged Reginald to develop a promotion that will increase weekend volume and increase occupancy and sales at the Princess Suites.

Case Study Questions and Issues

1. What steps might Reginald take to respond to Chris Wood's request for a promotion to increase weekend business?

2. How might Reginald develop a promotional strategy using the steps outlined in the chapter?

3. What would be reasonable financial results for the promotion? How did you determine these results?

4. What costs will Reginald incur in launching such a promotion?

5. How can Reginald ensure that the promotion will not adversely impact business from his current key customers?

- Many corporate companies seem to be booking large meetings in a much smaller time frame. It used to be where national sales meetings would be booked years in advance, but now we have large conventions book five to six months out.

- International market—Banquet catering menus are being revamped to cater to more international food items—meeting planners are requesting more custom menus or adding particular items to a meal function to meet the needs of their international group.

5. What role does marketing play within your company?

Marketing is used to create awareness and interest among potential guests. Mass marketing techniques are used to attract individual transient guests, and personal selling is used to obtain commitment from the group markets like associations and corporations.

6. If you could offer one piece of advice to an individual preparing for a career in the hospitality and tourism industry, what would you suggest?

Money isn't everything—go for a position or an opportunity that will open doors for you.

Be prepared to put in the hours!

industry profile

INTRODUCTION

In the competitive world of hospitality sales and marketing, the ability to effectively identify potential business, qualify the prospects, engage in personal selling activities, and eventually book the business is critical to the success of the property. The term *selling* is often used synonymously with the term *marketing*. Marketing encompasses all of the activities that are necessary in creating an exchange between a buyer and a seller. These activities include promotion, pricing, product design, and distribution. Personal selling is merely one component of the promotion mix, which refers to the personal communication of information to persuade a prospective customer to buy something (e.g., a product or service) that satisfies that individual's needs.[1] The range of activities that are under the umbrella of personal selling is quite broad. Sales managers communicate with clients and prospects by means of the telephone, personal sales calls resulting from appointments, cold sales calls without appointments, and contacts with clients at trade shows, professional meetings, and conventions.

Sales Roles

Sales jobs can vary widely in their nature and requirements, even within the same company or industry. This chapter focuses mainly on hotel sales, but the fundamentals and techniques can apply to any type of hospitality or tourism sales. One of the main factors that can be used to classify sales positions is the extent to which the salesperson is responsible for creating sales and developing new accounts. **Order takers** are salespeople who ask customers what they want or respond to purchasing requests. This type of salesperson is most common in organizations that have high demand for their products and services, or organizations that engage in a great deal of mass advertising and use the pull strategy for promotion. In other words, customers seek them out. **Order getters** are salespeople who are responsible for creating sales and developing new accounts. They still service their existing accounts, but they are also expected to use sales strategies to obtain new accounts.

Many resort hotels and luxury properties enjoy good demand and have many repeat customers. The salespeople in these establishments are able to spend more time in the office responding to inquiries and following up with repeat customers. The goal is to create a good mix of customers who will maximize the firm's potential revenue over the long run. Conversely, hotels that do not have high demand because of various components of their product–service mixes find it more challenging to obtain group business.

Order takers
Salespeople who attend to customer inquiries and repeat purchases.

Order getters
Salespeople who are responsible for creating sales and developing new accounts. They still service their existing accounts, but they are also expected to use sales strategies to obtain new accounts.

When there is excess room capacity, lodging facilities require salespeople to be good order getters and create sales. It is important to note that some hotels do not target group markets, and even with excess capacity, they might choose to have only one salesperson, who acts as an order taker.

Some firms employ both order takers and order getters to obtain a customer mix. For example, **telemarketing** systems use the hotel's telecommunication technology, and trained personnel conduct marketing campaigns aimed at certain target markets. Hotels advertise a toll-free number that can be used by customers to contact the hotel. When calls are received, they are sent through the proper channels. Transient customers can be handled by reservations, and group business can be directed to the sales department. Once the call is in the sales department, it can be determined whether to use an order taker or an order getter. Hotels that focus on group business tend to have separate toll-free numbers for the sales department.

A **sales blitz** is another type of personal selling activity that targets specific groups within a condensed time frame. A sales blitz can be done in person or over the telephone, and hotels will often use staff members from different departments within the hotel. The goal of most sales blitzes is to make a large number of sales calls in a short period of time, with the objective of generating as large a number of qualified potential buyers as possible. Blitzes are often used to requalify prior clients who have not booked any business for a year or more.

The importance of sales has increased as the competitiveness of the group meetings business has intensified. Today, through the efforts of the major hotel corporations and professional associations such as the Hospitality Sales and Marketing Association International (HSMAI), sales and marketing professionals employed within the hospitality and tourism industry are better trained than ever before. They have to be to remain successful.

Profile of a Successful Salesperson

What makes a salesperson successful? A profile of a successful salesperson would reveal several factors that contribute to the individual's success. Courtesy pays a big part in making an individual successful. It is imperative that the sales manager always strives to make certain that the client is satisfied. This means having to expend some extra effort or occasionally doing something that is not routine. It might even mean bending the rules or standard operating procedures to ensure client satisfaction. Courtesy also means being able to smile and handle a difficult situation even when those around you are angry or in a panic.

Telemarketing

The use of telecommunication technology to conduct marketing campaigns aimed at certain target markets.

Sales blitz

A selling activity that targets specific groups within a condensed time frame.

A second aspect in the profile of a successful salesperson is complete knowledge of the product–service mix that is being sold. The salesperson should understand every aspect of the operation and should be able to answer any questions that the prospect might raise. For example, hotel salespeople should be knowledgeable about all facets of the hotel, including items such as meeting-room setup, booking policies and procedures, weight capacity of freight elevators, audiovisual capabilities of the hotel, and food and beverage skills and talents of the hotel's staff. However, if the salesperson is not able to provide the information requested by a customer or prospect, the salesperson should know where to get the information, or refer the customer to the right person.

A third part of the profile is professional appearance and behavior. This does not mean that the individual needs to be a "pretty face." Rather, this requires professional clothing, such as business suits, and good personal grooming. First impressions are critical in selling, and professional appearance can be a real asset in establishing rapport with a prospective client.

The desire and willingness to work is a fourth characteristic in the profile of a successful salesperson. Only a small percentage of sales calls and contacts will result in sales or signed contracts. A successful salesperson must have the perseverance to keep going and to keep asking for the business, even when many others have said no. Keep in mind that if one call out of ten results in a signed contract, a sales manager has been told no nine times before making a sale. For this reason, when a prospect says no, the sales manager should say "thank you," knowing that the next prospect might say yes. A conversation with one of the leading salespeople for a major manufacturing company revealed an interesting philosophy when he stated, "I'm not in sales, I'm in rejections. I get rejected a lot more than I make sales."

Another quality that is a real asset in sales is organizational ability. Keeping in constant communication with dozens of clients and keeping all of the many separate details straight requires superior organization. Also, there are several contact management software programs such as Act, Maximizer, or Microsoft Outlook that make it relatively easy for sales managers to maintain profiles for each of their clients. In addition, contact management capability is often part of the sales and catering software used in hotels and other meeting facilities. The ability to recall names and faces is also important. When a salesperson meets clients, it is imperative to remember their names, the company they work for, and other pertinent details. Following up with trace dates and the details of each client's contract calls for superior organizational skills.

A final quality that is an asset to the successful salesperson is a strong personality. This does not mean that to be successful in sales, you must be extroverted and the life of the party. Rather, it means that you need to have some warmth, some empathy, and the ability to make others believe in and trust you. If prospects do not feel comfortable with the salesperson, it is very unlikely that they will make a purchase.

Several studies have been conducted with the purpose of identifying the characteristics or traits of successful salespeople. The results of one such study are shown in Figure 14.1.[2] Hotel sales and marketing is a dynamic environment in which to work. It is demanding and full of challenges, but the rewards are commensurate with the efforts required. In the hotel industry, salespeople are normally referred to as *sales managers*, and the person responsible for the sales function is referred to as the *director of sales*. In larger hotels, the director of sales reports to the *director of marketing*, and in some smaller hotels the two

---

Impression Criteria

Appearance—neat and clean-cut

Dress—conservative and in good taste

Demeanor—confident and with a sense of humor

Attitude—friendly and sincere, possessing a "consumer is number one" orientation

Voice and speech—talks to express and not to impress; has well developed listening skills

"Can do" Criteria

Grades—upper 25 percent of graduating class

Curriculum—tendency to take advanced and more difficult courses

Extracurricular activites—has contributed to organizations, held offices, and volunteered

Related work experience—part-time and summer jobs; internships

Career goals—interest in marketing and well developed reasons for this interest

"Will do" Criteria

Character—integrity, self-reliance, loyalty, idealism, principles

Motivation—drive, perseverance, sense of responsibility

Ability to get along with others—likes people, cooperative, has constructive attitude and maturity

---

FIGURE 14.1 • *Characteristics of successful sales personnel.*

positions are combined into a *director of sales and marketing*. The remainder of the chapter will explore aspects of hotel sales and personal selling.

SELLING TO GROUP MARKETS

Before a single telephone call or personal sales call is made, the sales manager must begin to develop a clear understanding of the nature of the buyer: the meeting planner. **Meeting planners** plan meetings that will be attended by all sorts of individuals who are part of a vast array of groups, from large national associations to small local civic groups. Many meeting planners, especially those representing large associations and companies, are very knowledgeable professionals. They usually know as much or more about the operation of a hotel than an entry-level sales manager. At the other extreme are those individuals who only occasionally plan meetings and whom the sales manager must educate, as well as sell. Such is the challenge faced by the sales and marketing team—selling to many different individuals, each holding the title of meeting planner. Chapter 3 covers some of the complexities of organizational buying behavior when dealing with large-volume sales and buying units composed of more than one individual.

If sales managers are to effectively sell to the meeting planner, several things are necessary. First, sales managers must thoroughly understand the product–service mix that they are representing. They must know everything or be able to find the answers quickly to questions raised by the meeting planner. Second, they must know how to sell. Selling is a skill that is first learned and then refined. Few individuals are born to be in sales; for nearly everyone, selling is a learned skill. Selling in the hospitality industry is just like selling in other industries, especially service industries. One must learn to sell effectively.

FAB Selling Technique

One of the most common approaches to selling is to focus on the benefits that a product or service offers consumers. In selling benefits, the salesperson relates a product's benefits to the consumer's needs by stressing its features and advantages. This technique can be referred to as the **FAB selling technique**. The *F* refers to product features, or the physical characteristics of the product. The *A* refers to the advantages, or performance characteristics, that will be of benefit to the buyer. And finally, the *B* refers to the benefit, or favorable outcome, that

Meeting planners

A meeting planner is someone who plans meetings that will be attended by all sorts of individuals. Meeting planners represent a vast array of different groups, from large national associations to small local civic groups.

FAB selling technique

One of the most common selling approaches that focuses on the benefits that a product or service offers consumers. The F refers to product features, or the physical characteristics of the product. The A refers to the advantages, or performance characteristics, that will be of benefit to the buyer. The B refers to the benefit, or favorable outcome, that the buyer experiences.

TYPE OF CHARACTERISTIC	DEFINITION	IMPACT ON LARGE SALES
Features	Describe facts, data, and product characteristics	Neutral or slightly negative
Advantages	Show product strengths in relation to competitors' products	Slightly positive
Benefits	Show how product meets the customer's needs	Very positive

TABLE 14.1 • *Summary of FAB Selling.*

the buyer experiences. In other words, salespeople take the product's features and demonstrate how they can be advantageous to the buyer, resulting in the end benefit that is being sought. Table 14.1 summarizes the components of the FAB selling technique. This technique will be described using a hotel as an example.

FEATURES. All products have physical characteristics such as price, shape, color, and size. Hotel services are no exception. In the past, many firms attempted to sell products and services based on features, until they realized that it was more effective to focus on the benefits provided by the product or service. Many hotels have front desks, guest rooms, restaurants, pools, meeting facilities, and parking lots. Consumers can fill their basic needs at any of these establishments, but those that are superior in terms of performance have a competitive advantage when it comes to benefiting consumers. Figure 14.2 provides a **property analysis checklist** that can be used to evaluate a hotel's basic features.

ADVANTAGES. Once the basic features are determined, it is necessary to compare these features with the features of competitors' offerings to assess a firm's strengths and weaknesses. This analysis provides salespeople with the information that they need to persuade buyers. The salespeople should focus on the firm's strengths or the advantages associated with the product and stress its benefits to the consumer. However, it is important to determine consumers' needs and the benefits that they are seeking. Hotel chains train salespeople to know the property's physical characteristics, but it is also necessary to train

Property analysis checklist

A form used to evaluate a hotel's basic features such as location, guest room accommodations, meeting facilities, general facilities and services, and transportation.

Location

Rural or urban; location within city or town

Type of area: industrial, agricultural, political

Accessibility by highway and major carrier; by membership

Facilities for sharing and overflow; attractions for free time

Guest Room Accommodations

Total number and amount that can be committed; when they can be committed

Types of rooms: singles, doubles, suites, etc.; special rooms: nonsmoking, handicapped-accessible

Rate schemes: rack rates, discounted rates (volume, time of purchase, etc.), upgrades

General Facilities and Services

Public dining and lounge facilities

Entertainment, recreation, and fitness facilities

Business or corporate services: faxing, copying, shipping, etc.

Other services: room service, valet parking, laundry, etc.

Meeting Facilities

Total number and dimensions of meeting rooms; possible setups

Location and dimensions of exhibit areas

Equipment: tables, podiums, audiovisual, etc.

Banquet rooms and reception areas

Outside Facilities and Services

Restaurants and tourist attractions

Sports and recreation facilities (e.g., golf, tennis, etc.)

Additional business services

Transportation

Mass transit and taxis

Rental cars, charters, and sightseeing vehicles

FIGURE 14.2 • *Property analysis checklist.*

- **Annual convention for the entire membership.** This meeting is usually the largest that the association will hold. It will often include exhibits, especially within the trade association market.

- **Board of directors meetings.** These are typically held three or four times a year and are often quite elaborate. The expenditures per attendee are higher than for other association meetings.

- **Seminars and workshops.** Associations provide continuing education for the members, and these meetings are held throughout the year.

- **Committee meetings.** Associations operate by means of a volunteer committee approach, and each of the committees may need to meet several times a year.

The decision-making process and long lead time for the association market can be quite frustrating for the hotel sales manager. This market segment is often assigned to the most experienced sales manager or the director of sales because that individual's additional experience will prove beneficial in working with this market segment. The meeting planners working with the larger associations are normally quite experienced and professional, so the hotel's representative must be equally knowledgeable and experienced. The decision making is scattered among several people within an association. For example, the meeting planner may decide where to hold small meetings and workshops, but decisions about larger meetings such as annual conventions normally involve the executive committee and/or the board of directors. For this reason, the sales manager must be prepared for a lengthy decision-making

Conventions and association meetings provide huge opportunities for hotels and restaurants. Courtesy of Gaylord National Resort and Convention Center

104 00492

process. The initial contact may be with the association meeting planner, but it may take several weeks or months before the board of directors makes a final decision concerning the location for a large meeting.

The lead time for planning meetings can also be quite long. For the largest of the national associations, it is common for the site of the annual convention to be selected five to ten years in advance. Even smaller associations typically plan their annual conventions one to three years in advance. This lead time creates some real challenges for the sales and marketing staff. Even if a large annual meeting is booked now, the revenue will not be realized for quite some time in the future.

An association often uses its annual convention as a revenue-producing event; the revenue is then used to fund some of the association's annual operating expenses. For this reason, associations are sensitive about such negotiable items as meeting-room rental, complimentary room policies, food and beverage prices, and, in some cases, room rates. Keep in mind that association attendees will be paying their own expenses to attend meetings and may be very sensitive about prices for guest rooms, suites, and food and beverages.

Another popular component of the association market is the **SMERF group**. SMERF stands for a combination of several market segments: social, military, educational, religious, and fraternal. SMERF groups tend to be nonprofit groups that have limited budgets and volunteer meeting planners (i.e., not professionals). Therefore, these groups tend to be very price-sensitive and do not spend as much on rooms or food and beverage as other associations and corporate groups. Some of the SMERF meetings are small, but the total number of meetings that the SMERF market segment generates makes the overall contribution significant. Also, the SMERF segment is important to hotels because these groups are willing to book rooms during nonpeak periods in order to get a lower price. This allows hotels to maintain a decent occupancy rate and keep more full-time employees.

CORPORATE MARKET SEGMENT. The **corporate market segment** is very broad and is widely solicited by hotels. The corporate market is quite different from the association market segment. The differences include needs and objectives, the type and number of individuals in attendance, and the lead time required. Corporations hold many more meetings than associations do. The meetings tend to be smaller, have a much shorter lead time, are less price-sensitive, are subject to quicker site decisions, and involve fewer individuals in the decision-making process.

Corporate meetings are attractive to hotels for several reasons: they are held throughout the year rather than being concentrated in certain periods or months, and they do not require as extensive a use of meeting rooms as the

SMERF group

SMERF is an acronym for a combination of several market segments: social, military, educational, religious, and fraternal. SMERF meetings are frequently held in conjunction with nonprofit groups that are often working with a very limited budget.

Corporate market segment

This market segment is very broad and is widely solicited by hotels. Corporations hold many more meetings than associations. The meetings tend to be smaller, have a much shorter lead time, are less price sensitive, are subject to quicker site decisions, and involve fewer individuals in the decision-making process.

association market segment. The typical corporation meeting involves fewer than 50 attendees. Types of corporate meetings vary widely, including the following:

- **Training meetings.** With the advent of new technology, corporations frequently hold meetings to train new staff and provide up-to-date training for current staff. This type of meeting is perhaps the most common. Many hotels located near the offices of major corporations will solicit this type of meeting on a continual basis.

- **Sales meetings.** Most corporations maintain a sales staff that meets on a frequent basis. These meetings serve both to provide information to the sales staff and to motivate them. This is an excellent type of meeting to solicit because the group is normally less concerned about price than other types of organization. The corporation is concerned about providing attendees with convenience and comfort.

- **New product introduction meetings.** When a corporation introduces a new product, it is often done with great fanfare. The meeting is likely to be attended by dealers, corporate sales staff, and the media. This type of meeting can be very extensive and very price-insensitive.

- **Management meetings.** Management staff often need to get away from the place of business to meet and discuss issues in a quiet environment, where they will not be interrupted by telephones and other office distractions.

- **Technical meetings.** Technical specialists need to meet to discuss items of mutual concern. This type of meeting is less elaborate than the other types of corporate meetings.

- **Annual stockholders meeting.** All publicly held corporations are required to have annual stockholders meetings that may be attended by a large number of individuals. Some food and beverage events associated with this type of meeting can be very extensive.

- **Board of directors meetings.** These are perhaps the most elaborate and expensive, and they often feature extensive food and beverage presentations. They also require more expensive and specialized meeting rooms within the hotel.

Meeting planning within corporations is typically spread among several departments. Larger corporations tend to have many meetings and may have established meeting planning departments. However, in most corporations, meetings are planned by people with other areas of responsibility, such as marketing or human resources; sometimes independent planners are used. The decision making is usually rapid and does not involve as many individuals as the association market does. If the meeting planner is not the final decision maker, he or she is usually highly influential.

In addition to business meetings, **incentive trips** are often planned for corporations' employees as a reward for outstanding performance. Incentive meetings tend to be held at resort properties in exotic locations and aboard cruise liners. In many ways, incentive meetings are similar to association meetings. For instance, location and climate are very important, and there is an emphasis on recreation and relaxation. Also, attendance is voluntary, spouses often attend, and the trips must be heavily promoted to encourage employees to perform well in hopes of "winning" a place on the trip. The lead time for planning incentive trips is a year or more, they last four to five days on average, and they can be attended by anywhere from 10 to 1,000 people (the average is around 100). Business-related meetings are normally scheduled during these incentive trips for tax purposes (participants do not have to report business trips as taxable income), but those meetings are often canceled or ignored by the meeting attendees. However, incentive trips do resemble corporate meetings in that the decision making is centralized, a master account is used for billing, service is important, planners are not price-sensitive, and there are established guarantees for rooms and meals.

Incentive trip

Corporations also plan incentive trips for their employees as a reward for outstanding performance.

DECISION FACTORS. The association and corporate markets are natural segments for the group business market in hotels because of their clear distinctions in meeting characteristics. In addition, sales managers need to understand the factors that are important to each meeting planner in selecting a facility. Table 14.3 contains a comparison of the factors considered important by meeting planners for the two types of meetings. Although it is important to deal with each meeting planner on an individual basis, these responses for the average planner provide a place to start. As you can see, there are differences in the factors that are most important for the various types of meetings. Corporate planners are most concerned about the quality of food, followed by the ability to negotiate rates and the number, size, and quality of meeting rooms. Convention planners are most concerned about the number, size, and quality of the meeting rooms and sleeping rooms and the ability to negotiate rates. Finally, association planners tend to be in less agreement as to the most important factors, but the ability to negotiate rates is among them. These planners are also worried about the meeting rooms, the quality of the food, and the cost of the facilities. The top four in rank are the same for the three types of meetings, but the factors differ somewhat in importance.

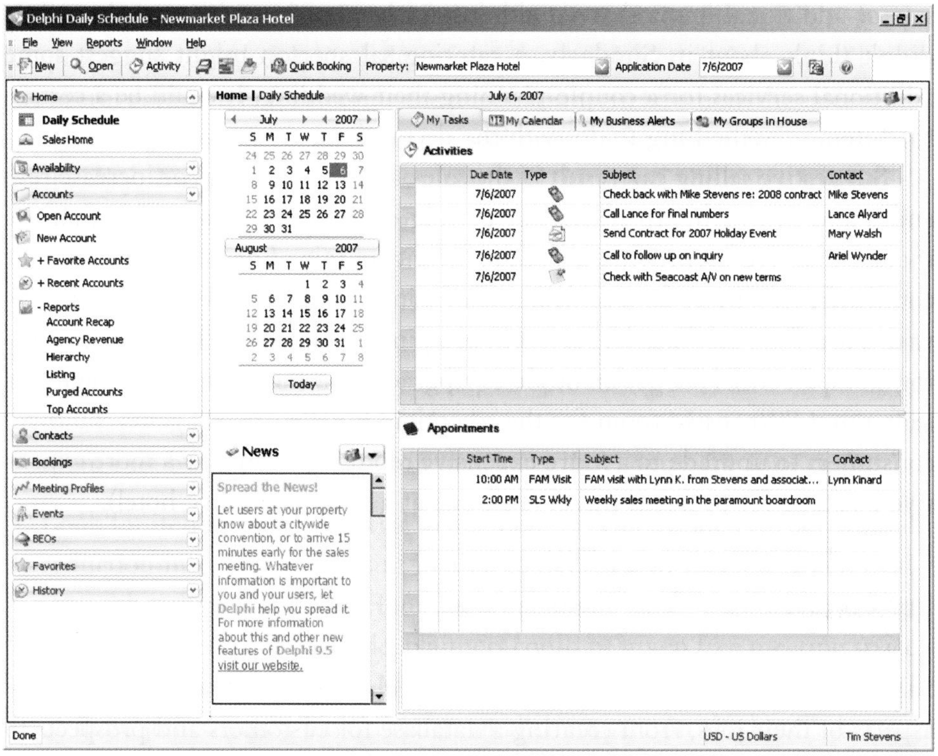

FIGURE 14.5 • *Delphi Screen. Courtesy of Newmarket International.*

programs for hotel sales; however, Delphi is currently the leader in market share for hotel sales departments. Salespeople in any industry using any computer software designed for sales will benefit from the automation of specific tasks and details.

ETHICAL ISSUES IN PERSONAL SELLING

As with most other areas of business, there is the potential for unethical behavior by salespeople. A firm's policies and practices should provide salespeople with a good understanding of acceptable behavior or conduct. When these policies are written and used in training, salespeople are more likely to uphold the firm's ethical standards. The following is a brief description of the most common types of unethical behavior among salespeople:

- **Sharing confidential information.** Salespeople and customers build close relationships over time that lead to the disclosure of confidential information based on trust. There is a potential for salespeople to share this information with a customer's competitors, either deliberately or accidentally, and so salespeople need to be cognizant of this possible breach. This behavior speaks to the character of the salesperson.

- **Reciprocity.** This refers to the mutual exchange of benefits between buyers and sellers. If a firm has a policy of reciprocity, it can be viewed as an exclusive tying arrangement, which is illegal. For example, a hotel might purchase supplies only from firms that agree to use its services for corporate travel.

- **Bribery.** Bribes in the form of monetary payoffs or kickbacks are unethical, if not illegal. Many U.S. firms find themselves at a disadvantage in international markets because their corporate policies and U.S. laws forbid them from offering bribes in countries where it is accepted as a normal business practice. Some meeting planners have coaxed hotels into giving them kickbacks from the room revenues for their meetings.

- **Gift giving and entertainment.** There is a fine line between gift giving, entertainment, and bribery. If the gift is being used to obtain the customer's business, then it amounts to a bribe. Gifts should be given only after contracts are signed, as a symbol of the firm's gratitude. Meeting planners are inundated with gifts in the form of hotel coupons and frequent guest points or even frequent flyer miles. Wining and dining clients is another popular sales technique. "Fam" (familiarization) trips provide meeting planners with free hotel rooms, airline travel, and entrance to tourist attractions or special events. In response, some firms have policies regarding the acceptance of gifts and entertainment by meeting planners and travel agents.

- **Making misleading sales claims.** In their pursuit of sales and quotas, salespeople may decide to provide customers or prospects with misleading information. It is not uncommon in hotel sales for a sales manager to promise meeting planners things that the food and beverage department cannot deliver. This results in some difficult negotiations at the time of the meeting. Another practice that is found in hotel sales departments is *blind cutting*. This refers to the practice of promising a certain quantity of rooms in a contract but then setting the actual room block at a lower amount to account for slippage or artificially high estimates from meeting planners.

- **Business defamation.** Salespeople sometimes make disparaging comments about their competitors when dealing with customers. Not only does this reflect poorly on the salesperson and the hotel, but in some instances it is actually illegal (e.g., slander or libel). It is very tempting to take a cheap shot at a competitor when making comparisons between properties or firms. However, salespeople should constrain themselves to answering specific questions with factual information.

The extent to which a firm is successful in deterring unethical behavior on the part of its employees will depend on how it treats employees who violate its policies and the level of support for the policies throughout the organization.

Summary of Chapter Objectives

This chapter has focused on a vital link in hotel sales and marketing: the sales and solicitation of group business. The initial section of the chapter examined the selling function and the attributes that make a salesperson successful. These attributes include courtesy, knowledge of the products and services, professional appearance, a strong desire for and willingness to work, and finally, a strong personality.

The role of the meeting planner was reviewed. Each meeting planner is different, and the needs and objectives of each group will be different, presenting a real challenge for the sales manager. However, common needs of meeting planners include costs, location, image and status, professional service, adaptability and flexibility, and professional operations and management. In working with a meeting planner, the sales manager should strive to build a solid working relationship based on trust and the hotel's ability to meet the meeting planner's needs and objectives. The sales manager should become a problem solver.

Selling effectively to group markets was discussed at length, especially as it relates to the needs and objectives of the association and corporate market segments. Characteristics of each of these markets were discussed and generalizations made. The FAB selling technique was introduced as a means of tying product features to advantages and benefits that can be marketed to prospective customers.

The personal selling process was presented, including four important steps: prospecting and qualifying, planning and delivering the sales presentation, handling objections, and closing the sale. Each step was explained and techniques provided for achieving the efficiency and effectiveness necessary to succeed. The importance of listening was discussed, and several options were presented for handling objections and closing the sale. Some additional personal selling tools, such as key account management, help salespeople expend their effort where the potential payback is greatest, and some tips were provided for improving negotiating skills. The use of information technology in sales was discussed.

Finally, the chapter discussed the ethical issues surrounding the personal selling process. There are many areas for potential abuse, including the sharing of confidential information, reciprocity, bribery, gift giving and entertainment, and business defamation. It is important for hotels and travel firms to establish a written code of ethical behavior that is conveyed to their employees during orientation and job training. There must be penalties for violating the firm's ethical standards, and the entire firm should support them.

chapter review

Pricing Objectives

Most of the possible **pricing objectives** can be grouped into four major categories based on goals related to financial performance, volume, competition, and image. These objectives are consistent with the organizational objectives discussed in Chapter 5 and must be considered when setting prices. A brief summary of the categories follows:

- **Financial performance objectives** focus on areas such as the firm's level of profitability, rates of return on sales and equity, and cash flow. Most large companies continually monitor these performance measures and find it easy to use these measures as benchmarks or objectives. It becomes relatively easy to see the role of price in these measures of firm performance.

- **Volume objectives** focus on sales and market share. These measures can be based either on the number of units sold or on the dollar amount of units sold. The sales measure looks at the firm individually, while the market share measure views the firm relative to the competition. Volume objectives are particularly common in the early stages of the product life cycle, when firms are willing to forgo profits in exchange for building long-term sales and market share. In addition, price competition stays strong in the maturity stage in an attempt to hold market share.

- **Competition objectives** focus on the nature of the competitive environment. A firm may want to maintain competitive parity with the market leader, widen the gap between itself and market followers, or simply survive. There is a good deal of head-to-head competition in the hospitality and tourism industry. For example, airline companies match each other's price changes so closely that the industry is often under investigation for price collusion.

- **Image objectives** focus on the firm's overall positioning strategy. A firm's position in the market is a direct result of its price–quality relationship as perceived by consumers. The hotel market can be segmented by price into economy, midmarket, and premium categories. Also, airline companies offer bereavement fares for emergency travel, and hotels offer discounts for guests with family members in the hospital. These discounts enhance the image of the firm.

Consumer Price Sensitivity

An important factor in setting price is **consumer price sensitivity**, or how consumers react to changes in price. Many situational factors affect a consumer's price sensitivity, and these factors can actually vary from one purchase decision to another. For example, a married couple may be less price-sensitive when choosing a restaurant for a special occasion than they would be if they were having a normal meal after work. The following summarizes the most common effects on consumer price sensitivity.[1]

PRICE–QUALITY EFFECT. In many situations, consumers use price as an indicator of a product's quality, especially when they do not have much experience with the product category. In this case, consumers will be less sensitive to a product's price to the extent that they believe higher prices signify higher quality. For example, overseas travelers often use price as a gauge of quality because they lack familiarity with the travel products in foreign countries. This pertains to all components of the travel product, such as hotels, restaurants, car rentals, and tourist attractions. This lack of information is one of the main reasons that consumers would use price as a signal of quality, along with the perceived risk of making a bad choice and the belief that quality differences exist between brands.

UNIQUE VALUE EFFECT. Consumers will be less price-sensitive when a product stays unique and does not have close substitutes. If a firm successfully differentiates its product from those of its competitors, it can charge a higher price. Consumers must remain aware of the differentiation and convinced of its value in order to pay the higher price. In essence, the firm's strategy is to reduce the effect of substitutes, thereby eliminating the consumer's reference value for the product. Resorts and health spas use this strategy by marketing themselves as one-of-a-kind properties. Similarly, many fine-dining restaurants use this approach and differentiate themselves on attributes such as the chef, the atmosphere, and/or the menu. Airline and car rental companies would have a more difficult time using this strategy because of the homogeneity of the products.

PERCEIVED-SUBSTITUTES EFFECT. Consumers become more price-sensitive when comparing a product's higher price with the lower prices of perceived substitutes for the product. Consumers must be aware of the other products and actually perceive them as substitutes. The prices for the substitutes help consumers form a reference price, or a reasonable price range, for the product. There are many perceived substitutes for products such as fast food, airline travel, car rentals, and hotel rooms. When there are a number of substitutes that consumers are aware of, there tends to be a downward pressure on price, resulting in a relatively narrow acceptable range for prices. For example, there are no significant price differences between products in fast-food restaurants or airline tickets for a popular route (e.g., New York to Chicago).

BROAD PRICING STRATEGIES

Economic value

Economic value equals the sum of a product's reference value and a product's differentiation value.

Reference value

The cost of the competing product that the consumer perceives as the closest substitute.

Differentiation value

The value to the consumer (both positive and negative) of any differences between a firm's offering and the reference product.

Skim pricing

This strategy involves setting high prices in relation to the product or service's economic value to most potential consumers. This strategy is designed to capture high profit margins from an exclusive segment of consumers that places a high value on a product's differentiating attributes.

Once a firm's pricing objectives are set, managers must identify the role that price will serve in the product's overall marketing strategy. Prices can be set high to restrict the firm's market to a limited segment of buyers, as in luxury hotels and fine dining restaurants (skim pricing); set low to attract buyers, as in economy hotels and fast-food restaurants (penetration pricing); or kept neutral to emphasize other aspects of marketing, as in midscale hotels and theme restaurants (neutral pricing).[2] Table 15.1 illustrates these strategies based on the relationship between price and economic value for the middle market of consumers. **Economic value** can be defined as the sum of a product's **reference value**, or the cost of the competing product that the consumer perceives as the closest substitute, and a product's **differentiation value**, or the value to the consumer (both positive and negative) of any differences between a firm's offering and the reference product.

Skim Pricing

A **skim pricing** strategy involves setting high prices in relation to the product or service's economic value to most potential consumers. This strategy is designed to capture high profit margins from an exclusive segment of consumers who place a high value on a product's differentiating attributes. Skim pricing is a preferred strategy when selling to the exclusive, price-insensitive market, and it results in higher profits than selling to the mass market at a lower price. For example, luxury hotels and resorts market hotel rooms with many amenities such as valet parking, laundry service, and golf. Most consumers are not willing to pay the higher prices associated with this level of service, but there is a smaller segment of consumers that places a high value on the additional amenities and will pay the higher prices. Similarly, upscale and fine-dining restaurants charge higher prices based on the menu, the

	RELATIVE PRICE	
PERCEIVED ECONOMIC VALUE	Low	High
Low	Neutral	Skim Pricing
High	Penetration Pricing	Neutral

TABLE 15.1 • *Strategies Based on Price and Economic Value.*

Luxury hotels and resorts add value to their offerings with amenities, such as golf. Courtesy Mobile Bay CVB.

ambience, the location, and the restaurant's reputation. In addition, many of the restaurants in this market segment offer valet parking.

Many service firms have limited capacity, and it may be necessary to maximize profits by managing supply and demand through higher prices. Skim pricing also tends to be used by firms whose variable costs represent a large portion of total costs and the product's price. There is little incentive to decrease cost per unit by increasing volume under this cost structure. From a competitive standpoint, skim pricing works best when a firm's product remains unique or is superior to competitive products in perceived quality. Once again, restaurants with good reputations, exclusive resorts, and airlines with limited business and first-class seating (especially on international flights) practice skim pricing.

Penetration Pricing

Penetration pricing involves setting low prices in relation to the firm's economic value to most potential consumers. This strategy works best on price-sensitive consumers who are willing to change product or service providers to obtain a better price. Firms using this strategy choose to have lower profit margins in an attempt to gain high sales volumes and market shares. Penetration pricing

Penetration pricing
This strategy involves setting low prices in relation to the firm's economic value to most potential consumers.

stays common among economy hotels that market to consumers who view the product as merely a place to sleep and have no need for additional amenities. However, firms must have the necessary capacity to accommodate the large volume in order to use this pricing strategy.

Most of the costs of providing the rooms in economy hotels are fixed. Normally, an economy hotel does not have a restaurant with room service or a concierge to help guests with travel plans. Similarly, quick-service restaurants do not have chefs, and food costs are relatively low. In both cases, the furniture and décor are fairly basic. The higher volume generated by the lower prices is expected to result in economies of scale and a lower cost per unit of providing the service. From a competitive standpoint, penetration pricing works best when a firm has a significant cost advantage over its competitors or when the firm is small and not considered a threat by its competitors. Charter airlines and small commuter airlines are examples of firms that can adopt a penetration pricing strategy and are not considered a threat by larger airline companies.

Neutral Pricing

Neutral pricing

This strategy involves setting prices at a moderate level in relation to the economic value to most potential consumers.

A **neutral pricing** strategy involves setting prices at a moderate level in relation to the economic value to most potential consumers. In other words, the firm makes a strategic decision to use attributes other than price to gain a competitive advantage (i.e., attributes related to product, promotion, and/or distribution). Another reason firms use this strategy is to maintain a product line that includes product offerings at different price levels. For example, many hotel chains have brands across all price categories such as budget/economy, mid-priced, upscale, and luxury. Therefore, one or more of their offerings will occupy the average price range with the basic amenities (i.e., low economic value) for full-service hotels. Franchising and the proliferation of chains in the hospitality industry often lead to homogeneous offerings with little differentiation and standard pricing across competitors in the same market segment.

A neutral strategy can be used by default, when a firm cannot use skim pricing or penetration pricing because of its cost structure or the market conditions. However, this strategy has become more popular with the growth in the value segment of consumers. In the hotel industry, many consumers do not want to pay high prices, but they do want some amenities such as restaurants and pools. Also, the Internet has simplified the information search process for consumers and it allows them to make quick price comparisons. For example, online travel agents obtain inventory from various companies and manage it based on the overall supply and demand for the product category and the market. Finally, a high price can actually be a neutral price when product value justifies the price to most potential consumers.

PRICING TECHNIQUES AND PROCEDURES

When management establishes prices, three approaches can be used, either individually or in combination with one another: cost-oriented pricing, demand-oriented pricing, and competitive pricing.

Cost-Oriented Pricing

As the name implies, **cost-oriented pricing** uses a firm's cost to provide a product or service as a basis for pricing. In general, firms want to set a price high enough to cover costs and make a profit. Two types of costs can be considered: fixed costs and variable costs. Fixed costs are those incurred by a company to remain in business, and they do not vary with changes in sales volume. For example, restaurants must invest in a building, kitchen equipment, and tables before they begin to serve customers. Variable costs are the costs associated with doing business, and they vary with changes in sales volume. For example, restaurants incur costs for food, labor, and cleaning that are directly related to the level of sales.

Break-even analysis can be used to examine the relationships between costs, sales, and profits. The break-even point (BEP) is the point where total revenue and total cost are equal. In other words, the BEP in units would be the number of units that must be sold at a given contribution margin (price-variable cost) to cover the firm's total fixed costs:

$$\text{BEP}_{\text{units}} = \frac{\text{Total fixed costs}}{(\text{Selling price} - \text{Variable cost})}$$

The break-even point in dollars can be calculated by multiplying the break-even point in units by the selling price per unit. Break-even analysis is a seemingly easy method for analyzing potential pricing strategies, but one must be careful to use only costs that are relevant to the decision so that the results are accurate.

Cost-oriented pricing

Cost-oriented pricing uses a firm's cost to provide a product or service as a basis for pricing.

Break-even analysis

Break-even analysis can be used to examine the relationships between costs, sales, and profits. The break-even point (BEP) is the point where total revenue and total cost are equal.

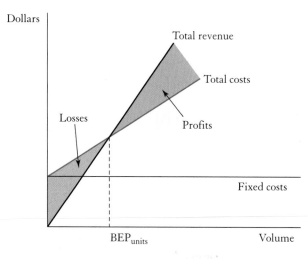

FIGURE 15.1 • *Break-even analysis.*

Figure 15.1 illustrates the relationships between costs, sales, and profits. As mentioned before, fixed costs are incurred regardless of sales. Therefore, they remain constant with changes in sales volume and are represented by a horizontal line. The total costs line intersects the fixed costs line where it begins on the vertical axis and increases with volume to account for variable costs. The total revenue line begins at the origin and increases with volume. The break-even point in units is the point where the total revenue line intersects the total costs line. When firms operate at volumes less than the break-even point, losses are incurred because total revenue is not enough to cover the total cost of producing and marketing the product. When volume exceeds the break-even point, firms will make a profit because total revenue exceeds total cost.

For example, suppose a family purchases a large home and renovates it for use as a bed-and-breakfast. The total fixed costs would be the $300,000 purchase price plus the $100,000 spent on renovations, or a total of $400,000. The owners estimate the variable costs to clean the rooms, restock supplies, and feed the guests at approximately $25 per day. If the owners were to charge guests $75 per night to stay at the bed-and-breakfast, the break-even point in units would be 8,000 room nights [400,000 / (75 − 25)]. If there were a total of 20 rooms and they obtained an average occupancy of 50 percent throughout the year, it would take 800 nights (a little over two years) to recoup their original investment. However, it is more likely that the purchase was financed over time, and the owners receive tax credits on the interest, expenses, and depreciation. Therefore, assuming the owners did not take salaries or hire additional workers, it is more likely that the yearly fixed costs are in the neighborhood of $30,000. The new break-even point would be 600 room nights [30,000 / (75 − 25)], which would represent 60 days at an average occupancy rate of 50 percent.

This example illustrates the benefit of using break-even analysis for setting the prices for new products. However, break-even analysis does not account for the price sensitivity of consumers or the competition. In addition, it is very important that the costs used in the analysis are accurate. Any changes in the contribution margin or fixed costs can have a significant impact on the break-even point. For instance, if the owners overestimated the price, and consumers are only willing to pay $50 a night, then the break-even point would change to 1,200 nights, or double the original estimate. Finally, the break-even formula can be easily adjusted to account for a desired amount of profit. The desired amount of profit would be added to the numerator (total fixed costs) and would represent the additional number of units that would need to be sold at the current contribution margin to cover the desired amount.

Cost-plus pricing is the most widely used approach to pricing in the industry. The price for a product or service is determined by adding a desired markup to the cost of producing and marketing the item. The markup is in the form of a percentage, and the price is set using the following equation:

$$\text{Price} = \text{ATC} + m(\text{ATC})$$

where:

ATC = the average total cost per unit and

m = the markup percentage / 100%.

Cost-plus pricing
Determining the price for a product or service by adding a desired markup to the cost of producing and marketing the item.

The average total cost per unit is calculated by adding the variable cost per unit to the fixed cost per unit. The fixed cost per unit is simply the total fixed costs divided by the number of units sold. For example, suppose a hotel has an ATC of $35 for turning a room and would like to have a 200 percent markup, which is reasonable for a full-service hotel. The selling price, or room rate, would be calculated as follows:

$$\text{Price} = \$35 + [(200 / 100) \times \$35] = \$105$$

This approach is popular because it is simple and focuses on covering costs and making a profit. However, management must have a good understanding of the firm's costs in order to price effectively. Some costs are truly fixed, but other costs may be semifixed. Semifixed costs are fixed over a certain range of sales but vary when sales go outside that range. In addition to the problem of determining the relevant costs, the cost-plus approach ignores consumer demand and the competition. This may cause a firm to charge too much or too little.

Target-return pricing is another form of cost-oriented pricing that sets the price to yield a target rate of return on a firm's investment. This approach is more sophisticated than the cost-plus approach because it focuses on an

Target-return pricing
Setting a price to yield a target rate of return on a firm's investment.

overall rate of return for the business rather than a desired profit per unit. The target-return price can be calculated using the following equation:

$$Price = ATC + (desired\ dollar\ return\ /\ unit\ sales)$$

The average total cost per unit is determined the same way as in the cost-plus approach, and it is increased by the dollar return per unit necessary to provide the target rate of return. This approach is also relatively simple, but it still ignores competitors' prices and consumer demand. For example, suppose someone wants to sell souvenir T-shirts in a tourist area of a popular destination such as the French Quarter in New Orleans. If he wants to make $30,000 a year, assuming the average total cost is $6.00 (cost per unit of T-shirts, cart rental, and license/permit) and he sells an average of 20 shirts per day, the price would be calculated as follows:

$$Price = \$6.00 + [\$30,000 / (20 \times 365)]$$

$$= \$6.00 + (\$30,000 / 7,300)$$

$$= \$6.00 + \$4.11 = \$10.11,\ or\ approximately\ \$10.00$$

The 20 shirts per day is an average, assuming some seasonality and variations due to weather. However, it is important to have accurate estimates for costs and sales in order to price effectively. In addition, the price should be compared with the competitors' prices in the area to make sure it is reasonable.

Demand-Oriented Pricing

Demand-oriented pricing approaches use consumer perceptions of value as a basis for setting prices. The goal of this pricing approach is to set prices to capture more value, not to maximize volume. A price is charged that will allow the firm to extract the most consumer surplus from the market based on the **reservation price**, or the maximum price that a consumer is willing to pay for a product or service. This price can be difficult to determine unless management has a firm grasp of the price sensitivity of consumers. Economists measure price sensitivity using the **price elasticity of demand**, or the percentage change in quantity demanded divided by the percentage change in price. Assuming an initial price of P_1 and an initial quantity of Q_1, the price elasticity of demand (ϵ_p) for a change in price from P_1 to P_2 can be calculated by:

$$\epsilon_p = \frac{(Q_2 - Q_1) / Q_1}{(P_2 - P_1) / P_1}$$

Demand-oriented pricing

The demand-oriented approaches to pricing use consumer perceptions of value as a basis for setting prices. The goal of this pricing approach is to set prices to capture more value, not to maximize volume.

Reservation price

The maximum price that a consumer is willing to pay for a product or service.

Price elasticity of demand

A measure of the percentage change in demand for a product resulting from a percentage change in price.

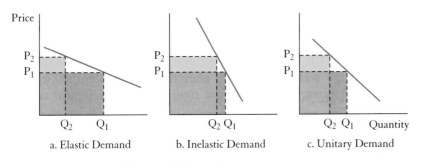

FIGURE 15.2 • *Price elasticity of demand.*

The price elasticity of demand is usually negative because price increases tend to result in decreases in quantity demanded. This inverse relationship between price and quantity demanded, referred to as the **law of demand**, is representative of most products and services. However, the demand for products and services can demonstrate varying degrees of elasticity (see Figure 15.2). The demand for products is said to be *elastic* ($\epsilon_p > 1$) if a percentage change in price results in a greater percentage change in quantity demanded. Conversely, the demand for products is said to be *inelastic* ($\epsilon_p < 1$) if a percentage change in price results in a smaller percentage change in quantity demanded. *Unitary elasticity* ($\epsilon_p = 1$) occurs when a percentage change in price results in an equal percentage change in quantity demanded. The absolute value of the price elasticity of demand is used to determine the type of demand.

In a market with elastic demand, consumers are price-sensitive, and any changes in price will cause total revenue to change in the opposite direction. Therefore, firms tend to focus on ways to decrease price in an attempt to increase the quantity demanded and total revenue. In a market with inelastic demand, consumers are not sensitive to price changes, and total revenue will change in the same direction. In this situation, firms tend to focus on raising prices and total revenues, even with a decrease in quantity demanded. In markets with unitary demand, price changes have no effect on total revenue and firms should base pricing decisions on other factors, such as cost. For example, suppose a theme park decreases its price of admission from $50 to $45 in an attempt to increase the number of visitors. After initiating the price change, the park observes an increase in the average daily attendance at the park from 10,000 to 12,500 people. The price elasticity of demand for this example would be calculated as follows:

$$\epsilon_p = \frac{(12,500 - 10,000) / 10,000}{(45 - 50) / 50} = \frac{.25}{.10} = 1.5$$

$$\text{Maximize} \left[\frac{\text{Actual revenue}}{\text{Potential revenue}} \right]$$

The potential revenue for a hotel would be the number of total rooms available for sale multiplied by the rack rate for those rooms. For instance, if a hotel had 200 rooms that all had a rack rate of $100, the potential room revenue for that hotel would be $20,000 per night. However, if the hotel had an occupancy rate of 70 percent and an average room rate of $80, then the actual revenue would be $11,200 [(0.7 × 200) × 80]. The yield in this case would be .56 (11,200 / 20,000). The goal is to maximize this figure or to get it as close to 1.0 as possible. What if this hotel offered more discounts and had an occupancy rate of 80 percent and an average room rate of $75? The actual revenue would have been $12,000 [(0.8 × 200) × 75], or a yield of 0.6 (12,000/20,000). As you can see, the potential revenue remains the same, but the actual revenue will change, depending on the level of discounts and the price sensitivity of consumers.

This example is simplified to demonstrate the basic use of yield management. In reality, hotels have different rooms with different rack rates, and many different market segments, including business, pleasure, or transient, and various group markets. Each of these major segments can be divided into smaller subsets. For instance, the group market can be segmented into

Hotels earn additional revenue through various on-site services, including the bar. Courtesy of Foxwoods Resort Casino.

association, corporate, and incentive travel. Hotels have created positions and, in some cases, departments that are responsible for revenue management. These individuals perform historical booking analysis and confer with the hotel's executive committee to determine discounting policies.

Another area that needs to be considered in determining a hotel's discounting policy is the additional revenue, other than room revenue, that is generated from guests. For example, hotels can earn additional revenue from the restaurant, bar, fitness center, parking, laundry services, room service, corporate services such as faxing and shipping, and catering for groups. Rather than analyze each guest, hotels look at the major market segments and calculate a multiplier that can be used to adjust room revenue for additional revenue potential. This is important because hotels must maximize the revenue they receive from all sources. For instance, it would be a mistake to sell the room to a transient guest who paid $10 more a night than a business traveler if the business traveler is likely to spend more than $10 a day for additional services. Similarly, turning down a group because of high demand among transient customers may result in a loss of revenue from catering services that would have been purchased by the group. However, in peak demand seasons, such as fall in New England, hotels can charge considerably more to transient customers than to groups, and it would be a mistake to book a group well in advance and forgo this additional revenue.

Yield management has had a major impact on the hospitality and tourism industry. Advances in computer technology have improved the ability to estimate demand and revenue. In addition, it has become easier to segment markets and employ selective discounting through vehicles such as the Internet. In the future, yield management programs will become more affordable for smaller operations. In fact, yield management systems can be developed using ordinary spreadsheet software. Finally, companies are working on resource management models that will analyze the revenue contribution from all sources in the hotel, rather than focusing only on guest rooms.

PRICING LAW AND ETHICS

Pricing practices are normally illegal if they are found to be anticompetitive or if they take unfair advantage of consumers. However, ethical standards are not as clear as legal standards developed through case law. Many people feel that although it is legal to maximize profits through pricing, it may not always be ethical. First, we will discuss the legal issues surrounding pricing decisions, and then we will present a typology that can be used for considering the ethical constraints on pricing.

Peter Carmichael *Operations Supervisor*

Six Flags New England • Springfield, Massachusetts

1. What are the major components or duties associated with your current position?

I currently oversee the rides, park services (cleanliness), and parking lot departments. I have also been responsible for the admissions (front gate), guest relations, and aquatics departments as well. Our biggest priority in any department is safety. I must oversee the department safety training program, proper daily record keeping and documentation, and department staffing levels. Other major responsibilities include tracking attraction throughput levels, attraction downtime, and monitoring the guest experience such as team member guest service and cleanliness standards.

2. What are the components of your position that bring you the most satisfaction? What about your position causes you frustration?

The most satisfying part of my job is the gratification I get from my guests having fun in the park. When I see guests screaming on a roller coaster, or children hugging a character in the park, I know that I had a major role in making that happen. My favorite thing to do at the end of the night is to stand near the main exit gate and ask guests how their day was. It is amazing how excited and how much fun our guests have during their visit.

The most frustrating part of my job is when I do not have the ability or power to make a guest satisfied with their experience. For example, if a child is not tall enough to safely ride an attraction, we are not able to make an exception just to make the guest happy, for obvious safety reasons. Although most guests understand the safety reasons behind the decision, and we offer alternative rides or options for the guests to be entertained, some folks simply aren't satisfied.

3. What are the most challenging aspects that you face?

Working in a seasonal theme park presents unique challenges. Hiring and training enough team members to open a park every April is a huge undertaking. However, working at a seasonal facility also has advantages. It provides a chance to retrain the returning team members, as well as gain the enthusiasm of brand new team members.

4. **What major trends do you see for your segment of the hospitality and tourism industry?**

There are a few trends that are obvious within the theme park and aquatics industry. Indoor aquatics facilities are becoming very popular right now. Also, family entertainment is also a huge trend within theme parks. Although the major thrill rides such as roller coasters are still being built, there is a large market for family rides and shows that the entire family can experience together.

5. **What role does marketing play within your company?**

Marketing, whether it is through print, radio, TV, or Web sites, is a key component when communicating to our audience. Through these avenues we communicate new attractions, special events, exciting shows and concerts, rides and New England's largest water park, Hurricane Harbor.

6. **If you could offer one piece of advice to an individual preparing for a career in the hospitality and tourism industry, what would you suggest?**

Gain as much experience as possible while in college. Although it may not be necessary to work for more than one park or company, it is a good idea to gain experience in as many departments as possible. For example, leadership interns at Six Flags New England, may spend one season in the Rides Department, transfer to Aquatics the next season, and also gain experience in Guest Relations. Most full-time management in a regional theme park manages multiple departments. Therefore, diverse experience, especially within an aquatics environment, is a huge advantage.

industry profile

INTRODUCTION

Tourism is one of the top industries in countries throughout the world, especially those without strong manufacturing industries. According to the World Tourism Organization (WTO), tourism represents around 35 percent of the world's export of services, and over 70 percent in least developed countries (LDCs).[1] The WTO estimated international tourist arrivals to be 846 million in 2006, and predict that figure to increase to approximately 1.6 billion by 2020. This is based on the average annual growth of 6.5 percent since 1950. The overall revenues from the international tourist arrivals totaled more than $733 billion in 2006.

A tourism destination offers both tangible and intangible products. The tangible products include the tourist attractions and facilities for lodging, dining, shopping, and parking. The intangible product is the image of the destination. The complexity of destination marketing is that tourists usually select among destinations based on the total set of destination attributes, not an individual firm's marketing effort. Therefore, in the increasingly competitive marketplace, marketing alliances between the private and the public sectors can create economies of scale for the destination. In the United States, tourism marketing alliances are often formed by a combination of agencies such as the convention and visitor bureaus, Chambers of Commerce, local governments, and tourism operators.

Destination Marketing Organizations

According to the Destination Marketing Association International (DMAI), destination marketing organizations (DMOs) are primarily concerned with promoting the long-term development and marketing of a destination, focusing on convention sales, tourism marketing, and service.[2] The two most common forms of DMOs are convention and visitors bureaus (CVBs) and tourism bureaus. In fact, DMAI changed its name from the International Association of Convention and Visitors Bureaus (IACVB) to better represent the function (i.e., destination marketing), rather than just one of the organizations involved in marketing destinations. DMOs market their destinations to business travelers, tour operators, meetings and event planners, and individual tourists.

Tourism bureaus are mainly government organizations that are funded through the government's revenue sources such as state and federal taxes (this could be referred to as provinces and national, respectively in other countries). These organizations are part of the government system that includes other divisions such as education, transportation, and defense. In the United States, convention and visitors bureaus are typically not-for-profit organizations that are funded through a combination of hotel taxes and membership dues. A small percentage (15 to 20 percent) of CVBs is either a government agency or a division of the Chamber of Commerce. Other funding sources include government grants, selling advertising and visitor center services, and donated services. However, CVBs do not normally charge customers for their services. Finally, the major expense for CVBs is advertising and promotion (including personal selling).

The membership of a CVB consists of organizations from the various stakeholders. The stakeholders for CVBs are those businesses who sell products or services that are attractive to associations and corporations that hold meetings and events, as well as the individual travelers. For example, obvious stakeholders would be hotels and other lodging facilities, convention centers, restaurants, and tourist attractions. Other, less obvious, stakeholders would be event organizers, shopping facilities, and convention services suppliers like decorators, entertainment companies, destination management companies (DMCs), and local transportation companies. CVBs are governed by a board of directors that follows a published list of bylaws. The major goals of CVBs are the following:[3]

- To encourage associations and corporations to hold meetings, conventions and trade show in the area

- To assist associations and corporations coordinating their conventions, seminars and trade shows in the area

- To provide services to tour planners, both domestic and international

- To provide leadership for the visitor industry, build the image of the area, and encourage marketing activities

- To provide additional support to travel writers to help sell the area

Destination Market Segments

The four primary market segments for CVBs are associations, corporations, tour operators, and individual travelers. Associations consist of social, military, education, religious, and fraternal (SMERF) groups, as well as industry trade groups. These groups can be local, regional, or national, and they all have meetings and events throughout the year. Associations hold conferences, which are smaller meetings normally focused on education and training, and conventions, which are large annual meetings for the national membership. Trade shows are conventions that include exhibitors that sell products to the association's members and their organizations. Many of these conventions are large enough to "sell out" a city and use most of the hotel rooms that are available. The most popular destinations for the largest conventions are Las Vegas, Chicago, Orlando, and Los Angeles because they have the necessary square footage for exhibitors and enough hotel rooms to accommodate all of the attendees.

Corporations also hold meetings and events throughout the year for sales training, advertising campaigns and product launches, board of directors, shareholders, and so on. Most of these meetings have less than 100 attendees, but there are a large number of these meetings relative to association meetings and conventions. Corporations are less price-sensitive than the other meeting groups and individual travelers. In addition, there is a better opportunity for more frequent repeat visitation. These characteristics all add up to make the corporate market a lucrative market for destinations that can acquire their business and loyalty. Corporations also hold picnics and holiday parties for their employees that are valuable pieces of business for the DMOs members or local partners.

Tour operators develop travel packages that they sell to individual travelers. These packages typically include airfare, lodging, and tickets to local attractions. Travel agents are also part of this market segment because they function as intermediaries between the tour operators and the final consumer when the tour operator doesn't sell directly to the consumer via mail, telephone, or the Internet. CVBs are responsible for organizing familiarization (Fam) tours for the tour operators and travel agents. The CVB approaches its local members (e.g., hotels and restaurants) to obtain donations in order to host the intermediaries free of charge. The goal is to "familiarize" the tour operators and travel agents with the destination so that they will promote the area to their clients and potential customers.

In addition, DMOs are concerned with providing information and promotional materials focused on the individual leisure traveler. DMOs promote events such as festivals and sporting events, cultural and heritage sites such as parks and museums, and recreational activities such as amusement parks, shopping facilities, and golf facilities. This is accomplished through mass communications rather than using the DMOs sales force. Placements in magazines and articles by travel writers are popular forms of marketing communications directed at this target segment.

DESTINATION PRODUCT DEVELOPMENT

Regional tourism products are developed by three different types of organizations: (1) individual service providers like amusement parks, (2) tour operators and travel agents, and (3) destination marketing organizations. Destination marketing organizations promote a number of different products, including convention centers, hotels, attractions, and events. In addition, DMOs promote transportation services and vendors/suppliers for meetings and events. Once again, the primary target markets for these products are the groups that hold meetings and leisure tour travel groups. The needs of the individual traveler are handled through mass communications, the DMO's Web site, and the visitors information centers located throughout the tourist areas. DMOs recognize the economic impact of bringing groups to the destination and focus a great deal of effort on acquiring this business. The main goal of the DMO is to increase visitor arrivals, resulting in an increase in hotel tax revenue and the additional spending on attractions, food, shopping, and transportation.

A large portion of the money received from hotel taxes is normally given to the convention and visitors bureau to use in promoting the destination. The CVB must create promotional materials like event planning guides and visitor guides that are distributed to organizations and individuals who make inquiries to the CVB by telephone, through the website, or via direct mail placements (i.e., drop cards) in magazines. Other support materials include signs and maps that are used by visitors to navigate the destination and its tourist areas. Finally, the CVB needs to hire full- and part-time employees to handle inquiries, sell to groups, staff visitor centers, recruit members, and take care of administration. One area that many destinations overlook, to their detriment, is the investment in infrastructure. This is a major part of product development and funds should be allocated to improve the destination's accessibility. For example, countries such as Vietnam and Cambodia have nice beaches but the infrastructure in these countries prevents them from competing with other Southeast Asian destination like Singapore and Thailand.

The first task in the product development process for the DMO is to take an inventory of all of the various elements (e.g., accommodations, attractions, events, etc.) that are available at the destination and determine the best way to market them in an attempt to create a **unique destination proposition**. The second task is to combine the various elements to create packages that will appeal to the various target markets. The last task is to develop marketing

Unique destination proposition (UDP)

A statement to describe the unique elements that are available at the destination in an attempt to differentiate it from other destinations.

programs that will be used to meet the needs of the potential visitors, including the communications plan. The overall goal of the product development process is to achieve an effective allocation of available resources to ensure economic sustainability. The following is a discussion of the common destination attributes that combine to form the product and are used by visitors to form their overall perceptions of the destination.

Destination Attributes

Destinations are a combination of tangible and intangible elements, or attributes, that define the location. The tangible elements consist of accommodations, restaurants, transportation, and shopping facilities. The visitors' perceptions of competing destinations are based on the number and quality of these tangible attributes. It is necessary to determine the weight, or importance, that visitors place on each of these attributes when positioning the destination using product development and marketing communications. However, it is difficult to make physical changes without an influx of capital from public and/or private sources. For example, international destinations that host the Olympic Games invest a great deal of time and resources in improving the destination's infrastructure and providing an adequate level of tangible elements such as hotels and sports venues. Other tangible elements include the destination's parks and historic sites. The United States has a national parks system and heritage sites such as battlefields, missions, and museums. Tourists visit places like the Grand Canyon in the United States and the pyramids in Egypt because of the natural beauty of these tangible elements. Destinations like Paris and London are popular because of the many historic sites and the overall scenery. Finally, the climate in the destination area also influences visitors. Many travelers prefer warm, sunny climates like Florida, California, and Arizona. Others prefer ski vacations in snow-ridden destinations like Colorado, Utah, and Vermont. However, natural disasters like hurricanes, tornadoes, and earthquakes can limit a destination's peak season.

The other set of elements that are used by visitors to evaluate a destination are the intangibles. The intangibles are important because they can distinguish one destination from another, even if the destinations enjoy the same number and quality of tangible elements. Perceptions are everything in marketing and DMOs must determine the visitors' perceptions of the overall appeal of the destination. Some areas of concern are crime, safety and security, crowdedness, friendliness, and cleanliness. It is often difficult to

Visitors choose destinations like Paris for the history of sites like Notre Dame Cathedral. Courtesy of Corbis Digital Stock.

overcome negative perceptions regarding these attributes because they are developed over time and can be based on information from reliable sources like friends and relatives who visited the destination. In addition, the media are influential based on how they cover certain news and events. That is why it is critical for DMOs to have a good relationship with the local and national media. Finally, there are other intangible elements like nightlife, adventure, and rest and relaxation that can help define a tourist destination.

The final decision to visit a destination is based on the visitor's overall perception of the destination, including the level of each of the tangible and intangible attributes, and his perception of the cost or value associated with the destination. This is similar to the decision-making process that consumers go through for other product and service purchases. First, there is need recognition, then some degree of information search, an evaluation of alternatives, and a final purchase decision. Tourism and travel are services and cannot be fully evaluated before purchased, or inventoried like tangible products. Therefore, there is a high potential for cognitive dissonance after the purchase, and before the actual consumption of the service. For example, many travelers purchase cruises and vacation packages several months in advance and must wait to enjoy the trip. In the meantime, they are exposed to advertisements, word-of-mouth, and news stories.

Destination Branding

Destination branding

Process of capturing the distinct elements of the destination and communicating them through components such as identity, personality, and image.

The goal of **destination branding** is to capture the distinct elements of the destination in the brand and communicating them through its components such as identity, personality, and image. This is accomplished by combining all of the attributes associated with the brand to form an identity that is unique and differentiates the destination from the competition. DMOs can start by conducting consumer research to determine the visitors' perceptions of the destination in terms of the destination's features and brand benefits. The destination brand benefit pyramid is used by many organizations to conduct this task.[4]

Level 1 – What are the tangible, verifiable, objective, measurable characteristics of this destination?

Level 2 – What benefits to the tourist result from this destination's features?

Level 3 – What psychological rewards or emotional benefits do tourists receive by visiting this destination?

Level 4 – What does value mean for the typical repeat tourist?

Level 5 – What is the essential nature and character of the destination brand?

In summary, these questions help to determine the key attributes or features that are associated with a destination, how these features benefit potential tourists or visitors, what value tourists and visitors place on travel to the destination, and the overall brand character or essence. Figure 16.1 is an example of

PLACES OF REMEMBRANCE. MOMENTS OF AMAZEMENT.
the river leads to many surprises.

SAN ANTONIO
DEEP. IN THE HEART.

VISITSANANTONIO.COM ★ 800·THE ALAMO

FIGURE 16.1 • *Destination Brand Advertisement. Courtesy of the San Antonio Convention and Visitors Bureau.*

a print advertisement that was used to launch the new San Antonio brand with the theme "Deep in the Heart."

The advantages of branding a destination are that it provides a means of communicating the destination's unique proposition, or identity, to potential visitors and differentiate the destination from competitors. It also helps the DMO to create a theme and a consistent message that can be communicated to the target markets using a combination of the brand's name, symbol, and logo. However, there are several reasons why branding destinations is difficult.[5] First, destinations are more multidimensional than most other products and services. Second, the market interests of the diverse group of stakeholders are heterogeneous. Third, there are politics involved in determining who will decide the brand theme and how they will be accountable. Fourth, DMOs lack direct control of the delivery of the brand promise by the local tourism community. Fifth, it is difficult to measure and monitor the brand loyalty of the visitors to a destination. Sixth, the scale and consistency of funding for destination marketing varies over the destination's life cycle.

Tourist Area Life Cycle

Tourist area life cycle

The tourist area life cycle is similar to the product life cycle for tourist destinations. Like products, destinations have a finite life and evolve through various stages of development.

Butler (1980) introduced the concept of a **tourist area life cycle**, which is similar to the product life cycle.[6] Like products, tourist destinations have a finite life and evolve through several stages of development, from introduction (exploration and involvement) to growth (development), maturity (consolidation), and finally decline (stagnation and poststagnation). However, just as with products, once a destination reaches maturity (stagnation) it can extend this stage by going through some changes and rejuvenating itself. This could involve adding more tourist attractions or accommodations, or targeting a new market. For example, many cities along beaches in the southern United States followed Fort Lauderdale, Florida, and targeted the spring break crowd from universities and colleges. Each stage of development has its own set of opportunities and threats for the local area. Figure 16.2 provides a graphical representation of the tourist area life cycle (TALC).

Exploration stage

The first stage in the tourist area life cycle occurs when there are a few adventurous tourists visiting sites with few public facilities. The visitors are initially attracted to the destination because of some natural physical feature.

EXPLORATION. During the **exploration stage**, there are a few adventurous tourists visiting sites with few public facilities. The visitors are initially attracted to the destination because of some natural physical feature. At this point, the destination only attracts a very specific type of visitor. The exploration stage of the tourist area life cycle is when the more adventurous travelers find destinations that aren't frequented by the masses. These travelers are normally looking for places that haven't become major tourism destinations. The new destinations don't have the infrastructures or the commercial enterprises that are found in the more established tourism destinations. One of the major appeals of the new destinations is the ability to interact with the resident populations and experience the local environment. These early tourists are welcomed by the host population, and some of the tourists decide to become residents. For example, Walt Disney World was started as a small theme park in a remote area around Orlando, Florida, in 1971. After visiting the park, tourists began to move to Orlando, and the city started to grow.

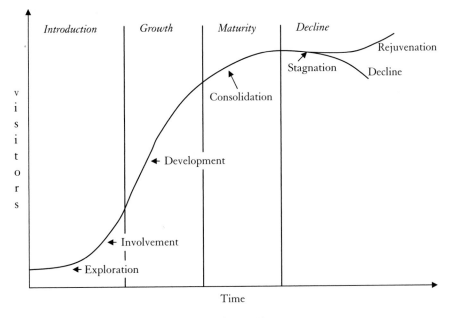

FIGURE 16.2 • *Tourist Area Life Cycle (TALC).*

INVOLVEMENT. As the destination moves into the **involvement stage**, there is limited interaction between tourists and the local community, resulting in only basic services. Increased advertising induces a pattern of seasonal variation and a definite market area begins to emerge. The involvement stage of the tourist area life cycle sees an increase in the number of tourists based on the word of mouth generated by the adventurous travelers. The number of tourism support businesses begins to increase, but most of the accommodations and restaurants are still owned and operated by local residents. There is not much planning for the regional development during this stage, often leading to the creation of a tourism organization to address the needs of the region. The local residents have more interaction with visitors that may enlighten them about the opportunities that exist for education, politics, and economic development. During this stage, there is an increase in the use of technology, and improvements are made to the local establishments.

DEVELOPMENT. The **development stage** is the last stage where there is continued growth in the number of visitor arrivals. There is a noticeable development of additional tourist facilities and increased promotional efforts. The destination experiences a shift in control of the tourist trade to outsiders, and the number of tourists at peak periods outnumbers the local residents. This results in some antagonism toward tourists. As this stage progresses, the interaction between tourists and local residents becomes less personal and more businesslike. For example, many support businesses such as hotels, restaurants, and other retail establishments emerged in the Orlando area due to the success

Involvement stage

The second stage in the tourist area life cycle occurs when there is limited interaction between tourists and the local community, resulting in only basic services. Increased advertising induces a pattern of seasonal variation and a definite market area begins to emerge.

Development stage

The third stage in the tourist area life cycle occurs when there is continued growth in the number of visitor arrivals. There is a noticeable development of additional tourist facilities and increased promotional efforts.

of Walt Disney World. Also, contractors moved to the area and a convention and visitors bureau was formed.

CONSOLIDATION.   Once the growth rate of visitor arrivals begins to decrease, the destination enters a **consolidation stage**. Tourism has become a major component of the local economy, and a well-delineated business district has begun to take shape. Some of the facilities are outdated and the destination tries to extend the tourist season. The consolidation stage of the tourist area life cycle is characterized by a shift from local control of businesses to more outside ownership and larger establishments. This causes the local economy to become more dependent on large corporations with a lack of empathy for the local population. More of the businesses are franchised and more people migrate to the area because labor is needed to support the increase in tourism. This results in more conflicts between the original residents and the new residents. In addition, the area becomes more crowded, and there are other negative impacts, like an increase in crime and pollution. Finally, there is an economic divide between the people who prosper as a result of the increased tourism and those who are directly involved. For example, the main industry for the island of Hilton Head, South Carolina converted from logging to tourism in the mid-1900s. However, many of the original residents couldn't afford the increase in taxes brought about by the increase in real estate prices. As a result, many of the residents lost their homes, or had to sell and leave the island where they were born and raised. Others were able to remain, but the cost of food and other basic necessities continued to rise, and the island's new residents had higher incomes and more luxurious lifestyles.

STAGNATION.   This leads to the **stagnation stage**, where peak numbers of tourists and capacity levels are reached. The destination has a well-established image, but it is no longer popular and the lodging facilities begin to erode and turnover. The stagnation stage in the tourist area life cycle is characterized by an abundance of tourism facilities and services. The market becomes saturated, and tourists' experience becomes less satisfying. In some cases, the negative impacts of tourism outweigh the benefits associated with the increase in visitation, and the local population loses its enthusiasm for entertaining tourists. The adventurous travelers who discovered the area are disillusioned by the commercialization and look for new destinations. Some of the less efficient firms go out of business, and the area is left with large franchises and chain operations. A destination can attempt to avoid or postpone a decline during **poststagnation** by finding a way to rejuvenate the area. This could include the addition of new attractions or focusing on a niche market. For example, the introduction of Walt Disney World rejuvenated the area when Cypress Gardens (an original attraction outside Orlando) started to show a decline in visitors.

Consolidation stage

The fourth stage of the tourist area life cycle occurs when tourism has become a major component of the local economy, and a well-delineated business district has begun to take shape.

Stagnation stage

The last stage of the tourist area life cycle where peak numbers of tourists and capacity levels are reached. The destination has a well-established image, but it is no longer popular and the lodging facilities begin to erode and turnover.

Poststagnation

The period in the tourist area life cycle after the beginning of the stagnation stage. Tourist destinations try to find ways to rejuvenate the area by adding new attractions or focusing on a niche market.

DESTINATION MARKETING COMMUNICATIONS

The basic communications process starts with a sender who encodes a message and then sends it through a medium chosen to reach a specific target public. The medium in this case would be in the form of an advertisement (print or broadcast), Web site content, or a sales presentation. Next, it is necessary for the message to be seen and/or heard, and decoded by a receiver. However, there can be some noise in the process that affects the clear communication of the message. This noise could be in the form of competing commercials or advertisements, direct mail clutter, lack of message effectiveness, and so on. The goal is to make sure the target public understands the message and acts on the message as intended.

Bureau Communications Plan

A comprehensive **communications plan** is composed of several individual plans designed for each of the target markets or "publics." It is important that the organization is proactive in its communications rather than merely responding to inquiries as they come in. The sales staff needs to actively seek out leads and continually prospect. In addition, the bureau should actively listen to its publics in order to determine their wants and needs. There should be an open dialogue between the bureau and these publics, including the local community. Finally, it is beneficial to create a theme for the destination that can be consistent throughout all of the bureau's communications. The theme should fit the destination's unique selling proposition and take advantage of its favorable destination attributes, thereby supporting the destination's brand and image.

Communications plan

An overall plan composed of several individual plans designed for each of the target markets or "publics" for a tourism destination.

The primary target publics include residents of the local community, tourists, attractions and hospitality firms, and the news media that cover the destination. The secondary target publics include residents of nearby communities and destinations, and their destination marketing organizations, and public segments such as the local government, schools, and medical facilities. There are three objectives:

1. Increase awareness, interest, and participation of the attractions and hospitality firms.

2. Increase awareness, interest, and participation of the residents.

3. Develop and maintain good relationships with the media so they can help to communicate the bureau's goals and objectives to the destination's target publics.

The bureau's communication goals and objectives are achieved through the use of carefully planned strategies. The strategies should utilize a multimedia and multilevel communication approach that consists of a variety of integrated marketing communications activities. These communication tools should involve the target publics in the process and gain their commitment for the desired outcomes. Finally, both qualitative and quantitative research techniques should be used to monitor the communications program and measure the effectiveness and the performance of the campaign.

Media Relations Strategies

DMOs are responsible for developing media relations strategies for each of the target publics. The most obvious plan is aimed at the customer markets. As previously mentioned, the DMO should create a separate marketing program, including communications, for each target market. The goal of the **customer plan** is to create awareness and interest in the DMO and the destination. The customer plan details the use of the organization's advertising and promotion, as discussed in Chapters 11 through 14. A separate plan is created for each of the destination's various target markets, including individual tourists, meeting planners, tour operators, travel agents, and corporations. Mass marketing techniques are used for individuals and families, and interpersonal communications are used for groups.

The **community relations plan** is developed to create a favorable environment in the local community within which the DMO operates. The members of this target group are the general public, the government, and the local media, including travel writers.

The **stakeholders relations plan** is aimed at producing business partnerships and alliances that result in additional revenue and marketing resources for the DMO. This target public includes the convention center, hotels, and other bureau members or local partners. In addition, local economic development and tourism-related agencies and businesses are part of this target public.

Customer plan

The component of the communications plan used to market the destination to various consumer segments such as individual tourists, meeting planners, and tour operators and travel agents.

Community relations plan

The component of the communications plan developed to create a favorable environment in the local community.

Stakeholders relations plan

The component of the communications plan developed to foster business partnerships and alliances.

The **crisis management plan** should be launched in the event of natural or manmade disasters, and any other factors that might raise public concerns and/or negatively affect local tourism and businesses. It is important to provide the pertinent facts in a timely manner.

The **internal relations plan** is aimed at improving employee morale and ensuring a positive and productive work environment. This component of the media relations strategies is normally handled by human resources rather than the sales and marketing department.

DESTINATION RESEARCH

The goal of research is to reduce the uncertainty surrounding managerial decisions. These decisions are made on a regular basis and included in the organization's marketing plan. There are four main objectives of research regarding tourism destinations:

1. What is the profile of the visitors, or potential visitors, that compose the target market(s) for the destination?

2. What is the overall value, or economic impact, provided by the target market(s)?

3. What are the attributes or characteristics associated with the destination that attract visitors, and how does the destination compare with other destinations on those attributes?

4. How should the marketing mix be composed for each target market? For example, what types of marketing communications should be used to reach the target markets, and what should the message be?

There are various research designs and methodologies that can be used to obtain the necessary information to answer these questions. However, it is important for the destination marketing organization to weigh the benefits of collecting additional information against the costs of collecting it, in order to choose the appropriate cutoff point in order to make a decision.

Some of the information is needed on a continual basis (e.g., monthly visitor arrivals, occupancy rates, and average daily rates), while other studies are only needed on a periodic basis (e.g., economic impact and forecasting, destination image, and inquiry conversion). Most of the information that is required on a continual basis is obtained through basic tracking and reporting

Crisis management plan

The component of the communications plan prepared in the event of a natural or manmade disaster.

Internal relations plan

The component of the communications plan developed to improve employee morale and the work environment.

methods. The more complicated studies that are conducted periodically are discussed in the following sections.

Economic Impact Studies

Tourism in many countries or regions is an industry that brings significant economic impacts to the local economy. Tourism not only contributes to the local economy monetarily by increasing foreign exchange and the purchase of goods and services, but also creates many job opportunities. In addition, tourism brings indirect effects to other industries that supply and support various tourism activities. There are several ways to estimate the economic impacts of tourism. An input-output model that multiplies total tourist expenditures by regional multipliers is the most commonly used method. The primary source of economic impact from tourism is derived from tourists' expenditures during their trips. The major categories of tourist expenditures are transportation, accommodations, meals, shopping, and tourist attractions. Changes in tourist expenditures can bring three types of effects to a local economy:

1. **Direct effect:** It refers to the effect brought to establishments and employees where tourists spend their money.

2. **Indirect effect:** It results from the need of tourism sectors to purchase from other industries in order to produce its output. Continuous interactions among sectors will be generated by these purchases until the money respent becomes negligible.

3. **Induced effect:** It is the income level increase as a result of tourism. A portion of the increased income will be respent on the final goods and services within the local economy.

Economic impacts of tourism come from the spending of tourists within the local area, change in regional incomes and changes in employment. To assess economic impacts, the local region is generally defined as all counties within a given radius of the destination, usually 30 to 60 miles. Satellite accounts and visitor survey input-output models are the two principal methods used for estimating the economic impacts generated from tourism.

Satellite account method
Process used to identify an overall estimate of tourism contribution to the state and national economies by reorganizing the account systems.

The **satellite account method** identifies an overall estimate of tourism contribution to the state and national economies by reorganizing the account systems. Using existing economic data and the implant action of tourism in an accepted system of accounts is the advantage of the satellite accounting approach. However, the disadvantage is that it is relatively more difficult to gather complete information necessary to extract tourism activity from national economic accounts. Furthermore, it is more difficult to apply the following method the national level or for subcategories of tourism activities.

The **input-output model** is a more common approach for estimating the economic impacts of tourism by directly surveying tourists to obtain data on their spending habits. The direct survey method is more applicable in estimating the impacts of a particular action on the local economy. By adapting appropriate economic ratios and multipliers, estimation of tourist expenditures can be transformed into the resulting jobs and income of a given region. The basic equations of the input-output model are as follows:

Tourist spending = Number of Visitors × Average spending per visitor

Economic impact = Number of Visitors × Average spending per visitor × Regional multipliers

Another more complicated and rigorous approach to estimate the income and jobs generated by tourism is the use of **multiplier analysis**. There are three types of multipliers:

1. **Output multiplier:** The ratio of change in total productive output of the total economy brought by the initial change in tourist expenditure.

2. **Income multiplier:** The change in income, such as wages, salaries and profits of the economy, resulting from the change in tourist expenditure.

3. **Employment multiplier:** The change of job opportunities associated with the change in total tourist expenditure.

The purpose of using multiplier analysis is to estimate the additional impact generated in a tourist destination for every dollar spent on the tourist product itself. Greater amount of local/regional resource utilization and lower proportion of imported goods that supply local consumption and production will result in a higher multiplier. Figure 16.3 provides a list of example questions that can be used in obtaining the necessary information for conducting an economic impact analysis.

The goal is to obtain information on total spending for the trip and then using the information on the size of the party and the length of the trip to convert the figures into per person per day so that the information can be compared over time and across market segments. In addition, there are often questions to determine the type of accommodations, attractions visited, where

Input-output model

A common approach for estimating the economic impacts of tourism by directly surveying tourists to obtain data on their spending habits.

Multiplier analysis

Procedure to estimate the additional impact generated in a tourist destination for every dollar spent on the tourist product itself.

1. How long did you stay in the Pioneer Valley?
   _____ days   _____ nights

2. Where did you stay during your visit?
   (Please name the lodging facility)
   ☐ Hotel _____
   ☐ Family/friends
   ☐ Bed & Breakfast_____
   ☐ Campground _____
   ☐ Other: _____

3. How many people were in your party?
   Adults _____   Children_____

4. Approximately how much did you spend on the following:
   Accommodations $_____
   Food $_____
   Tourist Attractions $_____
   Shopping $_____
   Transportation $_____
   Other (please specify) $_____

FIGURE 16.3 • *Economic Impact Sample Questions.*

they shopped, and where they dined. This information is useful to the CVB in recruiting members, obtaining government funding, and communicating the value of the organization to the local economy.

Destination Image Studies

Destination choice is influenced by an individual's perceptions of alternative possibilities (i.e., cities, regions, or countries). Therefore, it is important for a destination wishing to increase visitation to promote a coherent image. Destination image refers to the impressions a person holds about a destination in which he does not reside. Images can be formed through contact or experience, or they can be developed in the absence of contact. Perceptions about destination image are formed through advertising and promotions, news accounts, discussions with friends or relatives, travel agents, and past experiences. Destinations cannot easily change their physical attributes like the landscape or climate, so they must build their images around unique

How would you rate _____ on each of the following destination attributes?

	Poor				Excellent
Accommodations	1	2	3	4	5
Scenery	1	2	3	4	5
Shopping Facilities	1	2	3	4	5
Restaurants	1	2	3	4	5
Climate/Weather	1	2	3	4	5
Tourist Attractions	1	2	3	4	5
Historical Appeal	1	2	3	4	5
Safety and Security	1	2	3	4	5

FIGURE 16.4 • *Destination Image Sample Question.*

attributes that provide them with some type of sustainable competitive advantage. The destination, including its attractions, should be designed to meet the needs of the target market. Therefore, the diagnosis of the destination's strengths and weaknesses on salient attributes, relative to competitive destinations, is helpful in designing the tourism offerings and marketing programs. Figure 16.4 provides an example of a question that could be included in a questionnaire used in a destination image study.

The example only includes 8 attributes, but studies often include as many as 15 to 20 different attributes representing both tangible and intangible elements of the destination. Also, it is popular to put the attributes in the form of a statement (e.g., "San Antonio has many attractions" or "San Antonio has a good nightlife") and ask the respondent to provide his level of agreement on a scale ranging from "strongly agree" to "strongly disagree." Either way, it is possible to obtain respondents' perceptions of the destination on the attributes provided. The mean rating score for each attribute can provide the basic information regarding perceptions, or more sophisticated statistical methods like factor analysis and multidimensional scaling can be used to identify useful dimensions and create a perceptual map. The perceptual map can compare alternative destinations if the perceptions are gathered for them as well. These data are combined with the demographics and travel behaviors of the respondents to segment the market based on visitor profiles (e.g., seniors, families, etc.).

Conversion Studies

The purpose of the conversion study is to measure the effectiveness of the destination marketing organization's advertising and promotion. The most

San Antonio is known for the River Walk and many restaurants and nightlife
Courtesy of San Antonio Convention and Visitors Bureau.

important performance measure is the number of inquiries that are converted to visitors. Inquiries come to convention and visitors bureaus through three main sources: telephone, Web site, and drop cards placed in magazines. The goal is to measure the conversion rate on each of the three methods of inquiry to determine the most effective means of reaching the target market. The most popular advertising and promotion pieces for CVBs are the visitor's guide, magazine ads, and television ads, depending on the overall budget. In addition, there might be a meeting planner's guide, but many CVBs are only offering them in electronic version on the. This seems to be the preference for meeting planners because some of them deal with a large number of destinations and hotels, and they don't want to maintain large volumes of guides in hard copy form. Figure 16.5 provides a sample list of questions that can be used to measure the conversion rate for leisure travelers.

These questions obtain information on how respondents first became aware of the destination, if they decided to visit after receiving the promotion materials, the reason they didn't visit, and what other destinations they might have visited. In addition, there are questions about the purpose of the trip and how the visitors used the guide. Other questions that are important are the length of stay and the likelihood of visitation in the near future (return or first time). Finally, it should be noted that the information for all three types of studies can be part of one questionnaire: economic impact, destination image, and conversion. The questions for all three studies can be combined with questions about trip behaviors and visitor (or inquiry) profiles based on demographics and psychographics.

1. How did you first become interested in the Paradise Valley?

☐ Magazine   ☐ Friends/Relatives

☐ Internet   ☐ Newspapers

☐ Hotel/Restaurant brochures

☐ Other _____

2. After requesting information and receiving The Guide, did you visit the Paradise Valley?

☐ Yes (skip to #__)   ☐ No

3. If not, what were your reasons for not visiting the Paradise Valley?

☐ Cost   ☐ Alternative destination

☐ Distance   ☐ Personal Reasons

☐ Other _____

4. Did you visit an alternative destination? (please list)

_____

_____

(skip to # __)

5. For which of the following did you use The Guide? (check all that apply)

☐ Accommodations   ☐ Restaurants

☐ Tourist attractions ☐ Shopping

☐ Maps   ☐ Other: _____

6. What was the purpose of your trip to the Paradise Valley?

☐ Business   ☐ Business and Leisure

☐ Leisure (vacation) ☐ Family/Friends

☐ Visiting Colleges ☐ Other: _____

FIGURE 16.5 • *Conversion study sample questions.*

Summary of Chapter Objectives

This chapter is an overview of destination marketing. The main goal of the chapter is to introduce the reader to the destination marketing function and the organizations responsible for promoting tourism and travel sites. The most common destination marketing organizations (tourism bureaus and convention and visitors bureaus) are described, including the funding and operations of the organizations. There are four primary target market segments for DMOs: associations, corporations, tour operators, and individual travelers. The approach for marketing to these various target markets is discussed.

The next section of the chapter focuses on the destination product development process. The first step is to take an inventory of the product elements that exist at the destination (e.g., accommodations, attractions, and events). The tourist area life cycle helps the DMO to understand the evolution of the destination and see the timing of the addition of product elements. Next, the DMO must survey visitors (actual and potential) to determine their perceptions of the destination based on a group of destination attributes. Finally, the DMO must create a unique destination proposition that allows them to accentuate the destination's strengths and differentiate it from other destinations. Branding and positioning is used to develop an overall destination image that can be conveyed to potential visitors through a communications plan.

A communications plan is developed to integrate all of the marketing efforts of the DMO to ensure that they are consistent with the unique destination proposition and the theme for the destination. This plan includes campaigns targeted at both the primary and secondary publics. The most common publics are introduced and examples of applicable media relations strategies are examined. The chapter concludes with a discussion of the necessary types of destination research that should be commissioned by the DMO. The most popular studies are economic impact, destination image, and conversion.

Key Terms and Concepts

Communications plan

Community relations plan

Consolidation stage

Crisis management plan

Customer plan

Destination branding

Development stage

Exploration stage

Input-output model

Internal relations plan

Involvement stage

Multiplier analysis

Poststagnation

Satellite account method

Stagnation stage

Stakeholders relation plan

Tourist area life cycle (TALC)

Unique destination proposition

Questions for Review and Discussion

1. What are destination marketing organizations? What is their major function?

2. What are the two most common types of destination marketing organizations? How are they funded?

3. What are the target market segments for destinations?

4. How do visitors' perceptions of destination attributes affect the product development process?

5. What is the tourist area life cycle concept? How is it related to the product life cycle concept?

6. What is a communications plan? What are the target publics for the communications plan?

7. How is destination research used in the tourism and travel industry by destination marketing organizations?

8. What is a conversion study, and why is it important?

Notes

[1] World Tourism Organization, http://www.unwto.org/index.php.

[2] Destination Marketing Association International, http://www.destinationmarketing.org/page.asp?pid=21.

[3] Richard. B. Gartrell, *Destination Marketing for Convention and Visitor Bureaus*, 2nd ed. (Dubuque, IA: Kendall/Hunt, 1994).

[4] Steven Pike, "Tourism Destination Branding Complexity," *The Journal of Product and Brand Management*, 14 (4/5), (2005): 258–259.

[5] Nigel Morgan and Annette Pritchard, "Contextualizing destination branding." In Nigel Morgan, Annette Pritchard, Roger Pride (eds.). *Destination Branding: Creating the Unique Destination Proposition* (Oxford: Butterworth-Heineman, 2002), p. 31.

[6] R. Butler, "The Concept of a Tourist Area Cycle of Evolution," *Canadian Geographer* 24 (1980): 5–12.

Case Study

Paradise Valley Convention and Visitors Bureau

The Paradise Valley Convention and Visitors Bureau is the destination marketing organization for a second-tier city and its surrounding region, with annual visitor arrivals totaling 3,300,000. Bart Simpson is the executive director of the Paradise Valley CVB, and many describe him as outgoing and a bit of a cartoon character. The major objective of the CVB is to promote tourism for the region. The CVB publishes a promotional guide containing information on lodging, restaurants, entertainment, and tourist attractions. The guide is available free of charge by calling an 800 number, filling out a magazine insert, or requesting it through the Web site. Bart was curious about the conversion rate and wanted to know more about the destination's image and the economic impact of tourism. Therefore, he contracted with a research firm to conduct a survey of people who requested the guide. Questions 1 through 3 provide information on the conversion rate.

1. How did you first become interested in the Paradise Valley?

Options	Percent	Frequency
Magazine	30.7	119
Internet	6.4	25
Hotel/Restaurant brochures	3.1	12
Friends/Relatives	21.6	84
Newspapers	10.1	39
Other	28.1	109
Total	100	388

2. After requesting information and receiving *The Guide*, did you visit the Paradise Valley?

Yes <u>51.8%</u> ($n = 199$)   No <u>47.9%</u> ($n = 184$)

3. If not, what was your main reason for not visiting the Paradise Valley?

Options	Percent	Frequency
Cost	4.0	7
Distance	5.2	9
Alternative destination	26.6	46
Personal reasons	37.6	65
Other	26.6	46
Total	100	173

case study

The next section (Question 4) of the survey focused on the respondents' perceptions of the Paradise Valley based on 8 attributes. This information is intended to provide some insights into the destination image of the Paradise Valley.

4. How would you rate the Paradise Valley on each of the following destination attributes?

	Mean
Accommodations	3.75
Scenery	4.31
Shopping facilities	3.76
Restaurants	3.89
Climate/Weather	3.79
Tourist attractions	3.93
Historical appeal	4.13
Safety and security	3.99

(Note: results are based on a five-point scale ranging from 1 = poor to 5 = excellent.)

The final section of the study focused on the travel and spending behaviors exhibited by the respondents. The number of people in the party, the length of stay, and the amount spent on the various travel components can be useful in determining the economic impact of tourism for the region.

5. How many people were in your party?   <u>3.65 people (average)</u>

6. How long did you stay in the Paradise Valley?   <u>4.25 days (average)</u>

7. Approximately how much did you spend on the following during your trip?

Category	Mean
Accommodations	$185.60
Food	$143.95
Tourist Attractions	$60.95
Shopping	$134.50
Transportation	$40.40
Other	$13.50
Total	$564.75

(Note: the sum of the components doesn't equal the total because each component was averaged separately.)

Case Study Questions and Issues

1. What is the conversion rate for inquiries, and what were the main reasons for respondents not visiting? What strategies would you recommend for improving the conversion rate?

2. How did the respondents first become aware of the destination, and what effect would this have on your marketing strategies?

3. How would you describe the destination's image based on the results of the study? What type of market segment(s) would be the best target(s) for this type of destination? Explain your answer.

4. What are the expenditures per person per day on each of the travel components? What is the total economic impact of tourism on this region? Show your calculations and state your assumptions.

Glossary

Accessibility of market segments A criterion used to evaluate the effectiveness of market segmentation. The large target markets must be reachable, or accessible, through a variety of marketing communication efforts.

Acquisitions A firm can acquire the rights to new products or services by entering into a legal arrangement with another firm, thereby combining the two firms' products and services.

Active listening Active listening requires a person to hear and understand what the other person, or speaker, is trying to say, from the speaker's point of view. The person actually needs to understand the speaker, not merely hear what the speaker says.

Administered vertical marketing system A manufacturer or supplier attempts to control the flow of goods or services through the channel. This is usually associated with expert power in that distributors and retailers are willing to relinquish some of their control in order to benefit from the producer's knowledge and background.

Advertising Advertising consists of any paid form of nonpersonal presentation of ideas and promotion of ideas, goods, or services by an identified sponsor.

Advertising agencies Advertising agencies provide a wide variety of professional services, including campaign planning, market research, media selection and production, public relations, and campaign evaluations.

Advertising agency An independent firm that works for the client to produce creative work and media scheduling.

Advertising campaign An advertising campaign includes all forms of advertising held together by a single message or overall theme. A campaign is the overall plan or strategy that guides the development of all forms of advertising.

Advertising spot A short advertising message on a participating program.

Agate line A measurement by which newspaper and some magazine advertising space is sold, regardless of the actual type size used. There are 14 agate lines to an inch.

AIDA model The AIDA model has long been used in training sales personnel. To sell the prospect successfully, the sales manager must help move the prospect through each of the four steps of the AIDA model: awareness, interest, desire, and action.

AIO statements These statements refer to activities (e.g., hobbies and sports), interests (e.g., family), and opinions (e.g., politics).

Alliances Firms pool resources for a specific goal or purpose instead of combining ownership.

All-you-can-afford method The all-you-can-afford method is usually a last resort practiced by small firms that do not have the luxury of setting aside resources for promotion and advertising.

Asset revenue generating efficiency (ARGE) ARGE evaluates the relationship between actual revenue and maximum potential revenue. For example, within a hotel operation, the ARGE will examine the occupancy percentage and the average daily rate to determine the extent to which the revenue potential is being realized.

Association market segment The association market is very broad, ranging from large national and international conventions attended by thousands of individuals to very small but expensive board of directors' meetings.

Attitudes Learned predispositions to act in a consistently favorable or unfavorable manner.

Attribute data These data involve asking consumers to rate alternative brands on a predetermined list of attributes.

Augmented product The augmented product is the core product and peripheral services that combine to form the package of benefits offered by a product or service. It encompasses everything surrounding the service and its delivery, including intangible attributes such as accessibility and atmosphere.

Authentication Verifying the appropriate access by a user through the use of some combination of account numbers, passwords, and IP (Internet protocol) addresses.

Average daily rate (ADR) Average rate paid for occupied hotel rooms on a daily basis.

Barter A process of exchanging goods and services rather than money.

Bartering Individuals or organizations who exchange goods and services with one another.

Base rate The lowest rate for advertising in print media. This rate is for run of paper (ROP) and means that the medium, at its discretion, puts advertisements wherever there is space.

Behavioral segmentation This type of segmentation focuses on the behaviors that consumers exhibit in the marketplace.

Benchmarking A process whereby a firm establishes a level of performance by comparing current performance against past performance, or by comparing current performance against the performance of other companies or an entire industry.

Benefit segmentation This type of segmentation focuses on benefits that consumers are seeking when they purchase a product.

Bleed advertisement An advertisement that extends into all or part of the margin of a page.

Boston Consulting Group (BCG) matrix Most common, straightforward resource allocation model used in marketing. The matrix contains four cells based on two axes. The horizontal axis is labeled relative market share and the vertical axis is labeled as market growth rate. Each axis has two levels, high and low, resulting in four cells.

Boundary-spanning roles Roles that front-line employees (e.g., front desk clerks, waiters, flight attendants, travel agents) perform.

Brand The name, sign, symbol, design, or any combination of these items that is used to identify the product and establish an identity that is separate and unique from competitors.

Brand marks The symbol or logo design used to identify the product.

Brand names A part of the brand consisting of the words or letters that can be used to identify the firm.

Break-even analysis Break-even analysis can be used to examine the relationships between costs, sales, and profits. The break-even point (BEP) is the point where total revenue and total cost are equal.

Brochures Developed and used to supplement other forms of advertising and promotion; used in direct-mail campaigns in addition to being placed in hotels, restaurants, tourist attractions, and information centers.

Browser An application program that allows users to display HTML files obtained from the World Wide Web. Popular browsers include Internet Explorer, Firefox, Safari, and Netscape.

Business analysis Business analysis represents the qualitative and quantitative assessment of a firm's potential or a firm's strategies.

Business-to-business (B2B) E-commerce that involves one business selling to or creating an exchange with another business.

Business-to-consumer (B2C) The electronic form of retailing when a business sells a product or service to a consumer.

Buying center or buying unit Groups of people that influence buying decisions for organizations.

Cash cows Cash cows represent a specific business unit in the Boston Consulting Group Matrix. This category contains products with high relative market shares and low market growth rates. Products or divisions that are cash cows are the best source for positive cash flows because they have strong sales in established markets.

Causal methods These are often referred to as explanatory methods because they used historical data to establish the relationship between sales and other factors that are believed to influence sales. The other factors, or causal factors, can differ based on the level of the forecast.

Causal research   This is research used to define cause-and-effect relationships between variables.

Census   A sample consisting of the entire population.

Central reservation systems (CRS)   These are systems designed to improve the efficiency and effectiveness of the reservations function by providing a central point of contact for handling customers' requests in a timely fashion.

Channel length   The channel length equals the number of intermediaries between the manufacturer and the final consumer.

Channel power   The ability of one channel member to influence the behavior of other channel members in such a way as to get them to do things that they normally would not do. The most common forms of power are reward, coercive, expert, legitimate, and referent.

Channel width   Channel width represents the desired number of distribution channel partners required to provide the desired market coverage.

Circulation   The number of copies of a publication that get distributed.

Click-throughs   Number of images that are requested when an Internet browser clicks on an image or link, in order to access additional information. Click through rates are often less than 1 percent. Click-throughs are often expressed as unique page views.

Closed-ended question   A closed-ended question provides the respondent with options from which to select a response. It is much easier to collect and analyze information in this type of question. The respondents' answers are consistent and the data is in a form that is simple to record.

Coercive power   The ability to influence a channel member's behavior through the use of threats (e.g., restricted availability or access to products, or other unfavorable terms such as price or discounts).

Cognitive dissonance   Consumers may have second thoughts or negative feelings after they have purchased a product or service.

Cold calls   Personal sales calls made without prior arrangements or appointments.

Collateral materials   Include printed materials such as brochures, meeting planner guides, or other material.

Communications gap   This occurs when there is a difference between the service delivered and the service promised.

Communications plan   An overall plan composed of several individual plans designed for each of the target markets or "publics" for a tourism destination.

Community relations plan The component of the communications plan developed to create a favorable environment in the local community.

Compensatory strategies Consumers use a product's strength(s) in one or more areas to compensate for deficiencies in other areas. This strategy allows products' strengths to compensate for their weaknesses.

Competitive advantage An advantage over competitors obtained through lowering prices or including additional benefits that justify higher prices. The end result for either technique offers consumers greater value.

Competitive-parity method The competitive-parity method for establishing a budget involves direct comparison with the promotion and advertising efforts of major competitors.

Competitive pricing Competitive pricing places emphasis on price in relation to direct competition. This method assures that the price charged for products and services will be within the same range as prices for competitive products in the immediate geographic area.

Competitive structure A combination of buyers and sellers in a market.

Concept testing A written or oral description and/or a visual representation is shown to consumers in the target market.

Consolidated metropolitan statistical area (CMSA) A CMSA includes at least two PMSAs (Primary Metropolitan Statistical Area). A PMSA is an urbanized county or multi-county area with a population of more than 1 million individuals.

Consolidation stage The fourth stage of the tourist area life cycle is when tourism has become a major component of the local economy, and a well-delineated business district has begun to take shape.

Consumer adoption process Consumers will adopt new products at different rates, depending on their level of aversion to risk and change.

Consumer decision-making model This model consists of five stages that a consumer experiences when making decisions about the purchase of a product or service. The five stages consist of recognizing a problem, seeking information, evaluating alternatives, making a purchase decision, and evaluating the product or service after the purchase.

Consumer expectations Each individual consumer makes purchase decisions and has established, based on past experiences, a set of expectations for the performance of a product or service.

Consumer feedback This is the final area of performance evaluation and is a key element in understanding the results of financial results, based on how well the firm has met consumer needs.

Consumer price index (CPI)   A measure of the relative level of prices for consumer goods in the economy.

Consumer price sensitivity   Consumer price sensitivity reflects how consumers react to changes in price.

Consumer problem-solving techniques   Consumers typically use one of three types of problem-solving techniques when they encounter a problem: routine response behavior, limited problem solving, and extended problem solving.

Consumer-to-business (C2B)   The situation in which an individual seeks to sell products or services to a business, when consumers bid for products and services offered for sale by a firm.

Consumer-to-consumer (C2C)   Although not common in the hospitality and tourism industry, consumers selling directly to other consumers. Individuals selling or exchanging time-share units is an example of this type of exchange.

Contests   A contest requires some skill on the part of the participant to win prizes.

Continuous advertising   Continuous advertising refers to the practice of keeping the amount of advertising relatively constant over time. This type is appropriate for hospitality operations with very stable volumes.

Contractual vertical marketing system   A contractual vertical marketing system unifies the channel

members by means of a legal and binding contract. The firms agree to abide by the terms of the agreement, the goal of which is to realize cost economies that would not be possible if the firms independently operated.

Convenience sample   The most basic method of nonprobability sampling is the convenience sample because the researcher chooses a sample of population members that, in his or her opinion, represent the target population (e.g., professors use a class of students, or research firms intercept people at shopping malls).

Convention and visitors bureau (CVB)   Each major city or region within a state has a convention and visitors' bureau (CVB) that is responsible for promoting that city or region. Convention and visitors' bureaus work with local hospitality and tourism firms to secure conventions, meetings, and special events for the city or region.

Conversion study   A process to measure the effectiveness of the destination marketing organization's advertising and promotion by determining the number of inquiries that are converted to visitors.

Convivial dimension   This refers to the human element (e.g., body language, saying the guest's name) in the service delivery.

Cooperative advertising   Cooperative advertising involves two or more firms, one of which is often a national or regional chain, working together to sponsor an advertisement that provides benefit to all parties involved. Franchisees often participate as a second firm.

Copy testing   This involves pretesting the copy of an advertisement prior to running it in the media.

Core product   The core product represents the basic form of the product. It is the main benefit sought by customers in an attempt to satisfy their needs as recognized by the gap between the ideal state and actual state (e.g., within a restaurant, the core service is the food that will resolve the consumer's state of hunger).

Corporate market segment   This market segment is very broad and is widely solicited by hotels. Corporations hold many more meetings than associations. The meetings tend to be smaller, have a much shorter lead time, are less price sensitive, are subject to quicker site decisions, and involve fewer individuals in the decision-making process.

Corporate vertical marketing system   In a corporate vertical marketing system all of the participants are actually members of the same organization. The original firm either develops or purchases other firms at the various levels in the channel.

Cost per thousand (CPM)   The CPM, the oldest means for comparing media rates, examines the cost to reach 1,000 consumers through an advertising medium.

Cost/benefit analysis   Firms compare the costs of losing customers and obtaining new customers with the benefits of keeping existing customers.

Cost-oriented pricing   Cost-oriented pricing uses a firm's cost to provide a product or service as a basis for pricing.

Cost-plus pricing   Determining the price for a product or service by adding a desired markup to the cost of producing and marketing the item.

Coupons   The primary objectives for coupons are to stimulate trial of a firm's products and/or services by reducing the price, encouraging multiple purchases, and generating temporary sales increases.

Credence qualities   Attributes that are difficult to evaluate even after the service is consumed.

Crisis management plan   The component of the communications plan prepared in the event of a natural or manmade disaster.

Critical incidents   "Moments of truth" when customers interact with a firm's employees and have a positive or negative experience.

Cross-sectional study   A study used to measure the population of interest at one point in time.

Culture   Patterns of behavior and social relations that characterize a society and separate it from others. Culture communicates values, ideals, and attitudes that help individuals communicate with each other and evaluate situations.

Customer needs failures   These are based on employee responses to customer needs or special requests.

Customer plan   The component of the communications plan used to market the destination to various consumer segments such as individual tourists, meeting planners, and tour operators and travel agents.

Customer satisfaction   This occurs when a firm's service, as perceived by customers, meets or exceeds their expectations.

Decline stage   During the decline stage, the last stage in the product life cycle, industry sales and profits decline more rapidly, and the number of competitors gets reduced to those with strong positions.

Defensive strategy   A defensive strategy is used to counter the effects on an existing product from a competitor's new product.

Delivery gap   This occurs when there is a difference between the service delivery specifications and the actual service delivery.

Delphi technique   The Delphi technique involves collecting forecasts, developing composites, and sending the data to those participating several times until a consensus results.

Demand-oriented pricing   The demand-oriented approaches to pricing use consumer perceptions of value as a basis for setting prices.

The goal of this pricing approach is to set prices to capture more value, not to maximize volume.

Demographic segmentation   This type of segmentation focuses on demographics such as income, age, gender, and ethnicity.

Demographics   Characteristics that describe the population such as age, income, education, occupation, family size, marital status, and gender.

Descriptive analysis   An analysis using aggregate data to describe the "average" or "typical" respondent, and to what degree respondents vary from this profile.

Descriptive research   This is research that helps answer the questions who, what, where, when, why, and how.

Desired-objective method   The desired objective method involves developing a budget based on well-defined objectives.

Destination attributes   Combination of tangible and intangible elements that define the location.

Destination branding   Process of capturing the distinct elements of the destination and communicating them through components such as identity, personality, and image.

Destination image study   Diagnosis of the destination's strengths and weaknesses on salient attributes, relative to competitive destinations, is helpful in designing the tourism offerings and marketing programs.

Destination marketing organization (DMO) Organizations that are primarily concerned with promoting the long-term development and marketing of a destination, focusing on convention sales, tourism marketing and service.

Development stage The third stage in the tourist area life cycle is where there is continued growth in the number of visitor arrivals. There is a noticeable development of additional tourist facilities and increased promotional efforts.

Dichotomous question The simplest form of a closed-ended question is a dichotomous question, which contains two possible options. Examples include questions with "yes" or "no" answers or a categorical question such as gender with two possible responses, "male" and "female."

Differentiation value The value to the consumer (both positive and negative) of any differences between a firm's offering and the reference product.

Direct channel The manufacturer sells directly to the consumer, and the manufacturer performs all of the channel functions.

Direct marketing The firm contacts consumers at home or work with promotions.

Discretionary effort This behavior represents employee effort beyond the minimum requirements for his or her job.

Discretionary income An individual's income that is available for spending after deducting taxes and necessary expenditures on housing, food, and basic clothing.

Disposable income An individual's income that remains for spending after required deductions such as taxes.

Dissolve When one scene in a television commercial fades into the next, with the two showing simultaneously for a moment.

Distribution The manner in which the products and services are being delivered to consumers. It involves decisions related to the location of facilities and the use of intermediaries.

Diversification strategy A diversification strategy involves introducing new products and services into new markets. This strategy offers the most long-term potential, but it is also the strategy with the greatest degree of risk.

Dogs Dogs represent a specific business unit in the Boston Consulting Group Matrix. This category contains products with low relative market shares in industries and categories with low market growth rates. Dogs are the least attractive category in the matrix.

Domain name system (DNS) Each computer connected to the Internet has a unique name and number. The number is the IP address, and the name is the DNS.

Drive time The early morning and late afternoon/early evening hours when radio has its largest audiences and highest rates.

Dubbing Recording the sound portion of the commercial separately and then synchronizing it with the visual components.

Econometric models This model uses statistical techniques to solve a simultaneous set of multiple regression equations.

Economic impact study An analysis that is used to estimate the revenues that come from the spending of tourists within the local area, change in regional incomes and changes in employment.

Economic value Economic value equals the sum of a product's reference value and a product's differentiation value.

Economies of scale Cost efficiencies derived from operating at high volumes.

Electronic commerce (e-commerce) A term used to describe the buying and selling process obtained through electronic means such as the Internet.

Encryption Transmitted data are scrambled to prevent unauthorized access by users or hackers.

Entrepreneurial strategy Firms looking for new ideas that are generated internally through means other than research and development. Employees are a great source for ideas on improving existing products and services, and developing new products and services.

Environmental scanning Environmental scanning can be a formal mechanism within a firm, or merely the result of salespeople and managers consciously monitoring changes in the environment.

Evoked set A set of brands that will be considered in the final purchase decision.

Exclusive distribution The narrowest channel width where a firm limits the availability of its products or services to a particular outlet. This is common among independent operators in the hospitality industry.

Experience qualities Attributes that can be evaluated only after the purchase and consumption of a service.

Experiments A data collection process used to compare a control group with one or more treatment groups to determine if there are any differences attributed to the variable(s) being tested.

Expert opinion Marketers look to a panel of experts with knowledge of the industry and the marketplace to provide a forecast.

Expert power Expert power is the result of the superior knowledge of one channel member relative to another. Some hotels agree to pay commissions and employ independent hotel representatives because of their expertise in dealing with certain market segments.

Exploration stage   The first stage in the tourist area life cycle is when there are a few adventurous tourists visiting sites with few public facilities. The visitors are initially attracted to the destination because of some natural physical feature.

Exploratory research   This is research used to determine the general nature of the problem.

Exponential smoothing   This technique uses the trend line to predict future sales; however, it places more weight on the most recent periods.

External environments   The environments that influence the marketing process. The state of the economy, trends in society, competitive pressures, political and legal developments, and advances in technology reflect external environments and affect the performance of a product or service.

External influences   External influences include culture, socioeconomic status, reference groups, and household. All of these entities have an influence on the way a consumer progresses through the decision-making process.

FAB selling technique   One of the most common selling approaches that focuses on the benefits that a product or service offers consumers. The F refers to product features, or the physical characteristics of the product. The A refers to the advantages, or performance characteristics, that will be of benefit to the buyer. The B refers to the benefit, or favorable outcome, that the buyer experiences.

Facilitating products   Facilitating products are services that enable the customer to consume the core product. They must be present to make the product available where and when the customer wants it.

Fade in/fade out   The screen goes from black to the visual material, or the final visual shot is faded into black.

Family life cycle   The family life cycle uses age, marital status, and the number of children to create categories sharing common discretionary income levels and purchasing behaviors.

Firewall   A filter is used to monitor traffic between an organization's network and the Internet. This barrier can restrict access to certain IP addresses, applications or content.

Flighting media scheduling   Flighting media scheduling involves a schedule that is set up in spurts and stops. Periods of blitz advertising are used, with no advertising between blitzes.

Focus group   A group of 8 to 12 people who represent the population being studied and are brought together in an informal setting to discuss the issues surrounding the research problem.

Follow the leader   An approach that introduces competing products and services soon after the market leader introduces its products and services.

Franchisee A firm that obtains a license from another firm to use its name and business practices.

Franchising A contractual arrangement whereby one firm licenses a number of other firms to use the franchisor's name and business practices.

Franchisor The firm that licenses other firms to use its name and business practices.

Frequency The number of times the same audience-listeners, readers, or viewers-is reached. It is expressed as an average, since some people may see or hear an advertisement only once, while others see it a dozen times.

Frequent traveler programs Awards commensurate with level of use.

Fringe time The periods immediately before and after TV prime time, 4 P.M. to 8 P.M., and after 11 P.M. in all time zones except the Central time zone, where periods run an hour earlier.

General Electric (GE) matrix The GE Matrix is similar to the BCG Matrix in that it examines strategic business units based market attractiveness (i.e., market growth rate) and business strength (i.e., relative market share). However, the axes are based on a subjective measure composed of several indicators (e.g., product life cycle, competitor strategies, new technologies, and economic conditions) rather than just one objective measure as in the BCG Matrix.

Geographic segmentation This type of segmentation focuses on the consumer's geographic area of residence.

Global distribution systems (GDS) Systems used by hospitality and travel firms to facilitate transactions within the distribution channel.

Globalization Firms expand outside of their traditional domestic markets (i.e., expanding worldwide).

Goals Goals are broad statements of what the firm seeks to accomplish.

Gross rating points Gross rating points compare media vehicles and programs. This rating is calculated by multiplying the rating points (i.e., percentage of households, according to surveys, listening to a program or station at a particular time) by the number of times that program or station is heard or viewed during a given period, usually four weeks.

Growth stage The growth stage is evidenced by rapidly rising sales and profits and a decreasing cost per unit for providing the product or service.

Historical appraisal The historical appraisal starts by examining the market, looking at its size, its scope, and the market shares of the competitors.

Hospitality marketing mix Hospitality marketing mix consists of five components: product-service mix, presentation mix, communication mix, pricing mix, and distribution mix.

Hypertext A method of linking related information without a hierarchy or menu system.

Idea generation Ideas for new products can be generated internally as a assigned function for research and development groups, or result from brainstorming.

Imitative strategy An imitative strategy involves copying a new product or service before it can have a large impact in the market. This strategy is particularly appealing when the product or service is not unique or when it can be easily duplicated.

Implication questions Implication questions get the prospect to realize how any problems or dissatisfaction with the current supplier are negatively affecting his or her business.

Incentive trip Corporations also plan incentive trips for their employees as a reward for outstanding performance.

Inception stage The inception stage of the tourist area life cycle is when the more adventurous travelers find destinations that are not frequented by the masses. These travelers are normally looking for places that have not become major tourism destinations.

Indirect channel An indirect channel involves at least one intermediary that is responsible for one or more channel functions. This type of channel can exist in many forms, but it is not very common in service industries.

Inferential analysis An analysis of cause-and-effect relationships used to test hypotheses.

Information technology The use of computer systems and applications to improve operating efficiency and effectiveness.

Innovation An approach that seeks to be first to market with a new product or concept.

Input-output model A common approach for estimating the economic impacts of tourism by directly surveying tourists to obtain their spending data.

Intensive distribution The widest channel strategy is intensive distribution, where firms attempt to make products and services available through as many outlets as possible. This is a common approach among franchise operations that use mass advertising and realize economies of scale.

Intermediaries Intermediaries specialize in certain functions in the service delivery process and can add value to the service with their knowledge and expertise (e.g., travel agents, meeting planners, tour wholesalers and operators, and travel bureaus).

Internal influences These influences consist of personal needs and motives, experience, personality and self-image. They are not as observable and therefore are not as well documented and understood as external influences.

Internal marketing Internal marketing encompasses all activities used by a firm in an effort to improve the marketing effectiveness of its employees.

Internal relations plan The component of the communications plan developed to improve employee morale and the work environment.

Introduction stage The first stage of the product life cycle is called the introduction stage. At this point, the product has been through the new product development process. It has survived analysis and testing, and it was deemed worthy of market introduction.

Involvement stage The second stage in the tourist area life cycle is when there is limited interaction between tourists and local community, resulting in only basic services. Increased advertising induces a pattern of seasonal variation and a definite market area begins to emerge.

Judgment sample A judgment sample is slightly different in that the researcher makes a determination as to a subset of population members that will represent the population. This process is similar to the one used in choosing the members for a focus group.

Key account management Special attention given to customers who are producing the largest share of the revenue and profits or who have the potential to do so.

Knowledge gap This occurs when management's perception of what consumers expect is different from the consumers' actual expectations.

Law of demand The inverse relationship between price and quantity demanded is representative of most products and services.

Legitimate power Legitimate power is obtained through contractual arrangements that specify the members' expected behaviors. The most common form of legitimate power in the hospitality industry is franchising.

Local advertising Local advertising includes television, radio, print, and other media.

Longitudinal study A study used to measure the same population over an extended period of time.

Margin of error The difference between forecasted value and actual value.

Market demand Market demand for a product or service is the total volume that would be bought by a clearly specified customer group in a defined geographic area in a defined period.

Market development strategy A market development strategy focuses on developing new markets for existing products and services.

Market growth rate The market growth rate is usually based on average annual growth rate over the last few years, depending on the age of the industry, or category and can be viewed as a proxy for industry attractiveness, or future growth potential.

Marketing Marketing encompasses merging, integrating, and controlling supervision of all company's or organization's efforts that have a bearing on sales.

Marketing communications Marketing communications include a wide variety of approaches, which consist of, but are not limited to, advertising, promoting, direct marketing, telemarketing, and personal selling.

Marketing concept The marketing concept is based on the premise that firms determine customer wants and needs, and then design products and services that meet those wants and needs, while also meeting the goals of the firm.

Marketing information systems (MIS) The structure of people, equipment, and procedures used to gather, analyze, and distribute information used by an organization to make a decision.

Marketing management cycle The marketing management cycle involves marketing planning, marketing execution, and marketing evaluation.

Marketing mix The first layer around the target market, or consumers, is referred to as the marketing mix. The marketing mix has four components: price, product, place, and promotion, which are often called the four P's of marketing. Managers can control those variables.

Marketing planning Managers focus on three basic questions that should be addressed during this process: Where are we now? Where do we want to go? How are we going to get there?"

Marketing program Firms will manipulate the marketing mix variables (e.g., price, product, place, and promotion) to formulate strategies for a product or service that are used to form a marketing program.

Marketing research process A process used to collect information about consumers and markets.

Marketing strategy Marketing strategy encompasses the overall plan for achieving marketing objectives.

Market introduction The final stage in the new product development process is to introduce the new product to the entire market, or to roll it out market by market.

Market penetration strategy A market penetration strategy focuses on selling the existing product-service mix to the existing target markets. Most firms will attempt to increase the quality and consistency of the product-service mix as a means of increasing customer satisfaction, promoting brand loyalty, and increasing sales and market share.

Market segmentation Market segmentation is pursuing a marketing strategy whereby the total potential market is divided into homogeneous subsets of customers, each of which responds differently to the marketing mix of the organization.

Market share The percentage of the market that the firm's product-service mix will capture.

Maslow's hierarchy of needs Abraham H. Maslow identified five classes of needs and arranged them in the following order, from the lowest to highest level: physiological needs, safety needs, social and belonging needs, esteem needs, and self-actualization needs.

Mass customization When a firm customizes the experience for each individual consumer.

Maturity stage A stage within the product life cycle where the organization has expanded as much as the market will allow, and volume, measured in annual gross sales, will level off. Companies in this stage find that the market is often saturated and competition is increasing from alternative options.

Measurability of market segments A criterion used to evaluate the effectiveness of market segmentation. Measurability should be assessed from two perspectives: the overall size of the target market segment and the projected total demand or purchasing power of the target market.

Media planning process The media planning process involves four stages: performing a market analysis to determine the current situation, establishing its media objectives, developing media strategies to use in attaining the objectives, and evaluating the media program on a continual basis and adapting it to fit changing conditions.

Meeting planners A meeting planner is someone who plans meetings that will be attended by all sorts of individuals. Meeting planners represent a vast array of different groups, from large national associations to small local civic groups.

Menu engineering Analysis of menu items based on cost, volume, and profitability.

Menu sales mix analysis The simplest method used to evaluate menu effectiveness is to count the number of times that each item is sold.

Merchandising Merchandising creates an atmosphere to enhance consumer interest and service delivery.

Meta tags Keywords are used by search engines to identify content and then rank the content in order of relevancy for users. These key words are embedded into the coding of each Web page.

Metropolitan statistical area (MSA) The smallest urban area with an urban center population of 50,000 individuals and a total metropolitan population of more than 100,000. Metropolitan statistical areas are normally urban areas that are self-contained and surrounded by rural areas.

Milline formula   A formula used to compare the costs of advertising in different newspapers. It is customary to use the cost per line per million circulation, called the milline rate [(Line rate $\times$ 1,000,000) $\div$ Circulation = Milline rate].

Mission statement   A firm's mission statement defines its purpose and how to differentiate it from its competitors. It should provide managers with the general guidelines for decision making.

Monopolistic competition   A common, competitive structure where there are many buyers and sellers with differentiated products.

Monopoly   A competitive structure in an industry with one seller and many buyers.

Motives   A person's inner state that directs the individual toward satisfying a felt need.

Moving average   This technique uses short-term forecasts (e.g., monthly) and takes the average of the most recent periods to predict future sales.

Multiple-category question   A multiple-category question contains more than two options for the respondent. Demographic information like education and income is often obtained using these questions.

Multiplier analysis   Procedure to estimate the impact generated in a tourist destination for every dollar spent on the tourist product itself.

National advertising   National advertising is aimed at a national audience by using network television and radio, or national print media such as magazines or newspapers. This form of advertising normally promotes the general name of the chain, not individual locations or stores.

Natural or organic search optimization   This approach to optimization of Web pages is based on developing web pages so that the search engines will successfully find your content and position it prominently on search results.

Need-payoff questions   A set of questions focused on helping the prospect determine the positive outcome of purchasing your product (e.g., "If my hotel were to provide your attendees with better food and closer proximity to tourist attractions, do you think you would get better attendance and more registration fees?").

Needs   A time when a person lacks something or the difference between someone's desired and actual states.

Negotiating skills   Negotiating skills are a set of interpersonal and analytical skills that allows a person to create an exchange that results in the mutual benefit of the involved parties.

Neutral pricing   This strategy involves setting prices at a moderate level in relation to the economic value to most potential consumers.

New product committees New product committees consist of individuals representing cross-functional areas of the firm. Usually, representatives provide input from operations, marketing, finance, and accounting.

New product departments Some firms establish full-time new products departments. It is still important for members of this department to solicit input from all cross-functional areas of the firm.

New product development Developing new products and services is time consuming and risky, but it is essential to the continued long-term success of a firm.

Noncompensatory strategies Consumers place more emphasis on individual attributes and, in some cases, develop minimum thresholds to use in evaluating products and services. There are three main non-compensatory strategies that are used by consumers: conjunctive, disjunctive, and lexicographic.

Nonprobability sample Nonprobability samples are based on judgment and the selection process is very subjective.

Observation A process involving watching consumers and documenting their behavior.

Objectives Objectives are more detailed statements of what the firm intends to achieve. Well written objectives should state (1) what will be accomplished in measurable terms, (2) within what specific time frame it will be accomplished, (3) which individual or group will be responsible for achieving the objective, and (4) how the results will be evaluated.

Odd/even pricing Odd/even pricing involves setting prices just below even dollar amounts to give the perception that the product is less expensive (e.g., car rental agencies set prices like $79.95 rather than $80, and hotels use prices like $99 instead of $100).

Oligopoly A competitive structure in an industry with a few sellers and many buyers.

Open-ended question An open-ended question does not provide the respondent with any options, categories, or scales to use in answering the question.

Opinion leaders These leaders include both formal and/or informal leaders of reference groups, and their opinions normally influence opinion formation in others.

Opt-in and opt-out The approach to building e-mail distribution lists allows a consumer to elect to participate (opt-in) or remove his/her name from the distribution list (opt-out), giving the individual consumer control over the content of their individual mailbox.

Order getters Salespeople who are responsible for creating sales and developing new accounts. They still service their existing accounts, but they are also expected to use sales strategies to obtain new accounts.

Order takers Salespeople who attend to customer inquiries and repeat purchases.

Organizational buying A process used by organizations to determine needs (problem recognition), search for information, evaluate alternatives, make a purchase, and evaluate the purchase (postconsumption evaluation).

Outdoor advertising plant A company that buys or leases real estate (where it erects standard-size boards) or rents walls of buildings. It then sells use of space at these locations to advertisers.

Paid keyword search This approach involves paying the search engine companies to show advertisements for your site when users initiate relevant searches. Most search engines charges on a pay-per-click basis; that is, every time a user clicks on the advertising link, a fee is incurred.

Pay-per-click When online advertising is used, each time a user clicks on the advertisement and opens the advertiser's Web page, the advertiser pays the host of the advertisement. The cost of pay-per-click varies depending on the competitiveness of the Web site.

Penetration pricing This strategy involves setting low prices in relation to the firm's economic value to most potential consumers.

Perceived value This represents the perceptions that a consumer has about a product.

Percentage-of-sales method The method offers relative simplicity; a sales forecast is obtained, and a given percentage of this forecast is allocated to advertising.

Perception The process by which stimuli are recognized, received, and interpreted. Each individual consumer perceives the world differently.

Perceptual mapping A technique used to construct a graphic representation of how consumers in a market perceive a competing set of products relative to each other.

Perfect competition The competitive structure in an industry with many buyers and sellers of homogeneous products that are almost exactly the same.

Peripheral services Additional goods and services that expand the core offering and can be used to obtain competitive advantage.

Personal selling This is an interpersonal process whereby the seller ascertains, activates, and satisfies the needs and wants of the buyer so that both the seller and the buyer benefit.

Personality An individual's distinctive psychological characteristics that lead to relatively consistent responses to his or her environment.

Place This component, sometimes called distribution, refers to the manner in which the products and services are being delivered to consumers. It involves decisions related to the location of facilities and the use of intermediaries.

Point-of-sale (POS) displays These displays, usually seen at the counter of fast-food restaurants or as table tents in other types of restaurants, are designed to stimulate increased sales.

Point-of-sale systems A computerized system for recording sales and transactions.

Population The entire group, or target market, that is being studied for the purpose of answering the research questions.

Position statement Position statement describes the mission to the firm's external stakeholders (i.e., customers, suppliers, and the general community) in terms of the public's perceptions of the benefits offered.

Positioning statement Results from consumer research and perceptual mapping enable firms to develop a positioning statement. The positioning statement should differentiate the organization's product-service mix from that of the competition.

Positioning The process of determining how to differentiate a firm's product offerings from those of its competitors in the minds of consumers.

Poststagnation The period in the tourist area life cycle after the beginning of the stagnation stage. Tourist destinations try to find ways to rejuvenate the area by adding new attractions or focusing on a niche market.

Preemptible rates Charges for broadcast advertising spots that may be bumped to different time periods by advertisers paying higher rates. They vary in cost by the amount of notice the station must give the advertiser before moving an advertisement: the longer the notice, the higher the rate.

Preference data Data obtained by asking consumers to indicate their preferences for a list of alternative brands.

Premiums Premiums (i.e., giving away something) are used to bring in new guests, to encourage more frequent visits by current guests, and to build positive word of mouth about the operation.

Prestige pricing Prestige pricing is used by firms that have products with strong price-quality relationships in markets with inelastic demand. These firms set high prices and try to build value through other quality-related attributes such as service and atmosphere.

Price Price refers to the value placed by a firm on its products and services.

Price discrimination laws Price discrimination laws forbid firms from charging purchasers different prices for commodities of like grade and quality in an attempt to substantially lessen competition.

Price elasticity of demand A measure of the percentage change in demand for a product resulting from a percentage change in price.

Price lining   Price lining refers to the practice of having a limited number of products available at different price levels based on quality.

Pricing objectives   Pricing objectives can be grouped into four major categories based on goals related to financial performance, volume, competition, and image.

Primary data   Data that are collected for a current study or project and is tailored to meet the specific information needs for that study or project.

Primary metropolitan statistical area (PMSA)   An urbanized county or multicounty area with a population of more than 1 million individuals.

Privatization   A process whereby the government allows an industry or business to change from governmental or public ownership or control to a private enterprise.

Proactive strategies   These strategies anticipate changes in the marketplace.

Probability sample   Probability samples are more scientific, and a population member's chance of being selected can be calculated. Probability sampling methods include simple random sample, systematic sample, and stratified sample.

Problem questions   These questions are meant to uncover any problems or dissatisfaction the prospect has with the current supplier.

Procedural dimension   This refers to the procedures used in the service delivery process.

Product   The goods and services that are bundled together and offered to consumers.

Product bundling   An approach in which menu items are bundled with other items, often at a price that is less than if the individual items were separately ordered.

Product development strategy   The idea of developing new products for existing markets.

Product levels   Four product levels exist: the core product, the facilitating products, the supporting products, and the augmented product.

Product life cycle   The product life cycle theory describes how a product progresses from its infancy as a new product in development, through a growth phase, to a maturity phase, and then, eventually into decline.

Product line   Firms develop and maintain a portfolio of products and services.

Product managers   Manager who assume complete responsibility for determining marketing objectives and marketing strategies for a specific brand.

Product screening   After product ideas have been generated, the focus turns toward screening the list of potential products to select the ones with the greatest potential for success.

Product–service mix A bundle of goods and services offered by an organization.

Profit control data This is a function of sales and costs and should be broken down by market segment.

Projected demand The total market demand multiplied by the market share, or the percentage of the market that the firm's product–service mix will capture.

Promotional budgets Promotional budgets serve several useful and important functions: to provide a detailed projection of future expenditures; to provide both short- and long-range planning guides for management; and to provide a method for monitoring and controlling promotional expenses by comparing actual expenses against projections.

Promotional mix The basic elements include advertising, personal selling, sales promotion, and public relations. All of the elements are equally important.

Property analysis checklist A form used to evaluate a hotel's basic features such as location, guestroom accommodations, meeting facilities, general facilities and services, and transportation.

Prospecting and qualifying Identifying prospective clients is a critical activity if the sales manager's efforts are to be successful. In the process of identifying and qualifying prospects, hotel sales managers should determine whether prospective clients represent good prospects before they invest a large amount of time.

Psychographic segmentation Psychographics refers to segmentation based on lifestyle, attitudes, and personality.

Psychological pricing Setting prices based on consumer perceptions of value.

Public relations Public relations is a nonpersonal stimulation of demand for a product or service by providing commercially significant news about the product or service in a published medium or obtaining favorable presentation in a medium that is not paid for by the sponsor.

Publicity Any promotion that is not paid for is called publicity. Because the individual or group is not paying for the time or space, those involved do not have complete control and are at the mercy of the writer or producer.

Pull promotion strategy Pull promotion is aimed at stimulating the interest of consumers and having them pull the product through the channels of distribution. This puts additional pressure on the retail outlets or hospitality facilities to supply the products and services most in demand by consumers.

Pulsing advertising Constant low-level flow of advertising with intermittent periods of blitz advertising.

Purchasing power Consumers have the ability to purchase products and services.

Sales promotions Sales promotions include marketing activities other than advertising, personal selling, and public relations that attempt to stimulate consumer demand and increase sales. Sales promotions seek to accomplish several broad objectives and can be used for several reasons: to increase consumer awareness, to introduce new products and services, to increase guest occupancy and customer counts, to combat competitors actions, to encourage present guests to purchase more, to stimulate demand in nonpeak periods.

Salient attributes Attributes that are the most important to consumers in evaluating the alternative products or service offerings.

Sample size The chosen number of sample units to be included in a research study.

Sample The subset of the population that is drawn in such a way so as to represent the overall population.

Sample unit The basic level of investigation in a research study.

Sampling Sampling encourages the trial of new products. If consumers will at least try the product, it is believed that they are more likely to purchase it in the future. Sampling is also an excellent way to persuade consumers to trade up to more expensive products and services.

Sampling error The difference between the sample results and actual population measures.

Satellite account method Process used to identify an overall estimate of tourism contribution to the state and national economies by reorganizing the account systems.

Scaled-response question This form of a closed-ended question involves a statement or question followed by a rating scale. One of the more popular scaled-response questions is the Likert scale that has respondents indicate their level of agreement with a statement on a five-point scale, with 1 being "strongly disagree" and 5 being "strongly agree."

Search engine optimization Search engines, such as Google or Yahoo use automated crawlers that search Web pages for content, which is then reflected when a user does a search. Search engine optimization increases the probability of being recognized by the search engine.

Search feeds This approach is used when data describing your Web site is sent to the search engines and a fee is charged to ensure that your pages are part of the site engine's index.

Search qualities Attributes that the consumer can investigate prior to making a purchase.

Secondary data analysis The process of reviewing existing information that is related to the research problem.

Secondary data Data that have already been collected by another source and made available to interested parties either for free or at a reasonable cost.

Second but better strategy An adapted version of the imitative strategy where firms are responding to competitors' new products; however, the firm's primary goal is to improve on the initial product.

Segmented pricing The importance of price varies among consumers, and firms often use this variation as a means for segmenting markets. Then, a firm can choose to target one or more of these markets with specific marketing strategies tailored to each market.

Selective distribution Selective distribution refers to the middle channel width, where a firm uses more than one outlet but restricts availability of the product or service to a limited number of outlets.

Selling Focuses mainly on the firm's desire to sell products, and to a lesser extent on the needs of the potential buyer.

Service An intangible product that is sold or purchased in the marketplace.

Service blueprint A flowchart that details the delivery points of contact with customers.

Service failures Service failures are assigned to one of three major categories: (1) responses to service delivery system failures, (2) responses to customer needs and requests, and (3) unprompted and unsolicited employee actions.

Service gap The final gap that exists when there is a difference between customers' expectations of a service and their perceptions of the actual service once it is consumed.

Service quality A perception resulting from attitudes formed by customers' long term overall evaluations of performance.

Services marketing Marketing of services or promoting intangible items.

Showing A showing refers to the coverage of a market. A 100 showing is complete coverage of a market; a 50 showing is half of it.

Signature items Signature items portray specific menu items that are heavily promoted on the menu and for which a food service operation is known.

Similarity–dissimilarity data Similarity–dissimilarity data involve asking consumers to make direct comparisons between alternative brands.

Simple random sample This technique involves a totally random process where each population member has an equal chance of being selected. With this method, there is little chance of selection bias or sampling error.

Situation questions Questions aimed at gathering background information and facts about the prospect, his or her needs, and the organization he or she represents.

Skim pricing This strategy involves setting high prices in relation to the product or service's economic value to most potential consumers. This strategy is designed to capture high profit margins from an exclusive segment of consumers that places a high value on a product's differentiating attributes.

SMERF group   SMERF stands for a combination of several market segments: social, military, educational, religious, and fraternal. SMERF meetings are frequently held in conjunction with nonprofit groups that are often working with a very limited budget.

Spam   Any e-mail received that is unwanted or not desired by the recipient. It is estimated that up to 50 percent of the e-mail traffic could be classified as spam.

Specialty advertising Specialty advertising materials bearing the firm's name and logo can be given or sold to a targeted consumer.

SPIN selling   Neil Rackham developed the SPIN selling approach, which is an acronym for situation, problem, implication, and need-payoff questions. The idea is to prepare for the sale, investigate the prospect's needs, demonstrate your company's capabilities to meet those needs, and obtain a commitment.

Stagnation stage   The last stage of the tourist area life cycle where peak numbers of tourists and capacity levels are reached. The destination has a well-established image, but it is no longer popular, and the lodging facilities begin to erode and turnover.

Stakeholders relations plan   The component of the communications plan developed to foster business partnerships and alliances.

Standard operating procedures Management and staff follow these established procedures in a given operation or in a given situation.

Standards gap   The discrepancy that can occur between management's perception of what customers expect and how they design the service delivery process to meet those exceptions.

Stars   Stars represent a specific business unit in the Boston Consulting Group Matrix. This category contains products with high relative market shares in industries and categories with high market growth rates.

Strategic business unit (SBU) Strategic business units represent business centers consisting of products that share common characteristics and have the same competitors.

Strategic business units (SBUs) Brands or units that have their own sets of market conditions and competitors.

Strategic marketing plan   These plans result from a careful examination of a firm's core business strategy and primary marketing objectives.

Strategic window   Limited periods of time when marketing opportunities present themselves and the firm is in a position to take advantage of those opportunities.

Stratified sample The population is separated into different strata based on an important population characteristic and a sample is taken from each stratum using a random or systematic process.

Substantiality of market segments A criterion used to evaluate the effectiveness of market segmentation. The size of the segment must be reasonably substantial to warrant special attention to meet the needs of the segment and achieve the marketing objectives of the firm.

Suggestive-selling techniques Suggestive selling occurs when a service provider actively promotes one product over another to a consumer (e.g., a front desk employee suggests an upgrade to the concierge level over a standard room when a guest checks in at the hotel).

Supporting products Supporting products are additional goods and services that can be bundled with the core service in an attempt to increase the overall utility or value for consumers (e.g., concierge service, multilingual staff, 24-hour room service, and complimentary newspapers for business travelers).

Survey of buying intentions Firms use marketing research to ask potential customers about their future purchase intentions and then estimate future sales.

Surveys Data collection instruments designed to gather specific information for a particular research problem through a series of questions and statements.

Sweepstakes In sweepstakes, prizes are awarded solely based on chance.

SWOT analysis SWOTs are the basis on which strategic marketing plans are developed. Strengths and opportunities are leverage items on which firms develop competitive advantages. Conversely, weaknesses and threats are problem areas that must be minimized if the firm is to achieve maximum success.

System failures When a failure or service breakdown occurs in a core service provided by the firm.

Systematic sample A starting point is randomly chosen and then every nth member is selected for the sample.

Systems failure Failures in the core service offering of the firm. These failures are the result of normally available services being unavailable, unreasonably slow service, or some other core service failure that differs by industry.

Tactical marketing plan These plans focus on implementing the broad strategies that are established in the strategic plan.

Target-return pricing Setting a price to yield a target rate of return on a firm's investment.

Telemarketing The use of telecommunication technology to conduct marketing campaigns aimed at certain target markets.

Test marketing A common form of field experiment consisting of manipulations in the marketing mix at certain locations that represent the competitive environment and consumer profile of the overall population.

Time series analysis This method uses statistical techniques to fit a trend line to the pattern of historical sales. The trend line is expressed in terms of a mathematical equation that can be used to project the trend forward into future periods and predict sales.

Tourist Area Life Cycle The tourist area life cycle is similar to the product life cycle for tourist destinations. Like products, destinations have a finite life and evolve through four stages of development from inception (i.e., introduction) to growth to maturity, and finally into decline.

Trademark A trademark is the brand that has been given legal protection and is protected for exclusive use by the owner of the trademark.

Tradeouts When firms trade services in lieu of cash.

Trend extrapolation The simplest method for forecasting sales is the linear projection of past sales.

Unique destination proposition (UDP) A statement to describe the unique elements that are available at the destination in an attempt to differentiate it from other destinations.

Unique selling proposition (USP) Promoting a unique element of the product-service mix.

Unsolicited employee action Actions, both good and bad, of employees that are not expected by customers.

Up-selling A technique that involves getting consumers to buy items that are more expensive or provide a greater profit margin.

Value proposition How will the firm create value for the buyer? The value proposition defines how the firm will fulfill the needs of the consumer.

Venture teams These teams are similar to new product committees but are formed to complete a specific product assignment. Venture teams bring together expertise from operations, marketing, accounting and finance, and, if necessary, architecture and construction.

Vertical marketing system In a vertical marketing system, channel members work together as if they were one organization. Channel members work together to achieve a higher degree of efficiency, thereby reducing the overall costs of providing products and services.

Wheel of retailing The evolution of an organization from a low-end provider to a high-end provider.

Win-win relationship A situation that results when both parties are satisfied at the end of negotiations.

Word of mouth A spoken communication that portrays either positive or negative data.

Yield management Yield management programs are used to set prices that will maximize revenue, based on the costs of providing services and the price sensitivities of the consumers.

INDEX